Second
Corinthians

Second Corinthians

RAYMOND F. COLLINS

B
Baker Academic
a division of Baker Publishing Group
Grand Rapids, Michigan

© 2013 by Raymond F. Collins

Published by Baker Academic
a division of Baker Publishing Group
PO Box 6287, Grand Rapids, MI 49516-6287
www.bakeracademic.com

Printed in the United States of America

Library of Congress Cataloging-in-Publication Data
Collins, Raymond F., 1935–
    Second Corinthians / Raymond F. Collins.
        pages cm. — (Paideia : commentaries on the New Testament)
    Includes bibliographical references and index.
    ISBN 978-0-8010-3186-1 (pbk.)
        1. Bible. N.T. Corinthians, 2nd—Commentaries. I. Title.
BS2675.53C66 2013
227′.307—dc23   2012045437

13   14   15   16   17   18   19   7   6   5   4   3   2   1

For Timothy
and all those who walked with me on the road to Corinth,
in gratitude and appreciation

Contents

Figures

Foreword

Paideia: Commentaries on the New Testament is a series that sets out to comment on the final form of the New Testament text in a way that pays due attention both to the cultural, literary, and theological settings in which the text took form and to the interests of the contemporary readers to whom the commentaries are addressed. This series is aimed squarely at students—including MA students in religious and theological studies programs, seminarians, and upper-division undergraduates—who have theological interests in the biblical text. Thus, the didactic aim of the series is to enable students to understand each book of the New Testament as a literary whole rooted in a particular ancient setting and related to its context within the New Testament.

The name "Paideia" (Greek for "education") reflects (1) the instructional aim of the series—giving contemporary students a basic grounding in academic New Testament studies by guiding their engagement with New Testament texts; (2) the fact that the New Testament texts as literary unities are shaped by the educational categories and ideas (rhetorical, narratological, etc.) of their ancient writers and readers; and (3) the pedagogical aims of the texts themselves—their central aim being not simply to impart information but to form the theological convictions and moral habits of their readers.

Each commentary deals with the text in terms of larger rhetorical units; these are not verse-by-verse commentaries. This series thus stands within the stream of recent commentaries that attend to the final form of the text. Such reader-centered literary approaches are inherently more accessible to liberal arts students without extensive linguistic and historical-critical preparation than older exegetical approaches, but within the reader-centered world the sanest practitioners have paid careful attention to the extratext of the original readers, including not only these readers' knowledge of the geography, history, and other contextual elements reflected in the text but also their ability to respond correctly to the literary and rhetorical conventions used in the text. Paideia commentaries pay deliberate attention to this extratextual repertoire in order to highlight the ways in which the text is designed to persuade and move its readers. Each rhetorical unit is explored from three angles: (1) introductory matters; (2) tracing the train of thought or narrative or rhetorical flow of the argument; and (3) theological issues raised by the text that are of interest to the contemporary Christian. Thus, the primary focus remains on the text and not its historical context or its interpretation in the secondary literature.

Our authors represent a variety of confessional points of view: Protestant, Catholic, and Orthodox. What they share, beyond being New Testament scholars of national and international repute, is a commitment to reading the biblical text as theological documents within their ancient contexts. Working within the broad parameters described here, each author brings his or her own considerable exegetical talents and deep theological commitments to the task of laying bare the interpretation of Scripture for the faith and practice of God's people everywhere.

Mikeal C. Parsons
Charles H. Talbert

Preface

Just two days ago, I returned to the United States from a visit to Rome, where I participated in the twenty-second biannual meeting of the Ecumenical Pauline Colloquium held in the Benedictine Abbey of St. Paul's Outside the Walls. This year's colloquium was devoted to 2 Thessalonians and Pauline eschatology. Among the passages that we considered in detail was one from 2 Corinthians, insightfully presented by Morna Hooker, emerita of Cambridge, whose paper focused on 2 Cor. 5:1–10.

Inevitably, the identity of Paul's "we" arose in the discussion of the passage. Was Paul speaking about only himself, using some sort of editorial or apostolic "we"? Did he perhaps also have in mind Timothy, the coauthor of this letter, and/or other missionaries? Did he perchance offer a reflection on the possibility of his own death as a paradigm for the Christian believers, who were his addressees, to ponder?

Not only did the twenty-seven of us who participated in the colloquium have the matter of the significance of the "we" of 2 Corinthians to consider; we also weighed the matter of the coauthorship of 1 and 2 Thessalonians, asking ourselves about the extent to which Silvanus and Timothy (1 Thess. 1:1; 2 Thess. 1:2) contributed to these letters and to what extent the letters' characteristic "we" referred not only to Paul but also to Silvanus and Timothy.

Paul wrote his letters neither in a vacuum nor in isolation. His was a "team ministry." His letters, including the Second to the Corinthians, reflect that approach to the proclamation of the gospel. He sent the letter with which this commentary is concerned not only on behalf of himself but also on behalf of Timothy, his brother (2 Cor. 1:1). In this letter he speaks about how he was virtually lost without Titus and how much he relied on Titus in his dealings with the Corinthians, especially with regard to the collection that was to be made as a service to God's holy people in Jerusalem. Paul needed Timothy and Titus in order to function as an apostle of Jesus Christ.

No more than Paul was able to proclaim the gospel in spoken word and by written letter without the help of others have I been able to write this commentary on his gospel without the help of others. To begin, let me express my gratitude to James Ernest of Baker Academic and Brazos Press, who invited me to write this commentary at a time when I was still teaching at the Catholic University of America in Washington, DC. His support when the project was delayed due to a host of reasons beyond my control is particularly appreciated.

I must also thank those who helped to bring this study to its completion. The initial comments of Mikael Parsons, one of the general editors of the Paideia series, proved to be helpful indeed. Wells Turner, senior editor at Baker Academic and Brazos Press, and his team amazed me with their careful proofreading of the text. Rachel Klompmaker assiduously tracked down material for the illustrations, searching sometimes in vain for an illustration that I would have liked to include. To all of them I express my appreciation.

I am also grateful to colleagues at the Catholic University of Leuven in Belgium, particularly my dear friend Jan Lambrecht and his successor in Leuven, Reimund Bieringer. The latter, a former student, invited me to participate in the 2 Corinthians project that he cochairs within the Society of Biblical Literature. The contributions of these two scholars to the understanding of 2 Corinthians is well known to biblical exegetes and is reflected in these pages. Nonetheless, I value their friendship and their personal support even more than I value their exegetical contributions.

Finally, I would be remiss were I not to express my gratitude for the help, the support, and the challenges of "Timothy" who shared so much of this project with me and who so reminds me of Paul's own Timothy, if not his Titus.

Raymond F. Collins
Narragansett, Rhode Island
September 18, 2012

Abbreviations

General

BCE	before the Common Era (= BC)	hapax	hapax legomenon, term appearing
ca.	*circa*, approximately		only once
CE	the Common Era (= AD)	lit.	literally
cent.	century	mg.	marginal reading
chap(s).	chapter(s)	NT	New Testament
col(s).	column(s)	*olim*	formerly
frg(s).	fragment(s)	OT	Old Testament

Bible Texts, Editions, and Versions

Eng.	chapter/verse numbering in English versions
JB	Jerusalem Bible
KJV	King James (Authorized) Version
LXX	Septuagint, the Greek Bible
MT	Masoretic Text, the Hebrew Bible
NA²⁸	*Nestle-Aland: Novum Testamentum Graece.* Edited by Eberhard and Edwin Nestle et al. 28th rev. ed. Stuttgart: Deutsche Bibelgesellschaft, 2012.
NAB	New American Bible
NIV	New International Version
NRSV	New Revised Standard Version
REB	Revised English Bible
Theod.	Theodotion
UBS⁴	*The Greek New Testament.* Edited by Barbara and Kurt Aland et al. 4th rev. ed. Stuttgart: Deutsche Bibelgesellschaft / United Bible Societies, 1994.
Vulg.	Latin Vulgate

Ancient Manuscripts, Papyri, and Inscriptions

א	Codex Sinaiticus
B	Codex Vaticanus
BGU	*Aegyptische Urkunden aus den Königlichen/Staatlichen Museen zu Berlin: Griechische Urkunden.* 15 vols. Berlin, 1895–1983.
C	Codex Ephraemi Syri Rescriptus
I.Priene	*Die Inschriften von Priene.* Berlin, 1968.
P.Aberd.	*Catalogue of Greek and Latin Papyri and Ostraca in the Possession of the University of Aberdeen.* Edited by E. G. Turner. Aberdeen, 1939.
P.Alex.	*Papyrus grecs du Musée Gréco-Romain d'Alexandrie.* Edited by A. Swiderek and M. Vandoni. Warsaw, 1964.
P.Brux.	*Papyri Bruxellenses Graecae.* 2 vols. Brussels, 1974–91. Plus unpublished papyri at Brussels.
P.Laur.	*Dai Papiri della Biblioteca Medicea Laurenziana.* 5 vols. Florence, 1976–84.
P.Mert.	*A Descriptive Catalogue of the Greek Papyri in the Collection of Wilfred Merton.* 3 vols. London, 1948–67.
P.NYU	*Greek Papyri in the Collection of New York University.* 2 vols. Leiden, 1967; Wiesbaden, 2010.
P.Oslo	*Papyri Osloenses.* 3 vols. Oslo, 1925–36.
P.Oxy.	*The Oxyrhynchus Papyri.* 75 vols. 1898–2010.
P.Princ.	*Papyri in the Princeton University Collections.* 3 vols. 1931–42.
P.Tebt.	*The Tebtunis Papyri.* 5 vols. 1902–2005.
P.Wisc.	*The Wisconsin Papyri.* Edited by P. J. Sijpesteijn. 2 vols. Leiden, 1967; Zutphen, 1977.
P.Yale	*Yale Papyri in the Beinecke Rare Book and Manuscript Library.* 3 vols. 1967–2001.

Ancient Corpora

OLD TESTAMENT			
Gen.	Genesis	Ps(s).	Psalm(s)
Exod.	Exodus	Prov.	Proverbs
Lev.	Leviticus	Eccles.	Ecclesiastes
Num.	Numbers	Song	Song of Songs
Deut.	Deuteronomy	Isa.	Isaiah
Josh.	Joshua	Jer.	Jeremiah
Judg.	Judges	Lam.	Lamentations
Ruth	Ruth	Ezek.	Ezekiel
1–2 Sam.	1–2 Samuel	Dan.	Daniel
1–2 Kings	1–2 Kings	Hosea	Hosea
1–2 Chron.	1–2 Chronicles	Joel	Joel
Ezra	Ezra	Amos	Amos
Neh.	Nehemiah	Obad.	Obadiah
Esther	Esther	Jon.	Jonah
Job	Job	Mic.	Micah
		Nah.	Nahum

Hab.	Habakkuk
Zeph.	Zephaniah
Hag.	Haggai
Zech.	Zechariah
Mal.	Malachi

DEUTEROCANONICAL BOOKS

Bar.	Baruch
1–2 Esd.	1–2 Esdras
1–4 Macc.	1–4 Maccabees
Sir.	Sirach/Ecclesiasticus
Wis.	Wisdom of Solomon

NEW TESTAMENT

Matt.	Matthew
Mark	Mark
Luke	Luke
John	John
Acts	Acts
Rom.	Romans
1–2 Cor.	1–2 Corinthians
Gal.	Galatians
Eph.	Ephesians
Phil.	Philippians
Col.	Colossians
1–2 Thess.	1–2 Thessalonians
1–2 Tim.	1–2 Timothy
Titus	Titus
Philem.	Philemon
Heb.	Hebrews
James	James
1–2 Pet.	1–2 Peter
1–3 John	1–3 John
Jude	Jude
Rev.	Revelation

OLD TESTAMENT PSEUDEPIGRAPHA

Apoc. Ab.	Apocalypse of Abraham
Apoc. Mos.	Apocalypse of Moses (in L.A.E.)
2 Bar.	2 Baruch (Syriac Apocalypse)
1 En.	1 Enoch (Ethiopic Apocalypse)
2 En.	2 Enoch (Slavonic Apocalypse)
4 Ezra	4 Ezra
Jos. Asen.	Joseph and Aseneth
Jub.	Jubilees

L.A.B.	Liber antiquitatum biblicarum (Pseudo-Philo)
L.A.E.	Life of Adam and Eve
Let. Aris.	Letter of Aristeas
Liv. Pro.	Lives of the Prophets
Sib. Or.	Sibylline Oracles
T. Ash.	Testament of Asher
T. Benj.	Testament of Benjamin
T. Dan	Testament of Dan
T. Iss.	Testament of Issachar
T. Jos.	Testament of Joseph
T. Jud.	Testament of Judah
T. Levi	Testament of Levi
T. Naph.	Testament of Naphtali
T. Reu.	Testament of Reuben
T. Zeb.	Testament of Zebulun

DEAD SEA SCROLLS

Dead Sea Scrolls not listed here are cited by cave number followed by the letter Q (for Qumran) and the document number (e.g., 4Q175).

CD	Damascus Document
1QH	Hodayot (Thanksgiving Psalms)
1QM	Milḥamah (War Scroll)
1QS	Serek Hayaḥad (Rule of the Community / Manual of Discipline)
1QSb	Rule of the Blessings (1Q28b)
4QMMT	Some Observances of the Law (4Q394–399)

RABBINIC WORKS

The letters prefixed to the names of Mishnaic tractates indicate the following sources: Mishnah (m.), Tosefta (t.), Babylonian Talmud (b.), and Jerusalem/Palestinian Talmud (y.).

'Abot	'Abot
Ber.	Berakot
Gen. Rab.	Genesis Rabbah
Ketub.	Ketubbot
Pesiq. Rab.	Pesiqta Rabbati
Qidd.	Qiddušin
Soṭah	Soṭah

APOSTOLIC FATHERS

1 Clem.	1 Clement
Diogn.	Diognetus

Ancient Authors

ARISTOTLE
Rhet.   *Rhetoric*

DEMETRIUS
Eloc.   *De elocutione*
           (Peri hermēneias)

DEMOSTHENES
1, 2, 4 Philip.   *1, 2, 4 Philippic*

DIO CHRYSOSTOM
Alex.   *Ad Alexandrinos (Or. 32)*
Consuet.   *De consuetudine (Or. 76)*

EPICTETUS
Diatr.   *Diatribai (Dissertationes)*

EURIPIDES
Orest.   *Orestes*

HOMER
Il.   *Iliad*

JEROME
Epist.   *Epistulae*

JOHN CHRYSOSTOM
Hom. 2 Cor. *Homiliae in epistolam II ad Corinthios*

JOSEPHUS
Ant.   *Antiquities of the Jews*

LUCIAN
Cat.   *Cataplus*

GALL. *Gall.*   *Gallus*
Sat.   *Saturnalia*

ORIGEN
Cels.   *Against Celsus*

PHILO
Confusion   *On the Confusion of Tongues*
Dreams   *On Dreams*
Sacrifices   *On the Sacrifices of Cain and Abel*
Spec. Laws   *On the Special Laws*
Unchange-
able   *That God Is Unchangeable*

PLATO
Euthyphr.   *Euthyphro*
Phaedr.   *Phaedrus*
Pol.   *Politicus*

PLUTARCH
Apoph. Lac. *Apophthegmata Laconica*
Mor.   *Moralia*
Them.   *Themistocles*
Tim.   *Timoleon*

SENECA (THE YOUNGER)
Ben.   *De beneficiis*

THEODORET OF CYR
2 Cor.   *Commentary on Second Corinthians*

XENOPHON
Cyr.   *Cyropaedia*

Series, Collections, and Reference Works

ABD   *Anchor Bible Dictionary.* Edited by David Noel Freedman. 6 vols. New York: Doubleday, 1992.

BDF   *A Greek Grammar of the New Testament and Other Early Christian Literature.* Edited by F. Blass and A. Debrunner. Translated and revised by Robert W. Funk. Chicago: University of Chicago Press, 1961.

EDNT	*Exegetical Dictionary of the New Testament*. Edited by Horst Balz and Gerhard Schneider. 3 vols. Grand Rapids: Eerdmans, 1990–93.
PG	Patrologia graeca [= Patrologiae cursus completus: Series graeca]. Edited by J.-P. Migne. 162 volumes. Paris, 1857–66 (index, 1912).
PL	Patrologia latina [= Patrologiae cursus completus: Series latina]. Edited by J.-P. Migne. 221 vols. Paris, 1844–65 (with indexes).
TLNT	*Theological Lexicon of the New Testament*. By Ceslas Spicq. Translated and edited by James D. Ernest. 3 vols. Peabody, MA: Hendrickson, 1994.

Second Corinthians

Introduction

The ancient city of Corinth, described in Strabo's *Geography*, was destroyed by the Roman general Lucius Mummius in 146 BCE. A little more than a century later (44 BCE) Julius Caesar refounded the city as a Roman colony, Colonia Laus Julia Corinthiensis. In 29 BCE the Roman emperor established the province of Achaia, with Corinth as its capital. The geography of the area is roughly equivalent to the southern part of modern Greece.

The city was located at the crossroads of two major trade routes, one by sea, the other by land. Located on a narrow isthmus, Corinth controlled the port of Cenchreae to the east and the port of Lechaeum to the west. Corinth was therefore a port city with access eastward through the Saronic Gulf to the Aegean Sea and westward through the Gulf of Corinth to the Adriatic Sea. Seafarers departed from the ports of Corinth for such far-off destinations as Rome and Ephesus (cf. Acts 18:18–19). A north-south land route, the Peloponnesian Way, provided access between Corinth and the Roman province of Macedonia to the north. Strategically located at the juncture of these two important trade routes, the city of Corinth became a major mercantile and cosmopolitan center. In addition, the city hosted the biennial Isthmian Games, which celebrated the unity of the Greek people.

Paul's Missionary Visit to Corinth and His Correspondence with the Corinthians

Paul's missionary strategy led him to make use of the Roman routes, which provided access to important centers of population. Accordingly Paul stopped at Corinth during his second missionary voyage, somewhere around 50 CE. Luke gives a stylized account of that visit in Acts 18:1–18, but Paul's extant correspondence with the Corinthians offers no precise confirmation of the details of the visit as described by Luke.

Luke's account of the visit states that Paul stayed in Corinth a considerable time, about a year and a half (Acts 18:1–5, 11, 18). That Paul wrote letters to the church of God at Corinth confirms that he had been successful in evangelizing at least some of the Corinthians, a task in which he was joined by Silvanus and Timothy (2 Cor. 1:19; cf. 1 Cor. 1:1; Acts 18:5). His extant correspondence includes two letters to the Corinthians, but these were not the only letters that Paul wrote to the church of God in Corinth. First Corinthians 5:9 mentions an earlier letter in which Paul warned his addressees to shun sexually immoral people. Second Corinthians 2:3–4 mentions another letter, written by a stressed-out Paul (cf. 2:9; 7:8, 12). Thus the two extant letters to the Corinthians are but two pieces of a more extensive correspondence that included at least one letter from the Corinthians to Paul (1 Cor. 7:1).

The rest of the correspondence has been lost. All that remains are the two letters that are part of the NT, the so-called First Letter to the Corinthians and the so-called Second Letter to the Corinthians. Their enumerated titles do not refer to the sequence in which they were written; rather, in accordance with the stylometric principle at work in the compilation of the NT, 1 Corinthians is called "first" because it is longer than the other letter, the "second." It is commonly agreed, however, that 2 Corinthians was, in fact, written after 1 Corinthians. With sixteen chapters, 1 Corinthians comes immediately after Romans in the canonical NT, where it is followed by 2 Corinthians. With its 13 chapters and 256 verses, as the text was divided into chapters by Stephen Langton (1150–1228) and into verses by Stephanus (Robert Estienne, 1503–59), 2 Corinthians is the third-longest letter in the Pauline epistolary corpus.

The text of 2 Corinthians is well attested in the ancient manuscript tradition. The oldest more or less complete copy of the text is found on a papyrus that dates back to about 200 CE ($\mathfrak{P}^{46}$) and is now preserved in Dublin's Chester Beatty Library. This papyrus copy of the letter is missing only two verses, 11:11 and 11:22. Wear and tear on the papyrus has taken its toll, however slight the loss may have been. Another papyrus manuscript, dating from around 400 CE and also located in Beatty Library ($\mathfrak{P}^{99}$), contains considerable portions of the text, while some few verses are found on a seventh-century papyrus ($\mathfrak{P}^{34}$) now kept in Vienna's National Library.

Two of the oldest uncial manuscripts, the fourth-century Codex Sinaiticus ($\aleph$) and the fourth-century Codex Vaticanus (B), contain the letter in its entirety. Two of the fifth-century uncials are not as useful for studying the text of 2 Corinthians. The Codex Alexandrinus (A) contains only 4:14–12:6. The text found on a palimpsest (scraped and reused) manuscript, the Codex Ephraemi Syri Rescriptus (C)—the parchment containing 2 Corinthians was later reused to make copies of Ephraem's sermons—has suffered the fate of many a palimpsest. Only 1:1–2 and 10:8–13:13 have been preserved.

Paul's Letter

The text of 2 Corinthians preserved in the manuscript tradition has the form of a letter, a long one by ancient standards. It begins with an epistolary salutation (1:1–2) and concludes with a letter closing that resembles the closings of many Hellenistic letters.

Self-Revelation

Demetrius, one of the oldest theorists to write about the art of letter writing, declared: "The letter, like the dialogue, should abound in glimpses of character. It may be said that everybody reveals his own soul in his letters. In every other form of composition it is possible to discern the writer's character, but none so clearly as in the epistolary" (*Eloc.* 227). Paul, a Jew from Tarsus, was probably not aware of Demetrius's characterization of the letter, but the apostle to the Corinthians really does reveal his soul in 2 Corinthians.

He speaks about his being afflicted and in need of consolation. Paul mentions being weighed down and having a near-death experience, from which he was delivered by God. He refers to his sadness yet being able to rejoice. He speaks of his distress, anguish, and tears. He mentions his forgiveness of someone who has hurt him. He speaks about his restlessness and the many hardships that he has suffered. He speaks about his confidence and boldness, even when he is accused of timidity and levity. Paul tells of his love for the Corinthians, how he has opened his heart to them and they have not returned his love. He writes about his weakness and his boasting. Reluctantly he speaks about his visions and his revelations. He speaks about the thorn in his flesh and how he narrowly escaped the clutches of a regional king. He even talks about the difficulties caused by Satan. Most of all he speaks about his ministry, passionately and imaginatively. He defends the conduct of his ministry and his own personal integrity. An occasional oath punctuates his self-defense. Paul, in fact, reveals so much of himself in this letter that it can aptly be called the most personal of his letters.

The Spoken Word

The passion with which Paul writes is evident on every sheet of the ancient papyri manuscripts and in every chapter of our modern versions of the text. Paul's is the passion of the orator. His letters were dictated to an unknown scribe. He spoke his letters, rather than physically writing them himself. This was customary in the Hellenistic world. It was one of the reasons why Demetrius could compare letter writing with a dialogue. Yet Paul was no ordinary letter writer. He was an evangelist and preacher of the gospel. In secular terms he was an orator. In dictating this letter he used some of his customary rhetorical devices and the figurative language that his contemporaries considered to be persuasive.

Demetrius counseled against disconnected words and breaks in sentences. "Frequent breaks in a sentence," he wrote, "are not appropriate in letters. Such breaks cause obscurity in writing, and the gift of imitating conversation is less appropriate to writing than to speech in debate" (*Eloc.* 226). Yet Paul was engaged in a debate, to some degree with the Corinthians, to a greater degree with interlopers who introduced into the faith community at Corinth a gospel that apparently diverged from the gospel that Paul preached. The passionate debate in which Paul was engaged led to the disconnected words, omitted words, breaks in sentences, and interrupted thoughts that appear throughout the letter. Often he begins to speak about something, breaks the flow of his thought, and then returns to the original topic a verse or several verses later. Sometimes he uses participles, even a string of them, where verbs in the indicative are called for. In sum, Paul's passion sometimes interferes with the clarity of his expression of thought.

Much of the language of the letter is unusual for Paul. Unusual grammatical constructions are also to be found. The letter contains a large number of hapax legomena, words and phrases occurring here and nowhere else in his letters. Some, but not all, of these will be noted in the course of the commentary. Many of these hapax are not found elsewhere in the NT; some do not appear elsewhere in the entire Greek Bible. Some words in the letter seem to have been coined by Paul since there is no literary evidence for their use prior to their appearance in 2 Corinthians. One notable example is the composite word "false apostles," a single word in Greek (*pseudapostoloi*, 11:13). Paul also calls them "superapostles" (*hoi hyperlian apostoloi*, 11:5; 12:11). The incidence of this rare vocabulary may be due to the heat of the debate, as the novel "false apostles" exemplifies.

Unlike the theological debate to which the Letter to the Galatians attests, the debate in which Paul engages in 2 Corinthians is eminently personal. That he is engaged in a debate has probably contributed to his unusual vocabulary in yet another way. On occasion he seems to have borrowed some of the phraseology used by the interlopers.

Half a Conversation

Demetrius wrote that "Artemon, the editor of Aristotle's *Letters*, says that a letter ought to be written in the same manner as a dialogue, a letter being regarded by him as one of the two sides of a dialogue" (*Eloc.* 223). This is almost a truism, but the fact that it is true creates a difficulty for the interpretation of 2 Corinthians. Paul sometimes imparts new information to the Corinthians, with the result that we are hardly any more disadvantaged in understanding what he writes than were the Corinthians. This is certainly the case when he tells the Corinthians that he wants them to know about his near-death experience in Asia. To introduce the topic, he employs his customary disclosure formula: "We do not want you to be unaware, brothers and sisters" (1:8; cf.

8:1). The way he speaks about his visions and revelations (12:1–5) leads us to think that he had never before spoken about this issue.

On the other hand, there are experiences alluded to by Paul that were well known to the Corinthians. He speaks about his painful visit to the community, a visit so painful that he put off visiting again. He speaks about a tearful letter that he wrote. Presumably it was received and read by the Corinthians. He mentions a malefactor who was punished by the Corinthians. He mentions the collection for the saints that had started a year previously. Paul talks about Titus's visit to the Corinthians and how Titus had experienced the Corinthians' change of heart. He compares himself with the superapostles but does not really tell us much about them. There are so many other things that we would like to know about the situation in Corinth, but our only source of information is this letter, and it is just half of the conversation. Readers of the letter should be wary lest they consider facts to be self-evident or otherwise attested when the only source of information is Paul's hints and allusions.

In this respect we are considerably disadvantaged in comparison with the Corinthians. Not only had they experienced many of the things that Paul mentions and were therefore fully aware of what he was writing about, but they also had the letter read to them. There was no formal postal service in Paul's day. Letters were carried to their addressees either by a passing traveler co-opted for this task or by a trusted intermediary. Titus may have been the designated letter carrier who brought 2 Corinthians to the assembly in Corinth. In addition to reading the letter to the Corinthians, the letter carrier would have been available to fill in the gaps and answer questions. Both the letter writer and its recipients would have been aware of this additional source of information.

A Real Letter

Despite the difficulties that a modern interpreter encounters in trying to understand what Paul wrote, it is obvious that he was self-consciously engaged in the writing of a letter. None of his other letters draws as much attention to the writing of letters as does 2 Corinthians.

He speaks about the now-lost tearful letter, telling the Corinthians why he wrote it (2:3; 7:12) and his motivation in writing as he did (2:4, 9).

He writes about letters of recommendation, apparently because the interlopers came to Corinth bearing letters of recommendation (3:1–3). In this context he mentions the materials used in letter writing: ink and tablets. He says that he himself needed no letter of recommendation. Who could have recommended him, appointed to his apostolic task, as he was, by the will of God?

The recommendation of Titus and the other emissaries in 8:16–17, 23 has elements found in letters of recommendation and provides a hint that

Titus might have been the carrier of the letter. Frequently Hellenistic letter writers wrote letters of commendation on behalf of the letter carrier, attesting to the trustworthiness of the letter carrier and asking the recipients to provide the letter carrier with amenities and hospitality.

Finally, he speaks about the writing of this very missive. He tells the Corinthians that he writes only what they can understand (1:13). He tells them a bit about his purpose in writing (7:12; 13:10). And cleverly he tells them that he has no need to write to them about the collection (9:1). Then he proceeds to write about it.

The Course of Events

With the clues provided in the two letters to the Corinthians, it is possible to trace the course of events in Paul's relationship with the Corinthians. It is, however, impossible to determine with any precision when these events happened.

A First Visit and Two Letters

The beginning is obviously Paul's visit to Corinth during the course of his second missionary voyage (ca. 50 CE). Paul wrote a follow-up letter to the community, urging them to avoid immoral persons (1 Cor. 5:9). What led to the letter and what else, if anything, it said remain unknown to us. If the letter at all resembled Paul's other letters, it would have been somewhat long and would have addressed other topics. In any case, the issue of immorality seems not to have disappeared. Not only did Paul address the issue in 1 Corinthians, but he again alludes to it in 2 Cor. 6:16–7:1; 12:20–21.

Paul followed this letter up with another letter, occasioned at least partially by the report of Chloe's people (1 Cor. 1:11) and a letter that he had received from the Corinthians themselves. The tone of this letter (1 Corinthians) is clearly less harsh than the tone of 2 Corinthians. The letter addressed a whole host of issues, especially various issues that threatened the unity of the community. Among them was the pride that some people took in the spiritual gifts that had been granted them, displaying their sense of superiority vis-à-vis other members of the community. Toward the end of that letter, written from Ephesus around 53 CE, Paul announced his intention to return to Corinth, traveling by land from Macedonia (1 Cor. 16:5–9). His intention seems to have been to take a boat from Ephesus to Macedonia and then go to Corinth, probably traveling along the Peloponnesian Way.

A Second Visit and Another Letter

While he was in Ephesus, something happened in Corinth that led Paul to change his plans. We do not know how Paul found out about difficulties in

Corinth—he may have been informed by Timothy (cf. 1 Cor. 16:10–11)—but whatever the issues were, they were sufficiently serious for Paul to return directly to Corinth, most likely by sea. It remains possible, however, that Paul simply changed his mind, deciding to go first to Corinth and then travel north to the province of Macedonia.

In 2 Corinthians, Paul suggests two sources of the problems in Corinth. On the one hand, preachers arrived in Corinth with a version of the gospel not entirely consistent with Paul's. They seem to have disparaged his ministry. Among other things, they disdained the fact that he worked to support himself while he preached the gospel. Working to support oneself seems to have been, for them, beneath the dignity of a preacher of the gospel.

Another issue was caused by a miscreant, probably a member of the community, who created trouble for Paul or for someone who was very close to him. It is most likely the apostle himself who was offended. We do not know the precise nature of the offense, but the community was complicit in the offense insofar as it did not take the malefactor to task, at least for some time.

The visit did not go well. Paul was saddened and pained by what he experienced. The visit was probably short. Paul returned to Ephesus, his base of operations at the time. Lest another visit be equally difficult for him, Paul again changed his mind. He decided to send another letter to the Corinthians instead of visiting them as he had first intended to do (2 Cor. 2:1). This letter was probably delivered by Titus (8:6), whose main mission was most likely to continue the work of the collection announced in 1 Cor. 16:1–4. This was the tearful letter (2:3–4), which Paul sent to test the mettle of the community (2:9). Were they obedient in every respect?

Titus's Visit and Yet Another Letter, 2 Corinthians

Paul waited in Ephesus for a while, then went north to the port of Troas. Perhaps he had prearranged to meet Titus there. Paul used the time to evangelize the city (2:12), but he grew restless because Titus did not arrive. So Paul moved on to Macedonia (2:13), perhaps to Philippi, where there was a supportive community of believers. In Macedonia, Paul met Titus, who delivered a fairly upbeat report. On the one hand, the community had repented and taken steps—perhaps the measures taken were overly harsh measures!—to punish the miscreant. On the other hand, the members of the community were eager to receive Paul once again.

Titus's report cheered Paul up. There were, nonetheless, lingering difficulties. The interlopers were still around; at least their influence was still being felt insofar as Paul's authority continued to be called into question. Moreover, the issues of immorality and disunity seem not to have been totally resolved. The situation was, nonetheless, sufficiently calm for Paul to make three decisions. First, he would send Titus back to complete the work of the collection. Second, he would write a letter—extant 2 Corinthians—in which he would explain

9

and defend his ministry. The letter was probably written toward the end of 54 CE. Third, he would make another visit to Corinth, for which his letter would serve as preparation. Romans 15:25–31 suggests that this visit occurred when Paul arrived in Corinth to take the proceeds of the collection to Jerusalem.

Critical Issues

The historical-critical method of biblical interpretation began to be developed in earnest in the nineteenth century. The method seeks to determine the history of the text and the history behind the text. With regard to 2 Corinthians, one question of each sort has been especially debated in recent decades.

The History of the Text

The ancient manuscripts contain the text of 2 Corinthians, such as it appears in Greek in the edition of Nestle-Aland (NA[28]) and *The Greek New Testament* (UBS[4]). As is always the case with ancient manuscripts, there are some minor discrepancies among the various ancient texts. For the most part, the variants are due to scribal error, perhaps even erroneous "corrections" on the part of "knowledgeable" scribes. The editors responsible for the above-mentioned editions have resolved the issues to the best of their ability and have produced the Greek text on which modern translations are based.

There is, however, another issue with regard to the history of the text of 2 Corinthians that concerns contemporary critics. This issue is the unity of the text that has been handed down. Demetrius says that "there should be a certain degree of freedom in the structure of a letter" (*Eloc.* 229). Thus Paul cannot be blamed for producing a letter that does not evince the unity that is characteristic of an essay or a sustained argument in a court of law. There are, nonetheless, certain aspects of 2 Corinthians that have led many commentators to question whether the letter has any real structure at all. Is it so unstructured that it lacks any real unity?

As one begins to read Paul's letter, one finds that Paul has been smoothly developing his thought, talking about the sadness of his second visit, defending his change of travel plans, and mentioning his desolation at not finding Titus. Then suddenly, in 2:15, Paul interrupts his thought. Saying "Thanks be to God," he begins a long theological reflection. The theological reflection on Paul's ministry continues until 7:4, when his thought is suddenly interrupted once again, and Paul returns to the train of thought that he abandoned in 2:14. In 7:5 Paul talks about being in Macedonia, where he meets Titus and his sadness turns to joy. So 7:5 seems to follow naturally after 2:14.

The next strikingly abrupt transition occurs at 6:13. Paul has been speaking personally and somewhat emotionally to the Corinthians, telling them that his wide-open feelings for them contrast with their restricted feelings for him.

Suddenly he begins to tell them (6:14), using imaginative and then scriptural language, that they should not be in league with nonbelievers. Then in 7:2 he picks up the biological imagery of 6:13, asking the Corinthians to make room in their hearts for him. What he writes in 7:2–4 seems, logically, to follow immediately after 6:13.

Once back to Titus and the joy-producing report that Titus gave on meeting Paul, the apostle switches gears in 8:1. Instead of continuing to tell the Corinthians about the report, Paul says that he wants to give them some new information, treating an issue that has nothing to do with what he has been writing about. Without any apology for switching his train of thought, Paul says that he wants to tell the Corinthians about the Macedonians and God's gracious gift to them (8:1). Paul uses the example of the Macedonians to urge the Corinthians to participate in a collection on behalf of God's holy people in Jerusalem, an appeal that appears to have been interrupted because of the course of events narrated above.

The appeal continues throughout chapter 8, but in what is now the beginning of chapter 9, Paul introduces the topic of the collection as if for the first time. "For, to be sure," he writes, "it is superfluous for me to write to you about the service to the saints" (9:1). True, in chapter 8 he has talked about the practicalities of the collection, and in chapter 9 he provides a theological underpinning, but it is strange that he should seem to be bringing up the topic of the collection in 9:1 for the first time.

Then, having finished his remarks about the collection in 9:15, Paul begins to defend himself again (10:1). The tone of this self-defense is much harsher than the tone that he adopted earlier in the letter (1:3–2:1; 7:5–16). It hardly seems to be at home with the earlier passage, whose words were conciliatory. Moreover, it seems out of place after Titus's report that the Corinthians are ready to embrace Paul and presumably his message as well.

In sum, the extant text of 2 Corinthians has abrupt transitions (aporias) after 2:14; 6:13; 7:1; 7:4; 7:16; 8:24; and 9:15. For more than a millennium the text of 2 Corinthians was handed down without division into chapter and verse. For the modern reader of the text, chapter divisions inserted after 7:16; 8:24; and 9:15 soften the abruptness of the transitions. The contemporary reader has been conditioned by these divisions to think that Paul introduces new topics at what are now 8:1; 9:1; and 10:1.

During the historical-critical era of biblical scholarship, these abrupt transitions in the text have prompted scholars to look for some explanation. One proposal that has emerged is that extant 2 Corinthians is not a text that Paul dictated in one prolonged session. Rather, they opine, the text of 2 Corinthians that has been handed down through the centuries was not originally a single text but is a composite text compiled from as many as six different letter fragments. Some anonymous editor would have put them all together, using just one opening salutation and one letter closing, rather than incorporating a number of presumably similar opening salutations and letter closings.

Given the nature of the Paideia commentary series, it is not necessary to go into the variations on the compilation theory in any detail. An in-depth study of the issue would divert attention from the way that Paul spoke to the Corinthians through his letter and an understanding of what he wanted to tell them. Instead, I offer the opinion of Hans Dieter Betz as an example, actually a good example, of a theory suggesting that extant and canonical 2 Corinthians is the result of scribal compilation of earlier text fragments ("Corinthians, Second Epistle to," *ABD* 1:1148–54). Betz holds that the present text results from the compilation of six fragments of earlier texts, five of which come from letters written by Paul:

1. A lengthy and imaginative theological disquisition on Paul's ministry, the "first apology" (2:14–6:13; 7:2–4)
2. A harsh letter, the "second apology" (10:1–13:13), most likely the letter of tears to which Paul refers in 2:3–4
3. A conciliatory letter (1:1–2:13; 7:5–16) written on the occasion of Titus's uplifting report on the readiness of the Corinthians to embrace Paul
4. An "administrative letter" telling about the organization of a renewed appeal for support of the sainted poor people in Jerusalem (chap. 8)
5. A second "administrative letter" providing a theological rationale for the collection (chap. 9)
6. A later interpolation of a piece (6:14–7:1) that urges separation from unbelievers and was written by a hand other than that of Paul

According to this theory, the letter of tears has not been lost. It has been substantially preserved in 10:1–13:13. The idea that 6:14–7:1 is an interpolation is held not only by critics who hold that extant 2 Corinthians is a compilation of letter fragments; many other scholars also hold that 6:14–7:1 is a later interpolation into Paul's text. This issue will be discussed further at the pertinent place in the commentary.

Betz's compilation theory supposes a course of events that differs somewhat from the course of events that I have traced. In fact, most compilation theories require the reconstruction of a different course of events. Any construction of a course of events, including mine, is based on a reading of the texts. As a reading of the text differs, so the reconstruction of events must differ.

That the various compilation theories differ from one another weighs against the hasty embrace of any one of them. If the text was produced as a result of the compilation of letter fragments, the scribal effort was done very early in the history of the church. $\mathfrak{P}^{46}$ shows that 2 Corinthians has existed in its present form for the past eighteen centuries. The text that has been handed down will be followed in the commentary that follows.

The History behind the Text

My reconstruction of the course of events is, of course, history behind the text, but there is another issue that has intrigued scholars since the dawn of the historical-critical era of biblical scholarship, especially during the past several decades. That issue is the identity of Paul's opponents, the superapostles, as he disparagingly calls them in 11:5; 12:11. Who were they? Where did they come from? What was their theology? If they brought letters of recommendation (3:1), who was their sponsor? Why were they opposed to the Pauline mission?

Virtually the only source of information available to answer these questions is 2 Corinthians itself, but the letter does not provide sufficient information to satisfy our historical curiosity. It seems, however, that these opponents, whom I call "interlopers" since they came from outside the community (11:4), are not to be identified with the puffed-up persons with whom Paul takes issue in 1 Corinthians. The matters addressed in 2 Corinthians are different from the issues raised in 1 Corinthians. It is likely, therefore, that the interlopers arrived in Corinth after 1 Corinthians was sent. Moreover, the source of trouble in Corinth was different from the source of trouble in Galatia. Paul does not speak about the observance of the law and the issue of circumcision in 2 Corinthians. Accordingly, it would be a mistake to identify the intruders of 2 Corinthians with Paul's opponents in Galatia.

Paul readily admits that the interlopers are Jewish Christians (11:22–23a). Accordingly a number of scholars consider that they were Judaizers of one sort or another. That they appear as servants of righteousness (11:15) is another reason to pursue the line of reasoning that identifies the troublesome intruders as Judaizers. Paul's disquisition on Moses and the covenant in chapter 3 adds support to this kind of argument.

Other scholars take another tack, drawing attention to the fact that Paul spells out charismatic activity as the signs of an apostle. He also speaks about his visions and revelations (12:1–5), a topic that does not appear in any of his other letters. That these appear in a polemical context suggests that Paul is trying to match his opponents' claims to have been the beneficiaries of visions and revelations. Thus, a second group of scholars pursues a line of reasoning that identifies the interlopers as Spirit-people, as people who attribute special value to charismatic activity.

A third group of scholars tries to combine the two lines of reasoning. One recent attempt to do so was made by Thomas R. Blanton (2010, 150–51):

> Paul's missionary rivals espoused a standard covenant renewal theologoumenon. . . . They were individuals striving to mediate the renewed covenant between God and humans. Adherence to this covenant, they held, was facilitated by God's gracious gift of the spirit, a spirit that transformed human intentionality so that perfect obedience to the stipulations of the Torah could be construed as an attractive possibility.

In the end, we cannot identify the interlopers with any precision. Paul does not tell us much about their theology except to say that they preached another Jesus, another gospel, and another Spirit (11:4–5). Their attacks on Paul seem to be largely of a personal nature. They accuse him of walking according to the flesh (10:2). They say that his physical presence is weak and his speech contemptible (10:11). They question his integrity on a number of counts, particularly with regard to the collection.

In response, Paul does not directly address their different theology. He defends his ministry and his personal integrity. He seems to think that the interlopers have intruded into his territory (10:13–14). He acknowledges their greater rhetorical skill (11:6). He concedes that, nonetheless, they are Christian (10:7), indeed, servants of Christ (11:23). For the most part, Paul's arguments against them are personal, of the ad hominem variety. The interlopers peddle the word of God (2:17). Apparently they need letters of recommendation (3:1). They praise themselves and compare themselves to one another (10:12). They seek support and so burden the community (11:7–12). Paul describes them as seducers (11:3) and deceitful (11:13). He derides them as superapostles (11:5; 12:11) and calls them false apostles (11:13). They are servants of Satan who disguise themselves as servants of righteousness (11:15). Paul's caricature provides little help to us who would like to identify exactly who the interlopers were and how many of them there were.

The Structure of the Letter

The harsh connections noted above allow the letter, apart from its opening salutation and its epistolary closing, to be divided into five parts. It may be useful for us to review, in summary fashion, the way Paul develops his thought before we begin more intense scrutiny of what he has to say in this admittedly complex text.

The Letter Opening (1:1–2)

Introducing his fellow evangelist Timothy as a "coauthor," Paul begins his letter in a manner that was familiar to those who wrote and read letters in the Hellenistic world. He identifies his addressees as the assembly of God in Corinth but says that he wants the message to extend beyond Corinth, to those in the outlying districts of Achaia. He greets all of them with a greeting that bears a distinctively Christian character and is a hallmark of all his letters.

Ministerial Crises (1:3–2:13)

Instead of following up his letter with the customary thanksgiving, Paul opens the body of the letter with a beautiful prayer of praise suggesting that all has not been well for Paul. He prays to the God of all consolation, who has consoled him in the midst of all his afflictions. He gives thanks to God, who has delivered him from these afflictions, expressing the hope that he will be similarly delivered in the future. To give an example of his affliction, the apostle tells the Corinthians about his terrifying experience in Asia.

Then, intimating that he had a change of plans that caused some people to think of him as fickle, Paul tells about a seemingly previously unplanned visit to Corinth that made him sad. Someone in particular was the cause of his pain. So instead of returning to Corinth, where he feared that he might have another sad experience, Paul wrote the now-lost letter of tears to the Corinthians. He wrote the letter with distress and anguish. Through it all Paul hoped that his love for the Corinthians came through.

Apparently something of what Paul had written was taken to heart by the Corinthians. They punished the malefactor, perhaps excessively. Enough is enough, says Paul: now is the time for forgiveness and love. Paul adds that he himself has forgiven the troublemaker. Paul desires the reconciliation and encouragement of the malefactor lest this person fall into the wily clutches of Satan.

Shifting the train of thought from the Corinthians back to himself, Paul tells the Corinthians that he went to Troas to await the arrival of Titus. He had a good opportunity to evangelize in Troas, but he was restless because he failed to meet Titus and thus moved on.

Paul Explains and Defends His Apostolic Ministry (2:14–7:4)

With another abrupt change of thought, Paul offers thanks to God for a ministry that he describes in figurative language as his participation in a triumphal procession. He raises the issue of his being qualified for this ministry and responds that if he is qualified, it is only because God has made him capable of exercising the ministry. He is confident in the exercise of his ministry, but a problem looms on the horizon. Some people have arrived in Corinth bearing letters of recommendation. Paul needs no such letter because the faith of the Corinthians, available for all to see, is proof that he is qualified. They are Paul's letter of recommendation.

Having identified the service in which he and Timothy are engaged as a ministry of a new covenant, Paul begins to make a comparison with the ministry of the earlier covenant epitomized in the Exodus story of Moses and the stone tablets. That ministry was indeed glorious, but its ministry is passing away. The ministry of Moses is but a shadow of the ministry of the glory of Christ, the image of God. As servants of Jesus and ministers of the new covenant, Paul is able to commend himself and at least Timothy among his companions.

Paul is, however, aware of his own fragility and weakness. A comparison with vessels of clay is used to speak about his human condition. A rehearsal of some of the difficulties that were his during the exercise of his ministry further illustrates his human condition. But Paul has not succumbed to these difficulties. His difficulties allow the dying of Christ to be evident in his body. He has confidence for he believes in the resurrection. What he is doing will

15

result in life for the community and glory for God. As he continues to ponder his human condition, Paul does not lose heart. Various metaphors allow him to describe his mortality and the future that awaits him.

Then, turning his thought back to the Corinthians, Paul expresses his heartfelt love for the community. He wishes only that they would requite his love. They seem not to have done that. Somehow their affection for him is restricted. In the midst of his paternal appeal for love appears a seemingly intrusive passage that warns the Corinthians to avoid the kind of conduct that is associated with nonbelievers.

The Arrival and Report of Titus (7:5–16)

Resuming the thought that he has interrupted to speak about his ministry and himself as minister, Paul picks up on the idea of going to Macedonia. Having arrived in Macedonia, he received great consolation in the form of the arrival of Titus. The presence of Titus might have been enough, but the news that he brought was all the more encouraging. Titus has reported that the Corinthians are now eager for Paul; they have experienced a real change of heart. The harsh letter that he had sent has produced its effect; the pain that the Corinthians experienced on receiving it was short lived. Compounding Paul's joy is the fact that Titus is joyful. He too is encouraged by the obedience of the Corinthians.

Service to God's Holy People (8:1–9:15)

Paul then takes up another topic. He wants to tell the Corinthians about the grace of God given to the churches of Macedonia. That grace was their willingness to share what little they had with others, the "saints [in Jerusalem]." The apostle tells the Corinthians about the Macedonians' generosity because he wants to motivate the Corinthians to respond generously to the needs of the saints. That example might be enough, but Paul gives an additional model, that of the Lord Jesus Christ, who impoverished himself for our sake. Paul's idea is not that God's holy people in Jerusalem should become rich; it is rather that there should be parity among the churches. Who knows? Someday the Corinthians might need help.

Paul wants Titus to continue with the ministry of the collection, following a few directives that Paul sets down. Titus is ready and eager to take on the responsibility. Two companions are appointed to assist Titus: one known to the churches, who has once been Paul's traveling companion, and the other a person whom Paul has tested and found to be zealous. Paul expresses the hope that the collection will be successful and that the pride that he has in the Corinthians will prove to be justified.

With a somewhat formal introduction, Paul brings up the topic of the collection anew. He says that Titus and companions are an advance team and are to attend to the collection when the Corinthians' generosity will justify his pride in them. In this second go-around on the topic of the collection, God is the focal point of Paul's theological motivation. God has been generous to the Corinthians. God loves the one who gives generously. Through their generosity the Corinthians will demonstrate their obedience to the gospel and will glorify God. Throughout his exposition on the collection, Paul toys with the idea of "grace." It is the language that Paul uses to speak of the Corinthians' gift to the saints, but the terminology implies so much more than mere gift.

An Aggressive Taskmaster (10:1–13:10)

Paul's earlier defense of his ministry was relatively mild in tone. Now he tells the Corinthians that he is ready to be bold and aggressive. He employs the imagery of a military attack to describe how he is ready to defend the gospel against the sophistries that have been raised up against it. The Lord has given him authority. Paul stands ready to use that authority both in letter and in person, for building up but not for tearing down. There will be no difference between what he says and what he writes. Paul, however, is not reckless and unrestrained. He acts in accordance with the authority that the Lord has given him and the standards that God has established. If he has any boast, he can boast in the Lord, in what the Lord does through him.

He may have made a subtle swipe at the interlopers when he talked about maintaining standards and keeping within assigned boundaries, but he takes them on in earnest as he hurls a string of invectives at them. They are like the serpent who seduced Eve. The intruders may have taken umbrage at Paul's refusal to accept financial support from the Corinthians, but Paul doesn't want to burden the Corinthians because he loves them. But there is more. The interlopers have presented themselves as apostles of Christ when in fact they are pseudo-apostles and deceitful preachers. They are servants of Satan, who presents himself as an angel of light.

The intensity of Paul's argument increases as he follows the example of the interlopers and boasts about himself. It is foolish for him to do so, but he nonetheless does boast. His "fool's speech" passes in review all sorts of hardships and difficulties that speak about Paul's weakness. He offers two particular examples of weakness that are not mentioned in any of Paul's other letters: his narrow escape from the clutches of King Aretas in Damascus and the thorn in the flesh, a messenger given to him to keep him humble. Paul will not refrain from boasting about his weakness; he willingly exposes his weakness to the Corinthians for he wants them to know that power is perfected in weakness.

Having done what he had to do in the fool's speech, Paul announces that he is now ready to make another visit to the Corinthians, his third. By the time that he arrives, the collection should be completed. Paul offers a bit of defense on behalf of himself and Titus. He has not taken advantage of them, and neither has Titus. Citing his authority, Paul warns them against any lingering

17

signs of disunity and licentiousness. If he finds such signs on his arrival, he will be severe with them. This will build them up.

Paul's severity will be warranted, as he explains when he comes to the denouement of his speech. Just as Christ was crucified in weakness but lives by God's power, so Paul is weak but by God's power lives with Christ for the sake of the Corinthians. A short exhortation then reminds the Corinthians that Paul has not failed the test. He urges the Corinthians to test themselves lest, when he comes to them, he might need to be severe in exercising the authority that the Lord has given him.

The Letter Closing (13:11–13)

Paul's speech, the *homilia* that constitutes the body of the Second Letter to the Corinthians, comes to its conclusion on that note. Paul ends the letter with a staccato exhortation that recapitulates some of its main themes. He asks the Corinthians to extend greetings to one another and tells them, perhaps in a moment of enthusiasm, that all God's holy people greet them. At the end comes the final benediction, "The grace of our Lord Jesus Christ and the love of God and the fellowship of the Holy Spirit be with you all."

Outline of 2 Corinthians

The letter opening (1:1–2)

The senders of the letter (1:1a)

The recipients of the letter (1:1b)

The greetings (1:2)

Ministerial crises (1:3–2:13)

A prayer of praise and the Asian experience (1:3–11)

The berakah (1:3–7)

A near-death experience (1:8–11)

Paul's defense of his integrity (1:12–2:4)

The witness of conscience (1:12–14)

Defense against the charge of being fickle (1:15–22)

Skipping a visit to Corinth (1:23–24)

The tearful letter (2:1–4)

A disciplinary matter (2:5–11)

Frustration in Troas (2:12–13)

Paul explains and defends his apostolic ministry (2:14–7:4)

Anxiety and confidence (2:14–3:6)

A triumphal procession (2:14–17)

A letter of recommendation (3:1–3)

Paul's confidence (3:4–6)

A glorious ministry (3:7–4:6)

The ministry of righteousness (3:7–11)

Comparison with Moses (3:12–18)

Blindness of nonbelievers (4:1–4)

Proclaiming the Lord Jesus (4:5–6)

The present and the future (4:7–5:10)

Earthenware vessels (4:7–12)

Paul's faith (4:13–15)

Daily renewal (4:16–18)

The human condition (5:1–5)

Dwelling with the Lord (5:6–10)

A ministry of reconciliation (5:11–6:10)

Paul's confidence (5:11–15)

Reconciliation (5:16–19)

Ambassadors for Christ (5:20–21)

A short exhortation (6:1–2)

The exercise of Paul's ministry (6:3–10)

A plea for personal reconciliation (6:11–7:4)

Paul's open heart (6:11–13)

A scripturally based exhortation (6:14–7:1)

Paul's pride and joy (7:2–4)

The arrival and report of Titus (7:5–16)

Titus's arrival (7:5–7)

Further reflection on the painful letter (7:8–13a)

Titus's experience (7:13b–16)

Service to God's holy people (8:1–9:15)

The collection (8:1–24)

The example of the Macedonians (8:1–6)

The appeal (8:7–15)

Titus and his delegation (8:16–24)

A further appeal (9:1–15)

Concerning the delegation (9:1–5)

Final motivation (9:6–15)

An aggressive taskmaster (10:1–13:10)

Paul's missionary task (10:1–18)

Strategic warfare (10:1–6)

A warning (10:7–11)

Self-commendation (10:12–18)

On the attack (11:1–15)

The Corinthians' betrothal (11:1–4)

Paul is not inferior to the super-apostles (11:5–6)

The gospel for free (11:7–12)

The pseudo-apostles (11:13–15)

Boasting like a fool (11:16–12:13)

Putting up with Paul (11:16–21a)

A telling comparison (11:21b–23)

Paul's hardships (11:24–29)

The escape from Damascus (11:30–33)

Rapture to the third heaven (12:1–5)

A thorn in the flesh (12:6–9a)

Power in weakness (12:9b–10)

The peroration of a fool's speech (12:11–13)

Paul's third visit to Corinth (12:14–13:10)

The announcement (12:14–15)

A final defense (12:16–18)

Paul's fears (12:19–21)

Paul is ready nonetheless (13:1–4)

Exhortation and a prayer (13:5–10)

The letter closing (13:11–13)

Exhortation (13:11a)

Peace prayer (13:11b)

Greetings (13:12)

Epistolary benediction (13:13)

2 Corinthians 1:1–2

The Letter Opening

Introductory Matters

In Paul's Hellenistic world, letters generally began with an identification of the sender, a designation of the recipient(s), and a stereotypical greeting. Identifying the writer and the recipient at the beginning of a letter was particularly useful when letters were written on scrolls. The first words to be read as the scroll was unrolled identified both the person who had written the letter and the person for whom it was intended. Paul follows the custom of his day, beginning not only 2 Corinthians in classic fashion but all of his other letters as well.

Ancient letter writers sometimes added further information to the names of the sender and/or the recipient. When added to the name of the sender, this additional information was roughly equivalent to the signature block in a modern letter. Such information, called "titling" or "entitlement" (*intitulatio*), identified the relationship between the sender and the recipient and established the basis of the authority of the writer (*ēthos*) vis-à-vis those to whom he or she was writing (on *ēthos*, see the sidebar "Rhetorical Argument").

In the event that canonical 2 Corinthians is a composite document and thus an artificial letter, the editor responsible for compiling the text avoided repetition and saved valuable space on the papyrus or codex by

> **2 Corinthians 1:1–2 in the Rhetorical Flow**
>
> ▶ **The letter opening (1:1–2)**
> **The senders of the letter (1:1a)**
> **The recipients of the letter (1:1b)**
> **The greetings (1:2)**

21

Rhetorical Argument

Rhetoric, the art of persuasion, was well known in the ancient world. Rhetorical handbooks were written to help students of rhetoric. Works by Aristotle, Cicero, and Quintilian are among the most important of the surviving rhetorical manuals. These handbooks distinguish three kinds of rhetorical arguments, those from *ēthos*, *pathos*, and *logos*. An argument from *ēthos* is based on the authority of the speaker/writer vis-à-vis the addressee(s). The argument from *pathos* appeals to the addressee's self-interest or emotions. The argument from *logos* is rational, consisting of many different techniques that are spelled out in the manuals.

transcribing a single salutation. The chosen salutation identifies Paul as the author responsible for the content that follows and indicates that he has sent all of this material to the Christian community at Corinth. It does not necessarily follow that the salutations of the compiled texts were absolutely identical. The editor would have chosen a salutation that he considered appropriate, and in the case of 2 Corinthians, one similar to the salutation of 1 Corinthians.

Tracing the Train of Thought

The Senders of the Letter (1:1a)

1:1a. Paul identifies himself as an **apostle of Christ Jesus through the will of God** (1:1). In 1 Corinthians Paul wrote about the apostolate as the first of the Spirit's gifts to the church (1 Cor. 12:28). He identified himself as an apostle to the Corinthians, if not to others (1 Cor. 9:2). He is an apostle (*apostolos*, derived from *apostellein*, "send") to the Corinthians because he has been sent to preach the gospel to them. Paul is convinced that it is according to God's will that he was sent to the Corinthians. His language also suggests that he was sent to the Corinthians as the emissary of Christ Jesus.

The salutations and opening thanksgivings of Paul's Letters often anticipate some of the major themes of the correspondence. Second Corinthians is an apology for (i.e., defense of) and an extended disquisition on Paul's ministry to the Corinthians, his apostolate. Paul places the matter squarely before the Corinthians by introducing himself to them as an apostle of Christ Jesus, designated for this task by the highest possible authority, God himself.

Our **brother Timothy** joins Paul in greeting the Corinthians. Timothy is associated with Paul in the salutations of Philemon and 1 Thessalonians as well as 2 Corinthians. Together with Paul and Silvanus, Timothy has proclaimed the gospel to the Corinthians (2 Cor. 1:19). Identified in 1 Cor. 4:17 as Paul's beloved and faithful child, Timothy was sent to the Corinthians to remind them about how Paul had comported himself when he was among them. Since Silvanus is not named in the salutation of 2 Corinthians, it is likely that Silvanus was not with Paul when the letter was written.

Figure 1. Icon of the Apostle Paul.

Kinship language plays an important role in the rhetoric of several of Paul's Letters, especially 1 Corinthians, Galatians, 1 Thessalonians, and Philemon, but it plays a lesser role in 2 Corinthians—apart from 2 Cor. 8–9, where Paul takes up the matter of the collection on behalf of God's holy people in Jerusalem. Fully half of the occurrences of sibling language in 2 Corinthians appear in the context of this appeal (2 Cor. 8:1, 18, 22, 23; 9:3, 5).

Most English-language translations identify Timothy as "our" brother, but the pronoun *hēmōn* (usually translated "our") is not found in the Greek text (cf. 1 Cor. 1:1; 1 Thess. 1:1; Philem. 1). Paul is judicious in his use of pronouns. The absence of a pronoun in reference to Timothy suggests that Timothy is to be considered not only as brother to Paul but also as brother to the Corinthians.

Timothy as Coauthor

Second Corinthians can be described as what Jerome Murphy-O'Connor has called a "we-letter" (Murphy-O'Connor 1993). Paul's use of the first-person plural, especially in the first eight chapters of the letter, indicates that it is essentially a joint letter sent by Paul and Timothy to the Corinthians. Timothy shared with Paul many of the experiences recounted in the letter. Timothy's coresponsibility for the content and composition of the letter appears quite clearly in 1:13, where Paul begins to reflect on the fact that he is writing a letter and says, "We write." Obviously only one voice could dictate the words to the scribe who worked at the transcription of the text. The voice was that of Paul, but the contents came from Paul and Timothy. Thus it seems appropriate to speak of Timothy as the coauthor of this letter, at least until 9:1, when Paul begins to speak in the first-person singular.

The Recipients of the Letter (1:1b)

1:1b. Using the same formula that he employed in the salutation of 1 Corinthians (1 Cor. 1:2), Paul addresses the letter **to the assembly [*ekklēsia*] of God that is at Corinth.** Although *ekklēsia* is generally translated as "church," the word properly designates a gathering or assembly, a group of people called together for some purpose. As such, *ekklēsia* was a term in common use, where it especially referred to political assemblies and civic gatherings. Paul localizes the gathering to which he wants his letter to be read. The assembly was held in Corinth, the capital of the Roman province of Achaia.

Baker Photo Archive

Figure 2. A Map Showing Corinth, Capital of the Roman Province of Achaia.

The addressees, presumably called together to listen to the reading of Paul's letter, are theologically identified as "the assembly of God." The theological qualification distinguishes the addressees from other groups, such as civic assemblies or gatherings of local religious, funereal, and trade associations. It identifies the assembly as belonging to God, the one God of Paul's biblical tradition (1 Cor. 8:6), and underscores the situation of the Corinthian community within the history of salvation.

"Assembly of God" (*qĕhal-yhwh* / *hē ekklēsia tou theou*) is a biblical expression that identifies Israel as God's holy people. The epithet (cf. Deut. 4:10; Judg. 20:2; 1 Kings 8:14; Ezra 2:64; etc.) evokes memories of the people of God assembled in the desert at the time of the exodus, Israel's primordial experience of salvation (Deut. 23:1–8; Judg. 20:2; etc.). Paul's use of the term to describe the Christian community of Corinth associates them with Israel, suggesting that these Christians also participate in the history of God's saving his people.

Paul intended that his message also be heard by Christians who did not actually live in the city of Corinth. So he wrote to the Corinthians **together with all [*pasin*] the holy people who are in the whole [*holē*] of Achaia.** The double universal indicates that the apostle wanted his message to get around. How that message, the *homilia* of the letter, was to get around requires some consideration of the situation of the church at Corinth.

It is possible, but unlikely, that Paul intended this to be a circular letter, to be read not only in the metropolitan capital itself but also to other Christian congregations in Achaia, such as the fledgling church at Cenchreae (cf. Rom. 16:1), a short distance to the east of Corinth. It is more likely that Paul, well aware that his word would extend beyond those to whom it was immediately addressed (cf. 1 Thess. 1:8), wanted to encourage the dissemination of his message to Christians throughout the province.

That was made possible by the physical location of Corinth and its commercial and political status. Seafarers departing from the ports of Corinth stopped at a number of different ports around the Mediterranean basin. Travelers who trod the Peloponnesian Way easily made their way to and from Corinth, a center of mercantile and political activity.

Having spent considerable time in Corinth (Acts 18:5, 11, 18), Paul knew that Christian merchants and civic officials could bring his message to Christians in the outlying regions of Achaia as they went about their business. On the other hand, Paul also knew that people from throughout Achaia, not to mention other parts of the empire, came to Corinth to buy, sell, and trade as well as to conduct official business. Since it was a major market town, Corinth was always host to a fair number of visitors. Christians from other parts of Achaia may well have been part of the larger group that occasionally came together as a church, about which Paul wrote in 1 Corinthians (1 Cor. 11:18, 20).

The Greetings (1:2)

1:2. Having identified those for whom the contents of his letter was intended, Paul greets them with **to you be grace and peace from God our Father and the Lord Jesus Christ.** This signature greeting, replacing the stereotypical "be joyful" (*chairein*) of Hellenistic letters, was used by Paul in all of his letters except his oldest one, his first letter to the Thessalonians. The greeting probably had a liturgical origin and was appropriated by Paul because his letters were intended to be read to gatherings of believers.

Noteworthy for its binitarian monotheism—with a nod to Larry W. Hurtado (1998, 100, 114; 2003, 151–53), who speaks of the binitarian shape of early Christian devotion—the greeting is virtually a prayer in which Paul and Timothy ask God, identified as Father, and Jesus Christ, identified as Lord, to act in consort in conferring divine favor and covenantal peace upon those to whom the letter is addressed.

Theological Issues

Ecclesiology

The opening salutation of 2 Corinthians echoes a rather rich ecclesiology. The church (*ekklēsia*) is considered to be an event; it is a gathering of people that occurs at a specific time and in a particular place. Paul does not identify the venue of the gathering other than to say that the assembly takes place in the city of Corinth, but it is more than likely that the Corinthian believers gathered in the home of one of their number. They may have gathered specifically to hear the reading of Paul's letter, but it is also possible that their gathering provides an occasion for a "public" reading of the letter (cf. Acts 2:22; 1 Thess. 5:27).

Describing the gathering as the "church of God," Paul adds a salvific dimension to his understanding of the gathering and enables his addressees to consider themselves as a privileged assembly in the history of salvation. Though largely composed of Gentiles, the community can look to those who belonged to the generation of the exodus as their own forebears (cf. 1 Cor. 10:1).

That the members of the community belong to God receives further emphasis when Paul refers to all the holy people in Achaia. As a biblical description of the people of God, "holy" has cultic origins. It identifies a group of people set apart as God's own possession, to serve God's own purposes. Used in a plural form, the adjective indicates that not only is the community as a whole "holy" but also that each of its members is holy.

The salutation of 1 Corinthians specifies that the members of God's holy people have been made holy by Jesus Christ and that they are thereby designated as God's holy people (1 Cor. 1:2). Although properly describing the assembly at Corinth as belonging to God, the description of the Corinthians as holy also has an ethical component. They are expected to act as people who belong to God. Moreover, the identification of the Corinthians as holy reflects the fact that they have received the Holy Spirit, that is, the Spirit of sanctification. This gift is a dynamic presence leading the Corinthians to patterns of behavior that reflect their holy status.

Holy People (*hoi hagioi*)

Sometimes the Greek *hoi hagioi* is translated as "the saints" rather than as "holy people." These English translations are synonymous: "saints" has a Romance root, and "holy" has a Germanic root.

The community of believers recognizes the one God as Father and Jesus Christ as Lord. Since "Lord" precedes Jesus, a proper name, and "Christ" follows the name Jesus, "Lord" should be taken in a proper titular sense whereas "Christ" appears to be part of the proper name rather than being formally significant.

The bonds that bind the members of the assembly to one another are akin to family ties. Hence, Timothy is appropriately albeit metaphorically called "brother" (*ho adelphos*). The epithet points to the bonds of affection that link Timothy not only to Paul but also to the Corinthians, suggesting that similar bonds join all of them to one another.

Paul's ecclesiology highlights the importance of the local church, the local assembly. Paul does not, however, claim that the local assemblies exist in isolation from one another. Rather, the bonds of kinship that bind them together link them with other believers (cf. 1 Thess. 4:9–10). In the case of the church of God at Corinth, Paul notes that its members are in relationship with the other members of God's holy people scattered throughout the province of Achaia. Later in this letter Paul reflects on the link between the Corinthian believers and the "mother church" in Jerusalem (2 Cor. 8–9).

Writing to the Corinthians, Paul identifies himself as an "apostle." At this stage in the history of the early Christian communities, "apostle" was not yet used as a title. The designation identifies someone who has been sent on a mission, especially the mission of preaching the gospel in a place where it has not previously been proclaimed (cf. Rom. 15:20–21). The epithet connotes initial evangelization and the founding of a community of believers (cf. 1 Cor. 12:28), a role that Paul fulfilled vis-à-vis the community of Christian believers at Corinth (1 Cor. 9:2).

The rich ecclesiology of Paul's salutation provides contemporary believers with a paradigm for reflecting on their own church experience. To what extent do they consider themselves to be in continuity with Israel of old? How does their holiness manifest itself in appropriate patterns of behavior? Do they consider their relationship with other Christians to be that of brothers and sisters? Do they acknowledge the lordship of Jesus? Is the contemporary church faithful to its apostolic origins?

Christological Nomenclature

Paul uses the title "Lord" (*kyrios*) of Jesus in the epistolary greeting of 1:2. Commentators frequently note that this is Paul's preferred christological title. Paul writes, "We proclaim Jesus Christ as Lord" (4:5). By the time Paul wrote 2 Corinthians, use of the title in the opening salutation had become a standard feature of Paul's epistolary style. Paul reprises the title in 1:3, the first verse of the body of the letter, as a key word in "our Lord Jesus Christ," the apostle's most complete christological title (cf. 4:5; 8:9; and 13:13). Eighteen times in this letter the apostle uses the *kyrios* title of Jesus without mentioning Jesus's proper name.

The title was used in the Greek Bible to render the Hebrew Yahweh. Paul appropriates the title and uses it of Jesus. The title implies that Jesus has been raised from the dead through the Spirit, the power of God at work, and has entered into the divine sphere, where death reigns no more. Frequently, Paul uses the title as he anticipates the consummation of the kingdom. At the parousia Christ's lordship will be fully revealed. Between the resurrection and the

> ### Lord, *Kyrios*
>
> The absolute use of "Lord" in reference to Jesus occurs in 2:12; 3:16, 17 (2x), 18 (2x); 5:6, 8, 11; 6:18; 8:5, 19, 21; 10:8; 11:17; 12:1, 8; 13:10.

parousia, Jesus is Lord insofar as God acts in the world through Jesus. God exercises his lordship over all through Jesus, who is Lord. Christians are people who acknowledge not only that God is Lord but also that Jesus is Lord.

Paul's use of *kyrios* to describe who and what Jesus is represents a rhetorical tour de force. The people in the Greco-Roman world to whom Paul preached the gospel had an experiential understanding of someone being lord. The lord was someone who had the power of life and death over his servants. The lord was someone to whom servants owed complete obedience. Above all, the Roman emperor was lord. People's real-life experience of a lord gave them an initial basis for understanding what Paul meant when he identified Jesus as Lord, even if they did not grasp the full theological implications of the epithet.

In the berakah (*běrākâ*, "blessing," 1:3–7) Paul identifies Jesus as "Christ" (*Christos*). In 1:3 the apostle appends the Christ title to the name of Jesus (cf. 1:19; 4:6; 13:5), but later in the benediction he uses the title by itself (1:5). This isolated use of the Christ title will continue throughout the letter, where it occurs thirty-eight times. The absolute use of *Christos* is a characteristic feature of 2 Corinthians, distinguishing this missive from the other undisputed Pauline Letters.

The *Christos* title is a verbal adjective derived from the verb *chriō*, "anoint." "Christ" is not only synonymous with but also a true equivalent of "Messiah" insofar as both terms are transliterations of verbal adjectives, one in Greek, the other in Hebrew, used substantively and meaning "one who is anointed." Early Christian tradition associated the anointing of Jesus with his death and burial (Matt. 26:7, 12; Mark 14:3, 8; John 12:3, 7). In somewhat similar fashion Paul uses the *Christos* title of the human Jesus, who died and was raised from the dead.

> ### Christ, *Christos*
>
> The absolute use of "Christ" in reference to Jesus occurs in 1:5 (2x), 21; 2:10, 12, 14, 15, 17; 3:3, 4, 14; 4:4; 5:10, 14, 16, 17, 18, 19, 20 (2x); 6:15; 8:23; 9:13; 10:1, 5, 7 (2x), 14; 11:2, 3, 10, 13, 23; 12:2, 9, 10, 19; and 13:3.

The way the apostle uses *Christos* makes it an appropriate christological title in passages that underscore the solidarity existing between believers and the one in whom they believe. Indeed Paul puns on the title in 1:21.

PART 1

2 Corinthians 1:3–2:13

Ministerial Crises

Hellenistic letters typically begin with a health wish, sometimes complemented by a prayer of thanksgiving or replaced by such a prayer. A classic example is the second-century-CE letter of Apion, a soldier who writes to his father, greeting him, then saying, "I pray above all that you are healthy and strong, and that things are going well with you, as well as with my brother and my sister and her daughter. I give thanks to the Lord Serapis that he saved me when I was in danger on the sea." Paul generally follows the Hellenistic convention by following the salutation with a thanksgiving. The thanksgiving generally focuses on the community to which Paul is writing.

What follows the salutation of 2 Corinthians is about Paul: it is his prayer of praise to God. The prayer of praise is addressed to God, who encourages and consoles Paul in the midst of his afflictions and sufferings. The mention of Paul's afflictions introduces a motif that will recur throughout the letter. The first part of the letter introduces the Corinthians to a major crisis that Paul experienced in Asia, a crisis so severe that Paul feared for his life. A crisis of a different sort was the unrest that he experienced when he failed to meet Titus in Troas.

> ### 2 Corinthians 1:3–2:13 in Context
>
> The letter opening (1:1–2)
>
> ► Ministerial crises (1:3–2:13)
>
> Paul explains and defends his apostolic ministry (2:14–7:4)
>
> The arrival and report of Titus (7:5–16)
>
> Service to God's holy people (8:1–9:15)
>
> An aggressive taskmaster (10:1–13:10)
>
> The letter closing (13:11–13)

A crisis of another sort and the dominant theme of this first part of the letter is the grief that he experienced on the occasion of his second visit to the Corinthians. Not only was the experience painful for Paul, but also the abrupt change of plan occasioned by his second visit led to the accusation that he was acting in a fickle manner. The relationship between Paul and the Corinthians was definitely strained at that point. Paul therefore takes pains to defend his apostolic integrity.

2 Corinthians 1:3–11

A Prayer of Praise and the Asian Experience

Introductory Matters

Beginning the body of his letter with a prayer of thanksgiving, Paul seems to have followed a Jewish convention. The epistolary convention (cf. 2 Chron. 2:12; Eph. 1:3–14; 1 Pet. 1:3–5) reflects a broader Jewish practice, continued to this day (cf. Rom. 1:25; 9:5), in which blessing God, whose name has been invoked, is considered to be a very important duty. Indeed the Babylonian Talmud says that one should first offer praise and then pray (*b. Ber.* 32a). *Blessings* (*Berakot*) is the first treatise of the Mishnah, the Talmud, and the Tosefta.

Paul's prayer of praise is in the form of a berakah (MT: *běrākâ*, blessing), a kind of eulogy, a prayer similar in purpose to a doxology but with a different form. In the Greek Bible, the Septuagint (LXX), the berakah opens with a stereotypical formula, "Blessed be the Lord God of Israel, who . . . [*Eulogētos kyrios ho theos Israēl, hos . . .*]" (LXX: 1 Kings 1:48; 2 Chron. 2:11 [2:12 Eng.]; 6:4; Pss. 40:14 [41:14 Eng.]; 71:18 [72:18 Eng.]; see also Luke 1:68).

"Blessed" does not mean that humans are blessing God. "It is beyond dispute," Hebrews says, "that the inferior is blessed [*eulogeitai*] by the superior" (Heb. 7:7). In the biblical and Jewish tradition, God is declared blessed

> ### Flavius Josephus
>
> This historian says that King Eirōmos [Hiram of Sidon] wrote a letter to King Solomon that began, "It is proper to praise God for having given to you, who are a wise man endowed with every virtue, your father's royal power" (*Ant.* 8.53; cf. 2 Chron. 2:11–12; 1 Kings 5:7).

because he has imparted his blessings to the nation or to certain individuals (1 Sam. 25:32; Ps. 41:13 [40:14 LXX]; 1QM 14.4–5; 1QH 5.20; 10.14; etc.). In many of the biblical berakot (MT: *bĕrākôt*), the reason God is declared to be blessed is expressed in a relative clause. In this respect, Paul follows the biblical precedent when he writes about the God who encourages us in all our afflictions. Other Jewish berakot are prayers that God may impart his blessings on persons or things, for example, on those who are about to be betrothed (*b. Ketub.* 7b) or on those in mourning (*b. Soṭah* 7b). Paul's berakah is not a berakah of this type; the apostolic berakah is a confession that God is blessed.

The verbal adjective *eulogētos* used by Paul means to be well spoken of. Attentive to the syntax of the word, most biblical versions translate the word as "blessed" or "praised." The nature of the berakah as a prayer of praise leads some interpreters to translate *eulogētos* as if it were the noun "praise." In any case Paul's phrase, like the opening phrase in many such prayers, lacks a verb. Some verb must be supplied. Many English translations of 2 Cor. 1:3 and other biblical berakot supply the verb "be." Thus, "Blessed be the God and Father of our Lord Jesus Christ" (NRSV, JB, NJB; cf. KJV). When "be" is supplied in the translation of the opening words of a berakah, the berakah appears to be a prayer that God be blessed when in fact it is a prayer of praise and a declaration that God is indeed blessed, as those who are the beneficiaries of God's blessings are happy to proclaim. When the Greek adjective is translated as "praised" rather than as "blessed" and the verb "be" is supplied, the language of the translation is performative. The one who prays that God be praised is actually praising God.

Alternatively and perhaps preferably, "is" may be supplied as a verb in the principal clause of a berakah. Thus a common Jewish blessing begins, "Blessed are You, Lord our God, Ruler of the universe." The Lord God is declared to be blessed because he is the source of all blessings.

Effectively, the different approaches to the opening words of the berakah show that translation is not simply a matter of rendering words. It is also a matter of grappling with the syntax of an ancient language.

Tracing the Train of Thought

The Berakah (1:3–7)

1:3–7. Paul's prayer of praise initially appears to be almost a spontaneous sequel to his mention of the name of God. To this day pious Jews add a "blessed be He" when they mention the name of the Lord. Paul begins his prayer of praise in classic fashion, **Praised**

be God, but instead of identifying God as the God of Israel, he uses an explicative *kai* (**and**) to identify the God whom he is praising as the **Father of our Lord Jesus Christ** (1:3). The binitarian monotheism reflected in the greeting (1:2) receives new emphasis as Paul begins his prayer of praise. The title Lord (*kyrios*), used of God in the biblical *berakot*, is now used of Jesus, in keeping with Paul's customary usage.

Paul's identification of God as the Father of the Lord Jesus Christ achieves a double purpose with regard to the contents of his letter. First of all, the God whom Paul confesses is not to be understood apart from his relationship with Jesus Christ. Already the greeting (1:2) has implied that God and Jesus Christ act in consort. What God does vis-à-vis human beings is done through Jesus Christ. Jesus is Lord insofar as through him God exercises lordship over humanity. Second, the opening words of Paul's berakah put a focus on Jesus Christ, which will not be lost in the body of the letter, especially not in its conciliatory section, 1:3–2:13.

A second article (*ho*) introduces a further description of God, which reprises the "God and Father" language of the epistolary greeting. God, the Father of the Lord Jesus Christ, is **the Father of compassion**. "Compassion" is literally "mercies" (*oiktirmōn*). The plural implies that divine compassion is expressed in specific acts of mercy. The word occurs often in the Greek Bible as a translation of the Hebrew *rahămîm* (2 Sam. 24:14; Ps. 25:6; Isa. 63:15; Dan. 2:18 Theod.; cf. *T. Jos.* 2.3; Rom. 12:1). Described as the father of mercies, God is identified as the source of compassion. Being the source of acts of mercy is one of God's attributes (cf. Ps. 145:8–9), one by which God manifests a paternal attitude toward human beings.

The next descriptive epithet, **"God of all consolation"** (*theos pasēs parakaleseōs*), is similar to a longer formula found in the prayer of Rom. 15:5–6, "May the God [*ho theos*] of steadfastness and encouragement [*parakaleseōs*] grant you to live in harmony." The Romans' formula identifies God as the source of endurance and encouragement. Paul may have appropriated its language, as well as that of 1:3, from a liturgical doxology. In any and every circumstance, Paul looks to God as the source of encouragement, especially the encouragement that he needs and has needed in the situation that he is about to describe.

Paul has a predilection for speaking and writing in threes. His fondness for literary triads appears in a third use of the article (*ho*), this time introducing a participial clause that gives the motivation for Paul's prayer of praise. The God who is the source of all encouragement is one **who consoles us in all our affliction** (1:4). Paul specifies the liturgical language that he has just used to

Paraklēsis

Words derived from the prepositional prefix *para-* and the verb *kaleō* are among the most difficult words to translate in the entire NT. Readers of the Fourth Gospel are often confused about how best to identify the one whom Jesus is to send from the Father. Many translators take the easy way out by rendering the Greek *paraklētos* as Paraclete. There is, however, no easy way out when it comes to translating the noun *paraklēsis* that Paul uses in 1:3.

In the NT, the noun is very much a Pauline term. Eighteen of its twenty-nine occurrences appear in the undisputed Pauline Letters. The word rings throughout 2 Corinthians, where it occurs eleven times (1:3, 4, 5, 6 [2x], 7; 7:4, 7, 13; 8:4, 17). The connotations of the word run from "admonition" through "request" and "encouragement" to "comfort" and "consolation."

The related verb *parakaleō* occurs even more often in 2 Corinthians (1:4 [3x], 6; 2:7, 8; 5:20; 6:1; 7:6 [2x], 7, 13; 8:6; 9:5; 10:1; 12:8, 18; 13:11). When Paul uses the verb in a hortatory context, as he often does, *parakaleō* means "I urge [you to . . .]." In the first chapter of this letter, in which references to suffering and affliction are frequent, "consolation" and "console" seem best suited to capture Paul's thought.

describe God by applying the divine epithet to his own circumstances, challenging situations in which both he and Timothy have been involved. The use of "all" indicates that Paul has received consolation from God in each and every adversity that they have suffered.

God provides consolation and encouragement **to enable us** [Paul and Timothy] **to console people in any affliction with the consolation with which we ourselves are being consoled by God.** God's gift has a ministerial purpose. What Paul has received from God he is to give to others. There is something of a "chain reaction." As Paul has been consoled by God, he is to console others with the selfsame consolation that he has received.

The basis for what Paul writes lies in his conviction that his afflictions or sufferings share in the sufferings of Christ: **For just as the sufferings of Christ abound in us, so also our consolation goes beyond measure through Christ** (1:5). Expressing himself in this fashion, Paul introduces a christological paradigm that pervades the first part of his letter.

It is difficult to determine precisely what Paul means by the "sufferings of Christ" (cf. Phil. 3:10). It is not likely that Paul is referring to the kind of sufferings described in the Synoptic Gospels' Passion Narratives since, apart from the fact that Jesus's death was a death by crucifixion (1 Cor. 1:23; 2:2; Phil. 2:8), Paul does not make reference to the circumstances attendant upon Jesus's death. It is more likely that there is a corporate reference in Paul's expression. Paul considers his afflictions as the sufferings of Christ insofar as they are sufferings of the church, which he has described as the body of Christ (1 Cor. 12:12–27). These sufferings have been incurred for the sake of Christ. What Paul writes later in the letter suggests that he probably had in mind the apostolic sufferings that he endured while preaching the gospel of Christ.

Those sufferings are more than enough for Paul, but so too is the consolation that he is able to extend to others through Christ. To be sure, the analogy is not perfect, but Paul wants to underscore the superabundance of God's gifts manifest in the superabundance of the consolation that Christ has imparted to him and his companion. He and Timothy have been consoled beyond measure.

Thus far, Paul's focus has been on himself and Timothy. His repeated use of the first-person-plural pronoun is in keeping with this focus. Now Paul turns his attention to his addressees. Contemplating the possibility of two contrasting experiences for himself and Timothy, Paul says that each of the two experiences accrues to their benefit: **If we are afflicted, it is for your consolation and salvation. If we are consoled, it is** also **for your consolation at work in the patient enduring of those sufferings with which we too suffer** (1:6).

The Corinthians might be surprised that Paul considers his sufferings to be beneficial to them, but Paul affirms that his trials are doubly beneficial. On the one hand, Paul's sufferings are helpful as a source of consolation and encouragement for the Corinthians. The Corinthians can take heart from Paul's afflictions: they are not alone in suffering affliction. On the other hand, Paul sees his suffering as somehow fostering the salvation of the Corinthians. The mention of salvation gives an eschatological dimension to Paul's thoughts on consolation and affliction. Paul hardly considers himself to be their savior, but he may well be thinking that his sufferings will encourage the Corinthians to conform themselves to Christ and thus participate in salvation.

If Paul and Timothy are consoled, the Corinthians will be consoled and encouraged insofar as they will receive, from the missionaries' consolation, strength that enables them to endure sufferings similar to those of Paul and Timothy, all their afflictions being the sufferings of the body of Christ. Moreover, Paul will console and encourage the Corinthians, just as he and Timothy have been consoled and encouraged (1:4).

Paul is sure of what he has just said. He is confident that just as the Corinthians share in the sufferings of Christ, they will also share the consolation that Paul and Timothy have received as a gift of Christ: **And our** [in Greek, "of us"] **hope for you is firm in the knowledge that just as you share in the sufferings, so also you share in the consolation** (1:7).

Paul's language is dialogical; he writes about us and you. The pronouns recapitulate the first- and second-person-plural pronouns that permeate the passage. To express his confidence in and for the Corinthians, Paul uses an elliptical turn of phrase. His Greek simply says, "As you are sharers in the sufferings, so in the encouragement." Since Paul is expressing his hope, the encouragement that he expects for the Corinthians appears to have an eschatological dimension.

A Near-Death Experience (1:8–11)

1:8–11. Paul has every intention of trying to help the Corinthians understand what he has been saying. The initial "for" (*gar*) links what he is about to say with his benediction. The "disclosure formula" **for we do not want you to be unaware** (1:8; Rom. 1:13; 11:25; 1 Cor. 10:1; 12:1; 1 Thess. 4:13), with its double negative, indicates that he is imparting new information to the Corinthians. Appealing to them as his **brothers and sisters**, as he does only twice more in this letter (8:1; 13:11; cf. 1:2), Paul wants to share with members of his (fictive) family (see the section titled "Kinship Language" after my comments on 2:13) an experience that will help them understand how affliction can give way to consolation.

Paul mentions **the affliction [*thlipsis*] that we suffered in Asia**, without giving any further information as to what it was. This mysterious but difficult and troubling experience is an example of the afflictions that Paul and his companions have suffered for the consolation and salvation of the Corinthians (1:6). The plural may suggest that both he and Timothy have experienced something similar. If, however, the affliction was a matter of a serious problem affecting Paul's health, as seems likely, Paul's "we" would have been a literary plural, akin to the editorial "we" in contemporary literature.

Paul's language underscores the helplessness that he experienced at the time: **we were heavily weighed down, beyond our strength.** The experience brought him to the brink of despair, a psychological reaction that he seems not to have experienced in other situations: **so that we despaired even of life itself.** Only in 2 Corinthians does the apostle write about despair (*exaporēthēnai*; cf. 4:8). What he experienced in Asia was terrifying, life-threatening, and unique in Paul's life.

We would like to be able to analyze Paul's experience from a medical and psychological point of view, but the worldview of Paul and his contemporaries was different from ours. We examine the symptoms of an illness in an effort to determine its medical or psychological cause. The ancients looked at an illness and thought about its supernatural source. Using a rhetorically ascensive **indeed,** Paul describes his Asian affliction as a near-death experience, one in which **we experienced a death sentence upon us** (1:9). In no other place in his extant writings does Paul mention a death sentence (*to apokrima tou thanatou*). The rarity of his use of this kind of juridical language bespeaks the exceptional nature of his experience, his own helplessness, and the implied conviction that his situation was due to some supernatural power, the power of death (Rom. 8:38; 1 Cor. 15:26). The perfect tense of the verb that Paul uses in describing his experience of a death sentence shows that the experience continues to have an impact on his life.

We would like to know what happened in Asia, but ultimately all the textual clues lead up a blind alley. It may well be that Paul is referring to a serious

God Who Raises the Dead

The tradition of the Jewish berakah might have prompted Paul to characterize God as one who raises the dead. The Amidah prayer, or Eighteen Benedictions, was the key element in daily synagogal worship. Pious Jews recited the benedictions twice a day. The second berakah came to be known as the "Resurrection of the Dead" because it stressed the revival of the dead. There is nothing specifically Christian about the idea, which recurs in Rom. 4:17 (cf. Heb. 11:19).

Analogously, the idea of God as Savior, the one who delivers his people from evil, is a common motif in Jewish prayer. The notion is echoed in the final petition of Matthew's Jewish-Christian version of the Lord's Prayer (cf. the use of the verb "deliver" [*rhysai*] in Matt. 6:13).

physical ailment that he thought would prove fatal, but of this we cannot be sure. What we can be sure of is that it was a terrifying experience, one that led Paul to think that he was about to die, an experience that the apostle likens to a death sentence. His obvious emotion in recalling that experience is reflected in 1:8–11, a run-on sentence that is almost a hundred words in length.

Whatever it was that Paul experienced, the ordeal taught him a lesson. He experienced a death sentence **so that we might rely not on ourselves but on God who raises the dead.** The God who raises the dead is the God **who delivered us from such a great peril of death** (1:10). God delivered Paul from the peril that he faced. Paul seems to have interpreted his delivery from mortal danger as a harbinger of the resurrection of the dead. The lingering effects of the experience lead Paul to express his hope in personal and experiential fashion: **and who will deliver us.** Being delivered from the near-death experience made such an impression on Paul that he speaks of his deliverance three times within a single relative clause. Like the threat of death itself, Paul's hope is an ongoing experience. So Paul praises God **in whom we hope that he will continue to deliver us.** His reiteration of the idea that God will deliver him in the future is a faith-filled expression of hope, even if, at this point in the letter, the apostle is not yet speaking about his own eschatological salvation.

With somewhat convoluted terminology, Paul's thought turns again to the Corinthians. A clause, **with you helping us by prayer** (1:11), presumes and subtly asks that the addressees continue to pray for him. Their prayer is to be one of thanksgiving for the deliverance, described as a "favor" (*charisma*), that Paul has experienced: **so that [God] might be thanked on our behalf by many persons for the favor given to us with the** prayerful **help of [so] many.** Since many (*ek pollōn prosōpon*) apparently pleaded for Paul's deliverance from the death-defying experience, it is appropriate that many offer thanks to

God for the grace of deliverance that was granted Paul. In the quasi-liturgical context of Paul's berakah, Paul's "many" (*dia pollōn*) may have the Semitic connotation of all, who are not few in number. He may be suggesting that the entire community prayed for him and, despite the strain of the present relationship, Paul asks them to continue to pray for him.

Theological Issues

In the context of the berakah, Paul writes about prayer. He specifically mentions the prayers of petition (*deēsis*) and the prayer of thanksgiving (for which he uses the verb *eucharisteō*) offered on his behalf (1:11). This explicit mention of prayer arises from the prayerful context of the entire passage. Paul's berakah itself is a prayer of praise. His apparent allusion to the second berakah of daily worship recalls passages such as Deut. 32:39 and 1 Sam. 2:6 in the Greek Bible.

The Psalms, Paul's prayer book, provided the apostle with much of his language. Harvey (1996, 18) opines that the influence of the psalms is so pervasive in this passage that it is only the phrase "we despaired even of life itself," a poignant expression of personal distress, that is not influenced by the Psalter.

For example, in Ps. 38:6 the psalmist speaks of being "bowed down" under the weight of his iniquities and foolishness. In the Greek text (37:5 LXX) is the same verb that Paul uses to speak of his being weighed down (in 2 Cor. 1:8). Psalm 34, a psalm closely linked to the berakah, begins with "I will bless [*eulogēsō*; 33:2 LXX] the Lord." This psalm mentions "trouble" (34:6; *thlipsis* in 33:7 LXX) and twice speaks about being delivered (34:4, 7 [33:5, 8 LXX]), using the very verb later adopted by Paul (2 Cor. 1:10). Psalm 116 is a paean of praise to God, who has heard the psalmist's plea. As the psalmist waxes eloquent in praise, he speaks of his distress (116:3 [114:3 LXX]) and of being delivered (116:4 [114:4 LXX]) from death (116:8 [114:8 LXX]). This is the same kind of language that Paul uses to write about his God-initiated rescue from a nearly fatal experience.

Paul often uses biblical language to speak about his experience. The passages in Paul's Letters that come most readily to mind are passages from the books of the prophets Isaiah and Jeremiah and the book of Psalms. Paul's prayerful language of praise echoes that of Second Isaiah and psalms of confidence, such as Pss. 23; 71; 74; and 86. The words of the psalmist continue to inspire him as he speaks about his delivery from a life-threatening experience, especially since he does so in the context of a prayer of praise.

Like Paul, many Christian communities and many individual Christians continue to use these psalms in prayer. They are an important part of the liturgy of many Christian churches and constitute the bulk of the daily prayer in the Roman Catholic liturgy of the hours.

2 Corinthians 1:12–2:4

Paul's Defense of His Integrity

Introductory Matters

Second Corinthians 2:3–4 mentions an emotional letter that Paul wrote with tears in his eyes. The letter was occasioned by Paul's painful visit to Corinth and his encounter with an offender, an encounter to which the apostle makes reference in the following pericope. The difficult letter made a lasting impression on him. He mentions it again a few verses later (2:9) and comes back to it in 7:8, 12.

Some commentators (e.g., Bornkamm 1971; Furnish 1984; Betz, *ABD* 1:1148–50; Thrall 1977) think that the letter is substantively present in 2 Cor. 10–13, where Paul's tone is quite harsh. These chapters do not mention any visit to Corinth that caused pain to the apostle; nor do they mention any particular person who caused difficulty for Paul. Hence it is more than likely that the tearful letter has been lost.

That it existed at one time and has now been lost serves to remind us that we do not possess the entirety of Paul's correspondence with the Corinthians, let alone possibly additional correspondence with other communities.

Tracing the Train of Thought

The Witness of Conscience (1:12–14)

1:12–14. The ancients considered that baring one's soul, what we moderns call personal transparency, was an important feature of a letter. Paul did this in 1:8–11 but now adds that what he really wants to talk about is not himself and the perils that he faced but his relationship with the Corinthians: **For this is our boast: the witness of our conscience, that we conducted ourselves in the world in godly [in Greek *tou theou*, "of God"] integrity and sincerity, not according to fleshy wisdom but by the grace of God** (1:12).

Paul's own conscience can testify that whatever difficulties he faced were not due to any misconduct on his part. He acted with integrity and sincerity (*en haplotēti kai eilikrineia*). The two nouns, which are virtually synonymous, form a hendiadys. Paul acknowledges that God is the source of both qualities. If we seek a distinction between the two, "integrity" may relate to his personal ethic, while "sincerity" pertains to his uncompromised fidelity to the mission that God has entrusted to him. The motif of Paul's integrity plays out throughout the letter.

To make his point even more forcefully, Paul adds a clarifying contrast. The Greek wording of his clarification has a sharpness that is difficult to render in English. It begins with an explanatory *kai* ("and") that has been left untranslated and sets in opposition two prepositional phrases introduced by *en* ("in"). Paul says that his personal integrity and his single-minded devotion to his calling do not derive from his desire to conform to the standards of secular wisdom; rather, they come as a grace, a gift, from God. Paul describes ordinary, secular wisdom as "fleshy" (*sarkikē*); it belongs to the realm of flesh and blood, rather than to the realm of the Spirit. Adding **especially toward you,** Paul prepares for the apology that is to come. The Corinthians to whom Paul is writing enjoy a pride of place among those touched by his upright and single-minded behavior.

Then, in what seems to be a virtual aside, Paul begins to reflect on the fact that he is writing a letter to the Corinthians: **For we are writing to you only what you read and**

Hendiadys

Hendiadys is a figure of speech in which two closely related ideas are joined by the conjunction "and" (*kai*) rather than by a noun and an adjective or a noun and a qualifying noun in the genitive case. "Integrity and sincerity" is but one instance of Paul's use of this figure of speech (cf. Rom. 1:5). Paul occasionally coordinates two related verbs in similar fashion.

Paronomasia

Paul was a master rhetorician. As is the case with all of Paul's Letters, 2 Corinthians is a composition whose rhetorical appeal derives to a great extent from the apostle's deft use of rhetorical devices and figures of speech. Use of these devices is all the more important insofar as his addressees are listening to what he has written.

Paronomasia is a figure of speech that makes use of similar sounds. In some ways paronomasia is like a play on words insofar as similar sounds, words or stems of words, are placed in close proximity to one another in order to create a contrast. In English, "read and understand" is not an example of paronomasia, but Paul's Greek is a clear example of his use of this figure of speech. He writes, *Anaginōskete* [read] *ē kai epiginōskete* [and understand]. Paul's threefold employment of "understand" in 1:13–14 is another example of his use of this figure of speech.

understand (1:13). Paul does not write letters for the sake of writing letters; he writes so that his addressees will read the letter and understand it. That Paul states his intention in writing is all the more important since Paul is about to speak about his correspondence with the Corinthians. He does not want the present letter to be a source of miscommunication as has apparently happened in the past. Strikingly, he joins Timothy (cf. 1:1) with himself as the coauthor of this letter as he continues to write in the first-person plural.

Paul then turns his thought to what he hopes for the Corinthians. He hopes that they will understand: **I hope that you will thoroughly [*heōs telous*] understand that we are [*esmen*] your boast and you are ours on the day of our Lord Jesus Christ** (1:14). The apostle hopes that the Corinthians understand that at the parousia they will be one another's pride and joy. He writes **that we are your boast and you ours on the day of our Lord Jesus Christ**. Paul sees himself as a source of the Corinthians' pride, the object of their boasting on the day of the Lord Jesus. In turn, they will be the source of his pride (cf. Phil. 4:1; 1 Thess. 2:19).

Paul's use of the present tense assumes that they are already taking pride in one another. Paul hopes that this will last until the final times. In what is a virtual aside, **even as you have understood us partially,** Paul compares the future understanding for which he hopes with an element of partial

Parousia

The term "parousia" is a transliteration of the Greek *parousia*, which means "presence" or "arrival." Paul uses the term in its ordinary sense to refer to the arrival of Titus (7:6, 7) and his own presence. In 1 Corinthians and 1 Thessalonians he uses the term in a technical, theological sense to speak of the coming of Jesus as Lord on the day of the Lord.

understanding, which was then the Corinthians' experience (cf. 1 Cor. 13:12). In the space of just a couple of verses, ten words altogether, Paul has used the verb "understand" three times with three different objects: his letter, himself, and an eschatological experience in which he is a figure.

Defense against the Charge of Being Fickle (1:15–22)

1:15–22. In each of his letters Paul speaks about his travel plans. In this regard, 2 Corinthians is not an exception, but here he looks back on his previous plans. **With this confidence,** he writes, **I wanted to come to you first of all, so that you might have a second expression of my goodwill. For, having passed through you on my way to Macedonia,** I wanted **to come to you again on my way back from Macedonia and be sent by you on my way to Judea** (1:15–16). Confident that he has been praised by the Corinthians and well aware of how highly he regards them, Paul tells the Corinthians about his desire to pay them a couple of visits. In his earlier correspondence Paul expressed a desire to pay them a visit (1 Cor. 16:5–7), but there is no evidence that he told them about his desire to visit them another time after that.

Now Paul tells the Corinthians that another visit to them is at the top of his agenda. He wants to come to Corinth first of all. Another visit on the trip back from Macedonia, where Paul has founded communities of believers in Philippi and Thessalonica, would be an additional expression of his affection for the Corinthians. The visit would allow Paul to obtain provisions for the trip to Judea; properly supplied, he would be sent on his way (cf. Rom. 15:24; 1 Cor. 16:11). Visiting Corinth on his return trip would be another expression of Paul's affection for them. Implied in Paul's expression of his hope may be the thought that the Corinthians can be of some help in the final stages of collecting gifts for the poor in Jerusalem (1 Cor. 16:3–4; cf. 2 Cor. 8–9).

Paul seems to have changed his travel plans. Philosophical moralists contemporary with Paul, Epictetus in particular (*Diatr.* 2.15.4–8), urged that serious consideration be given to changing one's mind. Paul's changing his mind with regard to his travel plans rankled the Corinthians, prompting Paul to respond to their accusations with a pair of rhetorical questions: **So, wanting to do this, did I act with levity? Or do I want what I want according to the flesh, with the result that my "yes, yes" is also a "no, no"?** (1:17). Paul often contrasts "according to the flesh" (*kata sarka*) with "according to the Spirit" (*kata pneuma*). The contrast may be implicit in Paul's rhetorical question. If so, Paul is suggesting that he did not change his plans for any of the usual human reasons; he did so because he was moved by the Spirit to act as he did.

Chrysostom

Paul "is dependent on the Spirit's authority. Paul was not able to come to Corinth because it was not the Spirit's will for him to go there" (*Hom. 2 Cor.* 3.3).

The rhetorical questions call for a firm negative response on the part of the Corinthians. Paul's first question implies that he was not acting in some kind of arbitrary fashion; he wasn't vacillating. The second question suggests that his decision was not motivated by merely human considerations; he wasn't a weak person who speaks out of both sides of his mouth, saying yes and no at the same time. Paul's double yes and double no do not otherwise appear in the extant correspondence. The repetition most likely represents idiomatic usage; there is no need to find in Paul's expression any particular allusion to the dominical tradition that appears in written form in Matt. 5:37 (cf. James 5:12).

As he often does, Paul responds to his own rhetorical questions. He does so with an appeal to the fidelity and reliability of God and his Christ. **But God,** says Paul, is someone on whom we can rely. Affirming that God **is faithful,** Paul with some emphasis echoes a biblical tradition (Deut. 7:9) that is frequently reiterated in his correspondence with various churches (1 Cor. 1:9; 10:13; 1 Thess. 5:24). God's reliability grounds the reliability of Paul's word: **in that our word to you is not yes and no** (1:18). The "yes and no" indicate that Paul is responding to the accusation that he was speaking out of both sides of his mouth. But there is more than this at issue. Paul's "word" to the Corinthians is also the gospel message that he preaches (cf. 1 Cor. 1:18; 2:4; 15:2; 1 Thess. 2:13).

Paul continues to play with the yes-and-no theme as he affirms that there is no "yes and no" in Jesus Christ, the Son of God: **For the Son of God, Jesus Christ, the one proclaimed among you by us, Silvanus and Timothy and me, was not yes and no; in him there was only a yes** (1:19). Only here in the entire letter does Paul identify Jesus as "the Son of God." God is the first word in the Greek sentence. With emphasis placed on God in this way, the reader can continue to think about the God whom Paul has just affirmed to be faithful. To explain the reliability of God, Paul offers the example of the Jesus Christ of the kerygma. Jesus's yes is directed to God as Jesus consented to obey God and God's will for him (cf. Rom. 5:19; Phil. 2:8). Jesus's yes was a filial response to the Father. Jesus Christ is God's yes-man.

Paul's "word" to the Corinthians is about the Son of God, who was neither ambivalent nor unwavering in his obedience to the Father. In verse 18, Paul states that the word addressed to the Corinthians is "our word." He explains that the first-person plural refers to Silvanus and Timothy as well as to himself. This apostolic threesome preached at Corinth, from where they greeted the Thessalonians (1 Thess. 1:1).

Explaining his cryptic language about Jesus being a yes to God, Paul says, **For as many as are the promises of God, in him they are yes** (1:20). The promises of God were made to Israel, which counted the promises among its most important privileges (Rom. 9:4). Paul's turn of phrase suggests that the promises were virtually innumerable. In Jesus Christ all of God's promises to his people are confirmed and realized. In that sense, Christ is the yes to

---

Amen

"Amen" (*amēn*) is the Greek transliteration of a Hebrew and Aramaic term that means "so be it."

In biblical and Jewish tradition, "Amen" was a responsive affirmation employed in liturgical settings (cf. Neh. 8:6; *m. Ber.* 8.8). Paul acknowledges this customary use in 1 Cor. 14:16. He himself often adds a concluding "Amen" to the prayer formularies that he incorporates into his letters, the short berakot of Rom. 1:25 and 9:5; the doxologies of Rom. 11:36; Gal. 1:5; and Phil. 4:20; the wish-prayer of 1 Thess. 3:13; and the final wish-prayers of Rom. 15:33; 16:25–27; 1 Cor. 16:24 (mg.); Gal. 6:18; and Philem. 25 (mg.).

Second Corinthians is the only one of Paul's undisputed letters that lacks an "Amen" as the conclusion to a prayer formulary.

---

the promises. Paul immediately adds a corollary to this affirmation: **Whence, it is through him that the Amen is to the glory of God, through us.** Paul appears to be teasing out the implications of the congregation's use of "Amen," an acknowledgment that what has been said is reliable. The "Amen" is the congregation's yes to God's promises, a yes that has been enabled by Christ.

Figure 3. Paul's Travel Plans according to 1 Cor. 16.

The "Amen" is not merely a liturgical formula; it also expresses a way of life, characterized by fidelity and obedience to God. Christ, the very expression of God's faithfulness, enables the community to glorify God in what they say and do.

God has been a major focus for Paul's observations throughout the first chapter of the letter. Now that he has again mentioned God, Paul formulates a dense theological statement: **God is the one who strengthens us with you in Christ and who has anointed us, indeed,**

> **"In Christ"**
>
> "In Christ" (*en Christō*) is a common Pauline expression. Its appearance in 1:21 suggests a reference to the baptismal liturgy (cf. Rom. 6:3; cf. 1 Cor. 12:13; Gal. 3:27).

the one who has sealed us and has given the Spirit as a pledge in our hearts (1:21–22). The theological affirmation consists of four participles, each of which pertains to God's activity. The first participle is in the present tense, affirming God's ongoing strengthening of the evangelists and the community. The "us with you" underscores Paul's solidarity with the community and their common experience. In earlier correspondence with the Corinthians, Paul used the same verb ("strengthen," *bebaioō*) to describe Christ strengthening the community to the end (1 Cor. 1:8–9).

Figure 4. Paul's Actual Travels according to 2 Cor. 1.

Anointed

"Anointed" is the first of three aorist participles, joined together by *kai* ... *kai* ("and ... and"). This paratactic style is typical of Paul, the orator who dictates his letter, as is his use of a group of three. Those who wrote in Greek typically used more subordinate clauses than did Semitic authors, whose writings are often characterized by *parataxis*, the coordinate arrangement of words, phrases, and clauses. This run-on style is more typical of oral than of written forms of communication.

Punning on the word "Christ" (*Christos*, a substantivized verbal adjective derived from the verb *chriō*, "anoint"), Paul affirms that Christians have been anointed by God. Not only is this the only time that Paul uses the verb "anoint" but, apart from 1 John 2:20, 27, this is the only NT text on the spiritual "anointing" of Christians. The aorist participial form of the verb refers to some event in the past that has lingering effects. The anointing of 2 Cor. 1:21 (and of 1 John) refers to the gift of the Spirit in baptism—anointing was introduced as a baptismal ritual in the second century—a gift that continues to manifest itself in the mission of those baptized (cf. Luke 4:18).

The second member of Paul's triad is an affirmation that God has sealed us. The "us" (*hēmas*) continues to be the "us with you" of verse 21. A seal is a sign of ownership. As God has anointed his Christ with the Spirit, so he has anointed not only the evangelists but also believers with the same Spirit, inscribing them, as it were, with the character of Jesus (Stegman 2005, 361).

The third member of the triad describes the gift of the Spirit as a pledge. Paul's Greek, *ton arrabōna tou pneumatos* ("the pledge of the Spirit") uses a genitive of definition, an epexegetical genitive. The Spirit is the pledge. The image comes from the financial world, where it normally means something like "down payment," suggesting that there is more to come. The Spirit was given into the hearts of the Corinthians as well as the missionaries, given to them in the very core of their being. Granted as a pledge, the Spirit will continue to use the evangelists as his instruments and will continue to be active among the Corinthians.

The doubled image of the seal and the down payment symbolically expresses Paul's conviction that his work enjoys God's seal of approval and that the gift of the Spirit entails an ongoing experience for Paul and for the Corinthians.

Skipping a Visit to Corinth (1:23–24)

1:23–24. When Paul considers it important that his readers know something that cannot be verified by an appeal to some other source, he does not shy away from using a mild oath (Rom. 1:9; Phil. 1:8; 1 Thess. 2:5, 10). Wanting the Corinthians to know why he changed his travel plans, he swears, **I call upon God as [my] witness on my very being that it was to spare you that I did not**

come again to Corinth (1:23). Paul affirms that it was not out of self-interest but out of concern for the Corinthians that he changed his travel plans.

Paul's formulation echoes biblical language (see 1 Sam. 12:5–6; 20:42; but also Gen. 31:50; Judg. 11:10). Unlike the later rabbis, Paul does not hesitate to use the name of God (*ho theos*) as he swears. Later in the letter Paul will use different formulas to draw God into the truth of what he has to say (2 Cor. 11:31; 12:19).

As he tries to explain his conduct to the Corinthians, his personal integrity is at stake. Paul draws attention to himself with an emphatic *egō* ("I"). Since the Greek verb alone is sufficient to specify person and number, the use of the pronoun is not required. However, a personal pronoun can be added for the sake of emphasis. Paul does so and then compounds his personal investment in the truth of his statement by swearing on his own life. What exactly Paul means when he says that he wants to spare the Corinthians is, however, difficult to ascertain. Spare them from what? we might ask.

Paul then continues to describe his motivation by means of a rhetorical contrast. **Not that we lord it over your faith, but we are coworkers in your joy, for you are firm in your faith** (1:24). Switching from the emphatic first-person singular to the first-person plural, Paul denies that he and his companions are trying to boss the Corinthians around. Neither he nor Silvanus nor Timothy has any intention of domineering over the faith of the Corinthians. Their faith is not simply their belief: it is their life of faith, the dynamic and active faith of 1 Thess. 1:3.

Rather than domineering and lording over the Corinthians, the evangelists want to be coworkers (*synergoi*) with them. Paul is determined that the Corinthians understand the nature of their relationship. Rather than standing over the Corinthians as their bosses, Paul and his companions stand in a horizontal relationship with them. More often than not, when Paul uses "work" in its various forms (from the root *erg-*), he is referring to the work of the gospel. This is especially the case when he compounds the use of the root with *syn*, "with." The Corinthians are united with Paul and the other missionaries in the proclamation of the gospel, the fruit of which is joy.

The evangelical connotation of "coworkers" suggests that Paul has in mind something more than merely temporal joy when he writes about the joy of the Corinthians. Joy comes from God (Rom. 15:13) and his Holy Spirit (Rom. 14:17; Gal. 5:22; 1 Thess. 1:6). When Paul writes about joy, his language typically

The Explanatory "For" (*gar*)

An explanatory "for" (*gar*) introduces the codicil. This Greek conjunction appears four times in 1:23–2:4, making the pericope a tightly knit unit of thought. The expressions of Paul's thought follow closely one after another and are linked together by means of this conjunction. In 2 Corinthians Paul often uses this conjunction to join his thoughts together. An earlier example occurs in 1:8, where Paul's account of the Asian experience is joined to his prayer of thanksgiving.

refers to an experience of God's presence by those who belong to God. The Corinthians' "joy" refers to their lives as Christians, lived to the full.

Not only does the team of evangelists have no intention of domineering over the faith of the Corinthians; they also have no need to do so since the Corinthians stand fast in their life of faith, as the codicil explains.

The Tearful Letter (2:1–4)

2:1–4. Paul wanted to spare the Corinthians; now he adds that he didn't want to make them sad. This was a self-conscious decision on his part: **For I decided not to come to you again in sadness** (2:1). A strategically placed "again" (*palin*) evokes the memory of a previous visit that had caused Paul some personal pain and entailed sadness for at least some of the Corinthians. The mention of his own sadness contrasts sharply with the idea that he and his fellow evangelists are committed to the joy of the Corinthians. It also contrasts with the joy and happiness about which he will begin to write.

Continuing to write about sadness, Paul asks a rhetorical question. **For if I make you sad, is there someone who makes me glad other than the one whom I have saddened?** (2:2). Paul concedes that he has saddened some of the Corinthians, most likely on the occasion of his previous visit. In those circumstances, who can possibly cheer Paul up? Who can possibly take away Paul's sadness except the one whom he has saddened? The obvious answer is "no one."

The rhetorical "is there someone?" is necessarily in the singular. The Greek participles are in the singular, referring to the community itself rather than to any specific individual within the community. In the present circumstances no one but the Corinthian community itself can make Paul happy. A happy Corinthian church would make Paul happy.

Paul rarely uses the verb "gladden" (*euphrainō*). Apart from the verb's appearance in two Scriptures quoted by Paul, Deut. 32:43 (Rom. 15:10) and Isa. 54:1 (Gal. 4:27), this is Paul's only use of the verb, the only time that he uses it on his own. Connoting enthusiastic joy, the verb presumes a positive relationship of community between a person who is made glad and the one(s) who makes the person glad. Paul's rhetorical question expresses his desire that a warm community relationship exist between himself and the Corinthians.

As Paul continues to write about his relationship with the Corinthians, he explains why he sent a letter rather than visiting them: he wanted to avoid the grief that he experienced the last time that he was with them. **And I wrote to you for this**

Sadness

Sadness is a major theme in the first part of this letter, especially in chapters 2 and 7. Paul uses the noun *lypē* (sadness, pain, or grief) five times (2:1, 3, 7; 7:20 [2x]; cf. 9:7) and the verb *lypeō* (sadden, cause pain or grief) eleven times (2:2 [2x], 4, 5; 6:10; 7:8 [2x], 9 [3x], 11). Paul uses each of these words only twice in the rest of his extant correspondence.

very reason, lest, coming to you, I be made sad by those who should make me rejoice (2:3). Paul does not want to compound the sadness of his second visit, so he substitutes a literary presence for his personal presence and writes a letter to the Corinthians.

Paul is sure that at bottom he and the Corinthians share one another's joy (cf. 1:14). He is confident. Paul forces a single verb—the participle *pepoithōs*, followed by two clauses with syntactically different constructions—to do double duty ("confident . . . convinced"). He says that he is **confident in all of you and convinced that my joy is the joy of all of you**. The double use of the phrase "all of you" (*pantas hymas . . . pantōn hymōn*) is particularly striking. None of the Corinthians is beyond his purview; he expects all of them to share his joy reciprocally.

> ### The Threefold Purpose of the Hellenistic Letter
>
> Heikki Koskenniemi (1956) has shown that in addition to its specific purpose and message (*homilia*), a Hellenistic letter had two basic purposes. A letter was a way for an absent person to be present (*parousia*), and it was an expression of friendship (*philophronēsis*). Paul's writing about joy and explaining why he is writing to the Corinthians instead of paying a visit accomplishes both of these purposes.

Paul continues to express his attachment to the Corinthian congregation as he speaks about an earlier letter. **For I wrote to you from great distress and heartfelt anguish, with many tears** (2:4). As he often does, Paul uses three expressions to characterize his sadness as he writes the letter: great distress, heartfelt anguish, and many tears. Paul often writes about his distress (cf. 1:4, 8), but it is only here that he mentions his anguish and his tears. Each of the three expressions is accompanied by a qualifier that points to the intensity of Paul's sadness. His distress is great, his anguish heartfelt, and his tears many. The letter Paul wrote with such powerful emotion is often called "the tearful letter." Unfortunately it has been lost.

Having shared the emotions with which he wrote the letter, Paul employs a contrast to underscore what he really intends to do in writing the letter. The letter is being written **not to make you sad but to let you know the immeasurable love that I have for you**. This affirmation of Paul's love for the Corinthians enhances Paul's ethos, his profile, the authority with which he wrote and is writing. He not only loved and continues to love the Corinthians, but he does so almost excessively, immeasurably.

Theological Issues

The Faithful God

Gordon Fee writes that 1:15–22 is "one of the most God-centered, God-focused [passages] in the Pauline corpus" (1994, 289). The leitmotif of the subunit is the fidelity of God; its central affirmation is *pistos ho theos*, "God is faithful" (1:18). The pithy formula highlights one of the most prominent traits of the biblical God: his truth or fidelity (*'ĕmet* in Hebrew).

Throughout the subunit, Paul unpacks the idea of God's fidelity. The most prominent manifestation of God's fidelity is Jesus Christ, God's very own yes to his promises, the one who enables believers to express their own Amen to God. A second expression of the fidelity of God is the ministry of Paul, Silvanus, and Timothy, whose word is not a yes and no: instead, it is a simple yes. The gospel that they preach and have preached is an expression of God's faithfulness. A third expression of God's faithfulness is the gift of the Spirit. Through the Spirit, God has "christed" (*chrisas*, "anointed") Paul and the evangelists, enabling them to continue Christ's story. The participles describing the past and present activity of God in 1:21–22 point to the Corinthians. The baptized believers in Corinth are a fourth manifestation of God's faithfulness. These various manifestations of the faithfulness of God cohere to redound to the glory of God, as Paul says in 1:20.

The theocentricity of this pericope, manifest in Paul's unpacking the motif of God's faithfulness, highlights a focus on God, God's activity, and the human response to God's activity that permeates the entire letter. All too often the "theology" of Paul, that is, his "God-talk," is neglected or treated in cursory fashion in Pauline studies. This should not be the case. Paul has much to say about God in each one of his letters, not least in this Second Letter to the Corinthians, where God-talk, the explicit use of *theos* ("God"), appears in every chapter, some seventy-nine times in all.

Prior to his reflection on the fidelity of God, Paul has spoken to the Corinthians about his reliance on God (1:9). God willed that Paul should be an apostle (1:1). Paul and his companions were graced by God, particularly with the gift of a single-minded sincerity (1:12). Paul spoke to the Corinthians about God who is Father, the Father of the Lord Jesus Christ (1:2) and our Father (1:3). God has made the Corinthian community his very own (v. 1). God is the source of compassion and consolation (1:3), the one who enables the evangelists to console others even as they themselves have been consoled by God. God is the giver of grace and peace (v. 2). God is the Savior (1:10). God is praised (1:3), petitioned (1:11), and thanked (1:11). And God is the one who raises the dead (1:9).

Before reaching the end of chapter 1, the reader of 2 Corinthians has enough material to write a tome on Pauline theology. Nonetheless, Paul will have more to say about God as he continues to write this letter. The observant reader should be aware of Paul's focus on God throughout the entire composition. A similar theocentric focus is important for contemporary believers and perhaps even more so for those who preach the gospel, so well preached by Paul. It is almost too easy to forget about God when a believer is concerned about the mission of the church, the church itself, and Jesus. Jesus's focus was on God; so too was Paul's.

Eschatology

Toward the end of the last century J. Christiaan Beker (1980) argued that Paul's apocalyptic eschatology permeates all of his writings. Second Corinthians 1:14 provides a clue that this is so. Paul writes about boasting on the day of our Lord Jesus Christ.

The biblical prophets often spoke and wrote about "the day of the LORD," the "day of *yhwh* in the Hebrew Bible," *hē hēmera tou Kyriou* in the Greek Bible (Isa. 13:6, 9; Jer. 25:33 [32:19 LXX]; Ezek. 7:10; 13:5; Joel 2:1; 3:14 [4:14 LXX]; Amos 5:18, 20; Obad. 15; Zeph. 1:7, 14; Mal. 4:1 [3:19 LXX]). Depending on the perspective of a specific prophetic oracle, that future day was sometimes envisioned as judgment day (Amos 5:18–20); at other times it was construed to be a day of salvation (Joel 2:32 [3:5 LXX]).

In Paul's apocalyptic thought, that day, the day of the Lord, is the day when Jesus Christ, raised from the dead as Lord, will be fully manifest as Lord, assuming the title Lord (*kyrios*) that the Greek Bible used for *Yhwh*. The biblical day of the Lord became, for Paul, the day of the Lord Jesus Christ. The day of the Lord Jesus Christ will be a day of salvation. That this is the expectation of Paul and the Corinthians is implied by Paul's use of the pronoun "our" (*hēmōn*, absent from some manuscripts of 1:14) in the phrase, "the day of our Lord Jesus Christ." The qualifier indicates that when the Lord Jesus appears on that day, he will appear as the Lord of his people, that is, as their Savior and Benefactor.

In 1 Corinthians (15:23; 16:17) and in his Letter to the Thessalonians (1 Thess. 2:19; 3:13; 4:15; 5:23), Paul uses the Greek term *parousia*, meaning "presence" and by extension "coming," to refer to the presence, the parousia, of the Lord Jesus Christ on that day. Paul does not use the term in this technical theological sense in 2 Corinthians, but he does express a hope that the Corinthians will persevere in their understanding "until the end."

The phrase *eis telos* ("to the end") is a common Greek expression meaning "thoroughly" or "completely." The majority of commentators on 1:13 understand Paul's words *heōs telous* ("until the end," with a different preposition and the noun in the genitive rather than the accusative case) to be synonymous with the classic common expression, but in light of what Paul is about to say, his phrase may have an eschatological nuance. He may be expressing a hope that the Corinthians will persevere in their understanding "until the last things," that is, until the day of the Lord Jesus Christ. Perhaps, as Jan Lambrecht (2006, 27) suggests, Paul has deliberately intended a double entendre. He wants the Corinthians to persevere completely until the end.

The resurrection from the dead is an important element in Jewish apocalyptic thought. Paul echoes a Jewish prayer as he writes about God "who raises the dead" (1:9). For Paul the resurrection of Jesus from the dead was the decisive eschatological event. With Jesus's resurrection, the final era of salvation has begun. In a confession of faith, Paul attributes the resurrection of Jesus to the power of the Holy Spirit (Rom. 1:4). It is through the Spirit that God brings about the final era of salvation. That era has not yet fully run its course. Thus Paul can write about the Spirit "as a pledge" in our hearts (1:22). The presence of the Spirit in our hearts is, as it were, a down payment on the fuller reality that is yet to come.

Joy

Joyful language appears throughout the NT, in which the noun "joy" occurs fifty-nine times and the verb "rejoice" seventy-four times. "Joy," says Ceslas Spicq, is "the distinguishing characteristic of the Judeo-Christian religion" (*TLNT* 3:498). A large proportion of the occurrences of the word "joy" (*chara*) in the papyri are of Christian origin.

One third of the NT's use of joyful language appears in Paul, the noun nineteen times, the verb twenty-seven times. The apostle writes about joy in all of the extant letters with the exception of 1 Corinthians, but in none of his letters does he write about joy as much as he does in 2 Corinthians. The noun appears six times in 2 Corinthians, the verb eight times.

An overview of Paul's use of the language of joy quickly reveals that when he writes about joy, he is describing an experience that is not merely a good feeling, some warm fuzziness. True, Paul contrasts joy with sorrow or sadness (cf. 6:10), and he does so repeatedly in 1:23–2:4, but he also writes about joy in the midst of affliction (7:4; 8:2) and his experience of joy when he is weak (13:9). Thus Paul's joy has something of a paradoxical quality about it. There can be an experience of joy even in the most adverse circumstances.

For the apostle, joy is a gift from God (Rom. 15:13) and a fruit of the Holy Spirit (Gal. 5:22; cf. Rom. 14:17; 1 Thess. 1:6). Though not specifically identified as a charism, "spiritual gift," by Paul, joy is similar to the spiritual gifts in that as a gift of God joy is manifest in a characteristic pattern of Christian behavior. Linked with peace in Rom. 14:17; 15:13, and with righteousness in Rom. 14:17, "joy," like peace and righteousness, refers "to comprehensive, value-centered, complex behavior" and

---

Paul's Use of Joyful Language

The noun *chara*, "joy," is found in the following verses:

> 2 Cor. 1:15, 24; 2:3; 7:4, 13; 8:2
> Rom. 14:17; 15:13, 32
> Gal. 5:22
> Phil. 1:4, 25; 2:2, 29; 4:1
> 1 Thess. 1:6; 2:19, 20; 3:9
> Philem. 7
> but not in 1 Corinthians

The verb *chairō*, "rejoice," appears in the following verses:

> 2 Cor. 2:3; 6:10; 7:7, 9, 13, 16; 13:9, 11
> Rom. 12:12, 15 (2x); 16:19
> 1 Cor. 7:30 (2x); 13:6; 16:17
> Phil. 1:18 (2x); 2:17, 18, 28; 3:1; 4:4 (2x), 10
> 1 Thess. 3:9; 5:16
> but not in Galatians

"can stand for the sum of Christian behavior" (Berger, *EDNT* 3:454). This active aspect of joy may well characterize Paul's use of "joy" in 1:24.

Typically Paul uses "rejoice" in the first person to speak about his joy in the Christian communities to which he is writing (2:3; 7:7, 9, 13, 16; Rom. 16:19; 1 Cor. 16:17; Phil. 4:10; 1 Thess. 3:9). Used of Paul and his missionary team, "joy" acquires an apostolic nuance and is contagious. Paul rejoices when the Corinthians are led to repentance (7:9). Because he has confidence in them, he rejoices (7:16). The contagiousness of apostolic joy is a quality that appears when Paul writes about joy in 7:7, 13. This understanding of joy permeates what Paul has to say about joy in 1:23–2:4. For him, joy is a gift that is active and contagious.

Contemporary believers should remember just how important joy was for the apostle Paul. It was a gift of the Spirit that qualified the very existence of the believer. There is, of course, a place for "hellfire and brimstone" in Christian preaching, but this should not take away from the fact that the Christian experience is essentially a joyful experience.

2 Corinthians 2:5–11

A Disciplinary Matter

Introductory Matters

For a second time in Paul's extant correspondence with the Corinthians, the apostle addresses a disciplinary matter. Second Corinthians 2:5–11 and 1 Cor. 5:1–5 are similar in that they both speak about Jesus (albeit with different language), about Satan, and about the respective roles of Paul and the community. In both passages, Paul clearly states that it is the community's responsibility to take the initiative. Because of these similarities, most ancient, medieval, and Reformation commentaries interpreted the texts as if both were dealing with the same subject.

Yet the two passages differ from each other with regard to the specificity of the offense. In 1 Corinthians, the evildoer is identified as a man who was involved in an incestuous relationship with his father's wife. In 2 Corinthians, the evildoer is simply identified as someone who has been a source of grief for Paul and the community. The Corinthians surely knew who the person was (cf. 7:12) and what he had done, but we do not. A letter always assumes more than it states. That is generally not a problem for those who receive the letter, but it is a problem for us since we must remain in ignorance about the real situation. Unlike the Corinthians, we

> **2 Corinthians 2:5–11 in the Rhetorical Flow**
>
> The letter opening (1:1–2)
>
> Ministerial crises (1:3–2:13)
>
> > A prayer of praise and the Asian experience (1:3–11)
> >
> > Paul's defense of his integrity (1:12–2:4)
> >
> > ▶ A disciplinary matter (2:5–11)

have to be content with Paul's identifying the evildoer simply as "anyone" (*tis*, 2:5) and then as "him" (*ho toioutos*, "that one," in vv. 6, 7).

Tracing the Train of Thought

2:5–11. As Paul continues to write about the sadness that he and the community share, he turns his attention to someone in the community who has been a particular source of grief for him: **If someone has caused sadness** (2:5). The anonymous individual to whom Paul refers is most likely someone who had a role to play, perhaps the principal role to play, among those who made Paul's recent visit to Corinth such a painful experience for the apostle.

Paul's use of first-person-singular personal pronouns focuses the reader's attention on Paul himself, but Paul goes on to say that he is not the only one who has experienced sadness. The community has also suffered because of what has happened. Paul plays down his own sadness as he writes that the community itself has been saddened by the recent events: **he has saddened not me but, let me not exaggerate, all of you to some degree.** "All of you" (*pantas hymas*) picks up on a similar phrase in 2:3. As Paul draws attention to the sadness that the community has or should have experienced, he takes pains not to overstate his case. The parenthetical phrase "let me not exaggerate" and the qualifying phrase "to some degree" take some of the edge off what he is saying. The focus should not be on Paul since the entire community has been hurt in some way or another.

Many people in the Corinthian congregation seem to have already punished the evildoer, probably by shunning him in some way. Paul deems that to have been sufficient punishment: **punishment by most** of you **is enough for him** (2:6). Paul asks for no additional sanction simply because he, the apostle to the Corinthians, has been personally aggrieved by the evildoer. Rather, he is concerned that the sinner be forgiven and reconciled to the community. The time for punishment belongs to the past. Now Paul urges the community to adopt a new course of action. He asks them to forgive the sinner and encourage him: **now forgive and encourage him** (2:7).

Paul has the well-being of the evildoer in mind as he writes **lest he be overwhelmed by excessive sorrow.** Without the benefit of modern psychological insights, Paul seems to be aware that overwhelming remorse can be debilitating. The apostle urges the Corinthians not only to forgive and encourage the evildoer but also to love him lest he be overcome by remorse. **Therefore, I encourage you to reaffirm your love for him** (2:8).

Having interrupted his reflections on the difficult letter that he had written to the Corinthians in order to share with them some thoughts about how they should treat the troublemaker, Paul resumes his commentary on the earlier missive. **For this is why I wrote, so that I might know your character** (2:9). Some

---

The Epistolary Aorist

The epistolary aorist is a literary convention used in correspondence. In the indicative mood, the Greek aorist tense is basically a past tense. When an epistolary aorist is used, the event to which the verb refers is a past event by the time the reader receives the letter. It is not necessarily past at the time when the letter is being written.

---

scholars take the phrase "I wrote" (*egrapsa*) as an epistolary aorist, with the understanding that Paul is commenting on what he has just written. It is more likely, however, that Paul is referring to the tearful letter and his real reason for writing it.

The now-lost letter was written so that both Paul and the Corinthians might get to know one another better. He wanted them to know about his love for them (*tēn agapēn*, 2:4). As for himself, he wanted to know about their character (*tēn dokimēn hymōn*, 2:9). Paul's purpose clause is sometimes taken in the loose sense of "to test you," but this doesn't capture the real meaning of Paul's thought. He uses a Greek term (*dokimē*) that is very rare in Greek and is used only by Paul among NT authors (2:9; 8:2; 9:13; 13:3; Rom. 5:4 [2x]; Phil. 2:22). The proper meaning of the term, "proven character," must be retained in 2:9. Paul wants to know about the quality of their Christian life as he explains in the next clause, **whether you are obedient in every way.**

The obedience about which Paul writes here is not obedience to himself. Paul had no intention of being lord over the Corinthians' life of faith (1:24). For the apostle, "obedience" (7:15; Rom. 16:19) is a cipher for the Christian life. An authentic Christian life is lived in obedience to God; it is patterned after the obedience of Christ. Paul considers the Corinthians' renewed manifestation of love toward the evildoer as a sign of their obedience.

Not only does Paul urge the Corinthians to forgive the evildoer; he also joins with them in forgiving the one who has caused so much grief. **Whomever you forgive, I too forgive** (2:10). Paul has virtually discounted (2:5) the grief that he suffered: he wants the Corinthians to know that he is one with them in forgiving the evildoer. Not only is he one with them in forgiving the evildoer; he is also doing so for the sake of the Corinthians themselves. **Indeed, what I have forgiven, if I have forgiven anything, has been for your sake in the presence of Christ.** The introductory "indeed" (*kai gar*, v. 10) shows that

---

Obedience

Apart from 2:9, Paul uses the adjective "obedient" (*hypēkoos*) only in reference to Christ (Phil. 2:8). When Paul uses the verb "obey" (*hypakouō*) or the related noun "obedience" (*hypakoē*), he is speaking either about Christ's obedience to God (Rom. 5:19) or about believers' obedience to God (Rom. 6:12–16; Phil. 2:12), Christ (2 Cor. 10:5–6), or the gospel/faith (Rom. 1:5; 10:16; 15:18; 16:26). Paul's understanding of obedience is the background against which he writes about the obedience of the Corinthians.

Paul is about to explain why he has joined in the forgiveness that he wants the community to extend to the evildoer. To underscore the truthfulness of what he has said, Paul adds a few words that are almost a mild oath. Paul did what he did "in the presence of Christ" (*en prosōpō Christou*), that is, in the Lord's sight, or perhaps, with anticipated eschatology, before the judgment seat of Christ (5:10).

The rhetorical strategy is subtle. Paul has told the Corinthians that it is not his intention to lord it over their faith (1:24). So instead of forgiving the evildoer and asking the Corinthians to follow his example, Paul urges them to forgive and tells them that he joins with them in forgiving the evildoer. The subtlety of his strategy continues to be manifest as he draws attention to the forgiveness that he is extending with an emphatic "I" and then almost belittles his own action by saying "if I have forgiven anything." Paul's expressed concern is for the community. What Paul did in forgiving the evildoer was for the sake of the community (cf. 1 Cor. 5:5; Collins 1999, 213).

The reason why Paul wants to join with the community in forgiving the evildoer is the welfare of the community itself. He desires forgiveness **so that we might not be exploited by Satan** (2:11). The apostle does not want the wily Satan to rob the community of one of its members. If the congregation fails to forgive and reconcile, Satan will be victorious. He will have succeeded in removing one person from the community of believers in the city.

And the community should know this, **for we are not unaware of his designs**. Paul joins with the community in affirming that they know what Satan is up to. Satan is up to no good; he has designs against the community.

Theological Issues

Forgiveness

Paul is something of an innovator as he speaks about forgiveness in 2:5–11. The canonical Gospels often speak about forgiveness with the verb *aphiēmi*, the verb used in the Lord's Prayer, "Forgive us our debts as we also have forgiven our debtors" (Matt. 6:12; Luke 11:4). The root sense of *aphiēmi* is "take away," but Paul does not use the verb *aphiēmi* to speak of forgiveness except when

> ### John Chrysostom
>
> *"Paul lets the Corinthians take the lead and tells them that he will follow. This is the best way to soften an exasperated and contentious spirit."* (Hom. 2 Cor. 4.5)

> ### "Designs"
>
> In the NT "designs" (*noēmata*) is a Pauline word, appearing only in 2 Corinthians and Phil. 4:7. As often as Paul uses *noēmata* in the current correspondence (2:11; 3:14; 4:4; 10:5; 11:3), the term has a negative connotation (cf. Plato, *Pol.* 260D; Bar. 2:8; 3 Macc. 5:30). Hence the word is to be translated as "designs," or "plots," rather than by a neutral "thoughts," the product of thinking (Phil. 4:7).

he quotes Ps. 32:1 in Rom. 4:7. In 2:5–11, the vocabulary that Paul prefers to use when writing about forgiveness is *charizomai*, a verb that is used in the NT only in Luke-Acts and in the Pauline corpus. Paul uses the verb in all of his extant letters, with the exception of 1 Thessalonians. This verb connotes an aspect of forgiveness that is not inherent in *aphiēmi*.

Related to the noun *charis*, the basic sense of the verb *charizomai* is manifesting one's pleasure by giving. Hence, the verb is often used to mean "grant" or "give as a favor." Sometimes the verb is used in judicial texts with the meaning of "release" or "hand over to someone else." Paul generally uses the word to talk about God's gifts (Rom. 8:32; 1 Cor. 2:12; Gal. 3:18; Phil. 1:29; 2:9; Philem. 22), but in 2 Corinthians and only in 2 Corinthians, Paul uses the verb to connote a special kind of giving: the granting of forgiveness, forgiving (2:7, 10 [3x]; 12:13).

In the generations before Paul, the verb *charizomai* had not been used to mean "pardon" or "forgive." The use of the term with this connotation began in Paul's time. The writings of Paul's contemporaries, Josephus (*Ant.* 6.144) and Plutarch (*Brotherly Love* 17 [in *Moralia* 488F]), provide evidence that *charizomai* was beginning to be used to describe the forgiveness of offenses. Paul's own use of *charizomai* suggests that forgiveness is an act of graciousness, an act motivated by *charis*, graciousness. Paul writes about forgiving the evildoer in verses 7 and 10; in verse 8 he writes about extending love to the evildoer. In 2:5–11, Paul speaks about humans forgiving one another. He continues to do so in 12:13, where with great irony he suggests that the church might forgive his wrongdoing.

Paul's anonymous disciples, the authors of the deuteropauline letters to the Colossians and to the Ephesians, develop the theological implications of Paul's notion of forgiveness. They use Paul's term to speak of forgiveness among human beings, indicating that such forgiveness is the Christian response to God's forgiveness of sin (Col. 3:13; Eph. 4:32; cf. Col. 2:13), thereby echoing the fifth petition of the Lord's Prayer (Matt. 6:12; Luke 11:4), albeit using the language of the apostle who is the patronym of their letters.

Many people find it difficult to forgive, particularly when they have been personally hurt by someone who is close to them. It is so easy to be judgmental. Many times church communities suffer because their members fail to forgive one another for their perceived faults and feelings. Nonetheless, the Lord's Prayer and Paul's forgiveness of the troublemaker are a reminder that forgiveness is a hallmark of Christian existence. A failure to forgive harms the church, harms the world, and harms so many human relationships.

Satan

Commentators on Paul frequently draw attention to the apocalyptic matrix of the apostle's thought (see especially Beker 1980; 1982). Since Christ has been raised from the dead, the final times have been definitively inaugurated.

The hereafter is already here, even if it is not yet fully realized.

A common motif in apocalyptic thought is an eschatological showdown between God and the forces of evil. Satan, known by many names in Jewish and Christian apocalyptic literature, represents the personification of the evil and disorder over which God will ultimately triumph. Matthew's account of the temptation of Jesus calls this representation of evil "the tempter," "the devil," and "Satan" (Matt. 4:1–11). With the exception of 1 Thessalonians, in which the figure of "the tempter" (*ho peirazōn*) appears in 1 Thess. 3:5, Paul always calls this figure "Satan." The figure of Satan, almost always with the article in Greek (*ho Satanas*, "the Satan"), appears more often in 2 Corinthians (2:11; 11:14; 12:7) than in any of the other letters that Paul wrote (cf. Rom. 16:20; 1 Cor. 5:5; 7:5; 1 Thess. 2:18). Paul's Satan is the denizen of darkness (2:11) who causes evil, disorder, and dissension in the community. Satan is God's cosmic adversary. The church is a virtual battleground where a wily Satan attempts to seize and occupy God's turf.

> ### Apocalyptic Language
>
> Although we live in the final times, the fullness of the final times lies in the future. Obviously the future has not yet been experienced. The inspired imaginative language that the Bible uses to describe the final times is called "apocalyptic," an adjective derived from the Greek word *apokalypsis* ("revelation"). Use of this kind of imagery characterizes much of Jewish intertestamental literature.

Satan impedes Paul's work of evangelization (1 Thess. 2:18), but God can use Satan as an agent to keep Paul humble and attentive to his ministry (2 Cor. 12:7). A community might preserve its spirit by handing over a recalcitrant member to Satan (1 Cor. 5). For the most part, however, Satan appears in Paul's writings as in the rest of the NT, as a figure who is hostile to the church. Satan attacks the church and seeks to undermine God's plan of salvation. Paul describes false teachers who disturb the community as being under the influence of Satan (2 Cor. 11:14–15). Ever the tempter (see Job 1:6–12; 2:1–7), Satan may entice believers to marital infidelity if they try to follow a regime of undue asceticism (1 Cor. 7:5).

In the passage at hand, 2:11, Paul says that Satan might "rob" the community, depriving it of one of its members (see Wray and Mobley 2005, 132–33). If the community allows misguided righteousness to prevent its members from treating the evildoer with forgiveness and love, it will lose that person to Satan, God's adversary. In this regard, Paul observes that the community should know what Satan is up to. Satan is known for his wicked plots and designs. Accentuating Satan's craftiness as he does, the apostle may have drawn on the Gen. 3 narrative, a story to which Paul alludes in 11:3 and Rom. 16:20.

If the community heeds Paul's advice, Satan's attempted robbery will be foiled. This would be one small victory for the community and one small defeat for Satan, whose ultimate defeat is on the eschatological horizon for, says Paul, "the God of peace will shortly crush Satan under your feet" (Rom. 16:20).

Our contemporaries do not use the apocalyptic language that was so familiar to Paul and other Jewish writers. They readily identify Satan as a myth, as a figment of the imagination belonging to pre-Enlightenment thought. Nevertheless, evil continues to exist in our world and in the church. Paul had apocalyptic language to speak about evil and was able to do something about it. Today we need to find language to speak about the existence of evil in the world and in the church so that we can do something about it.

2 Corinthians 2:12–13

Frustration in Troas

Introductory Matters

In 1:12 the apostle Paul began to defend his reliability in the face of a change in his travel plans. By changing his plans, Paul caused some degree of consternation among the Corinthians. Notwithstanding either the change of plans or the painful letter that he sent, he remains steadfast in affirming his love for the Corinthians. Writing about these issues, the apostle bares his emotions, his sadness, his joy, and his desire to be cheered up.

In 2:12–13 Paul returns to the topic of his travels, telling the Corinthians about his recent trip. Most English-language translations render the text in at least two sentences, but there is only one long sentence in Greek. Those who read the text in Greek are aware of its peculiar syntax. Two features of the infinitive construction in verse 13 (*tō mē eurein me Titon*, "because I did not find Titus") are so unusual that they do not appear elsewhere in the NT. Paul's unusual turn of phrase does not, however, make it difficult to understand what he meant.

> ### 2 Corinthians 2:12–13 in the Rhetorical Flow
>
> The letter opening (1:1–2)
>
> **Ministerial crises (1:3–2:13)**
>
> A prayer of praise and the Asian experience (1:3–11)
>
> Paul's defense of his integrity (1:12–2:4)
>
> A disciplinary matter (2:5–11)
>
> ▶ Frustration in Troas (2:12–13)

Tracing the Train of Thought

2:12–13. Having shared his thoughts about the troublemaker, Paul returns to the topic of

61

The Gospel of Christ

"The gospel of Christ" (*to euangelion tou Christou*) is an expression that is found in every one of Paul's extant letters except the short note to Philemon (2:12; 9:13; 10:14; Rom. 15:19; 1 Cor. 9:12; Gal. 1:7; Phil. 1:27; 1 Thess. 3:2). Identifying "Christ" as the object of his proclamation, Paul implies that the good news of the gospel centers on what God has done in the death and resurrection of his Christ.

his travels, with details of place and purpose. The first stop on his agenda was a port city in Asia Minor: **Coming to Troas to preach the gospel of Christ** (2:12). Paul's use of an article with the proper noun highlights Paul's choice of Troas. Did he want to make the point that he went to Troas rather than to Corinth (see 1:23)? Or did he want to say that he had agreed to meet Titus in Troas (see 2:13)? In any case, the purpose of his visit to Troas was to preach the gospel of Christ.

Using a picturesque metaphor (cf. Acts 14:27), Paul tells the Corinthians that it was the Lord who provided him with the opportunity to preach as he did: **a door having been opened by the Lord**. The phrase, "in the Lord" (*en kyriō*) should be taken instrumentally, indicating that the door was opened "by the Lord." The "Lord" is Christ, as most often in Paul's Letters. On one level the image of the open door implies that Christ opened the hearts of those to whom Paul preached, so that the Pauline mission was effective (cf. 1 Cor. 16:9). On another level the metaphor evokes the social situation of the early church. From the earliest times, the gospel was preached in the homes (cf. Matt. 10:12) of those who were open to the good news. Shortly after Paul arrived in Macedonia, he preached in the homes of Lydia and the jailer in Philippi (Acts 16:14–15, 32). God's open-door policy, made effective in Christ, enabled Paul to preach the gospel.

Nonetheless, Paul was not at peace. **I was restless** (*ouk eschēka anesin tō pneumati mou*, "I did not have rest in my spirit"). The reason? **Because I did not find Titus my brother** (2:13). Paul was ill at ease because he had expected to find his fellow evangelist in Troas, and Titus was nowhere to be found. Paul's frustration may have been all the more compounded if he and Titus had previously agreed to meet in Troas.

Rather than stay in the region around Troas, an area that could also be called "Troas," Paul decided to go back to what we today call Europe: **So, despite the opportunity, having said good-bye to them, I went on my way to Macedonia.** With this decision, Paul physically moved closer to the Corinthians, but he doesn't explain the reasons for his decision to go to Macedonia. The way he writes about the decision indicates that there is some contrast between what Paul might have done and what he actually did. Going to Macedonia meant that he would forgo the opportunity for preaching the gospel that God's open-door policy had provided for him in Troas. Remaining in Troas would not settle Paul's personal turmoil.

After making the decision, Paul said good-bye (*apotaxamenos*, the only time that Paul uses this verb) to "them," presumably the hitherto unmentioned Christians of Troas. He then made his way to Macedonia. From Macedonia he then writes this letter to the Corinthians.

Theological Issues

Paul's Anthropology

Having already written at some length not only about his own emotions but also about the emotions of the Corinthians,

> **Note on the Composition of 2 Corinthians**
>
> Those who hold 2 Corinthians to be a composite document (e.g., Bornkamm 1971; Crafton 1991) generally believe that 1:1–2:13; 7:5–16; and 13:11–13 constitute one of its component fragments. Both 2:13 and 7:5 speak about rest. Hence, there would be a relatively smooth transition between 2:13 and 7:5.

Paul talks about his personal inner turmoil in 2:12–13. He says, "I did not have rest in my spirit." The rest about which he writes was not a matter of physical tiredness but something similar to the kind of restlessness that we describe as "tossing and turning" when we cannot sleep because we are worried about something. The restlessness that we experience by day manifests itself in twitching or the need to move about in one's chair or get up and walk. Either condition points to our psychosomatic nature. Paul's "I did not have rest in my spirit" is his way of saying that he was restless.

The word "rest" (*anesis*) rarely appears in the NT. Three of its five uses are in Paul, all of which are in 2 Corinthians (2:13; 7:5; 8:13; cf. Acts 24:23; 2 Thess. 1:7). In 7:5, Paul writes, "Our bodies had no rest [*oudemian eschēken anesin hē sarx hēmōn*], but we were afflicted in every way, disputes without and fears within." There is some similarity between 2:13 and 7:5. In both passages Paul writes about not having rest. In each case the restlessness is not the result of physical exertion; rather, it is a restlessness that we would say is due to psychological factors, frustration at not finding a friend in 2:13, arguments and fear in 7:5.

In 2:13 Paul writes about a lack of rest in his spirit (*pneuma*); in 7:5 he describes his flesh (*sarx*) as experiencing restlessness. That Paul apparently uses "spirit" and "body" interchangeably provides us with a valuable insight into the nature of Paul's anthropology, his understanding of the human being.

Paul uses a number of terms to talk about the human being, the most common of which are body (*sōma*), flesh (*sarx*), spirit (*pneuma*), soul (*psychē*), and heart (*kardia*). Paul's understanding of these terms is deeply rooted in his Jewish/Semitic background and harks back to OT usage. Semitic anthropology is basically holistic. Accordingly, the terms in Paul's anthropological lexicon do not designate different parts of the human being. Rather, each of them represents the whole human being, the whole human person, all the while drawing attention to one or another aspect or function of the human being. Thus in 2:13 his words about restlessness basically mean, "I was restless," while those of 7:15 mean "we were restless." In these two texts Paul uses different nouns to speak about restlessness, "spirit" in 2:13, "flesh" in 7:15; we moderns are content with the use of a personal pronoun.

What then is the particular nuance of Paul's use of the word "spirit" (*pneuma*) when it is used as an anthropological term, as in 2:13; 7:13? This usage must be distinguished from Paul's more common use of *pneuma* to refer to the divine Spirit, the Holy Spirit (cf. 1:22). Paul's "spirit" (*pneuma*) is not simply synonymous with "soul" (*psychē*; cf. 1 Thess. 5:23). "Spirit" is the total and complete human being in its capacity to transcend what is externally palpable or ascertainable; for example, in its capacity to feel or sense. "Soul" is the total and complete human being in its vitality, in its capacity to move and act.

Contemporary readers of Paul's Letters should be particularly attentive when they read passages in which Paul uses anthropological language. Influenced by a long tradition of Greek philosophy, Westerners tend to think somewhat dualistically. We separate matter from spirit and soul from body. But that is not the way Paul thought and wrote. His anthropology was holistic. Whichever term he used, he was writing about the whole human person, not some part of it. His different terms simply draw attention to one or another aspect of the person.

Comparisons are necessarily limited, but one might help in this instance. I know a woman named Mary Smith, who is a doctor, a wife, and a mother. Her patients call her "Doctor," her husband calls her "Honey," and her children call her "Mom." Yet there is only one Mary Smith. Doctor, wife, and mother are terms that identify the same human being but from different points of view. So it is with Paul's use of anthropological language. His terms speak of the human person from different points of view.

Kinship Language

Paul calls Titus "my brother" (2:13). The designation recalls Paul's use of "brother" as a "title" for Timothy in 1:1. Readers who are familiar with Paul's authentic correspondence are not surprised by Paul's describing Timothy and Titus in this way. Paul uses kinship language, especially the language of siblinghood, throughout the extant correspondence.

Paul's kinship language is obviously metaphorical; neither Timothy nor Titus was a blood brother of Paul. Neither is the famous but nameless evangelist of 2 Cor. 8:18 nor the tried and eager individual of 8:22 (cf. 12:18) related to Paul by blood. Paul calls each of these two unnamed individuals a brother; in 8:23 he jointly identifies them as "brothers." Certainly the entire Corinthian community cannot be counted among Paul's blood relations, but Paul addresses the Corinthians as his siblings in 1:8; 8:1; and 13:11.

Kinship language is by far the most common way that Paul refers to believers in his letters. He does this so frequently that many of the versions translate Paul's words with a paraphrase, lest the reader find Paul's repetitive usage tedious. Translating *adelphoi* as friends or using another paraphrase to render Paul's Greek may lead a reader to overlook the rhetorical nuances of the apostle's use of kinship language. Kinship language is language that properly belongs at home. Using kinship language to address a group of believers gathered in someone's home immediately establishes some affinity between Paul and his addressees as well as between his addressees and some third person or persons about whom Paul is writing.

Paul's use of kinship language is a significant element in the rhetorical strategy of Galatians and Philemon. Kinship language abounds in his 1 Corinthians and in 1 Thessalonians, especially in the oft-repeated formula of direct address, *adelphoi* ("brothers and sisters"). That 2 Corinthians uses this formula only three times is a sure sign that Paul's relationship with the Corinthians is less friendly than it was when he wrote the earlier letter to the same community.

When Paul describes Titus as "my brother," he underscores not only the latter's Christian faith but also the shared experience of Paul and Titus as they grew together in faith and worked together in evangelizing. In addition to Timothy and Titus, the only named individual person in the extant correspondence whom Paul calls "brother" is Epaphroditus (Phil. 2:25), with whom the apostle shared so much.

For the apostle Paul, the faith shared with another person makes that person a brother or sister. The relationship is fictive but real. It points to a common bond and some degree of affection. Paul uses kinship language to identify the bond that exists between believers in one local church and believers living in other Christian communities.

This kind of relationship continues to exist in the church at the present time. People in any specific congregation consider their fellow worshipers to be brothers and sisters, people upon whom they can rely in case of need. People of a congregation experience fraternal ties with believers in other congregations, perhaps a specific congregation in the inner city whom they have adopted or a sister church across the ocean whom they support and maybe even visit when the occasion allows. With an ecumenical perspective, Christians of one denomination refer to Christians of other denominations as their sister churches. Paul's use of kinship language goes a long way to explain the ties that link Christians with one another.

PART 2

2 Corinthians 2:14–7:4

Paul Explains and Defends His Apostolic Ministry

Second Corinthians 2:14 represents an abrupt change of thought from the reflection on his apostolic travels that occupied Paul in verses 12 and 13. Verse 14's abrupt transition from the preceding text is a major argument advanced by those commentators who hold that 2:14–6:17; 7:2–4 is an independent letter fragment that a later editor has incorporated into the canonical 2 Corinthians.

This section of the letter begins with a prayer of praise to God for the ministry that Paul describes in figurative language. His ministry is to speak God's word with sincerity. The defensive and apologetic stance that was apparent in the first part of the letter continues to appear in this part of the letter as Paul examines his ministry from different points of view, including his personal hardships.

2 Corinthians 2:14–7:4 in Context

The letter opening (1:1–2)

Ministerial crises (1:3–2:13)

▶ Paul explains and defends his apostolic ministry (2:14–7:4)

The arrival and report of Titus (7:5–16)

Service to God's holy people (8:1–9:15)

An aggressive taskmaster (10:1–13:10)

The letter closing (13:11–13)

2 Corinthians 2:14–3:6

Anxiety and Confidence

Introductory Matters

One of the features of this section of Paul's letter is the rapidity with which Paul changes the focus of his thoughts. Joseph A. Fitzmyer (1993, 68) explains this as the result of a free association of ideas "caused by catchword bonding, in which one sense of a term suggests another, and so the argument proceeds."

Despite the rapidly changing thought, a chiastic structure can be identified:

A Paul's capability (2:14–17)
    B The letter of Christ (3:1–3)
A′ Paul's capability (3:4–6)

The first subunit, 2:14–17, begins a section of the letter (2:14–5:10) that is characterized by a multiplicity of ever-changing metaphors. Almost without exception the metaphors are used to describe Paul's work of evangelization, contrasting his own understanding of his ministry with illegitimate or insufficient ways of preaching the gospel. In these first four verses Paul uses metaphors that appeal to the senses of sight, smell, and sound, making a rhetorical appeal to his readers in which he effectively urges them to contemplate his ministry with the entirety of their beings.

In the second subunit, 3:1–3, the thought goes from Paul to the Corinthians and then back to Paul, whose ministry is implicitly compared with Moses's role in service of the covenant. Readers of the letter are invited to look at what is being written and by whom.

The third subunit, 3:4–6, responds to the question about Paul's capability posed in the first subunit and continues the implied comparison with Moses by affirming that Paul is a minister of the new covenant. The subunit begins with Paul saying that he has confidence. The verb "have" at the beginning of a sentence will reappear in 3:12; 4:1; 4:7; and 4:13. Paul has confidence (3:4), hope (3:12), ministry (4:1), a treasure (4:7), and a same spirit of faith (4:13). The passages in the letter that deal with these topics are linked with 3:4–6 since they contain discussions about what Paul has.

Tracing the Train of Thought

A Triumphal Procession (2:14–17)

2:14–17. The prayer of praise in 1:3–7 took the place of the epistolary thanksgiving that the readers of Paul's Letters expect to find in his missives. With **thanks be to God** (2:14), the apostle finally introduces a formal thanksgiving motif into 2 Corinthians. Paul's expression of thanksgiving, "thanks be to God," is not unusual for him (cf. 8:16; 9:15; Rom. 6:17; 7:25), but the wording is different from the language of Paul's customary epistolary thanksgiving, "I give thanks" (Rom. 1:8; 1 Cor. 1:4; Phil. 1:3; Philem. 4) or "we give thanks" (1 Thess. 1:2; 2:13).

God is portrayed in two participial clauses, each of which makes use of a powerful metaphor that teases and puzzles the reader's imagination. With the phrase **who in Christ always leads us in triumphal procession**, Paul uses a word (*thriambeuō*; cf. Col. 2:15) to invite his readers to contemplate a triumphal procession. Triumphal processions were well known in the Greco-Roman world and so were not unknown to Paul. The eschatological scenario of 1 Thess. 4:16–17 portrays a triumphal procession; 1 Cor. 4:9 alludes to a procession in a theater. Typically Greco-Roman triumphal processions were organized to honor a victorious general and thank the god who was deemed responsible for the victory. Such processions often included a gaggle of prisoners on their way to death at the hands of their conquerors. Josephus, the Hellenistic Jewish historian more or less contemporary with Paul, describes one of these processions in the *Jewish War* (7.119–57; cf. Plutarch, *Romulus* 25.4–5, in *Lives*).

Paul invites his readers to contemplate a procession that includes his fellow missionaries and himself. The details of the procession are nonetheless

We and Us

The first-person-plural pronoun is used in different ways in this letter. "We" can refer to Paul and his fellow evangelists or, more restrictively, to the ones associated with him in writing and sending the letter. Occasionally Paul's "we" means all apostles of Jesus Christ. Sometimes Paul uses an editorial "we," which is basically equivalent to the first-person-singular pronoun, "I." At other times "we" can refer to Paul and his addressees or, more broadly, to Paul and his fellow believers. At still other times "we" embraces Paul and all human beings.

Scott J. Hafemann (1990, 12–16) takes the first-person-plural "us" in verse 14 as an epistolary plural, a kind of editorial plural, referring only to Paul, but it is preferable to take "us" as an ordinary plural. The marchers include Paul and his fellow missionaries, at least Timothy. Timothy greets the Corinthians in 2 Cor. 1:1 and is cited in 1 Cor. 4:17 (cf. 16:10–11) as Paul's emissary to the Corinthian community. Second Corinthians 1:19 refers to Timothy, along with Silvanus and Paul, as having preached the gospel to the Corinthians. This evidence suggests that Timothy, at least, should be included in the "apostolic we" of 2 Corinthians. Moreover, Phil. 1:1 portrays Timothy as a slave of Christ along with Paul himself. Accordingly one must not exclude Timothy from the band of enslaved prisoners evoked by the imagery of the triumphal procession.

difficult to identify, all the more so since Paul uses the word *thriambeuō* ("lead in triumphal procession") only once in his correspondence. The parade is a continuous procession that God has organized and directs. With "always" the apostle emphasizes the ongoing nature of the parade, whose route is that of Paul's missionary voyages.

The procession honors Christ, victorious over sin and death. Paul and his companions are vanquished and enslaved. Paul was taken by God at the moment of his call, and his companions at the moment that they embraced the missionary life. Since then Paul has been enslaved (Rom. 1:1; 1 Cor. 3:5; 4:1; 9:15–18; Phil. 1:1; cf. Titus 1:1) and subject to harsh conditions (2 Cor. 11:23–27), almost manipulated by God. He and his companions (cf. Phil. 1:1) participate in the parade under some constraint.

The second powerful metaphor in Paul's description of God appeals to his readers' sense of smell rather than their sense of sight. Paul's focus switches from an emphasis on the extended temporal character of his missionary activity to its geographic spread. Paul describes God as the one **who through us makes known the odor of his knowledge everywhere.**

Paul's use of aromatic imagery is unique in the extant correspondence. Paul may be asking his readers to think of himself and his fellow evangelists as incense bearers in the procession. From their censers arises billowing aromatic smoke. What God produces through him and his fellow missionaries is the gospel, the knowledge of him (*tes gnōseōs autou*), that is, the knowledge of Christ. For Paul, knowledge is experiential; it is far more than a noetic experience or mere intellectual knowledge. To know Christ is to experience Christ in one's life. Eventually knowledge of Christ entails being "in Christ," one of Paul's favorite ways of describing a Christian's authentic existence (cf. 5:17, 19; 12:2, 19). Through the apostolic endeavors of Paul and his fellow missionaries, God spreads the knowledge of Christ to every place (*en panti topō*; cf. 1 Cor. 1:2).

The juxtaposition of the two metaphors, with their appeal to different senses and their complementary references to time and space, involves Christ in two different ways. In the image of the triumphal procession, Christ is implicitly compared to a victorious general to whom Paul and his fellows are subservient. In the image of the aroma, knowledge of Christ is produced through the efforts of Paul and his companion missionaries.

The aromatic imagery takes a different turn in verse 15. In an explanatory clause beginning with **because**, Paul affirms that **we are the fragrance of Christ to God** (2:15). "Odor" and "fragrance" are biblical terms used to describe the pleasant smells that arise from sacrificial offerings (Gen. 8:21; Exod. 29:17–18; Lev. 1:9, 13, 17; Num. 15:3, 7, 10). Thus, Paul seems to be alluding to Christ's sacrificial offering of himself, which Paul and his companions exude through their apostolic ministry. The biblical language suggests that not only the participants in the sacrifice and the onlookers can smell the pleasant aroma, but also that the smell is pleasing to God himself, a sign that the offering is acceptable to God. Not only is Christ's sacrifice acceptable to God; so too is the ministry of Paul and his evangelizing companions.

The Smells

Paul uses two different terms to describe a smell, an olfactory experience: "odor" or "aroma" (*osmē*) and "fragrance" (*euodia*). It is difficult to translate the two words, which are rarely used by Paul. "Odor" appears only in 2 Cor. 2:14, 16 and Phil. 4:18; "fragrance" only in 2 Cor. 2:15 and Phil. 4:18. The distinction between the two terms has been made all the more difficult by Paul himself, who writes about a "fragrant offering" (*osmēn euodias*, Phil. 4:18; cf. Eph. 5:2). Most commentators and translators opt for "aroma" and "fragrance" as translations of the Greek terms in 2 Cor. 2:14–16, but they do not always agree about which Greek word is best translated by which English word.

I have opted for "odor" to translate *osmē* since the Greek word often suggests an unpleasant smell—although we occasionally speak of the "odor" of sanctity, which provides some indication of the ambivalence of "odor"—while the prefix *eu-* suggests that the experience of *euodia* is pleasant. So I have opted to render *euodia* as "fragrance."

Their ministry is exercised **among those who are being saved and those who are perishing.** The binomial expression recalls Paul's use of similar phraseology in 1 Cor. 1:18. The terms are eschatological, but Paul is convinced that both eschatological salvation and eschatological ruination are already under way at the present time. In 1 Cor. 1:18 Paul wrote that the message of the cross is discriminatory; the gospel message is foolishness to those who are perishing, but it is the power of God for those who are being saved. The discriminatory power of the gospel comes again to the

> ### "From . . . To"
>
> It is not likely that Paul is suggesting some sort of progress in death or in life with his "from [*ek*] . . . to [*eis*]" construction. The construction is a rhetorical formulation used for the sake of emphasis.

fore in 2 Cor. 2:16. As Paul continues with the aromatic imagery, a chiastic construction affirms that the aroma coming forth from himself and his fellow missionaries is **an odor from death unto death to the latter, an odor from life unto life for the former** (2:16). The experience of the same smell, meaning the hearing of the same gospel, has different effects on those who are being saved and those who are perishing. In the latter case, hearing the gospel message leads only to death; in the former case, the reception of the gospel leads to life.

"Death" and "life" do not refer to physical death and bodily life; the terms are to be taken in a theological, eschatological sense. The life-or-death response to the preaching of the gospel gives Paul occasion to ponder the weightiness of his responsibility. So he asks, **Who is sufficient for these things [*pros tauta tis hikanos*]?** When words formed from the *hikano-* root refer to humans, they have to do with the abilities of men and women. Hence, Paul's question really means, Who is capable of such activity? Who can possibly be up to the task? Who is really qualified for such a weighty responsibility? The positively phrased rhetorical question begs for a response. The appropriate response would be "no one." No one is up to this life-and-death responsibility.

Master of rhetoric that he was, Paul allows the reader of his letter to formulate his or her own answer. In the meantime, he offers an explanation that seems to be a digression: **For we are not, like so many** others, **peddlers of God's word** (2:17). Paul contrasts himself and his fellow evangelists with many others whom he considers to be mere shysters. They are hucksters, who hawk the word of God.

But, says Paul as he develops the contrast, **in Christ we speak with sincerity, like people who have come from God and are in the sight of God.** Speaking in close association with Christ (see 12:19), Paul and his fellow missionaries exhibit sincerity. It is obvious that Paul is implying that the majority do not speak sincerely. Paul, however, speaks the word of God faithfully, neither adding to it nor subtracting from it. To underscore his point, Paul makes two references to God. He affirms that he and his companions are "delegates" from God. They speak as they do because they have come from God and do

Peddlers of the Word

Describing the peddlers of God's word, Paul uses a Greek term (*kapēleuontes*) that does not appear elsewhere in the NT but was known to those familiar with philosophical debates. It was used to disparage pseudo-philosophers, especially Sophists, who delivered shallow lectures for monetary gain. Receiving pay for their lectures was one of the ways such philosophers supported themselves in the ancient world. Other philosophers were clients of a well-to-do patron, while some supported themselves by exercising a trade or begging. Paul preached the gospel free of charge. That was problematic for some Corinthians who thought, *People pay to listen to what is important.*

what they do because they are ever in the sight of God. Paul's choice of a verb to describe their speaking is the word *laleō*, which is sometimes used in the Greek Bible to connote inspired speech.

A Letter of Recommendation (3:1–3)

3:1–3. Paul apparently abandons his query about competency and qualifications in a reflection on what he has just written. His affirmation that he is speaking with sincerity, like someone who has been sent by God and does his speaking under the watchful eye of God, might sound like boasting. Paul addresses the issue head-on: **Are we beginning to commend ourselves?** (3:1). Is he really about to praise himself?

Typically commendation comes from someone else. And apparently there were some people in the community in Corinth who came with letters of recommendation. Paul asks whether he needs a letter of recommendation, as some people do: **Or do we need letters of recommendation either to you or from you, as some people do?** The "some people" of whom Paul writes are probably to be identified with the "many" who peddle God's word. They have come into the community bearing letters of recommendation. That these folk came to the Corinthians bearing letters of recommendation is a sure sign that they are outsiders. We do not know who purportedly wrote the letters that "some people" brought with them to Corinth, but they allowed these people, who are nameless as far as Paul is concerned, to establish a base of operation among the Corinthian Christians.

Paul's rhetorical question, the third such question within a few verses, demands a negative answer. Paul does not need a letter to introduce him to the Corinthians, nor does he need a letter of recommendation from them. The reason Paul doesn't need a letter of recommendation is that **you are our letter, written on our hearts** (3:2). For Paul, the only letter of recommendation that counts is the Christian community at Corinth.

The Corinthians would not have expected Paul to say that they themselves were the only letter that was needed, a letter that was firmly etched in the very depths of Paul's being, his heart. Hellenistic letters were typically written on papyrus, though some were written on leather or some other material. A letter written on the heart was a novel and striking idea. When Paul describes this letter as **known and read by all people,** he implies that he has talked about the Corinthian church. Paul does not hesitate to speak about one church to another church (8:1; 9:2; Rom. 15:26; 1 Cor. 16:1).

But there is more. Using a bit of exaggeration, he flatters the Corinthians, saying that the letter is known and read by everyone (*hypo pantōn anthrōpōn*). When Paul writes that the letter is read by everyone, he does not mean that everyone in his circles can read and write. Given the lack of literacy at the time, letters were generally read aloud to those who "read" them. The faithful community at Corinth is an unusual kind of letter. When Paul says that this letter is known and read by everyone, he really means that the faith of the community is well known and appreciated, especially among the churches.

Paul plays with the epistolary metaphor as he says that the Corinthians are a letter of Christ. The participial clause, **showing that you are a letter of Christ** (3:3), modifies the pronoun "you" at the beginning of the sentence. How can the letter be both "our letter" and a "letter of Christ" at the same time? The question need not be asked since Paul says that the letter of Christ is **serviced by us** (*diakonētheisa hyph' hēmōn*). More often than not in the Hellenistic

---

Letters of Recommendation

The letter of recommendation (*systatikē epistolē*) was well known in the Hellenistic world. Pseudo-Demetrius, the Hellenistic epistolographer, known for his classification of the kinds of letters written in the Greco-Roman Empire, cites the letter of recommendation immediately after the friendly letter in his list of twenty-one types of letters. The bearer of a letter of recommendation brought with him the authority of the letter writer, introducing the bearer of the letter to its recipient(s).

Letters of recommendation were often used in the early church. Luke tells us that the Christians of Ephesus sent Apollos on his way to Achaia bearing a letter of recommendation (Acts 18:27). What Paul wrote about Timothy and the household of Stephanas in 1 Corinthians has traits similar to those of a letter of recommendation (16:10–11, 15–16), as does what he was to write about Timothy and the two anonymous believers who were to accompany him to Corinth (8:17–24). From Corinth, Paul would later write a letter to believers in Rome, which included a recommendation of Phoebe, a deacon of the suburban church in Cenchreae (Rom. 16:1–2). Strikingly, these several NT examples all have the church at Corinth, either as the recipient of recommendations or as the location from which a recommendation came.

Dio Chrysostom

"For written ordinances, once the writing is erased, are done for in a single day.... Besides, while laws are preserved on tablets of wood or of stone, each custom is preserved within our own hearts." (Consuet. 3 [Or. 76])

world, letter writers dictated the content of their letters to scribes, who were responsible for the material transcription of their text. Paul compares himself to a scribe in the service of Christ, the author of the letter that is the Corinthian church. The aorist tense of the verb indicates that the letter writing took place in the past. Christ wrote the letter when Paul evangelized the Corinthian community.

Paul uses a striking contrast to highlight the nature of Christ's letter. It was written **not with ink but with the Spirit of the living God**. "Spirit of the living God" (*pneumati theou zōntos*) is not found elsewhere in the Bible; it speaks of God as "living," the primal trait by which God is identified in the Jewish Scriptures (see 1 Thess. 1:9; cf. 2 Cor. 6:16). The Spirit of the living God was at work in the writing of Christ's letter, the community of believers at Corinth.

The influence of the Jewish Scriptures on Paul is readily apparent in the following contrast. Christ's letter was written **not on stone tablets but on tablets that are hearts of flesh**. The stone tablets call to mind the tablets on which the Ten Commandments, an epitome of the prescriptions of the Mosaic covenant, were written. Moses prepared the tablets (Exod. 34:1; Deut. 10:1, 3), but it was God who wrote on them (Exod. 24:12; 34:1, 4, 27–28; Deut. 10:2, 4). Contrasting with these stone tablets are tablets that are hearts of flesh, human hearts. Paul's mention of writing on human hearts recalls the words of Jer. 31:31–33, where the prophet speaks of a new covenant and God's writing the law on the hearts of the house of Israel. On Sinai/Horeb, God wrote on stone tablets. God promised to write on human hearts in the renewal of the covenant. Paul now affirms that in Corinth the Spirit of the living God writes on human hearts.

Paul's Confidence (3:4–6)

3:4–6. These verses respond to the rhetorical question posed in 2:16, "Who is sufficient for these things?" Sometimes Paul allows his readers/listeners to formulate their own responses to his rhetorical questions, as was the common oratorical practice. On the other hand, he often answered his own questions. When he does so, he generally answers his question immediately, hardly giving his audience the opportunity to respond to the question. In a departure from his ordinary practice, Paul has delayed giving a response to the question posed in 2:16. Now he is ready to give his answer to the question Who is up to the task of evangelization?

The pericope centers on the notion of adequacy, expressed by different terms built on the Greek root *hikano-*, the adjective *hikanos* ("capable") in verse 5, the noun *hikanotēs* ("capability") in verse 5, and the verb *hikanoō* ("makes us capable") in verse 6. The noun and the verb do not appear elsewhere in Paul's extant correspondence. Apart from 2:16 and 3:5, the adjective appears only in 2:6 and 1 Cor. 11:30; 15:9. The Greek words could be used in reference to things or in reference to persons. Used of things, the adjective means "enough" or "sufficient" (see 2:6). Referring to persons, it means "competent," "capable," "adequate," "up to the task."

Paul begins to speak about his adequacy on a high note. **We have such [*toiautēn*] a confidence before God through Christ (3:4).** Typically Paul's contemporaries spoke of their confidence in other human beings (cf. 8:22); not so for Paul. He has confidence in the sight of God. "Such" refers back to what he has just written. Paul is confident that the Corinthians themselves are a letter of Christ and that he has had some role to play in the writing of the letter. His confidence is a mediated confidence; it comes to him through

---

More on Paul's Wordplays

Paul has a fondness for playing with words. He will often use a word, then return to that same word some verses later, using it in different ways so that he can capture the full measure of its connotations as he develops his argument. It is almost as if he treats the word like a gem that must be examined from different angles and from every facet so that its splendor can be fully appreciated.

Paul's playing with words in this fashion is an example of assonance, a figure of speech that features a close juxtaposition of similar sounds. The way Paul deals with competence in 3:4–6, using the Greek root *hikan-*, is a good example of this Pauline technique, but it is not the only example. Other examples in the passage are Paul's use of *gramma* ("letter"), which appears twice in 3:4–6 while its root appears in the participle *engegrammenē* ("written") of verses 2 and 3; and his use of *pneuma* ("spirit"), which also appears twice in 3:4–6, reprising the use of the same word in verse 3.

Paul continues to play with words in 3:7–11. The appearance of *gramma* ("letter") in verse 7 and *pneuma* ("spirit") in verse 8 echoes the sounds heard in the previous two pericopes. Verse 7's "on stone" (*lithois*) harks back to "on stone [*lithinais*] tablets" in verse 3. A highpoint of 3:4–6 is Paul's writing about himself and his companions as ministers (*diakonous*) of a new covenant. The idea of ministry is reprised in 3:7–11, where the word *diakonia* ("ministry") occurs four times. The pericope introduces the theme of glory (*doxa*), a word that appears eight times in the passage, while the related verb *doxazō* ("endow with glory," "glorify") appears twice.

This form of assonance continues into the following pericope when *doxa* ("glory") appears three times in verse 18. The face of Moses (*prosōpon Mōyseōs*), thematically introduced in 3:7, leads to the reappearance of Moses (*Mōysēs*) in 3:13, 15 and the mention of his face (*prosōpon*) in 3:13, 18.

Christ, who is actively present in the apostle's activity. Christ is the source of Paul's confidence.

Paul follows up his confident outburst with a disclaimer: **not that we are capable of considering anything as coming from ourselves** (3:5). Paul is not confident in his own abilities. Of himself he is not capable of doing anything; he is not even able to contemplate the possibility that something might come from himself. If he is at all capable, it is because God has given him the capability, **for our capability is from God.**

Human capability is always limited and specific. Some people are up to one task, but not up to another. Accordingly, God's enabling gift of capability given to Paul and his companions was a specific gift. God, **who made us capable to be ministers of a new covenant** (3:6), did not make Paul and his companions omnicapable; rather, God has enabled them for a specific task: to be ministers of a new covenant (*diakonous kainēs diathēkēs*).

The phrase "minister of a new covenant" appears only here in the NT. To be a minister suggests some kind of service, as the *diakon-* word group suggests. Words belonging to this group were used in reference to various kinds of service, including waiting on tables and providing health care. The Pauline churches used *diakonos* as a descriptive term to speak of leadership or ministry within the church (cf. 11:15; Rom. 16:1; Phil. 1:1), but it never lost its sense of service. Thus Paul can refer to himself and his fellow missionaries as "servants of God" (2 Cor. 6:4; cf. 1 Thess. 3:2; Rom. 13:4) or "servants of Christ" (2 Cor. 11:23; cf. 1 Cor. 12:5). In his earlier correspondence with the Corinthians, Paul asked the "Who are we?" question with regard to himself and Apollos and answered, "Servants through whom you came to believe" (1 Cor. 3:5).

Paul's service is in function of a new covenant. The Corinthians, for whose benefit Paul rehearses the etiological narrative of the institution of the Eucharist narrative in 1 Cor. 11:23–26, were familiar with a new covenant and its relation with the death of Jesus. The institution narrative mentions a new covenant (1 Cor. 11:25), a term apparently appropriated from Jer. 38:31–33 LXX (31:31–33 Eng.). The "new covenant," the realization of a divine promise, is a way of speaking about the eschatological relationship between God and his people that is effected in Christ.

To further characterize this covenant, Paul uses a contrast between a pair of qualifying genitives. The new covenant is **not of the letter but of the Spirit** (*ou grammatos alla pneumatos*). The alliteration of the Greek text strengthens the contrast for those who listened to it while it was read. The letter was a reference to the physical letters with which the covenantal prescriptions were inscribed in stone or, more broadly, to the Torah, reduced to its physical expression. In contrast with a mere textual covenant, the new covenant about which Paul writes is a covenant of the Spirit. Presumably Paul means to suggest that the new covenant is the result of the Spirit of God at work.

A text is powerless; but the Spirit of God is powerful. Further clarification ensues as Paul writes, **for the letter kills, but the Spirit vivifies.** The explanatory "for" indicates that Paul intends to explain why the covenant of the Spirit is superior to the covenant of the letter. A mere text "kills," not in the sense that it causes physical death but in the sense that it leads to sin and the kind of death that ensues (cf. Rom. 5:20–21). On the other hand, the Spirit of God gives life, eschatological life.

> ### John Chrysostom
>
> *"The law was spiritual, but it did not bestow the Spirit. Moses had letters but not the spirit, whereas we have been entrusted with the giving of the Spirit."* (Hom. 2 Cor. 6.2)

With this contrast Paul introduces a soteriological dimension into the task for which God has qualified him. Paul's new-covenant-related service is linked to the life-giving activity of the Spirit.

Theological Issues

God and the Preaching of the Gospel

As Paul begins what is arguably an apology, an argument of self-defense seemingly prompted by an opposition that comes from an ill-defined "many," he stakes a multifaceted claim for the role of God in what he does. The unit begins with Paul offering thanks to God.

Paul cites the name of God five times in the first subunit (2:14–17). The passage opens with Paul imaginatively affirming that God orchestrates the whole scenario. Paul and his companions are only slaves as they carry out the divine initiative. When they preach as they are constrained to do, they are, as it were, a pleasing fragrance rising to God.

By implication Paul suggests that what he and his inspired companions speak is "the word of God." This almost technical expression (see Acts 4:29, 31; 6:2, 7; 8:14; 11:1; 12:24; 13:5, 7, 44, 46, 48; 16:32; 17:13; 18:11; cf. Rom. 9:6; Phil. 1:14; 1 Thess. 2:13 [2x]), virtually equivalent to "the gospel," suggests that what Paul and his companions preach is the word that comes from God and is speech about God. God and what God does is the real object of the gospel, the good news.

Unlike those who peddle the word, Paul and his fellow missionaries come from God and do what they do in the presence of God. Because they are sent by God, God is the ever-present horizon of all that they do.

The second subunit (3:1–3) affirms the identity of the Corinthians as a letter of Christ. Paul is its scribe. He writes, however, not with ink but with the Spirit of the living God. In Paul's scribal work, his preparation of the letter, the Spirit of the living God is at work. Paul is able to minister to the Corinthians because the Spirit of the living God is active in his ministry. Strikingly, Paul affirms that the Spirit is the Spirit of the "living" God, thereby acknowledging that the God of whom he speaks is the God of his Jewish and biblical tradition.

The third subunit (3:4–6) responds to a question about Paul's ability that has been left hanging ever since he himself posed the question in 2:16. Paul speaks with confidence in the presence of God. Who is qualified for the ministry that is his? Of himself, Paul is not qualified. The capability that he has is from God, who enables Paul's entire ministry.

2 Corinthians 3:7–4:6

A Glorious Ministry

Introductory Matters

Midrash, derived from the Hebrew verb *dāraš* ("investigate"), is a method of biblical interpretation whose precise definition has been debated throughout decades of scholarship. Essentially it is a written commentary on a biblical text that seeks to apply the biblical text to a contemporary situation.

The scriptural echoes that abound in 3:7–18 constitute a midrashic interpretation of Exod. 34:29–35. The biblical narrative describes Moses as coming down from Mount Sinai with the skin of his face shining (a Hebrew word that the Vulgate mistranslates as "horned" in vv. 29, 30, 35) because he had been speaking with the Lord. He had in his hands the stone tablets on which the Lord's commands were written. Once he had spoken to Aaron and all the sons of Israel, who had been reluctant to approach him because of his face, Moses veiled his face. He removed the veil only when he entered into Yahweh's presence to speak with the Lord. Paul makes several allusions to the biblical narrative, but he quotes only a single verse: Exod. 34:34 in 3:16.

Paul's use of the biblical text is facilitated by the interpretive tradition of the passage, no insignificant part of which is that the Greek Bible, the one quoted by Paul in his letters, paraphrases the Hebrew *qāran* ("send out rays") as *dedoxastai* ("glorified"), the verb that appears in 3:10. The Syriac translation and the Aramaic targums paraphrase the biblical text in similar fashion.

Striking similarities with Paul's use of the biblical narrative can be found in the intertestamental *Book of Biblical Antiquities* (12). Like Paul, Pseudo-Philo presents the glory on the face of Moses as being ephemeral, Moses's covering his face so that it might not be seen, and a negative response to this behavior on the part of the Israelites.

Tracing the Train of Thought

The Ministry of Righteousness (3:7–11)

3:7–11. The subject of Paul's conditional clause, **if the ministry of death** (3:7), picks up on ideas expressed in the preceding verse, where Paul wrote about ministry and the killing power of mere letters. The ministry of death, implicitly the ministry of the old covenant (3:14), is described as having been **engraved in letters on stone**. In fact, it was not the ministry itself that was inscribed in stone. Rather, the terms of the covenant were written on stone. Typically, the terms of an ancient covenant were preserved for posterity's sake in written form on material that would not readily perish. In a covenant-renewal ceremony, the precepts of the covenant could then be read anew.

Stone was perfectly suitable for this purpose. Thus God gave Moses the tablets of the covenant, two tablets of stone, on which God himself had done the engraving (Exod. 31:18; Deut. 9:9–11). After Moses angrily destroyed the first set of stone tablets (Exod. 32:19; Deut. 9:15–17), God commanded Moses to cut two new tablets on which God would write his words (Exod. 34:1–4; Deut. 10:1–5). Deuteronomy 10:4 specifies that the words written by the finger of God were the "Ten Words," that is, the Ten Commandments that tradition has identified as the covenantal prescriptions of the Sinai or Mosaic covenant. The passive voice of Paul's "engraved" is a divine or theological passive, suggesting that God was the engraver; the perfect tense suggests that the covenant prescriptions enjoyed a somewhat permanent quality. Paul's midrash is based on Moses's coming down from the mountain with the second set of tablets.

The conditional clause was intended to affirm that the old covenant was, in fact, a glorious covenant. Despite the ministry of the old covenant being a ministry of death, the covenant itself was glorious for it **came in glory**. It came into being in glory not only because the precepts written on stone were given within a theophany, but also because those precepts reflected the will of God for his people.

To underscore the real glory of the old covenant, Paul notes that its glory was **such that the children of Israel could not gaze intently on the face of Moses because of the glory, transient as it was, of his face.** Paul alludes to

Exod. 34:30 LXX, which says that the face of Moses was shining with such glory when he came down from Sinai that the Israelites were afraid to approach him. Moses's face reflected the glory of the Lord, in whose presence Moses had been. Anticipating a comparison that he is about to make, Paul notes that the glory on Moses's face was going to disappear (*tēn katargoumenēn*, "transient as it was," in my translation). Some rabbis opined that the shining on Moses's face disappeared when Israel sinned, but their interpretation requires an inversion of the biblical narrative.

Felix Just, SJ/catholic-resources.org/Art/Dore.htm

Figure 5. Moses with the Stone Tablets and Light Streaming from His Head.

The main clause in Paul's sentences expresses the point that he really wants to make, namely, that the glory of the new covenant exceeds that of the old. He writes, **How much more surely will not the ministry of the Spirit exist in glory?** (3:8). Paul's argument from the lesser to the greater is an example of his use of the well-known *qal waḥômer* principle of biblical interpretation. The reader might have expected the ministry of death to be contrasted with the ministry of life, but Paul speaks of it as the ministry of the Spirit. This is Paul's ministry, the ministry of the life-giving Spirit (*zōopoiei*, 3:6).

Paul sustains his argument with a parallel a fortiori argument. **For if there is glory in the ministry of condemnation, how much more surely does the ministry of righteousness abound in glory** (3:9). An a fortiori argument with

---

Glory on Moses's Face in Jewish Tradition

From the early first century CE:
> "The light of his face surpassed the splendor of the sun and the moon.... And when he came down to the sons of Israel, they saw him but did not recognize him." (*L.A.B.* 12.1)

From the third century CE:
> "Even as no one can look at the sun as it rises, so no one could look at Moses." (*Pesiq. Rab.* 10.6)

The *Qal Waḥômer* Principle of Interpretation

The *qal waḥômer* principle is an analogy-based argument from the lesser to the greater, a kind of a fortiori argument. The principle was the first of Rabbi Ishmael's thirteen interpretive rules (*middôt*). Rabbis found the basis of the principle in Gen. 44:8 and Deut. 31:8. For them, ten uses of the principle could be found in Scripture itself (*Gen. Rab.* 92.7). Paul uses the principle in the form of an argument *a minore ad majus*, but Ishmael also considered arguments *a majore ad minus* as falling under the rule.

the "how much more surely" (*pōs mallon*) formula highlights the abundance of glory that comes with the ministry of righteousness. Whereas (some) glory belonged to the old ministry, an abundance of glory (*perisseuei . . . doxē*) belongs to the new ministry. Paul uses juridical language to qualify the contrasted ministries and, by implication, the covenants that they serve (cf. Rom. 5:15–20; see also 11:15). Condemnation (*katakriseōs*) is the antithesis of justification (*dikaiosynēs*); a verdict of guilt stands over and against a verdict of innocence.

Paul proceeds to explain what he has said about glory. **For indeed what was, in this case [*en toutō tō merei*]** (lit., "in part"), **endowed with glory has not been endowed with glory** (v. 10). His explanation is a paradox. We might have expected him to write, "what has been endowed with glory is no longer endowed with glory," using different tenses of the verb *doxazō*. But Paul uses the perfect tense in both instances. Hence the paradox: what has glory does not have glory. Paul resolves the paradox by adding **because of the surpassing**

Justification

The word "justification" (*dikaiosynē*) appears for the first time in this letter in 3:9. The Greek term is sometimes translated as "righteousness," but "justification" is the most common translation of the word when it appears in Paul's Letters. Justification is a major theme of Pauline theology particularly insofar as it has been developed by Paul in his letters to the Galatians and the Romans. In those letters particular nuances of justification are developed in the context of a dispute about the works of the law. That context is not the context of 2 Corinthians. It is inappropriate to interpret "justification" in this letter (3:9; 5:21; 6:7, 14; 9:9, 10; 11:15) in the light of the controversy addressed in Romans and Galatians. "Justification" must be taken in its ordinary sense, particularly in the light of the roots of the idea in the OT. "Righteousness" or "justification" is a matter of a right relationship between God and the people. Paul's ministry serves the goal of a proper relationship between humans and the God of the covenant.

glory (*eineken tēs hyperballousēs doxēs*). The glory of the new covenant exceeds that of the old.

This too demands an explanation: **For if what was disappearing** existed **with glory, how much more surely does what remains** exist **in glory** (3:11). Neither the conditional nor the main clause contains a verb, so one must be supplied. Previously Paul has written about the transient refulgence (radiance) on Moses's face: the glory on Moses's face was passing away (*tēn katargoumenēn*, 3:7). The transient glory on his face symbolized the entire dispensation affiliated with Moses, the old covenant. That too is disappearing, passing away, along with its glory. A contrast exists between what is vanishing (*to katargoumenon*) and what is permanent (*ton menon*). What abides is the new dispensation with the ministry of the Spirit, the ministry of righteousness. This new dispensation remains in glory.

The argument in 3:7–11 is tightly knit, consisting of a triad of interlocking comparisons and contrasts. Each of them contains the comparative formula "how much more surely." The second and third comparisons are joined to the earlier one by the explanatory particle (*gar*). Explanatory comments in verses 7 and 9 interrupt the flow of the argument.

Without these interruptions, Paul's argument is clear:

If the ministry of death came in glory, a fortiori the ministry of the Spirit exists in glory.

If there is glory in the ministry of condemnation, a fortiori the ministry of righteousness abounds in glory.

If what was to disappear existed with glory, a fortiori what remains exists in glory.

In effect, the glory ministry of the new dispensation is incomparable with the glory that characterized the old dispensation.

Comparison with Moses (3:12–18)

3:12–18. Moses was well known among Jews. After Abraham, Moses was the most revered figure in Jewish history. But Moses was not unknown in the Gentile world (see Savage 1996, 106–8). The apostle does not intend to disparage Moses in his trilogy of comparisons and contrasts (3:7–11); rather, his purpose is to highlight the glory of the ministry of the new covenant. Having done so, he continues his midrashic reflection on the Exodus narrative with thoughts about the veil mentioned in Exod. 34:33–35. Paul presents this as a conclusion to what he has just written.

Therefore, having such hope, we act very boldly (3:12). The fact that the new dispensation continues to endure in glory provides Paul with great hope. Encouraged in this way, he is able to speak out boldly. "Very boldly" is literally "with much boldness" (*pollē parrēsia*). The term "boldness" was well known in the Hellenistic world and connotes freedom of speech, openness, and the truth of what one is saying, even when the speaker faces some adversity.

Speaking boldly was a right of citizens and a quality attributed to great speakers (cf. 1 Thess. 2:2) such as Demosthenes (*1 Philip*. 4.51; *2 Philip*. 6.31; *4 Philip*. 10.53–54). If a speaker spoke with "boldness," a listener could have confidence in the truth of what was being said. Like the great Hellenists, Paul claims this quality for himself. But he may have something else in mind as well. In the biblical tradition, boldness is a quality of prophetic speech. The prophets spoke boldly since they uttered the truth of God.

Paul contrasts himself with Moses. Paul speaks openly; Moses hid himself. The apostle is **not like Moses, who put a veil on his face so that the children of Israel did not gaze intently at the end of what was passing away** (3:13). The negative comparison makes reference to Exod. 34:33–35, allowing Paul to continue the midrash on the Exodus text begun in verse 7. In fact, the purpose clause, "on his face so that the children of Israel did not gaze intently at the end of what was passing away," reprises almost verbatim the language of verse 7, where Paul used the wording to portray the glory of the old dispensation. Once again, Paul introduces the thought of something passing away and speaks of its end.

The Exodus text does not give a reason for Moses's veil, but Paul does. He describes Moses as hiding his face with a veil so that the Israelites would not see the old dispensation come to its end. In effect, Moses acted deceptively

Boldness (*parrēsia*)

"I am going to speak to you openly [meta parrēsias]; *I will not conceal anything."* (Demosthenes, *2 Philip*. 6.31)

"The righteous will stand with great confidence [en parrēsia] *in the presence of those who have oppressed them."* (Wis. 5:1)

"To find a man who in plain terms and without guile speaks his mind with frankness [parrēsiazomenon], *and neither for the sake of reputation nor for gain makes false pretensions, . . . to find such a man as that is not easy, but rather the good fortune of a very lucky city."* (Dio Chrysostom, *Alex*. 11 [*Or*. 32])

"Let those whose actions serve the common weal use freedom of speech [parrēsia] *and walk in daylight through the midst of the marketplace."* (Philo, *Spec. Laws* 1.321)

"We had courage [eparrēsiasametha] *in our God to declare to you the gospel of God in spite of great opposition."* (Paul, 1 Thess. 2:2)

whereas Paul acts with the integrity that is associated with boldness. Paul, however, does not want to place the blame on Moses. So he shifts perspective, attributing the real culpability to the Israelites (3:14). This kind of self-correction is not infrequent in the Letters of Paul, who sometimes gets carried away in his argument (e.g., 1 Cor. 1:16).

Fearing that he may offend his audience, Paul changed his tone. He uses a short remark to shift his focus and place the blame on the Israelites: **But their minds were hardened** (*epōrōthē*, 3:14). The verb, related to a word used to describe the kind of stone used in construction (*pōros*), appears to be introduced under the influence of what Paul has written about the stone tablets.

> **Rhetorical Self-Correction (*epidiorthōsis*)**
>
> Ancient rhetoricians used the term *epidiorthōsis* to describe a short and pithy statement that follows an unpalatable comment or argument (see Alexander, *De figuris* 1.4; Hermogenes, *De inventione* 4.12). Use of the literary technique enabled a speaker to provide evidence of his sensitivity to the audience. Paul uses the technique in 3:14 (cf. 7:3; 12:11; Rom. 3:5; Gal. 5:10). When such a corrective remark anticipates the offensive comment, it is called *prodiorthōsis*.

The metaphor, similarly related to other stones, also appears in Rom. 11:7–12 (cf. Rom. 11:25). It recalls the traditional biblical image of stony hearts (Exod. 4:21; 7:3; 14:4, 17).

Paul's use of the passive voice seems to suggest that God is the agent of the hardening (cf. Isa. 6:9–10; 29:10), but 4:4 indicates that Paul considers Satan, the god of this age, as the one who hardened the Israelites' hearts. Paul may have considered that Satan served as God's agent in hardening the Israelites' hearts.

A typical feature of the midrashic exposition of biblical texts is the application of the text to the author's present circumstances. Paul does this: **For until today during the reading of the old covenant the veil [*kalymma*]—which is not taken away [*anakalyptomenon*]—remains.** The veil, first introduced in verse 13, is reintroduced into Paul's exposition. It will serve as the motif around which Paul develops his midrash. The midrash uses "veil" metaphorically, the only usage of this metaphor and its pertinent terminology in his letters. It serves as an image of an inability to understand the word of God.

The scene evoked by Paul is the public reading of the Torah in the synagogue. Here 3:14 contains the oldest known use of the expression "old covenant" (*tēs palaias diathēkēs*, "Old Testament") in reference to a text. The terminology does not appear elsewhere in the NT. It appears here in contrast with "new covenant" (*kainēs diathēkēs*, 3:6), but the word "covenant" has a different connotation in each of the two cases.

Until this day, says Paul, during the reading of the Scripture, a veil falls over the face and is not taken away. The phrase "until this day" (cf. 3:15) introduces Paul's actualization of the Scripture, yet it does more than that. A

The Veil

Paul's midrash on Exod. 34 incorporates additional wordplays (*paronomasia*), especially as he toys with the idea of the veil on Moses's face.

The noun "veil" (*kalymma*):
3:13, 14, 15, 16
The verb "veil" (*kalyptō*):
4:3 (2x)
The verb "unveil"
(*anakalyptō*): 3:14, 18

similar phrase occurs in the citation of Deut. 29:3 LXX (29:4 Eng.) in Rom. 11:8. All three texts—Rom. 11:7–12 and 2 Cor. 3:14–15 as well as Deut. 29:4—say that within the covenantal context, the Israelites remain impervious to divine revelation. The veil that prevents understanding remains, says Paul, **because it is abolished** only **in Christ**. Christ has done away with the veil in the past, but it remains for Paul's contemporaries who remain in their unbelief. For them, the veil still needs to be destroyed.

To emphasize the point, Paul repeats himself with some modification. **Indeed, until now whenever Moses is read, a veil is placed on their hearts** (3:15). Metonymy allows the apostle to write about the reading of Moses rather than the reading of Scripture. Paul localizes the veil: it is placed over their hearts. This suggests that their hearts have been hardened (cf. 3:14) and evokes the scriptural tradition of hardened hearts. Like the ancient Israelites, Paul's contemporaries suffer from a kind of cardiosclerosis.

How can the veil be removed? Without asking the question, Paul introduces a passage of Scripture to give an answer. **"Whenever anyone turns to the Lord, the veil is removed"** (3:16). The Scripture is Exod. 34:34, "whenever Moses went in before the Lord to speak with him, he would take the veil off," but Paul's actualizing exegesis of the text leads him to adopt some modification. He applies the text to anyone rather than just to Moses. He uses "turn to," suggesting conversion, rather than "went in before." He says that the "veil is removed," as if by God, whereas the biblical text says that Moses removed the veil.

In the book of Exodus, the Lord is Yahweh, the God of Abraham, Isaac, and Jacob, but Paul generally uses the title (*kyrios*) for Christ, and that seems to be his meaning here. When anyone turns to Christ, a veil is removed, and thus that person is able to understand the word of God. If, however, Paul's readers understood the apostle to be quoting the biblical text, they might have understood "Lord" as referring to the God of Israel.

By way of explanation, Paul offers an interpretive comment, **and the Lord is the Spirit** (3:17). Concerning this passage, Chrysostom wrote, "He did not say 'the Lord is a Spirit' but 'the Spirit is the Lord'" (*Hom. 2 Cor.* 7.5). Other fathers of the church concur with Chrysostom in taking the passage as an affirmation that the Spirit is divine, but that is not Paul's point. Rather, Paul seems to be affirming a dynamic equivalence between Christ and the Spirit. It is by means of the Spirit that Christ acts in the present era of salvation. With this reference he returns to the pneumatological focus that characterizes his writing about the new covenant (see vv. 3, 6, 8, 18).

And where the Spirit of the Lord is, there is freedom continues Paul's explanation. Freedom is a major theme of Paul's Letter to the Galatians (see 2:4; 5:1, 13; cf. Rom. 6:18), but Paul only touches upon the idea of freedom in this passage, the only place in the letter in which he mentions freedom. Freedom entails freedom *from* the restrictive aspects of the old covenant—the veil has been removed for believers—and from the sin revealed by the law. Even more, freedom is freedom *for* something; it involves life, justification, and the transformation that comes with believers being in a situation in which they can contemplate the glory of the Lord.

Returning to the theme of the removal of the veil (see vv. 14, 16), Paul brings his argument to its conclusion: **And all of us, with face unveiled, contemplating as if in a mirror the glory of the Lord, are being transformed into the same image** (3:18). The focus is on all of us, that is, not only an apostle like Paul who has seen the risen Lord (1 Cor. 15:8; Gal. 1:16), but also the entire Christian community at Corinth. Believers at Corinth, "us," are implicitly contrasted with "them," that is, not only the Israelites of the exodus generation who could not look on Moses's face (v. 12; cf. Exod. 34:33, 35), but also Paul's Jewish contemporaries whose hearts are veiled when the Scriptures are read (v. 15). Because the veil has been removed by Christ, believers are able to contemplate the glory of the Lord, though not directly (cf. 1 Cor. 13:12).

"Contemplating as if in a mirror" (*katoptrizomenoi*) is a rare verb, found neither in the Greek Bible nor elsewhere in the NT. The word, a trove on Paul's part, is used to describe the singular experience of believers. In faith, believers

---

The Spirit of the Lord

Both nouns in the phrase "by the Spirit of the Lord" (*apo kyriou pneumatos*, v. 18) lack a qualifying article, yielding a pithy expression whose sense is difficult to determine precisely, as can be seen in the differing translations that appear in published English versions of the text and the works of commentators. Among these translations are the following:

The Spirit of the Lord	The Lord who is the Spirit
The Lord of the Spirit	The Lord, the Spirit
The Lord who is Spirit	The Spirit who is Lord

The phrase "the Lord is the Spirit" in v. 17, where both nouns have an article (*ho de kyrios to pneuma estin*), may have influenced some of these translations. My translation, "the Spirit of the Lord" (v. 18), reflects the pneumatological interest of the chapter as well as the theological notion that God and his Christ act by means of the Spirit.

Transformation

To speak of believers' transformation, Paul uses the verb "transform" (*metamorphoomai*). The verb is used by Paul only one other time (Rom. 12:2) and appears only four times altogether in the NT. The non-Pauline NT uses of the term are found in the Synoptic stories of Jesus's transfiguration (Matt. 17:2; Mark 9:2).

The verb first appears in the *Iliad* (2.319), and is often found in Hellenistic literature. Stories of transformation frequently appear in Hellenistic literature. Collections of such stories appear in Nicander's *Heteroeumena* (second cent. BCE), Ovid's *Metamorphoses* (early first cent. CE), and Apuleius's *Golden Ass* (second cent. CE). Paul's Hellenistic readership would be able to relate to the notion. Joseph A. Fitzmyer (1993), citing a number of Qumran texts such as 1QH 12 (formerly 4).5–6, 27–28; 1QS 2.2–4; and 1QSb 4.24–28, has shown that the idea of transformation was not foreign to the Jewish world.

---

have an experience of Christ that is metaphorically described as visual and results in believers being transformed into the same image (cf. Rom. 8:29).

The "same image" is undoubtedly that of Christ, but the expression has a double nuance. On the one hand, Christ is the image of God (4:4; cf. Col. 1:15); on the other, Christians enjoy a mirror image of Christ. The contemplation of the image of Christ provokes their transformation, but that is a process. Their transformation is, as Paul says, **from glory to glory**, from one degree of glory to another. The transformation is effected **as by the Spirit of the Lord**. The addendum comes as a reminder that the Spirit of Christ is the agent bringing about the transformation of believers.

Blindness of Nonbelievers (4:1–4)

4:1–4. Paul introduced his midrash on the exodus story as an inference from what he had written in 3:7–11. He wrote, "Therefore, having such hope, we act very boldly" (3:12). He now draws an inference from his extended midrash. **Wherefore, having this ministry to the extent with which we have been favored** (4:1). A switch in the reference of the first-person plural allows the apostle to return to the subject of his own ministry, whose integrity he has defended in 2:14–3:6. The comparative particle suggests that Paul has a ministry only insofar as he has received that ministry from God, but his main point is that God has gratuitously given the ministry to Paul. Appointing Paul to ministry is an act of mercy (*eleēthēmen*, hapax in 2 Corinthians) on God's part.

Since he is a beneficiary of God's graciousness, Paul says that **we do not lose heart** (cf. 4:16). **Rather** than being discouraged, **we have renounced hidden deeds of which one might be ashamed** (4:2). Paul is a man of personal and ministerial integrity. Expanding on the idea, Paul writes about his integrity, both negatively: **not acting in a cunning fashion nor falsifying the word of God**; and positively: **but** fully **disclosing the truth, we commend ourselves to every conscience before God.**

The contrast, a classic figure of speech, emphasizes what Paul has said about his integrity. The negative statements anticipate Paul's reaction to the charge that he has acted slyly, at least with regard to financial matters (12:16), and reiterate his affirmation that he is not one of those who peddle the word of God (2:17). These negative statements echo what Paul had written in his first letter when he said that his appeal did not come with deceit or trickery (see 1 Thess. 2:3–6).

"The truth" of which Paul writes is most especially the gospel message (see 6:7; 11:10; 13:8), but Paul's antithetical construction suggests that he wants his readers to understand that the gospel message is indeed "true." Proclaiming the truth as he does, Paul commends himself to everyone. He first raised the issue of his self-commendation in 3:1 and cited his own conscience as a witness to his integrity (1:12). Now he calls upon the conscience of everyone to attest to his forthrightness.

Despite Paul's personal integrity, not everyone accepts his message. To speak about those who do not accept his message, Paul again takes up the image of the veil, which he exploited in his midrash on Exod. 34. **And if our proclamation** [*to euangelion hēmōn*] **is nonetheless veiled,** he writes, **it is veiled for those who are perishing** (4:3; cf. 2:15). It is not only the Torah that can be veiled; the gospel message itself can also be veiled. As he raises this possibility, Paul may be responding to the accusations of people who say that some have not accepted the gospel because Paul has garbled the message and lacks eloquence and rhetorical skill (see 11:6). Paul rejects this kind of accusation out of hand, saying that those who do not accept the message are on their way to eternal ruin.

He blames Satan for their failure to believe. **In whose case**—that is, in regard to those who are perishing—**the god of this age has blinded the minds of unbelievers,** he writes (4:4). For Paul "this age" is the present evil age (see Rom. 12:2; 1 Cor. 2:6, 8; Gal. 1:4). The modified dualism of Paul's apocalyptic thought leads him to affirm that those who are hostile to Christ are under the control of various cosmic forces (see 1 Cor. 15:24–26), but nowhere is he as blatant as he is here when he affirms that the one whom he calls Satan (2 Cor. 2:11; 11:14; 12:7) is "the god of this age" (cf. MacRae 1968, 422). The god of this age stands in sharp contrast to the Creator God, who is Father. The god of this age is the cause of blindness; the Creator God is the source of light (see 4:6). Yet Paul's identification of those who are perishing as "unbelievers" (cf. 6:14–15) suggests that those over whom Satan has control are not total pawns. They have refused to believe and thus are complicit in their own blindness.

Paul writes about those who are blind in Rom. 2:19. In 2 Cor. 4:4, he writes about Satan causing blindness. Apart from the citations of Deut. 29:3 and Ps.

Paul's Modified Dualism

Paul is a faithful Jew. Throughout his life he was devoted to the one God of Israel, the God of his forebears (cf. 2 Cor. 11:2; 1 Cor. 8:6; Phil. 3:5). He also had an apocalyptic frame of thought, as did many of his Jewish contemporaries (Beker 1980; 1982). With them the apostle believed that demonic forces were at work in the world. In 2 Corinthians Paul writes about Satan (2:11; 11:14; 12:7) and Beliar (6:15). Until the consummation of the end time, there will be hostility between these powers and God.

Nonetheless, the one God is supreme. At the end, God's reign will be fully manifest; the demonic powers will be destroyed (cf. 1 Cor. 15:25–28). The way that Paul writes about the thorn in his flesh (2 Cor. 12:7) evinces his belief that God occasionally uses demonic forces for his own purpose. God's supremacy over creation—Paul does not suggest, as many dualistic thinkers do, that some beings were created by demonic forces or lesser gods—may be contested, but ultimately the one God is the supreme Lord of all.

68:24 LXX (69:23 Eng., MT) in Rom. 11:8, 10, these two are the only known instances of Paul's use of the blindness metaphor. In Rom. 2:19, Paul writes, "If you are sure that you are a guide to the blind, a light to those who are in darkness . . ." As in Rom. 2:19, use of the metaphor calls for a mention of its antithesis, light. So, commenting on the result of blindness, he writes, **so that they do not see the light of the gospel of the glory of Christ, who is the image of God.**

Light and darkness are traditional biblical metaphors used in reference to those who accept God and those who do not (cf. Isa. 42:6–7; 49:6; Luke 1:79; Eph. 5:8; etc.). Paul affirms that those who have been blinded by Satan cannot see the light (*ton phōtismon*), which he qualifies by means of a string of genitives. This style of writing is somewhat typical for a person whose Greek has been influenced by Hebrew. The light that unbelievers cannot see is the light of the gospel, which proclaims the glory of the risen Christ. In this regard they are quite unlike believers who, with faces unveiled, are able to contemplate the glory of the Lord and are transformed into the image of Christ (3:18).

Paul's description of Christ as "the image of God"—"Christ, who is the icon of God" (*hos estin eikōn tou theou*)—seems to depend on Jewish wisdom tradition but may also echo the Genesis tradition that humankind has been created "in the image of God" (*kat' eikona theou*, Gen. 1:27 LXX; cf. 1:26). Glory, reflection, mirror, light, image, and God—these terms shape the language with which Paul has crafted the imagery that he uses in 3:18; 4:4. This is also the language of passages such as Wis. 7:25–26: *Sophia* (wisdom) is "a pure emanation of the glory of the Almighty, . . . a reflection of eternal light, a spotless mirror of the working of God, and an image of his goodness."

The God of this Age

Paul employs the word "god" (*ho theos*) to designate the God of the patriarchs, the Father of Jesus. Grammatically a common noun, the word essentially functions as a proper name in Paul's Letters. The expression "the god of this age" does not, however, occur elsewhere in the NT.

Thus, Pelagius expressed ambivalence about how the Pauline and NT hapax should be interpreted:

> "The god of this world may be understood to be the devil, on the ground that he has claimed to rule over unbelievers. Or, on account of the attacks of the heretics, it may be understood to mean that God has blinded the minds of unbelievers precisely because of their unbelief." (*Commentary on the Second Epistle to the Corinthians* 4, in PL 30:781)

Some patristic authors, especially those who had been engaged in polemics against dualistic systems of thought, took Paul's words as a reference to God. Chrysostom, for example, comments: "The 'god of this world' may refer neither to the devil nor to another creator, as the Manichaeans say, but to the God of the universe, who has blinded the minds of the unbelievers of this world" (*Hom. 2 Cor.* 8.2).

Proclaiming the Lord Jesus (4:5–6)

4:5–6. Continuing to develop his thought in a stream of consciousness characterized by a loose association of ideas, Paul returns to the idea of the proclamation of the gospel that he introduced in verse 3. **For we do not proclaim ourselves, rather,** we proclaim **Jesus Christ as Lord and ourselves as your slaves for Jesus's sake** (4:5). The object of Paul's proclamation is not himself and his fellow missionaries; instead, it is Jesus Christ, whom Paul acknowledges as Lord. "Jesus" is the name of a human being. When Paul appends "Christ" as a title to the name of Jesus, he generally wants to draw attention to the death and resurrection of Jesus. When the apostle highlights the title "Lord," as he does here, he focuses on the risen Lord, whose manifestation is awaited at the parousia.

In and of itself, the title Lord (*kyrios*) suggests the designation of others as servants and slaves. So, using the title Lord, Paul is able to say that he (and his fellow evangelists) are "slaves." But in an unusual turn of phrase, Paul says he is a slave of the Corinthians, with respect to whom he does not exalt himself. Only here in the extant correspondence does Paul describe himself as a slave of the community (cf. 1 Cor. 9:19; 2 Cor. 6:4; 11:8). He functions as a servant for Jesus's sake. His service of the Corinthians takes place in his ministry of evangelization; he serves them as a minister of the new covenant.

Commenting further on his role as an evangelist, Paul returns to the theme of light, which he used in verse 4. **For the God who said "Let light shine out of the darkness"** [*ek skotous phōs lampsei*] **is the one who lets light shine in our hearts** (4:6). Paul intends to reference a scriptural text, but the exact wording of his quotation does not appear in the Greek Bible. Some scholars, such as Paul Barnett (1997, 225–26) and Mitzi Minor (2009, 82), find the reference in the creation story (Gen. 1:3), which has the advantage of evoking a context in which "image of God" occurs. Others prefer to see in the quotation a reference to Isa. 9:2 (9:1 LXX), where the phrase *phōs lampsei* appears. This has the advantage of evoking the concept of light that figures so prominently in the Deutero-Isaiah Servant texts, which Paul uses so often to speak about his own ministry (Rom. 10:16; 15:21; Gal. 1:15; etc.). Paul's nonliteral citation echoes both Scriptures.

"Our hearts" uses a personal pronoun in the first-person plural. The pronoun refers especially to Paul. Paul affirms that the God who has enlightened him—perhaps a reference to his Damascus experience—is the same as the God of the Scriptures. In doing so, he inserts his ministry into the broad context of salvation history, creation, and the renewal of God's people.

Paul's heart was enlightened for a purpose, **to spread the light of the knowledge of the glory of God in the face of Jesus Christ.** "To spread the light" appears in Greek as a simple prepositional phrase, *pros phōtismon*, "for the sake of light." Evoking the phrase in Isa. 49:6 in Deutero-Isaiah's third servant canticle, the phrase suggests the idea that Paul's enlightenment has a missionary purpose (see 2:14–16; cf. Gal. 1:15–16). That the phrase is to be interpreted in a missionary sense is confirmed by its parallelism with verse 4. Satan has

Knowledge of the Glory of God

In verse 6, as in verse 4, "light" (*phōtismon*) is qualified in Semitic fashion by a string of genitives. To understand Paul's thought, one must decide whether the first genitive, "of the knowledge" (*tēs gnōseōs*), is an objective or a subjective genitive. Is Paul talking about spreading light that consists of knowledge of the glory of God (as this commentary interprets the phrase), taking the genitive as an objective genitive? Or is he talking about light that comes from the experience of the glory of God? If the latter, Paul is talking about the light that is his because of his conversion experience.

Rather than interpret the phrase "for the sake of light" as a metaphorical description of Paul's work of evangelization, Margaret Thrall (1994, 318) takes the phrase to refer to the direct action of God. God let his light shine in Paul's heart to bring about an enlightenment produced by the knowledge of God's glory in Christ. She argues that the subject of the purpose clause is the subject of the main verb of the relative clause, *elampsen*, "lets light shine."

blinded the mind of unbelievers so that they do not see the light of the gospel of the glory of Christ; God has let light shine on hearts in order to spread the light of the knowledge of the glory of God on the face of Jesus Christ.

Theological Issues

Glory (doxa)

In Paul's day the meaning of the word *doxa* in ordinary parlance was "thought" or "opinion." In the apostle's Greek Bible, however, the word was used as a translation of the Hebrew *kābôd*. The principal connotation of the Hebrew term was "weight," that is, the weight of a person's rank or of the honor and esteem in which someone was held, especially because of power and wealth.

Since God was held in ultimate honor, *kābôd/doxa* came to connote an attribute of God, used particularly in reference to the manifestation of God's power in creating and ruling over creatures as well as his self-manifestation in theophanies. Biblical theophanies were described in terms that properly pertain to sense experience. The appearance of God was accompanied by fire and light (Exod. 24:17; Deut. 5:24; Ezek. 1:4, 13–14, 16, 22, 27–28; Isa. 60:1–3). Accordingly, biblical *doxa* often has "a touch of luminescence" (*TLNT* 1:366). Such usage is not attested outside the Greek Bible.

New Testament usage of the word is dependent on its appearance in the Greek Bible, the Septuagint. The term was used in reference to the glory of God but also, in a transferred sense, to the honor and esteem in which some persons were held. As a result "fame" and "reputation" came to be found among the connotations of the term in NT usage. Such usage paralleled other usage found in Koine Greek, where the term was used in reference to the high regard, opinion, or reputation in which a person was held. Strangely, however, Hellenistic Jewish writers like Philo and Josephus seem not to have been influenced by the Greek Bible in their use of *doxa*.

The term *doxa* appears frequently in the NT, being used in every book with the exception of Paul's short note to Philemon and the Johannine Epistles. A substantial number of these appearances occur in the Pauline Letters, Romans (16x), 1 Corinthians (12x), Galatians (1x), Philippians (6x), 1 Thessalonians (3x), and especially in 2 Corinthians, where the term occurs 19 times—64 times in all. The term appears another twenty times in the deuteropauline letters. Thus *doxa* is rightly styled a Pauline term since it appears in Paul more often than it does in the writings of any other NT author. In his writings the term has a wide variety of meanings, especially when it is used of humans.

Thirteen of the apostle's uses of *doxa* are to be found in 2 Cor. 3:7–4:6. Paul uses the related verb *doxazō* ("glorify") eleven times, two of which are in 3:10 (cf. 9:13). That the apostle's understanding of these terms in 3:7–4:6 reflects

Septuagintal usage is to be expected since the passage consists of Paul's midrashic reflection on an episode in the book of Exodus. The midrash culminates in the affirmation that Paul's mission is to spread the light of the knowledge of the glory of God in the face of Jesus Christ (4:6), through his preaching of the gospel. The glory of God and his Christ is the motivating force of Paul's every action. He does what he does for the glory of the Lord (8:19).

2 Corinthians 4:7–5:10

The Present and the Future

Introductory Matters

This passage begins with Paul asking his readers to contemplate a treasure contained in earthenware vessels. To this day the imagery is perhaps the most remembered and most frequently referenced image in the Pauline corpus. The apostle uses the image as he begins an extensive reflection on death.

Paul first mentions the subject of death explicitly in 4:10–12, where he writes, "carrying about the dying of Jesus in our body, . . . for we, the living, are always being handed over to death for the sake of Jesus, . . . so that the life of Jesus might be manifested in our mortal flesh; consequently, death is at work in us." This concentration of language pertaining to death is unusual in Paul's Letters. Paul often writes about death, but this is the only place in his correspondence where the words "dying," "death," and "mortal" come together in a single passage. Indeed, the words "dying" and "mortal" rarely appear in his letters. On the other hand, the term "dead"—most often used as a substantive plural ("the dead"), particularly in reference to Jesus's resurrection from the dead (*ek nekrōn*)—appears often in Paul's Letters (see Rom. 4:24; 6:4, 9; 7:4; 8:11 [2x]; 10:9; 1 Cor. 15:12, 20; Gal. 1:1; 1 Thess. 1:10; cf. Rom. 10:7) but does not appear in this passage and occurs only once in 2 Corinthians (1:9).

Paul's reflections on death should be considered within the context of a large body of Hellenistic literature that considers death. Biographers such as Plutarch in his *Parallel Lives* and Suetonius in his writings on various emperors, such as Augustus Caesar, Caligula, Claudius, and Nero, obviously had something to say about the deaths of their protagonists, as did the historian

Tacitus in his *Historiae* and Xenophon, who considered the death of Socrates in his *Apology of Socrates*. Seneca in *Apolocyntosis* and Martial in his *Epigrams* were authors of satirical pieces on death. Lucian wrote about death in *Dialogues of the Dead* and *The Passing of Peregrinus*. Among the philosophical moralists who took up the topic were Plato, especially when he wrote about Socrates's death in *Phaedo*, Cicero in his *Tusculanae disputationes*, and Plutarch. Hellenistic Jewish books that treat death are 2 and 4 Maccabees, as do some of the writings of Philo and Josephus, Paul's Hellenistic Jewish contemporaries. Manuel Vogel (2006) characterizes this body of literature as belonging to an ancient *ars moriendi* tradition. What Paul writes about death in this section of the letter belongs to the tradition as well.

Tracing the Train of Thought

Earthenware Vessels (4:7–12)

4:7–12. Having written about his ministry in glorious terms, Paul begins to take a different tack as he continues to defend his ministry. Turning from the ministry to those who minister, Paul writes, **We, however, have this treasure in earthenware vessels** (4:7). The "we" of whom he writes is himself in the first instance, but much of what he has to say pertains as well to his fellow evangelists and the believers to whom he is writing. The treasure is his important ministry (see 4:1), with all that this ministry entails. The image of earthenware vessels in which the ministry is contained suggests fragility (see

Earthenware Jars

The Dead Sea Scrolls, discovered in 1946–47, are ancient texts that were preserved in clay pots. The fragility of the pots led to the discovery of the scrolls. As the story of their discovery is told, a Bedouin boy tried to coax a goat out of a cave by throwing a stone at the animal. The stone hit and broke an earthenware vessel. The sound of the breaking clay led the boy to investigate. The rest is history, but the incident shows that texts were preserved in clay vessels and that these were indeed fragile.

Ps. 2:9) and weakness. The first metaphor, treasure, looks backward to verses 1–6; the second, earthenware vessels, looks ahead to verses 8–9.

Paul has been writing about writing (3:1–3, 7). He was surely aware that important texts were often kept in earthenware jars, whose fragility was well known. These jars were made in a pottery shop, often situated on the same marketplace where Paul plied his leatherworker's trade. One of his favorite biblical texts was the book of Jeremiah, which features the image of the potter making pots to be used as God sees fit (Jer. 18:6). Paul alludes to this and similar passages (see Isa. 29:16; 45:9) in Rom. 9:19–20. Hence the idea that pottery is available for use by its maker and owner could not be far from his mind.

The pictorial contrast between the treasure and the container was mentioned by Paul for a purpose, **so that** it becomes clear that **the superabundance of power is God's and not from us**. Paul's ministry is one of evangelization. He proclaims the gospel, which is the power of God (see Rom. 1:16; 1 Cor. 1:18). To describe the extraordinary nature of the power of the gospel, Paul writes about its "superabundance," a term that he alone among NT authors uses. He does so especially in 2 Corinthians (see 1:8; 4:17 [2x]; 12:7; Rom. 7:13; 1 Cor. 12:31; Gal. 1:13).

Baker Photo Archive

Figure 6.
Clay Jar from
Qumran Used
to Store Scrolls.

In contrast with God's extraordinary power is the weakness of the instruments that God uses. To make this point, Paul employs the first of the three hardship catalogs of 2 Corinthians (see 6:4–10; 11:23–33). The hardships could be overwhelming. Paul does not say that there has been an occasional hardship; rather, he emphasizes that he has endured the hardships **in every way** (4:8), a circumstance reinforced by the "always" of verse 10. Paul cites his multiple hardships both here and in 6:4–10 to show that he has not been broken by the difficulties that he has endured.

The hardships are arranged in a list of eight contrasting participles, the first generically pointing to a kind of difficulty that Paul is suffering, the second affirming that the apostle is not overcome by the difficulty. He begins by saying that he has been **afflicted but not crushed**. At the head of the list, being "afflicted" sums up and is the most important of Paul's hardships. In the opening prayer of praise (1:3–8), Paul has written about his afflictions and how God has consoled him in those difficulties. That thought suggests that God's power has saved Paul from being crushed. Paul's rhetorical ability is manifest when he uses a play on words in his second contrast. He is **perplexed**

Hardship Lists

A list of hardships similar to that found in 4:8–9 is a well-known Hellenistic literary form that is sometimes called a *peristasis* catalog. The Greek term sometimes means "difficult circumstances." Paul employs a number of these catalogs (4:8–9; 6:4–10; 11:23–33; Rom. 8:35; 1 Cor. 4:10–13; Phil. 4:12). Such lists were used by the Stoics and sometimes appear in diatribes of Cynic origin. Among the Stoics such lists were used to illustrate that they were staunch and invincible when faced with pain and the greatest of difficulties.

Occasionally the lists include antithetical expressions to highlight the writer's ability to withstand difficulty and opposition. Epictetus lauds the Stoic in this way: "Show me a man who though sick is happy, though in danger is happy, though dying is happy, condemned to exile is happy, though in disrepute is happy. Show him! By the gods, I would fain see a Stoic!" (*Diatr.* 2.19.24). See also Plutarch, *The Stoics and the Poets* 1 (in *Mor.* 1057D–E).

but not given to despair (*aporoumenoi all' ouk exaporoumenoi*). The subtlety of the apostle's language is almost impossible to render in English translation. Jan Lambrecht (2006, 72) makes an attempt to do so, suggesting "at a loss, but not utterly at a loss" as a translation that captures Paul's play on words.

Paul willingly admits that before the Damascus experience he persecuted the church of God (1 Cor. 15:9; Gal. 1:13 [cf. 1:23]; Phil. 3:6). Having received the light of the gospel, he himself became the victim of persecution (Gal. 5:11). He alludes to his having suffered persecution in the third antithesis, **persecuted but not abandoned** (4:9). The contrast echoes an antithesis found in 1 Corinthians: in another rehearsal of a number of hardships (4:10–13), Paul wrote, "When persecuted, we endure" (4:12). "Abandoned" occurs just twice in Paul's Letters. It is also found in Ps. 22:2, which Mark places on the lips of Jesus in his account of the passion (15:34). Then, with **struck down but not destroyed** (*kataballomenoi* [hapax in Paul] *all' ouk apollymenoi*), Paul concludes this short rehearsal of the difficulties that he has endured for the sake of his ministry.

Throughout the entire series, the emphatic and repeated "but not" draws attention to the second member of the antithetical phrases. The passive voice of the verb form in the second part of the antitheses, a "theological passive," suggests that God is the one who has not allowed Paul to be crushed and destroyed. God is the agent behind Paul's ability to withstand the troubles that he has endured. That Paul has not been destroyed indicates that he has not been totally wiped out; he has not died. What, then, does the apostle think about death? The rest of this section of the letter (4:10–5:10) provides the answer.

Paul begins with a christological reflection on his sufferings, **always carrying about the dying of Jesus in our body** (4:10). In this passage the apostle does not speak about the death of Jesus; rather, he speaks about the dying of Jesus (*tēn nekrōsin tou Iēsou*), the process and experience of dying. He sees his continual hardships as a reflection of and participation in the sufferings of the earthly Jesus. Paul's participation in Jesus's suffering results from his union with Christ. His letters provide occasional indications that he sees the believer's life as imitating the life of Jesus (see 8:9; Rom. 15:3; 1 Cor. 4:6–16; Phil. 2:4–8; 1 Thess. 1:6).

Paul is a paradigm of God's activity in Christ. As Christ died to bring life, so the apostle brings life through his own "dying." The purpose of his apostolic suffering is **so that the life of Jesus might be manifested in our body.** Unlike the Stoics, Paul has not rehearsed his sufferings in order to demonstrate his fortitude; rather, he wants the Corinthians to know that the reason for his suffering is so that the life and power of Jesus may be manifest. He does not separate the sufferings of the earthly Jesus from the resurrected life of Jesus. It is the dying and resurrection of Jesus that makes sense of Paul's difficult life. Jesus was crucified from weakness but lives by the power of God, as he says in 13:4.

The power of God is likewise manifest in the multiple hardships of Paul (see 4:7). Paul's sufferings do not deter him from his ministry; rather, they are an integral part of his ministry. They allow the power of God to shine forth through the fragility of his humanity. The power of God at work is the focus of the gospel message. It is not only the message itself but also the speaker of the message who must convey the message.

Paul's thought is difficult to understand, so he attempts an explanation: **For we, the living, are continually being handed over to death for the sake of Jesus** (4:11). It is a truism that once born, human beings have begun their journey to death. For Paul, his journey toward death is a life that is lived for Jesus's sake. His journey toward death, with all of its hardships, is under the control of God, who is handing Paul over to death. The verb that he uses, "being handed over" (*paradidometha*), appears in the Passion Narratives (Mark 9:31; 10:33; 14:18, 21) and is used by Paul when he writes about Jesus being handed over to death (Rom. 4:25; 8:32; 1 Cor. 11:23). Paul's use of this traditional language echoes the story of Jesus's passion here just as does the "dying of Jesus" (v. 10).

Paul reiterates the idea, affirming again that the hardships he endures while being handed over to death are **in order that the life of Jesus might be manifested in our mortal flesh.** The phrase repeats almost verbatim what he has just written, albeit with an anthropological corrective. His body (*tō sōmati hēmōn*, v. 10) is mortal flesh (*tē thnētē sarki hēmōn*, v. 11). The power of God that is revealed in the life of the resurrected Jesus is also revealed in Paul, in his mortal flesh.

The description of the subtle interaction between life and death that Paul has developed in verses 10–11 leads to a startling conclusion: **consequently**

101

death is at work in us, while life is at work **in you** (4:12). Paul's attention has quickly turned to the Corinthians. He tells them that the reason why he is being handed over to death, the reason why he endures his apostolic sufferings, is so that the Corinthians may experience the life of Jesus, the power of God, working within them. His ministry, with all its hardships, is an instrument whereby the power of God enables the life of the risen Jesus to be present within the community of believers. As Jesus experienced dying so that we might live, so Paul experiences his hardships so that the Corinthians might live.

Paul's Faith (4:13–15)

4:13–15. Often in 2 Corinthians Paul starts a subunit by mentioning one or another gift that God has given to him. Among Paul's gifts are confidence, hope, ministry, and treasure (see 3:4, 12; 4:1, 7). With language somewhat different from what he has been using, Paul refers back to what he has just been writing about. Now Paul writes about the spirit of faith that sustains him in his hardships. Explicitly citing Scripture for the first time in this letter, he writes, **because, having the same spirit of faith according to what is written, "I believed; therefore, I spoke"** (4:13). Paul generally introduces his quotations of Scripture with the verb "write" in the passive voice, but this particular lemma, "according to what is written," does not appear elsewhere in his correspondence. Psalm 115:1 LXX (116:10 Eng., MT) is the Scripture to which Paul refers. The apostle identifies with the psalmist; he has faith like that of the bard of old. The "faith" about which he writes is trust in God. The Spirit who engendered confidence in the psalmist is the Spirit who has moved Paul to trust in God despite the difficulties encountered in his ministry.

The words that Paul quotes in 4:13 come from a two-part psalm (Pss. 114–15 in the Greek Bible [116 Eng.]) that describes a righteous person whom the Lord has delivered from death. With his citation of the first words of Ps. 115 LXX,

---

Paul's Psalter

Paul's quotations from the OT generally follow the text of the Greek Bible, the Septuagint (LXX). It is well known that the enumeration of the psalms in the Greek Bible is different from that of the Hebrew Bible (MT), generally one less than the enumeration in the Masoretic Text. Thus the citation that Paul employs in 2 Cor. 9:9 is from Ps. 111:9 in his Greek Bible and matches 112:9 in the Hebrew text.

The Hebrew text of Ps. 116 is particularly problematic. The first part of the psalm (vv. 1–9) appears in the Septuagint as Ps. 114, while the second part of the psalm (vv. 10–19) appears in the Septuagint as Ps. 115. The psalm verse that Paul cites in 2 Cor. 4:13 is Ps. 115:1 as it now appears in the Greek Bible.

Paul indicates that he reflects on his own experience in the light of the psalm. As in 2 Cor. 4:6, Paul uses the Scriptures to interpret his ministry for himself and for others. He finds in the psalmist's righteous sufferer a paradigm for his own experience.

With trust in God, the righteous sufferer was able to speak. With a similar trust in God, Paul is able to continue his work of evangelization, his preaching. **We also believe; therefore, we also speak.** An emphatic "we" iterates his intention to apply the psalm to himself. Underlying the confidence with which Paul engages in his ministry is his core belief, the belief that God raised Jesus from the dead. Since he has used words with the root *pist-* to speak about faith in the sense of trust, he now uses **knowing** [*eidotes*] to speak about his belief **that the one who raised Jesus will also raise us, and he will present us with you** (4:14; cf. 2 Tim. 4:8). As is always the case in Paul's expression of faith in the resurrection of Jesus, he affirms that God is the agent of the resurrection of Jesus. His words echo those of early Christian creedal formularies (see 5:15 [cf. 1:9]; Rom. 4:24, 25; 6:4, 9; 7:4; 8:11, 34; 10:9; 1 Cor. 6:14; 15:4, 12, 15, 20; Gal. 1:1; 1 Thess. 1:10).

Paul does not understand the resurrection of Jesus to be an event unto itself. Rather, the resurrection of Jesus implies the resurrection of believers. The creedal formulas of Rom. 8:11; 1 Cor. 6:14; and 1 Thess. 4:14 proclaim this consequence as part of early Christian faith (cf. Rom. 6:5). Paul argued the point extensively in 1 Cor. 15. With firm faith (*eidotes*), he now reaffirms his conviction that God will raise us up—himself, his fellow missionaries, and the Corinthians—to stand before him. Paul's words express his belief that believers will be in the presence of God in the final age (see 1 Thess. 4:17). On the horizon, although not explicitly stated, is that judgment (cf. 5:10) is a feature of God's presence when the end times are definitively inaugurated.

Paul's thought about the eschatological life of the Corinthians hearkens back to 4:12. All that Paul suffers in the conduct of his ministry is so that the Corinthians might have life. **For all these things are for your sake,** he writes, adding a word about their ultimate purpose: **so that grace, having increased the thanksgiving of many people, will abound to the glory of God** (4:15). Paul's concluding words include more than one play on words that cannot be easily rendered in English translation. His thought is that the grace given to him leads many people to turn to the Lord and give thanks. Thus glory is rendered to God. All things considered, Paul's ministry is, through the medium of those who have embraced the gospel that he preached, for the glory of God, despite and because of his many apostolic sufferings.

Daily Renewal (4:16–18)

4:16–18. Having expressed his faith conviction, Paul repeats what he said in 4:1: **Therefore we do not lose heart** (4:16). Paul's apostolic sufferings do not make him discouraged. We would expect Paul to provide a reason why he is not discouraged. **On the contrary** makes it appear that Paul will supply the reason, but then he abruptly changes his thought (cf. 10:1). **If our outer person** [cf. Rom. 7:22] **is wasting away, our inner person is being renewed every day.** Like the process of death (4:10), personal renewal is a process that takes place day by day.

The shift in thought leads to a contrast between the "outer person" and the "inner person," one of a series of contrasts in a short subunit that focuses on Paul's present experience. The anthropological terms, probably taken from the Hellenistic culture in which he lived, are difficult to translate. Literally, the Greek terms signify "the outside" and "the inside," but Paul's thought does not abide the dualism of Hellenistic anthropology. What is outside, what can be seen, are earthenware vessels (4:7) and mortal flesh (4:11). What is inside, what cannot be seen, is a renewal that he has previously described as the Spirit-effected transformation from glory to glory (3:18). Each of the verbs used in reference to these anthropological terms occurs only here in Paul's extant correspondence.

The second contrast belongs to the semantic domain of weight and appears to reflect Paul's Semitic background. The apostle uses the notion of different weights to contrast tribulation and glory. The weights are qualified by temporal expressions that accentuate the contrast: **For the momentary lightness of our tribulation is producing an eternal weight of glory for us beyond all expectations** (4:17). Tribulation leads to glory. Paul's present affliction (see 4:8) is as nothing compared with eternal glory, which exceeds all human expectations and can only be a gift from God. Key to understanding the apostle's thought is the phrase "eternal weight of glory." "Glory" harks back to the glory that Paul has written about extensively in chapter 3; "eternal," also found in verse 18, prepares for what Paul will say about an eternal dwelling in chapter 5. The notion of weight has most likely been introduced because Paul's use of *doxa*

The Contrasts

Anthropology: outer person (*ho exō hēmōn*, a hapax construction in Paul) and inner person (*ho esō hēmōn*, 4:16)

Weight: light (*elaphron*, hapax in Paul) and heavy (*baros*, v. 17)

Time: momentary (*parautika*, hapax in NT) and eternal (*aiōnion*, v. 17)
      transitory (*proskaira*, hapax in Paul) and eternal (*aiōnia*, v. 18)

Sight: seen (*ta blepomena*) and unseen (*ta mē blepomena*)
     seen (*ta blepomena*) and unseen (*ta mē blepomena*, v. 18)

Process: wasting away (*diaphtheiretai*, hapax in Paul) and renewal (*anakainoutai*, hapax in Paul, v. 16)

Experience: tribulation (*thlipseōs*) and glory (*doxēs*, v. 17) ("glory") reflects Septuagintal usage in which *doxa* translates the Hebrew *kābôd*, which denotes heaviness.

Paul takes his next contrast from the semantic domain pertaining to the sense of sight. The experience that he has been describing is ours **who keep our eyes not on what is seen but on what is not seen** (4:18). His focus is not on the transitory that can be seen; it is on future invisible realities, **for what is seen is transitory, while what is not seen is eternal.**

The Human Conditon (5:1–5)

5:1–5. Paul continues his reflection on the human condition but changes his imagery. Rhetorical contrasts continue to characterize the expression of his thought. Previously Paul has used the image of an earthenware vessel (4:7) and has spoken about the outer person (4:16); now he uses the image of a tent to portray his human condition: **For we know that if our earthly dwelling, a tent, is destroyed** (5:1). The image of a tent conjures up ideas of fragility, a lack of solid protection, a transitory condition, and a stark existence. The image is biblical (Isa. 38:12; Ps. 52:5). Paul may have been especially indebted to Wis. 9:15 in his choice of this metaphor to describe his human condition. The destruction of the tent would be his death, about which he began to write in 4:10–12. That he uses a conditional clause to speak about his death may suggest that he continues to think that he may be alive at the parousia (see 1 Thess. 4:15, 17).

At bottom, Paul's reflections on death are based on his own experience. As he writes, he contemplates his own impending death. Yet his reflections are not merely autobiographical. His thoughts about death have import beyond himself. The plural that he uses is one that grammarians call a *pluralis sociativus*. His verbs in the plural pertain to himself, to Timothy (the coauthor of the letter, 1:2), and to those to whom he writes (i.e., believing Christians in Corinth). In a sense, his impending death is a paradigm for the Corinthians, who also face death, although perhaps not as immediately as Paul imagined his own death to be.

A tent can be compared to a real building, and Paul makes the comparison. After death, **we have a building from God, a dwelling not made by human hands, eternal, and in heaven.** Paul does not suggest that one's earthly body is not from God; rather, he wants to underscore that God alone produces the resurrected body. Paul points to the difference between the two phases of one's body by identifying the mortal body as a dwelling place (*oikia*, house) and the resurrected body as a building (*oikodomēn*), a less frequently used term. He uses one of his customary triads to describe this dwelling place. First, it is not made by human hands (*acheiropoiēton*, hapax in Paul), a description whose ultimate meaning is that the heavenly building is made by God. Second, unlike the tent, a transitory dwelling place, this building is eternal (cf. 4:17, 18).

Chrysostom on "Not Made with Human Hands"

"Once again Paul is alluding to the resurrection, which many of the Corinthians did not understand or accept. The earthly tent is our body. Admittedly, it was not made with hands, but Paul is simply comparing it with the houses we live in. He was not trying to make an exact contrast between the earthly and the heavenly but rather to exalt the latter in every possible way." (Hom. 2 Cor.10.1)

Third, whereas the tent is located on earth, this dwelling exists in heaven (cf. Phil. 3:20).

Paul the writer—and presumably Paul the preacher—is willing to mix his metaphors. As he continues to grapple with the mystery of human existence, he introduces the language of being clothed and unclothed into his discourse. His language is elliptical. **For indeed we are groaning in this** tent, our earthly body, **as we desire to put on our dwelling from heaven** (5:2). Only here in 2 Corinthians does Paul write about his groaning (vv. 2, 4; cf. Rom. 8:23). What causes him to moan is not so much his afflictions as it is his unfulfilled yearning, his desire to put on the dwelling from heaven.

Paul continues the imagery of apparel with an afterthought, **at least if we really put it on we will not be found naked** (5:3). The future tense of "will be found" refers to the time of the parousia. Then the person who has been clothed with the outer garment—Paul's image for the situation of dwelling in heaven—will not be naked. Paul's idea of nakedness is not that of a disembodied spirit that has rid itself of its mortal body. It is rather that of a body that is poorly clothed. It will be better clothed when it puts on the dwelling that is from heaven. Within this discussion of clothing, the image of not being naked at the parousia is an understatement; at the parousia a righteous person is clothed with a glorious body.

Paul clarifies what he has written. **For since we who are in the tent are weighed down, we groan** (5:4). The idea of being "weighed down" appears to have been introduced under the influence of Wis. 9:15 ("For a perishable body weighs down the soul, and this earthly tent burdens the thoughtful mind"), the passage that may also have inspired Paul's use of tent imagery. Why is Paul groaning (see v. 2)? His response—**because we do not want to take** clothing **off and be found naked; rather, we want to put** clothing **on**—echoes the idea of putting on a dwelling from heaven (v. 2b). The contrast between "take off" and "put on" (see v. 2b) adds additional emphasis to

Put On

"Put on" (*ependysasthai*), which means putting something on over something else, especially a piece of clothing over something else, is a rarely used verb, not appearing elsewhere in the Bible. The one who has been clothed remains the same but appears different because of adding another set of clothes.

2 Corinthians 5:3: A Problematic Verse

There are only seven words in the Greek text of 5:3 in NA[28]/UBS[4], but there are two important text-critical issues. One is that the introductory particles "at least if" (*ei ge*) are found in this edition, but some ancient manuscripts, especially 𝔓[46] and Codex Vaticanus (B), read "since" (*eiper*) instead of the two particles.

The other is that the participle "took off" (*ekdysamenoi*) is found in NA[28]. With this reading of the text, Paul's statement is paradoxical, "if we really take it off, we will not be found naked." However, 𝔓[46], Codex Vaticanus, several other ancient manuscripts, and the majority of medieval manuscripts read "put on" (*endysamenoi*). On balance, the sense of the passage seems to require "put on" as the more appropriate reading of the manuscript tradition.

Further discussion of these issues can be found in Margaret Thrall (1994; 2000, 1:373–80), Bruce Metzger (1994, 511), and Jan Lambrecht (2006, 83).

his thought. Paul wants to put on the resurrected body, symbolized by the heavenly building.

Ultimately the reason for Paul's groaning, the reason why he wants the body to be changed, is **so that what is mortal may be swallowed up by life.** Paul personifies life. His words resonate with what he wrote in 1 Cor. 15:54, citing Isa. 25:8, "When this perishable body puts on imperishability, and this mortal body puts on immortality, then the saying that is written will be fulfilled: 'Death has been swallowed up in victory.'" He is looking for the day when resurrected life engulfs mortality, when resurrected life will destroy mortality. Paul does not anticipate the destruction of the mortal body; what he desires is the destruction of mortality itself.

Paul brings this part of his exposition on the human condition to a conclusion with a bit of theological reflection: **And the one who has prepared us for this very reason is God, who has given us the pledge of the Spirit** (5:5; see 1:22). This statement of principle pertains to all believers, but the Greek text lacks a verb. At its center is "God," sandwiched between two participial clauses. The personal pronouns in the first-person plural, "us," certainly have a broader scope than his previous use of the first person principally in reference to himself. The first-person plural refers to all believers.

Paul's emphasis is on the gift of the Spirit to us, a down payment and guarantee of resurrected life. Resurrected life is a life of participation in the resurrected life of Jesus. Paul said that Jesus "became a life-giving Spirit" (1 Cor. 15:45). With the gift of the Spirit as a pledge of resurrected life, a gift presumably given in baptism, God has prepared believers for their acquiring a dwelling in heaven.

Ellipsis

Ellipsis, from the Greek *elleipsis*, meaning "defect" or "deficiency," refers to an idea that is not fully expressed grammatically. The reader/listener must supply what has been omitted. A common form of ellipsis is the omission of the verb "to be," as in 5:5, where the Greek text has no word corresponding to the "is" of my translation. Ellipsis is often found in letters not only because letter writers in the ancient world used ordinary speech in the dictation of their letters but also because the author ordinarily assumes that he and the addressee(s) share common knowledge of some things.

For Paul, letter writing is a manner of speaking (Collins 2000). Ellipses abound in 2 Corinthians, not only because Paul is dictating his thoughts but also because of the agitated tone echoed in much of what he has to say.

Dwelling with the Lord (5:6–10)

5:6–10. With **therefore** (*oun*) Paul seems to be on the verge of drawing a conclusion from what he has just written, but in fact he abruptly changes the direction of his thought as he takes up another aspect of the human condition. Present existence is a matter of being apart from the Lord. **Remaining ever confident and knowing that dwelling in the body, we dwell apart from the Lord** (5:6). Jerome Murphy-O'Connor (1989, 106) opines that "dwelling in the body, we dwell apart from the Lord" is a Corinthian slogan inserted into the letter by Paul to highlight a possible misinterpretation of what he has said in 5:1–5. Paul cited Corinthian slogans in order to correct and nuance their claim with good effect in 1 Corinthians. That the verbs "dwell in" (*endēmeō*) and "dwell apart from" (*ekdēmeō*) occur in Paul only in 5:6, 8–9 gives Murphy-O'Connor's suggestion some plausibility.

Despite his mortal circumstances and the fragility of his earthenware condition, Paul remains confident that he will put on the glorious resurrected body. For him, that is a matter of faith, as he says in an aside—**Indeed, we walk [*peripatoumen*] with faith and not with sight [*dia eidous*]** (5:7)—that forms the center of a chiastic construction in verses 6–8.

Paul's "walking" is a metaphor. He is not talking about placing one foot ahead of the other as he moves from one place to another. Rather, he is talking about a way of life, a way of acting and behaving. Apart from its appearance in Philodemus, the first-century-BCE philosopher and poet, a metaphorical use of "walk" (*peripateō*) does not appear in Hellenistic literature. Paul's use of the metaphor (see 4:2; 10:2, 3; 12:18) derives from the Hebrew Bible's use of *hālak* ("walk") to describe the way one lives one's life. While in this life, Paul lives and acts with belief and trust in God. Sight of what Paul does not see and cannot see in his present existence, that is, God face to face, remains

---

Anacoluthon

Transliterated from the Greek *anacolouthon,* meaning "not following" or "inconsistent," anacoluthon is a technical term that refers to syntactical incoherence or inconsistency. The word is especially used in reference to a shift in a single sentence from one construction to another. Some forms of anacoluthon are idioms of common speech, but the presence of anacoluthon is considered to be incorrect in studied prose.

"On the other hand, when a natural conversational tone is imitated, as in Plato, it is quite inoffensive and can even be allowed in epistolary study provided that it does not impair understanding. The latter is a limit which Paul, it seems, quite often violated" (BDF §458). Anacoluthon is common, even "flagrant" (BDF §467) in Paul. This is particularly evident in 2 Corinthians, where Paul's emotions seem to get the better of him as he writes.

---

for the future. The Pauline aphorism applies not only to himself but also to all believers.

Verse 8 completes the chiastic structure of Paul's expression of thought and adds a corrective nuance to what the apostle has written in the first part of the chiasm. Reprising the thought of his ever-present confidence, he adds, **Yes, we are confident and would rather dwell apart from the body and dwell with the Lord** (5:8). The chiasm then appears thus:

confident, dwelling in the body	we dwell apart from the Lord (v. 6)
confident, dwell apart from the body	and dwell with the Lord (v. 8)

Hellenists would have been familiar with the use of "dwell apart" as a metaphor for death. Paul incorporates the idiom into his discourse on death, but he does not exploit the metaphorical sense of the term in his first use of it. Present existence is dwelling in the body and apart from the Lord; future existence is dwelling apart from the body and with the Lord. The aorist tense of the infinitives in verse 8 evinces Paul's desire to begin to dwell with the Lord (cf. Phil. 1:21–24). The Lord is the risen Christ (see 2 Cor. 4:14; Phil. 1:23; 1 Thess. 4:17). Being with the Lord is what the future life is all about. Being with the Lord is the reality of salvation.

The apostle spells out the implications of his desire by drawing an inference from what he has written: **Wherefore, we also aspire, whether dwelling in** the body **or dwelling apart from** the body, **to be pleasing to him** (5:9). Occasionally Paul includes an exhortation to be pleasing to God in his hortatory remarks (see Rom. 12:1–2; 14:18; Phil. 4:18). The elliptical style of verse 9 requires that "body" be supplied as the object of the verbs that he has used in verses 6 and 8. What does it mean to aspire to be pleasing to the Lord in the future

Figure 7. The *Bēma* in Corinth. The Acrocorinth (Greek *akros*, "highest, topmost") sits atop the mountain that rises in the background. In the foreground is the *bēma*, a raised platform where public officials gave speeches, heard legal cases, and rendered judgments. Gallio sat on the *bēma* when he judged Paul (Acts 18:12, 16, 17). In 2 Cor. 5:10 Paul mentions a *bēma* on which Christ will sit.

life? The aspiration would seem to be a given. Perhaps Paul was not as careful as he might have been in his choice of words. The contrast between the two dwelling situations suggests that Paul intends to say that in whatever situation he may be, he aspires to be pleasing to the Lord.

Exhorting his addressees, Paul sometimes mentions divine sanctions. For example, he appends a remark about not inheriting the kingdom of God to the list of vices that he cites in 1 Cor. 6:9–10. Here he says, **For it is necessary for all of us to appear before the judgment seat of Christ** (5:10). That he writes about judgment in his disquisition on death suggests that his reflections are intended to serve a paraenetic purpose for those who read them. The reality of a future judgment by Christ serves as motivation for all of us to strive to please the Lord while we are dwelling in the body. Paul directs his remarks to his fellow believers; he is not writing a theological tract on eschatology in which he might consider the future of those who do not believe. He wants believers, particularly those who are listening to the reading of his letter, to remember that they will appear before the judgment seat (*bēma*) of Christ on the day of the Lord.

Paul had the experience of facing a judgment seat. Luke tells us that Paul was brought before the judgment seat of the proconsul Gallio when he was in Corinth (Acts 18:12, 16, 17). In Rom. 14:10, Paul says that we will all stand before the judgment seat of God. In 5:10, Paul indicates that Christ will act as God's vice-regent in judging believers (cf. Rom. 2:16), much as Gallio served as the emperor's vice-regent when Paul was judged.

As Jan Lambrecht (2006, 86) observes, the verb that Paul uses to describe the appearance before the divine tribunal is a strong term and connotes that all will be judged according to what they really are (cf. 1 Cor. 4:5). The purpose of their appearance before the divine tribunal is **so that each one is recompensed** [*komisētai*] (hapax in Paul) **according to what they did in the body, whether good or evil.** "Do good or evil" is an expression that Paul also uses in Rom. 9:11. The phrase "in the body" (*dia tou sōmatos*) indicates that it is a person's behavior during their mortal existence that is subject to divine judgment.

Theological Issues

Jesus

Paul rarely uses the name of Jesus without the qualification of one or another christological title. His unadorned use of the title principally refers to Jesus in his earthly life. There are twelve such uses of an unqualified "Jesus" in the undisputed letters. Six of the occurrences appear in other letters (Rom. 3:26; 1 Cor. 12:3; Gal. 6:17; 1 Thess. 1:10; 4:14 [2x]). The remaining six appear in chapter 4 of this letter (vv. 5, 10 [2x], 11 [2x], 14). The "Jesus" of the last four of these uses is the risen Jesus, whom he identifies with the earthly Jesus.

There may, in fact, be a seventh use of an unqualified Jesus in chapter 4. According to the Greek text of the confessional formula of verse 14 in NA[28]/UBS[4], Paul says that God raised the Lord Jesus (*kyrion Iēsoun*), but "Lord" (*kyrion*) is not found in some of the oldest and most reliable manuscripts, especially 𝔓[46], Codex Vaticanus, and some of the ancient versions, particularly the ancient translations of the Greek text into Coptic and Latin. Moreover, the ancient scribes had a tendency to multiply sacred names. The title "Lord Jesus" rarely occurs in the Corinthian correspondence. When it does appear, it is in the context of a disputed issue (see 11:31; 1 Cor. 9:1; 11:23). My translation of 4:14 reflects the opinion that the shorter reading is to be preferred.

In sum, seven of Paul's unadorned uses of "Jesus" are to be found in 2 Cor. 4. The concentration of this usage in a passage in which Paul is reflecting on his own ministry shows that the apostle can understand

Evil

"Evil" (*phaulon*) appears in only these two places in Paul's extant correspondence (Rom. 5:11; 2 Cor. 5:10). Thus it is not surprising that many ancient copyists—including those who transcribed 𝔓[46], Codex Vaticanus, and the majority of medieval manuscripts—used the more common *kakon* ("bad" or "evil") rather than *phaulon*.

his ministry, with all its suffering, only in the light of the paradox of Jesus's death and resurrection. The resurrection of Jesus provides him with hope as he conducts his ministry in the midst of any number of hardships. The dying of Jesus provides him with motivation and a paradigm for his ministry. Using the unadorned name of Jesus, without the qualification of a christological title, allows Paul to focus on the earthly Jesus. When he turns his attention to what lies ahead, the eschatological judgment, he uses the Christ title since it draws attention to the human Jesus who has been raised from the dead.

The way Paul meditates on his life and death is similar to the way many Christians think about life and death when they realize that their earthly life is coming to an end. That Jesus died but was raised from the dead gives them hope and confidence in the waning weeks of life.

Eschatology

Commentators sometimes raise the question of whether Paul is consistent in the exposition of his eschatology. Specifically they ask whether Paul has changed his mind since he wrote about the parousia and the resurrection of the dead in 1 Cor. 15. Occasionally other passages, most often 1 Thess. 4:13–18; Phil. 1:21–24; and Phil. 3:20–21, are brought into the discussion.

Unfortunately, the discussion often overlooks the fact that Paul was not a systematic theologian. Rather, his theological outlook appears in letters that by their very nature are ad hoc compositions in which Paul responds to issues at hand. The issue in 1 Corinthians is that some have said that there is no resurrection of the dead (1 Cor. 15:12). Paul responds with the affirmation that Christ has been raised from the dead and addresses the issue of the transformation of the body in response to those who would undermine belief in the resurrection by asking what kind of body the dead will have when they are raised (15:35).

Paul's point of departure for discussing death and future life in 2 Corinthians is his weakness as a minister of the gospel and as a human being. Whatever power he had came from God and not from himself. This led in stream-of-consciousness fashion to his reflection on his death and the future life. The number of elliptical constructions and anacolutha in 4:7–5:10 point to the less-than-systematic development of Paul's thought in the passage. Paul's lack of consistency in the passage indicates that his thought has not been developed systematically. What he writes in this passage is not consistently coherent in itself, let alone fully consistent with what he writes about the same topic in other circumstances.

A second factor that is often overlooked is the metaphorical language used by Paul to describe the resurrection and the future life. Since neither Paul nor anyone else, other than Jesus, has experienced the resurrection and the hereafter, Paul's language is necessarily figurative. And Paul is not disinclined to mix metaphors in his discourse on death and the future life. He writes about clothing, housing, and travels. Such mixing of metaphors contributes to the lack of consistency in Paul's thought and exposition.

Apocalyptic language, an exercise in religious imagination, was the language used by many of Paul's Jewish contemporaries to speak about the future. Paul occasionally uses apocalyptic language for this purpose. Here he uses metaphor. Metaphor and apocalyptic use imagery to describe what humans have not experienced. The language is necessarily rich but also necessarily imprecise.

As has been noticed by several commentators, the language of Paul's exposition in 4:7–5:10 evinces the influence of Hellenistic thought. His references to the outer person and the inner person, nakedness and clothing, dwelling in the body and dwelling apart from the body—all use language with which a Hellenist would be familiar. Even the notion of future recompense in accordance with one's deeds would not have been unfamiliar to Hellenists.

> ### Plato on Judgment
>
> *"The rest, when they have finished their first life, receive judgment, and after the judgment some go to the places of correction under the earth and pay their penalty, while the others, made light and raised up into a heavenly place by justice, live in a manner worthy of the life they led in human form." (Phaedr. 249A–B)*

Although Paul borrows Hellenistic idiom for expounding his thought in 4:7–5:10, the reader cannot help but be aware of the tension that Paul experiences between his present mortal life, which is being ever more conformed to the life of Jesus, and the future for which he longs. In that future life with Christ will be complete. Articulating his several thoughts on death and the future life, Paul reflects on somatic existence in a way that is radically different from common Hellenistic thought. He does not look upon the body as something that will be rejected in the future life; rather, the body will be transformed because it will be clothed differently from how it is clothed at the present.

The reader can hardly help but observe that it is God who takes care of the future, not only of Paul's future but also the future of all believers. Paul's discourse on death is a meditation, as it were, on his own mortality, but it is not irrelevant to other believers, who also have mortal bodies.

2 Corinthians 5:11–6:10

A Ministry of Reconciliation

Introductory Matters

With an inferential "therefore" (5:11), Paul begins to write about his ministry. His discourse is as much expository and paraenetic as it is apologetic. The highlight of his exposition is his description of his ministry as a ministry of reconciliation (5:18). Some scholars, particularly some German commentators in recent decades (notably Ernst Käsemann [1971]), have expressed the view that the core section of this exposition on ministry—particularly the passage on reconciliation (5:18–21), with perhaps the exception of 5:19b and 5:20c—has been appropriated by Paul from an earlier, preexisting tradition. As is typical in the discussion of an author's use of source material, the arguments are based on unusual vocabulary, a difference in theology from that which appears in other writings by the same author, and the appearance of a structure different from the structures and style of the adjoining passages in the document. On the basis of these arguments, it has been claimed that 5:18–21 is essentially a hymn that Paul has taken over from an earlier tradition.

Yet 2 Cor. 5:18–21 follows smoothly after the preceding sentence in Paul's text, it lacks a hymnic structure, and it is addressed neither to God nor to his Christ. The passage, moreover, contains no hapax legomena and, if the vocabulary and style are not Paul's most familiar choice of words and style, they are not absent from his extant correspondence. On balance, the theology is remarkably consistent with Paul's theology, particularly the representative role of Christ in Pauline soteriology. In sum, the proposed arguments do not prove that Paul has taken 5:18–21 over from a preexisting oral or written source, and certainly not from a hymn.

A related issue concerns the possible influence of the fourth Servant Song in Second Isaiah (Isa. 52:13–53:12) on Paul's exposition of the theme of reconciliation. Paul was well acquainted with the Servant Songs. He occasionally cites from the Servant Songs in his letters (cf. Rom. 10:15–16; 15:21) and seems to have been influenced by them from time to time in many of his letters. Although 2 Cor. 5:18–21 contains no verbal allusion to the fourth song, the idea that Paul's thought might have been influenced by this canticle in Deutero-Isaiah is not to be excluded.

A related matter is the quotation from Isa. 49:8 in 6:2. The words are part of an oracle appended to the second Servant Song (Isa. 49:1–6). The words belong to the Servant tradition. In Second Isaiah the words are descriptive, referring to the Servant. In Paul the words have paraenetic import. They are an element in Paul's appeal to the Corinthians to respond to God's grace in the "now" (6:2b) of their salvation.

> **2 Corinthians 5:11–6:10 in the Rhetorical Flow**
>
> The letter opening (1:1–2)
>
> Ministerial crises (1:3–2:13)
>
> Paul explains and defends his apostolic ministry (2:14–7:4)
>
> > Anxiety and confidence (2:14–3:6)
> >
> > A glorious ministry (3:7–4:6)
> >
> > The present and the future (4:7–5:10)
> >
> > ▶ A ministry of reconciliation (5:11–6:10)
> >
> > > Paul's confidence (5:11–15)
> > >
> > > Reconciliation (5:16–19)
> > >
> > > Ambassadors for Christ (5:20–21)
> > >
> > > A short exhortation (6:1–2)
> > >
> > > The exercise of Paul's ministry (6:3–10)

Tracing the Train of Thought

Paul's Confidence (5:11–15)

5:11–15. Paul further develops the thought about the eschatological judgment expressed in 5:10, applying it to himself as he writes, **knowing, then, the fear of the Lord** (15:11). Although he uses a participle in the first-person plural, Paul is writing about his personal experience, as is indicated by the singular "I hope" in the following clause. His knowledge of the fear of the Lord is not just theoretical, not something that a young Paul might have learned at the feet of Gamaliel, who explained the Scriptures to him (Acts 22:3). For Paul to have knowledge of the fear of the Lord means that the fear of the Lord is something that he has taken to heart, something that motivates his behavior.

As a wise man, Paul conducts his life and his activity in awe of the ever-present Lord. The judicial imagery of the previous verse (5:10) suggests that Paul has evoked the biblical notion with a particularly Pauline nuance. First of all, the "Lord" to whom his phrase makes reference is none other than Christ, who was mentioned in the preceding verse. In addition, 5:10's mention of the

The Fear of the Lord

The "fear of the Lord" is a well-known biblical idea that refers to the awe that human beings experience in the presence of God (cf. Pss. 34:11; 111:10; Prov. 1:7; 2:5; 8:13; 9:10; 10:27; 14:26; 15:16, 33; 19:23; Sir. 1:12; Eccles. 8:12–13; 12:13; etc.). The fear of the Lord is a way of speaking about a person's profound reverence in the presence of God.

judgment seat suggests that, for Paul, the biblical concept is not without some sense that the Lord in whose presence a person stands in awe is a judge. The Lord's judgment might well provoke fear in those who do not follow his ways.

Motivated by the fear of the Lord, Paul tells the Corinthians about his relationship to them and his relationship to God: **we are trying to persuade people and are well-known to God.** As he writes, Paul makes use of the contrast between humans (*anthrōpous*) and God (*theō*). With regard to humans, Paul is trying to convince them of the truth of the gospel. The verb in the present tense indicates that, by his preaching, Paul is attempting to persuade people, without specifying anything about his success or lack thereof. He has in mind principally the Corinthians themselves, some of whom have succumbed to the rhetoric of the so-called superapostles (11:5; 12:11) and a gospel other than the one that Paul preached and that they had initially accepted (11:4). In addition to persuading the Corinthians about the gospel, Paul also needs to convince them of his own apostolic integrity, assailed as it is in so many different ways. This is an ongoing effort on Paul's part, as the expression "we are persuading" implies; the verb has the sense of continually trying to persuade.

For the benefit of the Corinthians, Paul affirms that his apostolic integrity is perceived by God: his integrity is known by God. In the previous verse, Paul writes about appearing before the judgment seat of Christ. At the time of the future judgment, people's actions, whether good or evil, will be fully known to Christ. Now the apostle uses the same verb (*pephanerōmetha*) to speak about his openness and transparency before God. The verb is in the perfect tense to affirm that Paul was transparent to God in the past and that his transparency continues into the present. It is not only what Paul did or does that God knows; God also knows Paul's motivation, why he did what he did and why he does what he does.

Adding a complementary thought, **and I hope to be well known in your consciences,** Paul expresses the hope that in the depths of their consciences the Corinthians will be as convinced of Paul's apostolic integrity as God is. He hopes that they will fully appreciate what he has done among them and what he continues to do even as he writes to them. Paul wants them to know that his motivation and intentions are upright, despite the tensions that have arisen between him and some members of the Corinthian community.

Paul's defense of his apostolic integrity is not intended to build himself up in the eyes of the Corinthians; he is not looking for praise from the Corinthians.

We are not again commending ourselves to you (5:12), he writes, echoing the thoughts that he expressed in 3:1–3. What Paul writes about his transparency before God and the Corinthians is not intended to be self-commendation; rather, Paul writes to **give** the Corinthians **an occasion to boast about us so that you might have something to say to those who boast about externals and not about** what lies within **the heart.**

The integrity of Paul's ministry has been called into question. How can the Corinthians provide a rebuttal to those who are questioning the authenticity of the one who is apostle to them (1 Cor. 9:2)? Revealing himself to his addressees, the church of God at Corinth, Paul gives them an occasion and opportunity to boast about him and his ministry, to be proud of him and his apostolic ministry. Paul writes elliptically: his Greek says only "so that you might have something to those who boast." A verb of speaking must be supplied in order to make sense of what he says.

Those before whom the Corinthians are expected to boast about the integrity of Paul's ministry are people who seem to be more concerned about appearances than about what lies within the heart. Anthropological terms express the contrast. Paul writes about the face (*prosōpon*) and the heart (*kardia*). The contrast is between what can be seen and what cannot be seen, between outward appearances and what lies deep within the human person. Those who boast about outward appearances are most likely those who have taken issue with Paul's ministry, the superapostles, with their letters of recommendation (3:1) and their charismatic and wonder-working activity (12:12).

Contrast continues to dominate Paul's writing as he shares with the Corinthians a reflection on his own activity: **If we are beside ourselves, it is for God; if we have our wits about us, it is for your sake** (5:13). What Paul means by being beside himself is not entirely clear.

Lying behind Paul's words might be a slur launched against him, an accusation, among others, that Paul is some kind of madman. If Paul is being assailed in this manner, he is facing one of the accusations brought against Jesus (Mark 3:21, with the same verb that Paul uses in 5:13). However, neither this letter nor any of Paul's other extant correspondence clearly indicates that this kind of accusation was being made against Paul.

On the other hand, Paul's words might be Paul's own reference to the way he has responded to his critics. If this is how Paul's words are to be interpreted, he is saying that although others find him defending himself excessively, God knows the purity of his intentions. He is defending himself, as he does, for the sake of God. While possible, such a line of interpretation appears to be a bit of a stretch.

It is more likely that Paul is referring to his charismatic activity—sometimes an ecstatic experience, at other times akin to an ecstatic experience—suggesting a comparison between himself and his adversaries who seem to have boasted about their charismatic prowess. If Paul has any charismatic ability, that ability

117

More on Explanatory "For" (*gar*)

The second word in verse 14 is *gar*, "for." In English the conjunction must appear at the beginning of the sentence or clause; in Greek the conjunction appears as the second word in the sentence, in the "post-positive position." Most often the word introduces a truly explanatory comment on what has just been written; at other times, the connection between what follows the conjunction and the preceding discourse is relatively loose. Paul uses the construction about seventy times in 2 Corinthians. I have chosen not to translate the *gar* of verse 14, preferring to indicate its presence in the Greek text by saying that what Paul is about to say, he writes "by way of explanation."

is God's gift, and Paul exercises the gift in the manner that God wants.

Paul then turns his attention from God to Christ as he proclaims that **the love of Christ controls us** (5:14). By way of explanation of what he has just written, Paul speaks about the love of Christ. The love of Christ about which he writes is not his love for Christ; rather, it is the love that Christ has for him. The genitive is a subjective genitive (*hē agapē tou Christou*), indicating that the love comes from Christ. The love that Christ has for the apostle overpowers him. It takes control of him and directs him to do what he does. Paul's verb can be translated in different ways, but in the context of this letter, the connotation of the verb (*synechei*) is "taking control of and directing." Essentially Paul is saying that the love of Christ provides direction and energy for his apostolic activity.

Paul continues to describe himself as he articulates an affirmation of his credo. Rather than using the vocabulary of the *pist-* word group, "faith," "belief," Paul writes about a conviction that he has definitively reached for "us," **who have come to this conclusion**, he writes, **that one has died for all**. The one who has died is Christ, who has died for all of us. The order of the Greek words "one for all" (*heis hyper pantōn*) makes the point even more strikingly than the English translation does, which requires that the verb be placed between the contrasting "one" and "all."

The *hyper* formula, occurring three times in verses 14–15, contains a soteriological "for" (*hyper*) that brings to mind the language used by Paul when he writes about the death of Christ elsewhere in his correspondence, particularly in Rom. 5:8, "Christ died for us" (cf. Rom. 5:6; 8:32; 14:15; 1 Cor. 11:24; 15:3; 2 Cor. 5:21; Gal. 1:4; 2:20; 3:13). Christ died on behalf of all of us. One of us represents all of us. The death of Christ is representative, vicarious, and expiatory.

> Christ: has died for all, *hyper pantōn* (2 Cor. 5:14)
> has died for all, *hyper pantōn* (v. 15)
> died and was raised for them, *hyper autōn* (v. 15)

This affirmation does not represent the full range of Paul's convictions. Since Christ died (*apethanen*) for us, **therefore all have died** (*apethanon*). The inference that Paul draws from his expressed conviction shows that "for all" also implies that all of us somehow participate in the death of Christ. There is, nonetheless, a shift in the meaning of the verb. Christ's death for all was his physical death, his death on the cross. All of us have not physically died. When Paul says that all have died, the verb is to be taken in a metaphorical sense. The apostle is referring to our death to sin, which results from Christ's atoning death on the cross. At bottom is an Adam-Christ typology similar to that of Rom. 5:15. As Adam died, so Christ died, and we all die.

Reprising the language of his expressed conviction, **and he died for all**, Paul explains the purpose of Christ's death. Christ died **so that the living live no longer for themselves but for the one who died and who was raised for them** (5:15). "The living" refers to Christians, those who are alive in Christ. The sense of the participle is metaphorical. Earlier Paul spoke about death in a physical sense and then about death in a metaphorical sense. Now he writes about living in a metaphorical sense and then about living in a physical sense. Christians live—that is, conduct themselves during the course of their lives—not for their own sakes but for the sake of Christ, who died and rose. They live not in a self-centered and self-interested fashion; rather, they live for the sake of Christ.

One and many was the dominant antithesis in Paul's speaking about the death of Christ; dying and living is the dominant antithesis as he writes about Christians. Believers have died to sin because of Christ; now they live for the sake of Christ, who died and was raised for them (1 Cor. 15:4–5; 1 Thess. 4:14).

Reconciliation (5:16–19)

5:16–19. Having expressed his conviction about the death of Christ, Paul writes about an epistemological change that has taken place in him. Paul no longer sees things the way he once did. **So, we no longer know anything according to the flesh** (5:16). The initial "so" refers back to what Paul wrote in verses 14–15, especially his words about Christ's controlling love. That love has changed the way Paul looks at things. By means of the emphatic pronoun "we," he stresses that he is writing about his own experience.

"No longer" (the Greek *apo tou nyn* is, lit., "from now on") does not suggest that Paul's way of looking at things differently began as he was writing to the Corinthians. His changed way of understanding began when Christ's love took hold of his life. From that time he no longer looks at things in a merely human fashion, *kata sarka*, "according to the flesh." He, like all believers, can no longer judge things in a fleshy manner because he is a new creation.

A primary example of the change in his way of understanding and key to that change is his different appreciation of Christ: **If we too once knew Christ according to the flesh, we no longer know** him in this way. At one time Paul viewed Christ in a merely human fashion, specifically, perhaps, as

---

Paul's Use of "in Christ" and Similar Phrases

"In Christ" (*en Christō*): 2:14, 17; 3:14; 5:17, 19; 12:2, 19; Rom. 9:1; 16:7, 9, 10;
   1 Cor. 3:1; 4:10, 15a, 17b; 15:18, 19, 22, 31; 16:24; Gal. 1:22; 2:17; 3:14, 26; Phil.
   1:13; 2:1, 5; 4:7, 19, 21; 1 Thess. 2:14; 4:16; 5:18; Philem. 20, 23.
"In Jesus Christ" (*en Iēsou Christō*): Rom. 3:24; 6:11, 23; 8:1, 39; 15:17; 16:3; 1 Cor.
   4:15b; Phil. 1:1, 26; 3:14.
"In the Lord" (*en kyriō*): 2:12; 10:17; Rom. 14:14; 16:2, 8, 11, 12 (2x), 22; 1 Cor. 1:31;
   4:17a; 7:22, 39; 9:2; 11:11; 15:58; 16:19; Gal. 5:10; Phil. 1:14; 2:19, 24; 3:1; 4:1, 2,
   4, 10; 1 Thess. 3:8; 4:1; 5:12; Philem. 16, 20.
"In him" (*en autō*): 1:19, 20; 5:21; 13:4; 1 Cor. 1:5.

---

a violator of the law and a deluded preacher whose disciples departed from
what Paul believed to be the canons of Jewish orthodoxy. Consequently Paul
persecuted the church (1 Cor. 15:9; Gal. 1:13). Now Paul has a different idea
about Christ; he no longer understands Christ as he did in the days when, as
a zealous Pharisee, he persecuted the church of God.

Paul's changed appreciation of Christ has consequences. It has led him to a
new appreciation for those who believe in Christ. **So, if anyone [*tis*] is in Christ,**
he writes, **that person is a new creation** (5:17). The language is pregnant and
elliptical. He expresses his thought with only seven words. His pithy affirmation
lacks the verb to be in the conditional clause as well as in the principal clause.
In Greek the principal clause has only two words, "new creation" (*kainē ktisis*).

Referring to believers as those who are "in Christ" (*en Christō*), Paul uses
one of his most characteristic expressions. The phrase means much more than
a bland "Christian" or "believer" might suggest; it points to the union between
the believer and Christ, the believer's participation in Christ.

Describing the believer as being a "new creation," Paul capitalizes on a
biblical (Isa. 43:18–19; 65:17; 66:22) and Jewish notion that points to God's
eschatological and all-encompassing renewal. The idea was prevalent in Jewish apocalyptic literature (*Jub.* 4.26; *1 En.* 72.1; *2 Apoc. Bar.* 32.6; 44.12; 57.2;
4 Ezra 7.75) and the Qumran texts (1QS 4.25; 1QH 5.17–18 [formerly 13.11–
12]). The expression "new creation" occurs in *Jub.* 4.26 and 1QH 5.17–18
(formerly 13.11–12), but Paul is the only NT author to use the idiom (cf. Gal.
6:15). He sees the final times as having begun in Christ's death and resurrection; hence he can affirm that those who are in Christ already participate in
the eschaton, albeit not fully.

Typically, thoughts of the new creation are cosmic in scope (cf. Rom. 8:19–
23). Thus the idea of a new creation leads Paul to say, **The old things have
passed away; behold, there have come into existence new things.** Contrasts
continue to dominate the expression of Paul's thought. In verse 17 the contrast

is between old things (*ta archaia*) and new things (*kaina*). The apostle expresses his thought in a chiastic structure (A-B-A′), "old things" and "new things" being the outside elements, with the verbs in the center, separated from one another by "behold" (*idou*), which serves almost as an interjection.

Paul's language is reminiscent of Isa. 43:18–19, where the prophet contrasts a new order with an order that is about to pass away. In 2 Cor. 5:17 Paul reprises Second Isaiah's vocabulary, notably in the expressions "old things," "new things," and "behold" (LXX). Paul sees the eschatological expectation of a new creation as being fulfilled in Christ. Christ's death and resurrection mean that the old order has passed away, to be replaced by a new order that has already come into existence. Writing "there have come into existence new things," Paul uses a verb in the perfect tense (*gegonen*), indicating that what has happened in the past is continuing to have an impact on the present. The new order of things has come into existence and continues to come into existence, even as it has not yet been fully realized.

Paul puts what he has written in verses 14–17, with its christocentric focus, into theological perspective as he writes, **All this** [*ta panta*, all things] **is from God** (5:18). All that Paul has just written about has its origin in God. Then Paul qualifies God in a fashion that is unique within the extant correspondence. Paul tells the Corinthians that God is the one **who reconciled** [*tou katallaxantos*] **us to himself through Christ.**

Introducing this new concept into his discourse, Paul changes the meaning of "us" (*hēmas*). Since verse 14, he has made use of an editorial first-person plural; his "we" has really meant "I." Now he uses the first-person plural to speak of himself and his addressees, indeed, all humankind. God has reconciled all humankind to himself. The past tense (aorist) of the participial expression indicates that the reconciliation took place at some definite time in the past. That reconciliation took place through Christ indicates that reconciliation took place in the Christ event, that is, in the death and resurrection of Christ.

The meaning of the first-person-plural pronoun, "us," switches once again as Paul speaks about the implications for him of God's reconciling activity. God **gave us**, he writes, **the ministry of reconciliation.** He uses the term "ministry" (*diakonia*) almost as a technical term to identify his own apostolic ministry. Earlier in the letter he described that ministry as a ministry of a new covenant (3:6), a ministry of the Spirit (3:8), and a ministry of righteousness (3:9); now he speaks about his ministry as a ministry of reconciliation (*tēn diakonian tēn katallagēs*). The task that God has entrusted to Paul is proclaiming that God has reconciled the world to himself through Christ's death and resurrection (cf. 1 Cor. 15:1–5). As a prophet, Paul was called to embody the content of his proclamation in his very being, in the way that he acted. His ministry of reconciliation is therefore effected not only in the gospel that he preaches but also in the apostolic suffering through which he participates in the suffering of the dying Christ (1:5; 4:10; Phil. 3:10).

A Matter of Grammar

The first few words of the Greek text of 2 Cor. 5:19 contain two major cruces, two difficulties for the interpreter of the text. The first two words, *hōs hoti* (cf. 11:21; 2 Thess. 2:2), which I have translated "that is," can be variously interpreted. Grammatically, the emphasis might lie on *hōs*, stressing the idea of a comparison; alternatively, the emphasis could lie on *hoti*, drawing upon its causal connotation. Since the two words appear together, their interpretation cannot be a matter of either-or. "That is" brings two clauses into a comparative relationship that allows the second to be seen as an interpretation of the first.

The second crux concerns the relationship among "God," "was" (*ēn*), the "in Christ" formula, and the participle. Some take the words "God was in Christ" as a theological-christological affirmation of the incarnation. This is a notion that is otherwise foreign to Paul, so even though the verb is separated from the participle by three Greek words, I have opted to take the verb + participle as a periphrasis and to take "in Christ" as a phrase qualifying the verb, describing the means by which God effects reconciliation.

Paul repeats himself, paraphrasing and further developing to some degree the thought that he expressed in verse 18: **that is, in Christ God reconciles the world to himself, not counting their transgressions against them but placing the word of reconciliation in us** (5:19). The first part of the verse (5:19a) reprises the thought of verse 18b. The parallelism between the two clauses suggests that the meaning of the phrase "in Christ" is essentially instrumental, basically synonymous with the earlier "through Christ," although the idea of God's presence in Christ cannot be far from Paul's consciousness.

The parallelism confirms that the "us" of verse 18b refers to all humankind. In verse 19a "us" is paraphrased as "the world," an expression that in this instance refers not to the cosmos as such but rather to the inhabitants of the cosmos, especially insofar as they are sinful, as the following clause suggests: **not counting their transgressions against them.** The double use of the personal pronoun, "their" and "them," unfolds the personal connotation of "the world." In this context "the world" is used metonymously for the world's inhabitants. That Paul speaks of the world points to the universal scope of reconciliation. All people have been reconciled to God in Christ.

Verse 19b expresses a new idea, one that does not appear in the previous verses. Paul brings the notion of the forgiveness of sin into the development of his thought on reconciliation. Rather than saying that God has forgiven human beings their sins, Paul uses the language of accounting to say that God has not reckoned their transgressions against them. His language appears to have been influenced by Ps. 32:1, a verse that Paul quotes verbatim in Rom.

4:7–8. Paul says, in effect, that God has not made a list, one list for each person, of offenses that could be counted up. God has chosen not to keep tabs on human beings in this way.

A modern reader of Paul's letter might have expected Paul to write about the "sins" that human beings commit. He does not do so. For the apostle, sin (*hamartia*) is a superhuman power that holds human beings under its control, almost manipulating them to do various forms of evil. "Transgression" (*paraptōma*, v. 19), on the other hand, designates an individual sinful act committed by a human being (cf. Rom. 4:25). God has decided not to keep track of these individual transgressions.

With regard to Paul, God has entrusted the apostle with the task of preaching the gospel, the good news of reconciliation. He describes God as **placing the word of reconciliation in us**. This is a new way for Paul to describe his apostolic mission. The description is parallel to verse 18c, where Paul talks about his ministry of reconciliation. Now he focuses on the communicative aspect of that ministry. It began with God placing the message of reconciliation within Paul in a fashion that is similar to the word of God coming to various biblical prophets. The message is that God has reconciled all humankind to himself through Christ and that the sins of men and women are not "counted" against them.

Sin

Paul generally uses the word "sin" (*hamartia*)—a word that occurs most often in the Letter to the Romans—to refer to a kind of demonic power that takes hold of human beings, leading them to commit the immoral acts that he calls "transgressions" (*paraptōmata*, a word that Paul rarely uses in the plural). Almost 90 percent of Paul's uses of the word *hamartia* are in the singular and have this sense. In the Corinthian correspondence, the word occurs twice in 1 Cor. 15:56 with this sense. Lying behind 2 Cor. 5:19 is the presupposition that Christ has conquered sin in the sense of a superhuman power that leads humans to commit individual transgressions.

Apart from the two occurrences in 1 Cor. 15:56, "sin" is mentioned only five other times in the extant Corinthian correspondence. In 1 Corinthians Paul twice employs "sins" in the plural (*hamartiai*), but the vocabulary is not properly his own. In 1 Cor. 15:3 it is part of a creedal formula, whose wording antedates Paul. The apostle has received the creed from earlier Christian tradition. Paul's other use of the plural "sins" is found in 1 Cor. 15:17, where it is clearly dependent on the wording of the creed cited just fourteen verses earlier.

In 2 Cor. 11:7 Paul uses "sin" in the singular to refer to a possible transgression on his part. Second Corinthians' other two uses of "sin" in the singular (5:21–22) are exceptional and will be explained in the exegesis of those verses.

Ambassadors for Christ (5:20–21)

5:20–21. The term **therefore** (5:20) signifies that Paul draws an inference from what he has written about his ministry of reconciliation and about God having placed a message of reconciliation within him. What are the implications of his being a minister of reconciliation for the Corinthian believers? Paul responds in language that the Corinthians can understand. **We are ambassadors** (*presbeuomen*), he writes. Paul uses the verb *presbeuō* only in 5:20, but the idiom was well known in Classical and Post-Classical Greek, where it had the meaning "to be ambassador" or "to function as an envoy." The verb connoted both a role and the exercise of that role. Being an ambassador entails being named or commissioned to serve in that capacity, speaking on behalf of the commissioning authority, and expecting to receive the respect that is owed to the authority. Conveying a message on behalf of the sending individual or group, an ambassador represents that authority. Paul's ministry of reconciliation is a function of his ambassadorial role.

Paul's use of this language, unusual for him, is appropriate in a letter written in difficult circumstances. The language has a twofold function within Paul's *apologia pro ministerio meo* (defense of my ministry). On the one hand, the language suggests that as an ambassador, Paul has faithfully delivered the message of the one who sent him and that he continues to do so. On the other hand, Paul is deserving of respect, respect that has sometimes been lacking, as the upcoming list of circumstances (6:4–10) will make abundantly clear.

Qualifying his ambassadorial role as being **for Christ**, Paul affirms that he is an ambassador for the sake of Christ; but even more than that, he is an ambassador who represents and takes the place of Christ. Christ has fulfilled a ministry of reconciliation through his death and resurrection. Who is to continue the ministerial service of reconciliation now that Christ has died and been raised? Who is to continue that ministry? Paul, who is an ambassador in lieu of Christ.

Adding **as if God were making an appeal through us,** Paul specifies that God is the ultimate authority behind his ambassadorial role. God has entrusted to Paul the message that he is to convey. If the Corinthians choose to reject Paul, they are ultimately rejecting God because God appeals to the Corinthians through Paul. "Making an appeal" (*parakalountos*) is a verb with a wide range of meanings, the most common of which are "encourage" and "urge." It can also mean "console" or "appeal" (see the sidebar *"Paraklēsis"* at 1:3). In diplomatic documents, the stuff with which ambassadors are familiar, *parakaleō* often means "make an appeal," not

The Quotation Marks

Marks of punctuation do not appear in the Greek texts of ancient NT manuscripts. Thus the Greek text of 5:20 does not include quotation marks. I have used quotation marks in my translation since Paul offers a succinct summary of God's appeal by pleading with the Corinthians, saying "Be reconciled to God."

on the basis of one's own authority but on the basis of the sending authority. Using Paul as his spokesperson and his ambassador, God makes his appeal.

Paul fulfills his ambassadorial role **for the sake of Christ**—a repetition of the formula with which the verse began. The appeal is simply phrased: **We beg you, "Be reconciled to God."** The short exhortation sums up the gist of what is expected of the Corinthians in response to the message of reconciliation. It is the core of God's appeal to them. The exhortation implies that Paul considers his addressees to be in a situation of some alienation from God. The introductory formula, "We beg you," uses a verb (*deometha*) that Paul sometimes employs to speak about his apostolic mission (cf. 8:4; 10:2; Gal. 4:12). The verb has a nuance of please. "Please," says Paul, "be reconciled to God." Paul's plea does not include a mention of those to whom the appeal is addressed, but the second-person plural of the exhortation indicates that "you" is to be supplied. As God's spokesperson, he pleads with the Corinthians to be reconciled to God.

A dense and particularly meaningful theological affirmation follows after Paul's appeal. God **made the one who did not know sin** to be **sin for our sake** (5:21). As in the affirmation about Christ in 5:14, Paul refers to Christ anonymously in 5:21. Christ is the one who did not know sin. With this affirmation Paul is declaring not that Christ had no intellectual knowledge of sin but that Christ had no personal experience of sin. "Know" retains the biblical connotation of experience; Christ did not experience sin; he is the sinless one (see Heb. 4:15; cf. 1 Pet. 1:19; 3:18). Nonetheless, God has **made** him **sin** for our sake.

The participial phrase "the one who did not know sin" is the object of the verb, but the Greek text lacks a designated subject. The implied subject is God; since verse 18 Paul has been writing about God's activity. But what does the apostle mean when he says that God has made Christ sin for our sake?

Some commentators, dating back to patristic times—Augustine, Ambrose, Cyril of Alexandria, Thomas Aquinas, John Calvin, and more recently, Léopold Sabourin and Stanislaus Lyonnet (1970, 250–56, 419–24), Ralph P. Martin (1986, 140, 157), and Linda L. Belleville (1996, 159)—think that "sin" (*hamartia*) means "sin offering." After all, Paul is not disinclined to use sacrificial language and cultic terms to describe Christ's death (cf. Rom. 3:25; 1 Cor. 5:7), and Paul's Greek Bible occasionally uses *hamartia* to speak about a sin offering (Lev. 4:25, 32, 34; cf. Lev. 4:21, 24; 6:18 [6:25 Eng.]; Num. 6:14). It is, however, unlikely that Paul is describing Christ's death as a sin offering. He does not do so anywhere else in his extant correspondence. Moreover, the "sin

Sin Offering

In the Leviticus passages, *hamartia* serves as the translation of the Hebrew idiom *ḥaṭṭā't*, which means "sin offering." The Hebrew *ḥaṭṭā't* is one of several different Hebrew words that can be translated as "sin." These different terms are not necessarily synonymous; each has its own particular nuance.

Gregory of Nazianzus on 5:21

Christ was "sin itself [*autoa-martia*]" (*Oratio XXXVII in Matt XIX,1–12*, in PG 36:284).

offering" interpretation would require that the meaning of *hamartia* change radically within an expression consisting of just four Greek words (the sequence in Greek is *ha-martian hyper hēmōn hamartian*). Finally, Paul contrasts *hamartia* with *dikaiosynē*, "righteousness." A contrast between sin and righteousness is easily understood, but what would a contrast between a sin offering and righteousness mean? The terms are hardly antithetical.

"Sin" really means sin. Sin is human sin, and God made Christ sin for our sake. Somehow God made Christ a sinner on our behalf. This does not mean that God forced Christ to commit sin. Rather, Paul is affirming that God had Christ enter into solidarity with sinful humanity (Rom. 8:3). Christ suffered and died as though he were a sinner. Death was a punishment for sin. Christ suffered a punishment for sin (Rom. 5:12; 6:23).

Using a soteriological *hyper* formula similar to the one that he employed in verses 14 and 15, Paul adds that God made Christ sin **for our sake** (*hyper hēmōn*). Christ's sinlessness remains intact since Christ's being made sin was "for our sake," for us. Christ was made sin as the representative of sinful humanity. Made sin, Christ took away our sin. Paul is referring to Christ's death, a punishment for sin.

Christ took away our sin **so that in him we might become the righteousness of God**. God made Christ sin so that we might become the righteousness of God. That we become the righteousness of God is the reason why God made Christ sin. Paul begins his expression of this thought with an emphatic "we," drawing the readers' attention to the fact that he is still talking about the "we" of "for our sake," that is, all humankind.

God's purpose in making the representative of humanity to be sin is that all of humanity might become the righteousness of God. The "righteousness of God" is an abstract concept that Paul uses in place of more concrete and personal language. He is saying that we are justified by God. We are in a right relationship with God; our justification comes from God. Hence we are a manifestation of the righteousness of God. When Paul says that "in him" we might become the righteousness of God, he is affirming that

Chiasm

Paul's pregnant description of God's activity in verse 21 is described in a tightly knit chiasm (A-B-C-B'-A'). The outside elements of Paul's Greek refer to Christ without using his name: "the one who did not know sin," "in him." Within these references to Christ is an emphasized reference to humanity, "for our sake" (*hyper hēmōn*) and "we" (the emphatic *hēmeis*). At the center of the Greek text, we read "[God] made so that" (*epoiēsen hina*), God did something in order that . . . we might be justified.

The Righteousness of God

The meaning of "the righteousness of God" (*dikaiosynē theou*) in Paul's Letters has been much disputed throughout the ages, especially since the time of the Reformation. The issues that arose in Paul's relationship with the Corinthians are not, however, those that he addresses in his letters to the Galatians and the Romans. What Paul means by "the righteousness of God" must be interpreted within the context of Paul's discussion with the Corinthians rather than in the light of his controversy with the so-called Judaizers.

In addition to the exegetical and theological discussions related to the interpretation of *dikaiosynē* and the related Greek words that belong to the *dikaio-* word group, there is an another issue, one that arises from the translation of the Greek into English. The English language has been enriched by its rootedness in both Germanic and Romance sources. Many of our synonyms exist because we use words rooted in both the Germanic and Romance traditions to express the same or very similar ideas. When translating into English and dealing with Greek words in the *dikaio-* word group, we thus must choose between terms related to "right" and "righteousness" from the Germanic tradition, or terms related to "just" and "justification" from the Romance tradition. This compounds the difficulty of finding adequate vocabulary with which to express the apostle's rich and complex notion of *dikaiosynē*.

Christ is the means of our justification. Because of Christ's death and resurrection, humanity's state of sin has been exchanged for a condition of justification.

To fully understand this affirmation of believers becoming the righteousness of God, we must grasp its eschatological and ethical connotations. Our righteousness means that the era of salvation has begun. It began when Christ died on the cross and was raised, in consequence whereof we have been justified. "Righteousness" is not a static concept. It is a matter of a relationship, of being in a proper relationship with God. Transformed by the righteousness of God, we express our righteousness by the way we behave in relationship to God and to those with whom God is in relationship, meaning all those who constitute humankind.

A Short Exhortation (6:1–2)

6:1–2. So, working together, we also urge you lest you receive the gift of God in vain (6:1). With these words Paul continues to exercise his ambassadorial role. He introduces his appeal with an introductory phrase, "working together"; thus he is cooperating with God in making this appeal (cf. 1 Thess. 3:2). This cooperation is a consequence of Paul's ambassadorial role. God makes his appeal through Paul (2 Cor. 5:20). Reminding the Corinthians about his ambassadorial role enhances Paul's *ēthos* and the rhetorical force of his

127

appeal. The reminder brings to the fore something that is only implicit in his epistolary "we appeal to you," "we urge you" (*parakaloumen*; cf. 1 Thess. 4:1, 10; 5:14). Use of "we appeal to you" in this way is a feature of Hellenistic diplomatic letters.

The appeal that Paul is about to make is in addition to the one that he has already made. The emphatic "you" (*hymas*) stresses the idea that Paul, the ambassador to the Corinthians, is making his and God's appeal directly to them. They are urged not to receive the gift of God in vain. In this epistolary context, the gift of God, God's grace (*charin tou theou*), appears to be the righteousness of God with which the Corinthians were justified by God in consequence of Christ's redemptive death (2 Cor. 5:21).

That gift brings with it an ethical responsibility to which the Corinthians seem not to have been fully responsive. Paul fears that the gift may go for naught and so urges the Corinthians not to allow the gift that they have received to be a gift received in vain. Would the Corinthians neglect the powerful impact of God's gift? With his words, Paul urges the Corinthians to lead the kind of life that is appropriate to their new condition, that of being justified by God.

To bolster his appeal, Paul echoes Isa. 49:8: **"At the favorable time, I heard you; on the day of salvation, I helped you"** (6:2). The Scripture is introduced not in Paul's typical fashion, with the customary "as it is written" (cf. 8:15; 9:9), but by **for he says** (cf. 6:16). The lemma that Paul uses points to the Scripture as God's word. As God's legate, Paul is conveying God's message to the Corinthians.

Isaiah 49:8 is cited as it appears in the Septuagint, Paul's Greek Bible. In its Deutero-Isaiah context the passage is part of an oracle about Israel's return from exile. The two parts of the verse are in synonymous parallelism: the one is basically a paraphrase of the other. For those who have been exiled, the return from exile begins a new era of salvation for Israel. It is another occasion for Israel to experience God's saving action in its history. For Israel, the return from exile was truly a day of salvation.

Paul is, however, not overly concerned with the historical circumstances to which the oracle applies. Like other Jewish writers of his time, Paul applies biblical texts to the situation of himself and his addressees. **Lo, now is the favorable time; lo, now is the day of salvation!** Paul uses the Isaiah text christologically and in actualized fashion. Paul believes that the final age, the time of salvation, has dawned with the death and resurrection of Christ (cf. 5:17), and he reads Scripture in this light. Paul comments on the Bible's "favorable time" (*kairō dektō*) with a doubly augmented prefix form of "favorable" (*euprosdektos*), which underscores the notion that the acceptable time, the appropriate time, is really a good time, truly a beneficial era. The day of salvation is truly a favorable time. The repeated soteriological "now" (*nyn*) affirms that the day of salvation is a present reality.

"Lo" (the demonstrative particle *idou*), the command that introduces both parts of Paul's scriptural commentary, summons the Corinthians to pay attention to the "now" in which they live. Their "now" is a time of salvation. Their "now" is qualitatively different from the time in which they have previously lived. Their "now" is the eschatological present, the era of salvation that has been inaugurated with Christ's redemptive death and resurrection. Their now is the time in which they must live in accordance with the empowering gift of God's righteousness.

The Exercise of Paul's Ministry (6:3–10)

6:3–10. Before describing his ministry as a ministry of reconciliation (5:11–14a), Paul had written about the transparency of his ministry and its controlling force. Carried out in fear of the Lord, Paul's ministry was directed by the love of Christ. Now Paul returns to the subject of his ministry. With **giving no occasion for taking offense in any way, lest the ministry be blamed** (6:3)—Paul's Greek words begin the single long sentence of verses 3–10—he affirms that he does not want the ministry of reconciliation to be compromised by any action on his part. The double negative—*mēdemian en mēdeni*, literally, "nothing in no way"—underscores the apostle's intention not to have the ministry compromised by anything that he might do. He would do nothing whatsoever that would lead anyone to stumble or take offense and thus negate, even partially, the effectiveness of his ministry.

On the other hand, he says, **in every way we commend ourselves as ministers of God** (6:4a). "In every way" (*en panti*) is antithetical to "in no way" (*en mēdeni*), sharpening the contrast that Paul is making. In the presence of people, Paul wants to give no offense whatsoever; before God, Paul wants to serve as an effective minister in every way. Paul has hitherto denied that he is engaged in any form of self-commendation. Nonetheless, as a minister of God, he can commend himself but only insofar as he is serving God. The formulation of 6:4 enables Paul to accentuate the idea that it is as a minister of God that he commends himself.

Self-Commendation

In 6:4 Paul writes about commending himself as a minister of God. Previously, Paul has basically said that he is not engaged in promoting himself (3:1; 5:12). His Greek clearly distinguishes between self-commendation that is not acceptable and self-commendation that is. When he writes about unacceptable self-commendation, an exercise in vainglory, he places the object before the verb (*heautous synistanein*, 3:1). When he writes about acceptable self-commendation, he places the object after the verb (*synistantes heautous*, 6:4).

> **Paul's Three Sets of Hardships**
>
> *Personal anguish:* affliction, distress, and dire straits
> *Difficulties caused by others:* beatings, imprisonments, and riots
> *Self-inflicted difficulties:* labors, sleepless nights, and hunger

Paul then proceeds to describe the way in which he has exercised his ministry. Not everything was under his control. Far from it! There was a lot with which he had to put up. Endurance was required (cf. Rom. 5:3–4). Paul begins the description of his ministry with reference to the kind of endurance that was required of him, **with great endurance**, and then cites a variety of circumstances that required this great endurance: **in affliction and distress, in dire straits, with beatings, in imprisonments, in riots, in labors, with sleepless nights, without food** (6:4b–5).

Paul has a predilection for threes and so offers a list of three groups of three to describe the adversity that he has faced during the exercise of his ministry. The first group describes Paul's experience of this adversity. He has exercised his ministry in circumstances that brought affliction and distress. Sometimes he ministered in dire straits (a translation that tries to capture the nuance of constriction in Paul's *en stenochōriais*). Paul uses virtually synonymous nouns in the plural form to tell the Corinthians that his experience of hardship in the exercise of ministry was not a onetime occurrence. Personal hardship was something that Paul experienced more than once during the course of his service to God.

In catalogs of this sort—a list of circumstances, generally hardships, as well as in lists of virtues and vices—rhetorical effect is achieved by cumulative impact; thus, it is not particularly useful to try to distinguish one item on the list from another. Accordingly, it is not necessary to search through Paul's autobiographical references (e.g. 1 Thess. 2:2) or the Acts of the Apostles (e.g., 13:50; 14:19; 16:22–24; 17:5; 18:12; 19:29) in order to identify specific circumstances that Paul experienced as affliction, distress, or dire straits.

> **In Affliction and Distress**
> **(*en thlipsesin, en anankais*)**
>
> The two nouns are in the plural. In the singular, they are paired in 1 Thess. 3:7. "Affliction" introduces the short hardship catalog in 4:8–9. When used in the singular, "affliction" occasionally has the nuance of eschatological afflictions, the difficult circumstances that precede the coming of the day of the Lord. Paul's use of the plural in 6:4 suggests that he had several particular experiences in mind.

A distinction, however, is to be made among beatings, imprisonments, and riots. Acts 16:22–24 describes magistrates in Philippi having Paul and Silas flogged and put into a cell, where they were held in stocks. In 2 Cor. 6:5 Paul mentions his imprisonments (cf. 11:23), but Acts mentions only the Philippian imprisonment as having occurred before the time Paul wrote 2 Corinthians. Clement of Rome cites Paul's patient endurance and mentions that Paul was seven times imprisoned. Clement's "seven" may be a symbolic number meaning many times rather than an accurate count of how often the apostle was imprisoned.

Having mentioned the hardships that others inflicted on him, Paul cites the hardships that he voluntarily took on for the sake of the gospel. He mentions in particular his labors, his sleepless nights, and his going without food. Paul's "toils" (cf. 11:23) refers to the energy- and time-consuming work that Paul engaged in for the sake of the gospel. Included among Paul's toils was the manual labor, his job as a leatherworker, that he undertook in order to be able to preach the gospel free of charge (1 Cor. 15:10; Gal. 4:11; Phil. 2:16; 1 Thess. 3:5). That Paul went without food does not mean that he practiced some sort of religious fast as he pursued his ministry; rather, it indicates that he was deprived of the opportunity to eat properly as he exercised that ministry. Food deprivation and sleepless nights are also mentioned in Paul's hardship catalog of 11:23–29 (v. 27).

Paul contrasts his hardships with various qualities of his ministry. He exercised his ministry **with sincerity, with knowledge, with magnanimity, with generosity, with the Holy Spirit, with unfeigned love, with the word of truth, and with the power of God** (6:6–7b). Each of the eight terms is introduced by the preposition *en*, which is here better translated as "with" than by the normal rendition, "in." These eight qualities are easily divided into two groups of four.

The first four—sincerity, knowledge, magnanimity, and generosity—are readily identified as virtues. Paul spoke about his sincerity in 5:11, where he wrote about his transparency before God and the Corinthians; now he uses a classic term, "sincerity" (*en agnotēti*), to describe the forthrightness of his ministry. His knowledge is not so much a result of his experience and learning as it is a gift of the Spirit (cf. 1 Cor. 12:8; 13:2, 8). His magnanimity is a kind of godlike forbearance (cf. Rom. 2:4; 9:22). His generosity, likewise a divine attribute (Rom. 2:4; 11:22), refers to Paul's goodness and kindness.

Even more clearly than the first group, the next set of four qualities affirms that Paul exercises his ministry as a result of the gifts that God has given him. Each of the

> ## Clement of Rome
>
> *"By reason of jealousy and strife, Paul by his example pointed out the prize of patient endurance. After that he had been seven times in bonds, had been driven into exile, had been stoned." (1 Clem. 5.6–7)*

> ## Paul's Two Sets of Assets
>
> *His virtues:* sincerity, knowledge, magnanimity, generosity
> *His gifts:* the Holy Spirit, unfeigned love, the word of truth, the power of God

Three Contrasting Experiences

Armaments on the right and on the left
Honor and dishonor
Slander and good repute

qualities in this second group is conveyed by a two-word expression, a noun and a qualifier. Paul preaches through the power of God's Holy Spirit (cf. 1 Thess. 1:5). His unfeigned love is a gift of the Spirit (cf. Rom. 12:9, with the same qualification, and Gal. 5:22). The word of truth is yet another way for Paul to describe the message that God has entrusted to him, the message that he has previously described as a message of reconciliation (5:19), the good news itself. Finally, Paul notes that he preaches with the power of God. Sometimes Paul associates the power of God with the Holy Spirit at work (cf. 1 Thess. 1:5). That seems to be his intent here.

The next set of circumstances outlined by Paul is set off from the first two by a shift in preposition. Paul introduced each of the previous circumstances of his ministry using the preposition *en* ("in"); now he introduces a group of three pairs of contrasting circumstances using the preposition *dia*, which I have translated "with": **with the armament of righteousness on the right and on the left, with honor and dishonor, with slander and good repute** (6:7c–8b).

All three of the contrasts employ opposites to convey the idea that Paul exercised his ministry in every sort of circumstance, but the first is noteworthy for its military metaphor. The Stoics often used military imagery to portray their speaking forth the truth as a battle to be waged. The armament of righteousness describes arms used for the sake of righteousness (cf. 10:4). Those held in the right hand would be offensive weapons, those in the left defensive weapons (such as a shield). The evangelist must proclaim the gospel and defend its truth against those who would undermine it (cf. 2 Tim. 4:2; Titus 1:9).

Using a chiasm (A-B-B′-A′), Paul says that he conducts his ministry in circumstances that bring him honor and dishonor, slander and praise. Slander and praise are the verbal expression of the honor and dishonor that Paul has experienced. He knows all too well that honor quickly turns to dishonor and suspicion, as it did in Galatia (Gal. 4:12–20) and most probably in Corinth as well.

CristianChirita/Wikimedia Commons

Figure 8. A Roman Soldier. In 6:7 Paul talks about armaments on the right and on the left. This stone relief shows a Roman soldier with a sword in his right hand and a shield on his left arm.

Paul then gives a fourth set of circumstances, a list of seven, using an antithetical construction for each. Each member of the series is introduced by the comparative particle *hōs*, **as**, referring specifically to the first phrase in the contrast. Each of the contrasting expressions contains a verb form, a participle with but one exception ("we live"). The seven contrasts—*kai* (generally "and" but here translated as "yet" for the sake of contrast) is the contrasting conjunction in five of the antitheses (1, 2, 3, 4, 7), and the weaker *de* ("and" or "but," though here also translated as "yet") in two of them (5, 6)— are parallel with one another. Paul writes,

> **Paul's Seven Additional Contrasting Experiences**
>
> Deceiving yet truthful
> Unknown yet well known
> Dying yet still living
> Punished yet not put to death
> Grieving yet ever rejoicing
> Poor yet enriching many
> Having nothing yet possessing everything

as deceiving yet truthful, as unknown yet well known, as dying yet we live, as punished yet not put to death, as grieving yet ever rejoicing, as poor yet enriching many, as having nothing yet possessing everything (6:8c–10).

This series of antitheses portrays the complex and paradoxical nature of Paul's apostolic ministry. With the exception of the first, "deceiving," all fourteen traits are an accurate description of Paul's ministry. As for the first, Paul is not deceitful (cf. 1 Thess. 2:3), even if some may have doubted his sincerity because of his change of travel plans (2 Cor. 1:15–17) or because they thought that the collection on behalf of the saints was a way for him to take advantage of them (12:16–18). Throughout this letter to the Corinthians, he has defended the sincerity and authenticity of his apostolic ministry. He has received the word of truth (6:7). Then, toward the end of the letter, Paul says of his ministry, "We are unable to [do] anything against the truth, only for the sake of truth" (13:8).

Unlike the great orators, philosophers, and civic officials, Paul is unknown to the world at large. Nonetheless, he is known to God (5:11; cf. 1 Cor. 13:12) and to the believers in Corinth. The next phrase, "as dying yet we live," alludes to Ps. 118:17 (117:17 LXX): "I shall not die, but I shall live, and recount the deeds of the LORD." Paul had at least one near-death experience (1:9). His dying refers to his mortality (cf. 4:16), yet it also recalls that Paul bears the dying of Christ in his body (4:10). That Paul is alive with the life of Christ is highlighted by the grammatical form of "yet we live." The Greek particle *idou* ("behold"), which I have not translated, provides emphasis to this affirmation. There can be no doubt that Paul is alive with the life of Christ.

The allusion to Ps. 118 continues as Paul writes about his being punished yet not having suffered the punishment of death. The psalmist says, "The Lord has punished me severely, but he did not give me over to death" (Ps. 118:18). The psalmist is speaking about the undeserved sufferings of the good person inflicted by God as a form of divine discipline (cf. Heb. 12:5–7, citing Prov.

3:11–12). Paul's allusion to the words of the psalmist suggests that, with the psalmist, he believes that his sufferings have come from God.

Throughout his ministry, Paul has had occasions to be sad and occasions to be joyful. His relationship with the Corinthians occasionally led Paul to experience considerable grief (2:1, 4). Throughout it all he has found joy in his sufferings (Phil. 2:17). In some ways every human life consists of sadness and joy, but Paul relates these qualities to his ministry. In some respects the joy-sadness antithesis is the lot of all Christians (cf. 1 Thess. 1:6). Their joy, like his, is a gift of the Spirit (Gal. 5:22).

The final two antitheses are virtually two sides of the same coin. Paul's poverty was real. He supported himself by his work as an artisan (1 Cor. 4:11–13; 1 Thess. 2:9), an occupation never well paid in the ancient world. Despite his poverty (cf. 2 Cor. 11:9, 27), he was able to enrich many other people (*pollous ploutizontes*). Despite his poverty, he had everything (*panta katechontes*).

A phrase in the Cynic philosopher Crates's *Letter to the Wealthy* sounds similar to Paul's final words. Crates writes, "Although we possess nothing, we have everything." Paul's "riches" contrast with Paul's material poverty, but these riches are metaphorical expressions. The riches that Paul gives to others are the spiritual riches of the gospel that he preaches (cf. 9:11; 1 Cor. 9:11). Crates's possessions are his freedom from reliance on material things; Paul's possessions are the spiritual riches that God has given to him (cf. 12:9a; Rom. 8:32). Paul's and Crates's similar statements have radically different meanings.

Theological Issues

Reconciliation

Among NT authors, only Paul and his disciples write about reconciliation, using the words that belong to the reconciliation word group.

Etymologically, the noun "reconciliation" (*katallagē*) and the verb "reconcile" (*katallassō*) are related to *allos*, the adjective meaning "other" or "another." The noun means "exchange"; the verb means "change one thing

---

The Reconciliation Word Group in the New Testament

The noun *katallagē* ("reconciliation"): Rom. 5:11; 11:15; 2 Cor. 5:18, 19
The verb *katallassō* ("reconcile"): Rom. 5:10 (2x); 1 Cor. 7:11; 2 Cor. 5:18, 19, 20
The verb *apokatallassō* ("reconcile"): Col. 1:20, 22; Eph. 1:16 (Along with the majority of biblical scholars, I believe Colossians and Ephesians to have been written by disciples of Paul. Hence I consider the use of the intensive verb *apokatallassō*, "reconcile," to be post-Pauline usage.)

for another." In antiquity, these words were principally used in reference to the exchange of money, changing money from one currency to another, just as the traveler who goes from one country to another must do today. Sometimes the words were used in a metaphorical sense, in reference to human relationships. Thus Aeschylus, Herodotus, and other Greek writers use the noun to describe enmity that has been exchanged for friendship, and they employ the verb to speak about making one's enemy into one's friend.

In ancient literature, Paul's use of the terms to describe a change of relationship between God and humankind is singular. In 1 Corinthians Paul writes about the reconciliation of a woman to the husband from whom she has been separated, using the verb *katallassō* that was commonly used for marital reconciliation (1 Cor. 7:11). Apart from this single instance of Paul's use of a "reconciliation" word in its ordinary sense, Paul always attributes a theological sense to reconciliation. His theology of "reconciliation" first comes to expression in 2 Cor. 5:18–20 (cf. Rom. 5:10–11). This theology has five characteristic features:

1. Theological reconciliation is a divine activity. God takes the initiative and is the principal agent of reconciliation. Second Maccabees uses "reconcile" to speak about humans reconciling themselves with God (2 Macc. 1:5; 5:20; 7:33; 8:29). Paul does not speak in this fashion. For the apostle, reconciliation is always a matter of God reconciling humans to himself. God is the agent of reconciliation and the goal of reconciliation. Reconciliation is not something that humans can accomplish. Paul does not generally use periphrastic constructions, but he does so in 5:19a in order to emphasize, in a way that a more common formulation of his thought would not allow him to do, that it is God who reconciles the world to himself.

2. The object of reconciliation is humankind, identified as "us" (5:18) and as "the world" (5:19). Colossians 1:19–23 articulates a theology of cosmic reconciliation, but notions of cosmic reconciliation are not foremost, if at all present, in 2 Cor. 5:18–20. For Paul, the world is the world inhabited by human beings, the world in which the power of sin is at work, as Paul makes clear when he writes about human transgressions. The object of God's reconciling activity is sinful humanity. Sinful human beings are the beneficiaries of God's reconciling activity.

3. Christ is the means by which God reconciles the world to himself. Reconciliation is "through Christ" and "in Christ." Each of the phrases highlights the instrumentality of Christ in reconciliation, but "in Christ" highlights the notion that reconciliation is a divine activity more so than does "through Christ." Christ's instrumentality was effected when God made Christ sin in order that we be reconciled to God. Christ became sin when he died on the cross. In Pauline usage the Christ title (*Christos*)

normally points to the death and resurrection of Christ. In 5:11–20, Paul uses the Christ title seven times without further qualification (5:14, 16, 17, 18, 19, 20 [2x]), thus four times in 5:18–20.

4. Paul has been entrusted with a ministry of reconciliation. He fulfills his ministry in his person and in his proclamation. As God's ambassador, Paul announces the message of reconciliation. His ambassadorial task is to announce that God has reconciled the world to himself through Christ. Paul is the means by which God conveys this message to humans. Using his ambassadorial authority and the power of his rhetorical skill, Paul begs his addressees to be reconciled to God and proclaims that the time for doing so is *now*.

5. Reconciliation is a reality. The tenses of the verb *katallassō* in verses 18 and 19 show that reconciliation has already occurred, as does the reference to the death of Christ, a reality of the past. Reconciliation has taken place. God has done what God had to do. He has reconciled the world to himself.

There must be a human response. Paul's ministry of reconciliation is to enable that response; he speaks about God's reconciliation of humankind and appeals to the Corinthians to be reconciled to God. The Corinthians must accept the word of reconciliation proclaimed by Paul. They must also be reconciled to Paul, God's ambassador, since the one who rejects an ambassador rejects the authority of the one who sent the messenger.

The Theological Nature of Paul's Apostolic Ministry

The opening lines of 2 Corinthians point to God as the source and strength of Paul's ministry. He begins the letter by identifying himself as an apostle through the will of God. He identifies his addressees as an assembly that belongs to God. His prayerful greeting is that they receive grace and peace from God (1:1–2). Shortly thereafter Paul breaks into a prayer of praise addressed to God, whom Paul describes as the father of compassion and the God of all consolation. The merciful Father consoles Paul in the midst of his various tribulations (1:3).

A theological frame of reference dominates Paul's description of his ministry in 5:11–6:10. He begins by affirming his openness before God. The fashion in which Paul exercises his ministry is fully known to God. The apostle subtly compares himself with those who boast about externals rather than prizing what lies within the heart, the depth of the human person known only to God (1 Thess. 2:4; Jer. 11:20; 17:9–10).

Paul's ministry takes place in the eschatological age, the final times that have come into existence with the death and resurrection of Christ. The old things have passed away; a new reality has come into existence (5:17). The renewed person is a new creation. The language of "new creation" epitomizes the fulfillment of prophetic expectations. The adjective "new," appearing twice in 5:17, has eschatological connotations throughout the NT. In Christ a new age has dawned. All this, says Paul, is due to the activity of God (5:18a). This new era is the day of salvation (6:2), the *now* of our salvation. Paul preaches the gospel in God's new time of salvation.

If Paul has any charismatic gifts or enjoys any ecstatic experiences, these are the result of God's relationship with Paul. They are for God's sake, not for Paul's sake, not even for the sake of the Corinthians (5:13). In 6:6, Paul acknowledges, almost in passing, that he has received the charismatic gift of knowledge. Later in the letter he will write about an ecstatic experience (12:1–4).

God has given Paul the ministry of reconciliation (5:18c) and entrusted to him the message of reconciliation (5:19c). The message that he has received is a message of truth (6:7), a message that Paul has spoken truthfully (6:8c). In effect, God is speaking through Paul. Paul is God's spokesperson, as the apostle himself affirms in 5:20.

The message of reconciliation is a message about God's reconciling activity. Paul proclaims that God has reconciled the world to himself through Christ. Moreover, the core of his preaching (cf. 1 Cor. 15:3–5) is that the Christ who died was raised by God. There is a hint of this core preaching in 2 Cor. 5:15. The passive voice of "who was raised" is a theological passive; Jesus was raised for us by God.

Paul has exercised and continues to exercise his ministry as the servant of God (6:4). With the power of God (6:7b) and with the gift of the Holy Spirit (6:6e), he has been able to preach the gospel. The sweeping overview of the circumstances of his ministry in 6:8c–10 portrays, in its positive aspects, the effect of God's action on Paul, ambassador of Christ, spokesperson of God.

Paul's Circumstantial Catalog

Before he was a letter writer, Paul was a preacher of the gospel, an orator, whose purpose in preaching was to convince his audience of the truth of the gospel message (5:11). As an orator, Paul employed many of the same techniques used by philosophical moralists and politicians. These speakers often made use of lists of virtues to portray a good person, lists of vices to portray an evil person, and lists of hardships to build up the rhetorical *ēthos* of an orator by demonstrating his endurance in the face of adversity. As a group, the Stoics were among the most notable to use these kinds of lists, both in their spoken appeal and in their writings.

Paul undoubtedly used such lists in his proclamation of the gospel, for they appear here and there throughout his letters. Catalogs of virtues are found in Galatians and Philippians, of vices in Romans, 1–2 Corinthians, and Galatians, and of hardships in Romans, 1–2 Corinthians, and Philippians.

When lists of these sorts were used by the Stoics and Paul, they were typically both generic in character and adapted to the rhetorical situation in which

137

Paul's Lists

Catalogs of Virtues

In Paul: Gal. 5:22–23; Phil. 4:8

In the deuteropauline letters: Eph.
4:2–3, 32; 5:9; Col. 3:12; 1 Tim.
3:2–4; 3:8–10, 11–12; 4:12; 6:11, 18;
2 Tim. 2:22–25; 3:10; Titus 1:8; 2:12;
Heb. 7:26

Catalogs of Vices

In Paul: Rom. 1:29–31; 13:13; 1 Cor.
5:1, 10–11; 6:9–10; 2 Cor. 12:20–21;
Gal. 5:19–21

In the deuteropauline letters: Eph.
4:31; 5:3–5; Col. 3:5–8; 1 Tim. 1:9–
10; 6:4–5; 2 Tim. 3:2–5; Titus 1:7; 3:3

Hardship Catalogs

In Paul: Rom. 8:35b, 38–39; 1 Cor.
4:10–13a; 2 Cor. 4:8–9; 6:4–10;
11:23–29; 12:10; Phil. 4:12

---

the list was presented. Some virtues, vices, and hardships appeared so often on the lists that they could easily be described as the characteristic vocabulary of one or another kind of list. On the other hand, "one size fits all" was not the norm. Each list was created by its author in such a way that it pertained to the particular rhetorical situation.

The use of hardship catalogs is a characteristic feature of 2 Corinthians. Four lists of this type occur within its thirteen chapters (4:8–9; 6:4–10; 11:23–29; 12:10). Of these, the longest is clearly the twenty-eight-item list—not counting the ten contrasting items—found in 6:4–10. Since the publication of Rudolf Bultmann's doctoral thesis in 1910 (*Der Stil der paulinischen Predigt und die kynisch-stoische Diatribe* ["The Style of Paul's Preaching and the Cynic-Stoic Diatribe"]), Paul's lists of apostolic hardships have frequently been compared to Stoic hardship lists. These lists sometimes used an antithetical structure, but Paul's list differs from theirs insofar as he does not present himself as one who has risen above or conquered adversity. He is not a stoic Stoic, who rises above adversity and boasts about it. Paul is one who acknowledges the adversity that has made the exercise of his ministry difficult for him.

A few other scholars compare Paul's hardship lists with lists found in apocalyptic Jewish writings. These Jewish writings do not, however, use the antithetical format such as appears in 6:8–10. Moreover, those lists do not give evidence of the eschatological tension that characterizes all of Paul's writings, a hint of which can be discerned in 6:4–10.

Lists of tribulations appear in a wide spectrum of literature during the Hellenistic era, including not only Stoic and Jewish apocalyptic writings but also other Hellenistic literature, works of Pharisaic Judaism, and some early gnosticizing literature. Paul's lists are comparable to these but differ from them in several significant respects, notably with their eschatological perspective and an emphasis on the gifts of God, as is particularly apparent in the hardship catalogs of 2 Corinthians.

I have identified the list that appears in 6:4–10 as a circumstantial catalog, a list of circumstances, corresponding to the German *Peristasenkataloge*. The Greek word *peristasis* ("standing around") was used in reference to a crowd or a set of circumstances. Typically the circumstances are difficult; hence, many commentators designate lists of this sort as hardship catalogs or tribulation lists.

Yet the list in 6:4–10 is not really a list of adverse circumstances. The second set of circumstances—sincerity, knowledge, magnanimity, generosity, the Holy Spirit, unfeigned love, the word of truth, and the power of God—forms a list of virtues and gifts that God gave Paul for the exercise of his ministry. These virtues and gifts are similar to the charismata about which Paul wrote at length in his First Letter to the Corinthians (1 Cor. 12–14). The third set of circumstances is a mixed bag. The military metaphor shows Paul to be a persuasive orator. That he has enjoyed honor from some and is held in good repute shows his preaching to have been successful to some degree.

In the fourth set of circumstances, the antithetical construction places emphasis on the second element. Paul describes himself as truthful, well known, living in Christ, not put to death, always rejoicing, enriching many, and possessing everything that he needs and wants. This is hardly a panorama of circumstances to be feared or avoided. These circumstances, highlighted by means of the rhetorical contrast, constitute grounds for rejoicing.

Describing Paul's apostolic ministry as it does, the list of circumstances in 6:4–10 forms a kind of literary inclusion with 5:11, where Paul begins to speak about his efforts to persuade people. In 5:20 he identifies the capacity in which he has undertaken this effort, namely, as Christ's ambassador through whom God is appealing to people, specifically to the Corinthians. The unit comes to a close with Paul's complex description of the circumstances in which he has conducted his ministry of proclaiming the gospel.

Like the Stoic hardship catalogs, Paul's list of circumstances is intended to enhance his rhetorical *ēthos*. He wants the Corinthians to be aware of the sincerity and authenticity of his ministry, as well as of his personal commitment to it, no matter the personal cost. To limit the purpose of the catalog to the narrow enhancement of Paul's authority is, however, to narrow the specific function of this list in the overall argument of 2 Corinthians.

The list also has a paraenetic function. It encourages the Corinthians to be steadfast in their commitment to the Christian faith. They are in danger of being conflicted by the superapostles and perhaps others who would lead them astray. Paul offers them himself as an example of someone who is resolute in the face of adversity as he fulfills his Christian calling. Citing examples was a well-known technique in Hellenistic rhetoric, and Paul was not averse to offering himself as an example to be imitated (cf. 1 Cor. 11:1; 1 Thess. 1:6).

Paul's exemplarity goes beyond his plea that the Corinthians be steadfast in their commitment to Christ. Cumulatively the many positive elements in Paul's list, eighteen in all, provide a description of Paul's life as a Christian and apostle. This panorama provides another type of example that the Christians of Corinth would do well to emulate. The positive aspects of Paul's apostolic ministry constitute, as it were, a catalog of "virtues" to be imitated.

If the circumstantial catalog of 6:4–10 serves a paraenetic purpose, the lists of hardships in 11:23–29 and 12:10 have a theological purpose. They illustrate Paul's weakness, through which the power of God is manifest.

Although the circumstances of contemporary believers are radically different from those of Paul, we have much to learn from Paul's use of hardship catalogs. One lesson to be learned is that God sustains us with many gifts even in the midst of what sometimes seems to be overwhelming adversity. Another lesson is that these hardship lists illustrate the fragility of the human condition. Despite human weakness, God can and does work through people who remain steadfast in their loyalty to him.

2 Corinthians 6:11–7:4

A *Plea for Personal Reconciliation*

Introductory Matters

The passage begins with Paul expressing his heartfelt emotions for the Corinthians and asking them to requite his love for them (6:11–13). The tone of Paul's expression changes abruptly as he tells the Corinthians, in very strong terms, not to associate with unbelievers. He supports his exhortation with a string of scriptural passages, in a manner that is rare for Paul and does not occur elsewhere in this missive.

Almost two centuries ago Christian August Gottfried Emmerling (1823, 73–79) observed that 6:14–7:1 fits uneasily in its present context. Twelve years later Karl Schrader (1835, 300–306) opined that the verses were not written by Paul. Since that time scholars have disagreed among themselves about the Pauline provenance of the passage. Not only is its context problematic, but the passage also contains a number of terms not otherwise found in Paul's Letters, and its thought seems to be quite different from that of the apostle Paul.

A new piece was added to the puzzle in 1947 with the discovery of the Dead Sea Scrolls. The separatist attitude of 6:14–7:1 is similar to that found in the scrolls. The opposition to idols, the use of catenae of biblical texts, and the reference to Beliar are paralleled in the scrolls. These several factors coalesced in a growing consensus that the passage was a non-Pauline interpolation into the letter. Many scholars, otherwise convinced that 2 Corinthians is a single letter, were open to the idea that 6:14–7:1 was inserted into the letter at some other time.

The Strange Language of 6:14–16a; 7:1

Terms that do not occur elsewhere in the NT: be unevenly yoked (*heterozygeō*), Beliar (*Beliar*), defilement (*molysmos*), harmony (*symphōnēsis*), agreement (*synkatathesis*)

Terms that do not occur elsewhere in Paul: purify (*katharizo*), part (*meris*), the ruler of all (*pantokratōr*)

Terms used by Paul but with a differing meaning: flesh and spirit (*sarx kai pneuma*), acting (*epiteleō*), holiness (*hagiosynē*)

In recent decades, however, a growing number of scholars have taken issue with the hypothesis that this pericope is a post-Pauline interpolation. Scholars such as Margaret E. Thrall (1977), Jan Lambrecht (1978), and Jerome Murphy-O'Connor (1987) have written well-reasoned articles to advance the view that not only are the ideas of 6:14–7:1 those of Paul but also the passage fits its current epistolary context. A variant of this approach holds that 2 Cor. 6:14–7:1 substantially represents a pre-Pauline composition that the apostle emended and incorporated into his letter. Supporting the contention that the passage belongs to the letter that Paul wrote is the fact that it is not absent from any of the ancient manuscripts of the text.

Particularly problematic for the interpretation of the passage are the first two significant expressions, "unevenly yoked" (*heterozygountes*) and "unbelievers" (*apistois*). The contextual issue is crucial to the meaning of these keywords. The first word is one of several terms in the passage that do not occur elsewhere in Paul's writings—nor, for that matter, in any other NT text. The term is obviously metaphorical, but what does it mean in this context? Etymologically the term refers to mismatched animals whose different size and strength leads them to pull on a yoke in different ways. What, specifically, is the yoke to which the term is referring?

The second term is one that Paul uses only in the Corinthian correspondence,

---

2 Corinthians 6:11–7:4 in the Rhetorical Flow

The letter opening (1:1–2)

Ministerial crises (1:3–2:13)

Paul explains and defends his apostolic ministry (2:14–7:4)

  Anxiety and confidence (2:14–3:6)

  A glorious ministry (3:7–4:6)

  The present and the future (4:7–5:10)

  A ministry of reconciliation (5:11–6:10)

  ▶ A plea for personal reconciliation (6:11–7:4)

    Paul's open heart (6:11–13)

    A scripturally based exhortation (6:14–7:1)

    Paul's pride and joy (7:2–4)

where it appears frequently—eleven times in 1 Corinthians (6:6; 7:12, 13, 14 [2x], 15; 10:27; 14:22 [2x], 23, 24) and three times in 2 Corinthians (4:4; 6:14, 15). The term *apistos*, "unbeliever," usually designates someone who does not proclaim Jesus as Lord, but is that the meaning of the term in 6:14, 15? If Paul is telling the Corinthians not to associate with unbelievers, how can his thought be reconciled with what Paul has so clearly expressed in 1 Cor. 5:9–10, namely, that the only way of avoiding the immoral of this world is to leave the world entirely? Has his thinking changed so radically in the space of a few short years?

Etymologically, the term means not-faithful, *a-pistos*. Could it be that this passage, with its strong language, is a warning to the addressees to stay away from those who are not faithful to Paul, who are disloyal to him?

Tracing the Train of Thought

Paul's Open Heart (6:11–13)

6:11–13. In the body of his letters, Paul frequently appeals to his addressees as brothers and sisters, but rarely does he appeal directly to the congregation, as he does here, calling them "Corinthians" (cf. Gal. 3:1; Phil. 4:15). Then he says, **Our mouth is open [*aneōgen*] to you, Corinthians, our heart wide open [*peplatyntai*]** (6:11). The language is metaphorical. The open mouth symbolizes Paul's frankness and sincerity in speaking to the Corinthians. His wide-open heart bespeaks his emotions, his tremendous love for the Christians of Corinth (cf. 1 Cor. 16:24).

There is more than enough room for the Corinthians in Paul's wide-open heart; **You are not constricted [*stenochōreisthe*] in us** (6:12), he writes. You don't occupy a tiny, cramped space in our heart. But, says he, you Corinthians have only the smallest place for us in your hearts; **you are constricted [*stenochōreisthe*] in your feelings**. The anthropological imagery is noteworthy. Paul goes from the mouth, to the heart, to the gut. To symbolize feelings, Paul uses a word (*splanchnois*; cf. 7:15) that properly refers to the vital organs, the stomach, heart, lungs, liver, spleen, and kidneys. Since these vital organs are the most intimate parts of the human being, Jews like Paul used the term to speak of the emotions that lie deep within the human being.

What a contrast between Paul's feelings toward the Corinthians and their lack of emotional attachment to him! So he makes a fatherly appeal to them: **I am speaking to you as children; reciprocate by opening up [*platynthēte*] your hearts** (6:13). He wants his Corinthian children to have the same kind of affection for him as he has for them. Paul will again use parental imagery to speak of his relationship with the Corinthians in 12:14–15; there, too, he will speak of his love for the Corinthians (cf. 2:4; 8:7; 11:2).

A Scripturally Based Exhortation (6:14–7:1)

6:14–16b. Then comes a strong and unexpected negative exhortation: **Don't begin to be unevenly yoked with unbelievers [*apistois*]** (6:14a). The phrase includes a metaphor not otherwise found in the NT. The tense of the verb suggests that something is on the verge of happening. The negative exhortation presents a sharp contrast with the preceding positively phrased exhortation. The Corinthians should have a positive relationship with Paul; they should not embrace an inappropriate relationship with unbelievers.

Some (e.g., Collange 1972, 305; Rensberger 1978, 29–31, 41–44; Martin 1986, 196) think that *apistois* means "disloyal" [to Paul] rather than "unbelievers," but the word occurs only in Paul's Corinthian correspondence and always refers to those who do not believe. That is undoubtedly the meaning of the word in 6:14. Paul's agricultural imagery reflects biblical agricultural law, which strongly prohibits mixing animals (Lev. 19:19; Deut. 22:9–11).

Paul's topical exhortation is supported by a series of five rhetorical questions, each of which demands a negative response. **For what do righteousness and lawlessness have in common? Or what does light share with darkness? What harmony is there between Christ and Beliar? Or what part does the believer have with the unbeliever? What agreement does the temple of God have with idols?** (6:14b–16a). Answering "none" to each of the questions allows readers to convince themselves that there is no way they can be in partnership with unbelievers. The rhetorical repetition requires that the awaited responses become sequentially more emphatic. Deep within, Paul expects a rising crescendo of no's.

Each of the questions begins with an interrogative adjective followed by a noun. Although the nouns are not strictly speaking synonyms of each other, each of them belongs to the same semantic word group. Finding five such nouns represents a rhetorical tour de force on Paul's part. It is no wonder that some of them do not appear elsewhere in the Pauline correspondence. Of the five "synonyms," four of them do not appear elsewhere in Paul's writings; "share" (*koinōnia*) is the only exception.

My translation attempts to reflect the singularity of each term; to do so with a readable rendering led me to sometimes give a translation that does not use a noun. The meaning of all the questions is this: "What does X have in common with Y?"

"Lawlessness," "darkness," "Beliar," "unbeliever," and "idols" constitute a virtual mosaic of images to describe the unbeliever. "Lawlessness" is a term rarely used by Paul (cf. Rom. 4:17; 6:19

Paul, Father of the Corinthians

"I am not writing this to make you ashamed, but to admonish you as my beloved children. For though you might have ten thousand guardians in Christ, you do not have many fathers. Indeed, in Christ Jesus I became your father through the gospel." (1 Cor. 4:14–16)

[2x]), but it is an apt description of the lifestyle of those who live in total disregard of the law, of any law whatsoever. But in this context, where "lawlessness" is contrasted with "righteousness," as it is in Rom. 6:19, the term probably refers to those who pay no heed to the Jewish law.

Light is contrasted with "darkness" (*skotos*). In the biblical tradition, darkness, particularly darkness contrasted with light (cf. Isa. 5:20; 59:9), is a powerful image. Darkness symbolizes the absence of God or divine displeasure. Gentiles dwell in darkness. The contrast between light and darkness appears in intensified fashion in the Dead Sea Scrolls, especially in the *Manual of Discipline* and the *War Scroll*. According to these texts the children of righteousness walk in the light, while the children of falsehood walk in darkness (cf. 1QS 1.9–11; 3.13; 1QM 13.1–6, 9–12; cf. 1 John 1:6). The contrast between light and darkness is dear to Paul, who uses it in 4:6 and has exploited it in 1 Thess. 5:4–5 (cf. Rom. 13:12). In Rom. 2:19 darkness characterizes the existence of those who do not know God, those who don't have a real experience of God.

> ### Light and Darkness at Qumran
>
> *"From of old you appointed the Prince of light to assist us, and in his hand are all the angels of justice, and all the spirits of truth are under his dominion. You made Belial for the pit, angel of enmity; in darkness is his domain, his counsel is to bring about wickedness and guilt."* (1QM 13.10–12)

Beliar is another name for Belial, a well-known figure in the Dead Sea Scrolls who also appears in the *Testament of the Twelve Patriarchs* and other intertestamental literature. According to the worldview of the Dead Sea Scrolls, the sons of light are engaged in a struggle with the sons of darkness, as Belial and those who walk in darkness try to overcome them (1QS 3.20–25; 4Q117 2.7; 3.8). Belial is an angel of darkness who tries to entice people into apostasy and immorality (1QM 13.10–12; CD 4.12–19). This Satanic figure appears in the NT only in 2 Cor. 6:15, where he stands in marked contrast with Christ.

The unbeliever is contrasted with the believer, who should have nothing to do with idols. In 1 Corinthians, the apostle urged the Corinthians to flee from idol worship (10:14). Romans 1:21–32 offers a dramatic presentation of the various kinds of immorality that Paul deems to be the consequences of idolatry.

Lawlessness, darkness, Beliar, and idols belong to the mosaic of realities that characterize the existence of the unbeliever, someone who does not believe in God, a pagan. This mosaic sheds light on the meaning of being mismatched with unbelievers. The yoke that joins animals of different sizes and strength—that is, when they are unevenly yoked—becomes problematic only when the animals begin to move. It is when the animals are prodded to plow or turn a millstone that it becomes apparent that they cannot act in consort with one another. This seems to imply that Paul made use of the imagery to urge the

Corinthians to avoid the behavioral patterns, the mores, of unbelievers, those with whom they would be "unevenly yoked."

Each piece in the mosaic of realities associated with unbelievers has an ethical dimension. Lawlessness is inherently an ethical concept. In itself, darkness is not an ethical notion, but "walking in darkness" has strong ethical connotations. Paul urges God's holy people in Rome to put aside works of darkness (Rom. 13:12) for, as he said in his first letter, we do not belong to darkness (1 Thess. 5:4–5). In light of the ethical connotations of the mosaic pieces associated with the unbeliever, it may well be that the initial exhortation "Don't begin to be unevenly yoked with unbelievers" is not so much a demand that the Corinthians avoid all contact with unbelievers as it is a piece of moral exhortation: Christians are to avoid the forms of behavior that are associated with the demonic Beliar and the worship of idols. In Rom. 1:22–32 Paul gives a detailed description of the kinds of behavior that are the consequence of idol worship.

Contrasted with the mosaic of elements that characterize unbelievers is a mosaic of elements that characterize believers. Contrasted with lawlessness is righteousness, a rich notion that focuses on the right relationship with God and with others that is made possible because of the death and resurrection of Jesus. It is a gift from God that entails living in accordance with one's relationship with God and with others.

In the natural order of reality, light is contrasted with darkness, just as it is in Paul's biblical and theological construct. Describing believers as "children of light" (cf. Luke 16:8; John 12:36), Paul educed the ethical consequences of

---

Beliar/Belial

Beliar in the NT: 2 Cor. 6:15

Beliar in the *Testaments of the Twelve Patriarchs*: *T. Reu.* 4.11; 6.3; *T. Levi* 18.12; 19.2; *T. Jud.* 25.3; *T. Iss.* 6.1; *T. Zeb.* 9.8; *T. Dan* 4.7; 5.1, 10–11; *T. Naph.* 3.1; *T. Ash.* 1.8; 3.2; *T. Jos.* 7.4; *T. Benj.* 3.3; 7.1–2

Belial in other intertestamental literature: *Liv. Pro.* 4.6, 20; 17.2; *Jub.* 1.20; 15.33; *Sib. Or.* 2.167; 3.63, 73

Belial in the Dead Sea Scrolls: 1QS 1.18, 23–24; 2.5; 1QH 11.28–29, 32; 12.13–14; 13.39; 14.21; 15.3; 1QM 1.1, 5, 13, 15; 4.2; 13.2, 4, 11; 14.9; 15.3, 17; 16.11; 17.15; 18.1, 3; CD 4.15; 5.18; 8.2; 12.2; 4Q88 10.10; 4Q286 frg. 7, 2.1–6; 4Q175 line 23; 4Q171 2.10–11; 4Q176 frgs. 8–11, line 15; 4Q174 frgs. 1, col. 1, 21, 2, lines 8–9; frgs. 1, col. 2, 3, 24, 5, line 2; frg. 4, line 3; 4Q177 2.4; 3.8, 10; 4.9, 11–12, 14, 16; 5.5, 10; 4Q253 frg. 3, 2; 4Q225 frg. 2, col. 2, line 14; 4Q390 frg. 2, col. 1, line 4; 4QMMT C 29; 5Q13 frg. 5.2; 11Q13 2.13, 25; 3.7

this reality. Christians are to put on a breastplate of faith and love and, for a helmet, the hope of salvation (1 Thess. 5:8).

If Beliar represents the single overarching figure in the existence of an unbeliever, Christ has that role in the life of the believer. Not only is "Beliar" a hapax in the NT, but the contrast between Christ and a demonic figure is not otherwise replicated in the NT. Strikingly, the contrast is not between Beliar and the Lord; it is between Beliar and Christ, an epithet that occurs here without an article, as it so often does in 2 Corinthians. Typically the epithet highlights the reality of Christ insofar as he has died and been raised from the dead. If Christ is a name with a titular connotation, as well may be the case, the essential Jewish character of the series of questions is even further in evidence than it otherwise would be.

The believer (*pistos*) is contrasted with the unbeliever. The substantive adjectives in the singular should be taken as generic singulars; the terms refer respectively to all believers and to all nonbelievers. Paul often refers to the nonbeliever (*apistos*), but 2 Cor. 6:15 is the only instance in the extant correspondence where *pistos* means believer. Typically Paul uses the term as a simple adjective, sometimes in reference to God, who is faithful (1:18; 1 Cor. 1:9; 10:13; 1 Thess. 5:24).

Idols are compared with the temple of God, providing a clear Jewish monotheistic perspective on the entire series of rhetorical questions. At this time in history, the temple in Jerusalem, the referent of 6:15, was still standing. It had not yet been destroyed. The explanatory punch line, **for we are the temple of the living God** (6:16b), provides a new frame of reference for the moral imperative.

The explanation reprises the positive element of the fifth antithesis, specifying that the temple is the temple of the living God, that is, the God of the Judaic tradition in whom Christians believe. The emphatic "we" situates the Corinthians over against "them," nonbelievers, although some commentators think that the contrasting group is that of the intruders who entered the Corinthian community and were not loyal to Paul.

The image of the community as the temple of the living God echoes the use of similar cultic imagery in 1 Cor. 3:9–19 (cf. 1 Cor. 6:19) as well as the use of the temple metaphor in the Dead Sea Scrolls. In both cases the imagery suggests that the community is somehow a replacement temple, characterized by holiness, which sets it apart from the profane, unclean, and immoral. The explanation builds on the fifth antithesis but hearkens back to the initial exhortation. Believers should not enter into an inappropriate relationship with nonbelievers because they, Paul's "we," are the temple of the living God. The five antitheses, intercalated between the exhortation and its explanation, provide rhetorical support for the exhortation.

6:16c–18. A complex catena of scriptural citations enhances the moral argument. It adds an argument from divine authority to the "logical" argument

147

that has been developed thus far. The introductory lemma, **just as God said** (6:16c), is atypical for Paul. Generally he uses "as it is written" (e.g., 8:15; 9:9) or a variant thereof, for example, "according to what has been written" (4:13), as the formula of introduction when he cites Scriptures.

The scriptural passages—Ezek. 37:27 paralleling Lev. 26:12; Isa. 52:11; and Ezek. 20:34 with 2 Sam. 7:14—are arranged in a classic A-B-B′-A′ (vv. 16c–d, 17a–b, 17c, 17d–18) chiastic structure so that the emphasis falls on the central hortatory citations. The framing passages, with their respective promises, provide theological underpinning for the exhortations.

> I will dwell among them, and I shall walk among them
>> And I will be their God, and they will be my people.
> Therefore depart from among them
>> And separate yourselves, says the Lord.
> And do not touch what is unclean;
>> Then I will welcome you
> And I will be to you like a father
>> And you will be to me as sons and daughters.
> Says the Lord, the Ruler of all. (6:16c–18)

Each of the scriptural passages loosely follows the wording of the text in the Greek Bible, the Septuagint. Some modifications were introduced under the influence of other scriptural passages and the editor's redaction. The first citation is an amalgam of texts found in Ezek. 37:27 and Lev. 26:12, that is, a reference to God dwelling among his people—echoing the temple motif in 6:16—and the well-known covenant formula ("I will be your God, and you will be my people").

The first promise is followed by an exhortation based on Isa. 52:11, the center of the chiasm and the support for the preceding argument, with its series of rhetorical questions. An initial conjunction, "therefore," has been added to relate the exhortation inferentially to the temple and covenantal promise. The prophetic text originally referred to Israel's return from exile and urged the returnees to maintain ritual purity. The redactor has inserted "says the Lord" (*legei kyrios*) in the middle of the quotation, thereby creating a double exhortation and the A-B-B′-A′ structure. The adapted text no longer refers to a physical journey and ritual impurity; in context, the passage refers to a moral separation and moral impurity.

The second promise, "I will welcome you, and I will be to you like a father, and you will be to me as sons and daughters," like the first, is also an amalgam, a combination of Ezek. 20:34 and 2 Sam. 7:14. The use of these scriptures in the catena also represents an adaptation of their original meaning. The passage from Ezekiel originally referred to Israel's return from exile. Now it appears as the Lord's promise to those who heed the exhortation to avoid moral impurity. The text from 2 Sam. 7:14 was originally a promise made to

David in regard to Solomon, who was to succeed him on the throne of Israel. The redactor has modified the text so that in its present context the Scripture pertains to Corinthians who eschew moral impurity.

The modification has affected both the number and the person of the text. Instead of "I will be a father to him, and he shall be a son to me," it now reads "And I will be to you like a father; and you will be to me like sons and daughters." The addition of "daughters" may have been under the influence of Isa. 43:6, another return-from-exile text (cf. Isa. 56:5; 60:4).

> **Chrysostom on "What Is Unclean"**
>
> *"Unclean things refer to adultery and fornication in the flesh and to evil thoughts in the soul. We must be delivered from both."* (Hom. 2 Cor. 13.17)

The end of the catena is signaled by the expression "Says the Lord, the Ruler of all," which forms a literary inclusion with the introductory "just as God said" and reprises the "says the Lord" formula at the center of the catena. "The Lord" normally appears as a christological title in the Pauline Letters; here the epithet is used of the God of Israel, just as it is in the Greek Bible.

The addition of "ruler of all" (*pantokratōr*) provides a climax and adds heightened urgency to the message of the catena, that is, that God, who is Lord of all, will keep the promises that he has made to his people, in this case, the Christians of Corinth, if they avoid immorality. Apart from 6:18, the epithet "ruler of all" is found in the NT only in the book of Revelation where, as here, it always refers to God, generally identified as "the Lord God" (Rev. 1:8; 4:8; 11:17; 15:3; 16:7; 19:6; 21:22; cf. 16:14; 19:15).

7:1. The inference—**Therefore, my beloved**—drawn from the oracular message summarizes its content: **having these promises, let us purify ourselves from all defilement of flesh and spirit, acting in a holy way in the fear of God** (7:1). The apostle often uses "beloved" (*agapētoi*) as a form of direct address (see Rom. 12:19; 1 Cor. 10:14; 15:5; Phil. 2:12; 4:1 [2x]; 1 Thess. 2:8; Philem. 16) and will do so one other time in this letter (12:19). The appearance of the formula in 7:1 echoes its use in 1 Cor. 10:14, where Paul urges the Corinthians to flee from idol worship. Its appearance here is most appropriate since Paul has just avowed his affection for the Corinthians (6:11–12) and urged them to requite his love in kind (6:13; cf. 7:2, the next verse in the extant letter).

The promises, addressed by God to the Corinthians, are those mentioned in the scriptural catena, God's dwelling among his people, God's parental and covenantal relationship with the people. Unlike other passages in Paul's letter that speak of God's promises (1:20; cf. Gal. 3–4), 7:1 makes no mention of the realization of the promises through Christ. These promises are presented as a reason why the Christians of Corinth should heed the exhortation that follows. The exhortation is phrased negatively in the principal clause with a verb in the imperative mood (indicating what is to be removed) and positively in a subordinate clause with a participle (indicating what is to be pursued).

The negative portion of the exhortation uses the language of ritual purity, "Let us purify ourselves from all defilement," to urge moral cleansing. The cleansing is to be complete; both the adjective "all" and the antithetical pair, "flesh and spirit," point to the complete purification to which the readers of the exhortation are being urged. The positive counterpart, "acting in a holy way" (*epitelountes hagiōsynēn*, lit., "accomplish holiness") of the negative exhortation also uses language that usually belongs to the ritual domain. The verb (*epiteleō*, lit., "accomplish") was commonly used in reference to ritual performance, as it was by Philo (*Dreams* 1.215) and Josephus (*Ant.* 4.123; 9.273); the noun (*hagiōsynē*) properly designates the quality of having been removed from profane usage and dedicated to the Lord. With these ritual overtones, the terminology of the double exhortation coheres with the first of the promises and the affirmation that Christians are the temple of the living God.

In the Pauline writings, holiness is typically a gift from God, effected by the Spirit. As such, it is not something that humans can accomplish; hence the verb *epiteleō* does not have its usual meaning, "accomplish," in 7:1. Some passages in Hellenistic texts (e.g., *Let. Aris.* 133, 166) suggest that the word sometimes means "act." That would seem to be its meaning in 7:1. The exhortation urges those who hear it to act in a manner that is in accord with their holy condition, their belonging to the Lord (cf. Rom. 6:19). They should do so in the "fear of God" (cf. 5:11), an expression that calls to mind the biblical notion of "the fear of the LORD" (Isa. 11:2). Quoting Ps. 35:2 LXX (36:1 Eng.), Paul uses the phrase "fear of God" in Rom. 3:18. The expression suggests the awe of a human being in the presence of God rather than fear of punishment. Tobit 4:21 stresses the ethical aspect of the fear of God, while other ancient texts describe those who act righteously as "fearing the Lord [or God]" (see, e.g., *Jos. Asen.* 8.9; 22.8; 27.2).

Paul's Pride and Joy (7:2–4)

7:2–4. These verses continue the thought of 6:11–13, with its plea that the Corinthians requite Paul's affection for them. Continuing the spatial imagery that has dominated his earlier plea, Paul begs the Corinthians to **make room for us** (7:1), virtually repeating what he has just said in 6:13, "Open up your hearts." Paul backs up his plea with three reasons, negatively expressed. Using litotes, rhetorical understatement, he says, **We have wronged no one; we have corrupted no one; we have taken advantage of no one.** The thrice-repeated "no one" is emphatic. Paul says that there is not a single person in the Corinthian community who has reason for withholding love from Paul and his companions. In 12:17–18 he will again profess that he did not take advantage of his addressees.

Then, speaking personally, in his own name, he adds, **I have not pronounced judgment; I previously said that in our hearts we die with you and live with you** (7:3). At times Paul may have spoken harshly to the Corinthians, but he was not condemning; he was not pronouncing judgment on anyone in the community. In fact, he has begged the Corinthians to forgive the one who has wronged him, just as he himself has forgiven that malefactor (2:5–10).

Paul's switch from the singular to the plural is striking. He speaks, but he is not alone in his affection for the Corinthians. His heartfelt relationship with the Corinthians (cf. 3:2; 6:11) is shared by his fellow missionaries, who also die and live with the Corinthians.

> ### "Make Room for Us"
> ### (*chōrēsate hēmas*)
>
> Paul's use of "make room" in 7:2 is another example of how he plays with words, using the well-known rhetorical device of *paronomasia*. "Make room" (*chōrēsate*) has the same root as the twice-repeated "you are constricted" (*stenochōreisthe*, 6:12). Both verbs are in the second-person plural. With the exception of the latter's appearance in 4:8, neither verb appears elsewhere in Paul's extant correspondence.

On first sight the pairing of the verbs appears to speak of profound affection. Paul's language seems to be the language of deep friendship (cf. Malina and Pelch 2006, 150). Even today we speak of living and dying with someone. The words are particularly fitting for marital and romantic relationships. Similar expressions were used in antiquity. But Paul does not write about living and dying. He writes about dying and living. The sequence of the two verbs (*synapothanein*, "to die together"; *syzēn*, "to live together"), both compounded with *sy(n)-* ("with"), suggests that Paul's thought is profoundly theological. He and his companions are one with the Corinthians in their participation in the death of Christ and their common sharing in the life of Christ.

Having affirmed that there is no reason for the Corinthians to be stinting in their affection for him and his fellow missionaries, Paul says: **I have spoken frankly to you; I take great pride in you** (7:4). The parallelism between the two clauses is clearer in Greek than it is in my translation. Paul then adds another pair of parallel clauses: **I have been filled with consolation; I am overflowing with joy.** The Corinthians cannot fail to notice Paul's telling them about the magnitude of his sentiments. "Much" is the first word of each sentence in the first pair of sentences, both of which lack the verb "to be." My translation is a paraphrase. Translated literally, the elliptical sentences would read as follows:

> much frankness of mine for you (*pollē moi parrhēsia pros hymas*)
> much boasting by me about you (*pollē moi chauchēsis hyper hymōn*)

The first word of each sentence in the second pair of sentences is a verb that speaks about being full, even overflowing. As Paul reminds the Corinthians of

---

Living and Dying with Another

Horace to Electra

"With you I would love to live, with you I would gladly die." (*Odes* 3.9.24)

Electra to Orestes

"With you I shall choose to die and live." (Euripides, *Orest.* 307–8)

Chrysostom

"Paul mentions both dying and living, in order to preserve the right balance. For there are a lot of people who will sympathize with others in their misfortunes, but when things turn out well for them [others], they become jealous and do not rejoice on their [others'] behalf." (*Hom. 2 Cor.* 14.1)

---

his sentiments toward them, the keywords that he uses—"frankness," "boasting," "consolation," and "joy"—have echoed throughout the letter.

Paul's final words of verse 4, **in all our affliction**, recall the circumstances rehearsed in 6:3–10. Despite his manifold afflictions, Paul wants the Corinthians to know that he is filled with consolation and joy. "I have been filled" and "I am overflowing" are respectively in the perfect and present tenses, showing that Paul is talking about his real sentiments as he is writing to the Corinthians.

Theological Issues

Whether written by Paul, redacted by Paul, or later interpolated into canonical 2 Corinthians, 6:14–7:1 possesses a particularly rich theological content.

Scripture

Apart from the Letter to the Romans, the apostle Paul rarely strings together a number of passages from the Jewish Scriptures. Catenae of scriptural passages appear in Rom. 3:10–18; 9:25–29; 10:18–21; 11:8–10, 26–27, 33–36; 15:9–12; and a short catena appears in 1 Cor. 15:54–55. Although Paul does quote from the OT in his other letters, including 2 Corinthians, the passages are not strung together in this fashion.

The lemma "just as God said" does not otherwise appear in Paul's Letters. Its language, nonetheless, reflects the formula that introduces the citation of Isa. 49:8 in 6:2, as does the redactional phrase "says the Lord" that appears at a central point in the catena and again at its end, where, along with the introductory lemma, it creates a ring construction around the entire series of quotations. The switch from the aorist tense in the initial lemma to a present tense in the second and third formulas serves to actualize the text. The Scriptures do not so much pertain to the past as they have present relevance for the Corinthian community. And the Scriptures are, as the lemmas suggest, the word of God. Through them the word of God is directed to the Corinthians.

The catena begins with the idea that God dwells among the Corinthians, thus making them the dwelling place of God, the temple of God. This idea echoes 1 Cor. 3:16. Two principal theological motifs and a hortatory inference emerge from the arrangement of the texts. The return-from-exile motif of Isa. 52:11 and Ezek. 20:34 (cf. Isa. 43:6), now applied to the Corinthians, suggests that theirs is a new experience of salvation, comparable to Israel's return from exile. The covenant motif of Ezek. 37:27 and Lev. 26:12, "I . . . will be your God, and you shall be my people," coheres with the idea that Paul is a minister of the new covenant (3:6). The paraenetic inference suggests that the Corinthian church is a holy people, called to be separated from the profane and immoral.

It is particularly striking that this collection of texts, which originally applied to the Jewish people, is now applied to a community whose membership is largely Gentile. No longer are Gentiles restricted to the court of the Gentiles; they are a constituent element of the temple in which God dwells. To them belong the experience of salvation and the (re)new(ed) covenant. They are God's holy people (cf. 1:1), set apart from and challenged to separate themselves from the kinds of behavior that characterize those who do not know God.

The catena of scriptural citations represents an actualized use of Scripture. It takes passages that properly belonged to one historical context and applies them in another. Believers continue to use the Scriptures in this way since the Scriptures are, as it were, the written constitution of God's people. Proper application of the text requires, however, that there be some analogy between the situation of the past and the situation of the present.

God

The rich theology that undergirds the catena and its framework should not be lost in the intensity of discussing the authenticity of the passage. The scriptural catena highlights the notion that God is revealer. He has spoken to his people through the prophets and continues to speak to them through the scriptural texts. The uncharacteristic lemmas of 6:16–18 (cf. 6:2) highlight the idea that the Scripture is the word of God. This word has abiding relevance (cf. Deut. 5:3). In sum, God has spoken in the past and continues to speak in the present. This points to God's fidelity to the word that he has spoken. Among the divine utterances are the promises that God makes to his people. These promises focus on God's covenantal relationship with his people.

God is identified both as "God" and as "Lord." The designations occur together in several biblical texts, especially the covenant formularies of Exod.

20 (vv. 2, 5, 7, 10, 12) and Deut. 5 (vv. 2, 6, 9, 11, 12, 14, 15 [2x], 16 [2x]). As an appellation, the biblical "God" highlights divine transcendence. The transcendent God has, nonetheless, deigned to dwell among his people, making them the temple of God, the dwelling place of God. The use of "Lord" underscores the claim that God has to the allegiance of his people. It is therefore significant that "says the Lord" is inserted into the hortatory citation of Isa. 52:11. Not only does the insertion create a second unit of exhortation; it also adds the weight of authority to the ban on defilement.

In 6:18 the addition of *pantokratōr* ("the ruler of all"), otherwise translated as "Almighty" or "All-powerful," adds emphasis to the exhortation. The Lord of all requires obedience of his subjects. An additional nuance, not to be neglected, is that the Lord who speaks in the Scriptures is not only the Lord of Israel but also the Lord of all, thus including Gentiles.

Key elements of salvation history are present in the passage's use of covenantal language and its allusions to Israel's return from exile. Neither the title "Savior" nor the epithet "Redeemer" appears in this passage, but these designations appropriately apply to the God to whom the passage draws attention. God has chosen a people and led them out of exile, a situation of being alienated from God. God is the Savior and Redeemer of Israel; God is the Savior and Redeemer of his holy people.

The traditional covenantal formula that speaks of God and his people is rephrased in the paternal-filial imagery that designates God as Father and the people as God's sons and daughters. Use of the image in the passage represents an expansion of the notion that Israel is God's son (e.g., Hosea 11:1) and an actualization of the biblical imagery.

The God of 6:14–7:1 is the Lord who demands that his people live in a manner consistent with their relationship with him. A covenantal relationship with the Lord places ethical demands on the people. The references to the temple and the allusions to ritual purity and ritual impurity provide a lens through which this demand can be imaged. God's demand that his people live ethically is summed up in the exhortation to act in a holy way in the fear of God. Their holy way of life is to be consistent with and reflect the holiness of their God.

154

PART 3

2 Corinthians 7:5–16

The Arrival and Report of Titus

Paul had expected to meet Titus in Troas in Asia Minor. Disappointed that the intended rendezvous has not taken place, Paul announces his intention to travel east to Macedonia (2:13). Thereupon he continues his letter with a long and many-faceted digression on his ministry.

In 7:5 Paul resumes the train of thought that he abandoned in 2:13, telling the Corinthians about his arrival in Macedonia. The resumption of his earlier thought in 7:5 is one of the major reasons many critics—including Jean-François Collange (1972), Jeffrey A. Crafton (1991), and Franz Zeilinger (1992)—hold that 1:1–2:13 and 7:5–16 are a single letter fragment, while 2:14–7:4 is a fragment of a different letter.

2 Corinthians 7:5–16 in Context

The letter opening (1:1–2)

Ministerial crises (1:3–2:13)

Paul explains and defends his apostolic ministry (2:14–7:4)

▶ The arrival and report of Titus (7:5–16)

Service to God's holy people (8:1–9:15)

An aggressive taskmaster (10:1–13:10)

The letter closing (13:11–13)

Introductory Matters

Reprising many of the motifs of 1:3–2:13, this section of Paul's letter is readily divided into three subunits, forming a chiastic structure (A-B-A′). The pattern is well known to readers of Paul's letter, having been employed by Paul in 1 Corinthians and several times in the current missive.

The first (7:5–7) and third (7:13b–16) subunits are directly concerned with Paul's description of the arrival of Titus and the feelings that ensued. The central unit (7:8–13a) is a digression in which Paul returns to the topic of the letter that upset the Corinthians (2:3–4, 9). That the letter achieved its intent was the basis of Paul's consolation (7:5–7) and Titus's joy (7:13b–16).

Tracing the Train of Thought

Titus's Arrival (7:5–7)

7:5–7. With the words, **and when we came to Macedonia** (7:5), Paul returns to the account of his frustrating travels, which he abandoned in 2:13. Since physical and social circumstances all but precluded solitary travel in Paul's day, it is hardly likely that he would have traveled by himself to Macedonia. Moreover, 2:13 gives no indication that he intended to do so. Thus the first-person plural pertains to Paul and his traveling companions, his fellow missionaries.

After arriving in Macedonia, Paul initially experienced no physical or psychological relief. **Our flesh**, he writes, **enjoyed no rest; we were afflicted in every way.** His first words are reminiscent of what he writes in 2:13, thereby confirming the continuity of this passage with what he has written in chapter 2. There he writes about his spirit's lack of rest; now he says that his flesh had no rest. In Paul's anthropological vocabulary, each of the terms is used to speak of the human person in its entirety. He was conflicted from without and from within; he was afflicted in all sorts of ways (see 7:4b). He met with **struggles on the outside** and had **fears on the inside**. Paul may have encountered these difficulties in Philippi, a Macedonian city that he had evangelized. His outer struggles were most likely conflicts with some of the inhabitants of the area, perhaps some who were adversely affecting the Christian community there (see Phil. 3:2).

But God who consoles the lowly (7:6) provided Paul with the relief that he sought. In 1:3, Paul praised God as the source of all consolation. Now he himself was to experience that consolation once again, for God **consoled us with the arrival of Titus.** Paul has said that he was filled with consolation (7:4b). Now he explains how he was consoled. The presence of Titus was, for Paul, a manifest expression of divine consolation. But there was more to God's consolation of Paul than the mere physical presence of Titus. That Titus was consoled by the Corinthians also elevated Paul's spirits. The apostle was consoled **not only with his arrival but also with the consolation with which he was consoled in regard to you** (7:7).

What brought such consolation to Titus? **He told us about your longing, your regret, and your zeal for me.** Spelled out in a rising crescendo, the Corinthians' threefold reaction was a source of encouragement for Titus. Perhaps he was surprised by their change of heart. The Corinthians even longed to see Paul, perhaps fearing that he would not visit them again (see 2:1). They regretted their previous treatment of Paul. And they demonstrated their zeal for Paul, perhaps by their punishment of the malefactor (2:5–11).

Titus told Paul about the current feelings of the Corinthians. The "announcement" compounded Paul's joy. **I rejoiced all the more**, he writes. The consolation with which God consoled Paul led to the apostle's joy, one of God's many gifts (see Rom. 14:17; 15:13; Gal. 5:22; cf. 1 Thess. 3:9). Joy is a gift that God often gives to those who are afflicted or troubled (7:4; 8:2; 1 Thess. 1:6), as Paul has been. The God of all consolation turned Paul's affliction into joy.

Further Reflection on the Painful Letter (7:8–13a)

7:8–13a. With Titus's announcement that the Corinthians had experienced a change of heart, Paul begins to reflect a bit more on the letter that he had sent them (see 2:3–4, 9): **For if I grieved you with my letter, I don't regret it** (7:8). The apostle realizes that the letter had the desired effect. He wrote to test the Corinthians' character (2:9); their present longing, regret, and zeal have proved their mettle. As a result, Paul has no regrets about having penned the letter—at least he does not have any present regrets. An aside, **and if I did regret it**, suggests that Paul did entertain some regrets about the letter, but they have now vanished, for **I see that that letter grieved you for only a little while**, and **now I rejoice**.

Paul was happy with a divine joy, not because the Corinthians were troubled by his letter, if only for a short time. **Not because you were sad**, he writes, **but rather because your sadness led to a change of heart [*metanoia*] for you were sad according to God, with the result that you suffered no loss from us in any way** (7:9). Their sadness was measured by God's standards. It was, to repeat the formula used by many commentators, a "godly" (*kata theon*) sadness. Paul uses the image of economic loss (*zēmiōthēte*) to say that the Corinthians suffered no harm as a result of Paul's letter.

A Chiasm within the Chiasm

A The letter that caused sadness (v. 8)

   B The Corinthians' godly sorrow (vv. 9–12)

A′ The letter that caused sadness (v. 13a)

Sadness in the Sight of God

Three times Paul writes about sadness or grief "according to God," twice with a verb (7:9, 11), once with a noun (7:10a). Most commentators translate the expression as "godly," but this is a weak translation and does not adequately capture the full meaning of the qualifying phrase. The phrase seems to refer to sorrow that is according to God's standards or sorrow that is experienced in the presence of God, probably both at the same time. Over and against sadness in the sight of God is a type of sadness that belongs to this world (7:10b).

On the contrary, their sadness was productive, **for sadness in the sight of God** (*kata theon*) leads to conversion; it **produces a change of heart [*metanoian*] that is not to be regretted since it leads to salvation** (7:10). The Corinthians' hearts have been changed, as Titus's report affirms. Paul uses a pithy Greek phrase (*eis sōtērian ametamelēton*) to characterize this change of heart. He says that the reason the conversion of the Corinthians is not regrettable is that their change of heart leads to salvation.

But, Paul writes in order to distinguish godly sadness from worldly sadness, **worldly sadness produces death.** Whereas godly sadness eventually leads to salvation, worldly sadness leads to death. The death about which Paul is writing is not physical death. He uses "death" in a metaphorical sense. Worldly grief, grief according to the standards of this world, leads to spiritual death.

The distinction between godly sadness and worldly sadness having been made, Paul continues his reflection on the grief that the Corinthians experienced. The change of heart that it produced is manifest in many ways, as Paul explains. **Look how much earnestness this very sadness before the eyes of God produced in you, not only that but also defense, indignation, fear, longing, zeal, and punishment** (7:11).

Paul's first words indicate that he wants to pursue further the nature of the godly grief that the Corinthians experienced. The enthusiasm that was generated in him as a result of Titus's report is evident in the way he describes the effects of the Corinthians' conversion. He begins by describing their newfound zeal for him, drawing their attention to how great it was. There quickly follows in staccato-like fashion a series of an additional half-dozen experiences, linked one after another by the Greek *alla* ("but also").

He speaks of their "defense" (*apologian*), not an apology in the modern sense of the term but an attempt to clear themselves of any accusation of lingering rejection of Paul or of harboring false teachers. They were indignant either at themselves for having treated Paul the way that they did or at the wrongdoer whom Paul is about to mention (7:12). Their fear may have resulted from the realization that they faced the wrath of God for the way they acted. Titus has reported about their longing and their zeal for Paul (7:7). And they have punished the wrongdoer (see 2:5–11), perhaps excessively.

For the modern reader, it is difficult to ascertain exactly what Paul is referring to with each of these terms, but the Corinthians would have known what he meant. Paul spells out a whole series of things; the cumulative effect would have convinced the Corinthians of Paul's enthusiasm at the news he received from Titus.

Then, restraining himself as he adopts a more sober tone, Paul affirms that his addressees are now purified. In the past they may have been guilty because of their attitude and their behavior toward Paul, but now that they have had a change of heart, they are innocent: **in every way you have proved yourselves to be innocent in this regard**, that is, in the matter at hand. As the letter continues, it will become obvious that there are nonetheless still some issues to be resolved (see 12:20–13:4).

The enthusiasm generated by the report of the Corinthians' change of heart leads Paul to digress from the topic at hand to the letter that he wrote them (7:8). Returning to the topic of the painful letter, Paul speaks about its real purpose (cf. 2:9): **And if I wrote to you, it was not for the sake of the wrongdoer, nor was it for the sake of the one who was wronged, but it was so that your zeal for us might be apparent to you** (7:12). Paul did not write to the Corinthians so that they might act in his stead in punishing the malefactor, nor did he intend any self-vindication. Rather, he wrote his letter to test the Corinthians' character, to find out whether they were loyal to him. The present zeal of the Corinthians shows to the Corinthians themselves that in their heart-of-hearts, **in the presence of God**, they are loyal to the apostle.

Wherefore we are consoled (7:13a). Rather than experiencing any regret because he wrote his letter (7:8), Paul experiences consolation. The letter achieved its purpose; it has been effective in producing a demonstration of loyalty on the part of the Corinthians. This brings consolation to the apostle.

Titus's Experience (7:13b–16)

7:13b–16. Paul has been virtually carried away as he enthusiastically describes the consolation that he experienced despite having sent the Corinthians a letter that caused them grief. Their change of heart has allowed him to consider that letter in a new light. Now he returns to the subject of Titus, who has brought the great news to Paul. Paul's own joy (see 7:7) was compounded by his awareness of Titus's joy: **With our consolation we rejoiced all the more at the joy of Titus because his spirit was refreshed by all of you** (7:13b). Paul's enthusiasm continues to be manifest as he writes hyperbolically about Titus's being cheered up and encouraged by all the Corinthians.

Titus seems to have had some hesitation about going to Corinth as Paul's emissary. Would he be received as Paul had been received? Before Titus's departure for Corinth, Paul had to encourage him. To Titus Paul boasted about the Corinthians. The encouraging report with which Titus returned meant that Paul's boast was on target; he did not regret his attempt to encourage

Titus: **If I boasted to him about you, I had nothing of which to be ashamed** [*ou kateschynthēn*] (lit., "I was not ashamed"; 7:14). Paul spoke only the truth to the Corinthians. What he had told Titus about the Corinthians with so much pride also proved to be the truth: **and as we told you everything truthfully** (cf. 13:8), **so our boasting about you to Titus has also proved to be the truth.**

Paul had to encourage Titus before his departure. Now **his feelings for you have increased all the more** (7:15). Using Semitic idiom as is his custom, Paul says that Titus's affection (*splanchna*, "bowels"; cf. 6:12) for the Corinthians continues to grow **as he recalls the obedience of all of you, how you received him with fear and trembling.** The phrase "fear and trembling" is a biblical idiom typically used in reference to human beings in the presence of God (see Exod. 15:16; Isa. 19:16; Phil. 2:12). Paul appropriates the phrase to describe a tense situation (see 1 Cor. 2:3; cf. Eph. 6:5). The situation at Corinth must have been tense. Not only was Titus on edge; so too were the Corinthians. Nonetheless they manifested their loyalty to Paul. Their obedience was evident. Titus's affection for the Corinthians grew as he remembered and told the story of the Corinthians' loyalty to Paul and their obedience to God.

And, says Paul, **I rejoice that I am able to depend on you in every way** (7:16). For the fourth time in this passage, Paul speaks about the joy that he experiences because of the Corinthians (7:7, 9, 13, 16). This joy engenders Paul's complete confidence in the Corinthians. On this happy note, the apostle not only completes his report on Titus's return but also prepares the way for the appeal that he is about to make (2 Cor. 8–9).

Theological Issues

Consolation and joy are the dominant themes of 7:5–16. Paul uses the verb "console" (*parakaleō*) four times, the noun "consolation" (*paraklēsis*) twice, the verb "rejoice" (*chairō*) four times, and the noun "joy" (*chara*) once. The motifs pick up the final words of the previous section of the letter, in which Paul says, "I have been filled with consolation; I am overflowing with joy in all our affliction" (7:4).

Consolation and joy are gifts of God. Paul begins 7:5–16 by mentioning how downhearted he had been. He was beset with difficulties and was suffering turmoil within. Such was Paul's human situation before God's intervention. Reprising the description of God with which he began the letter, Paul identifies the intervening God as "God who consoles the lowly" (7:6). The descriptive language recalls that Paul has previously described the Father as the "God of all consolation" (1:3). That Paul will invoke God in this fashion, as he does in Rom. 15:5, indicates not only that God is the source of consolation but also that this divine attribute provides the lowly and downtrodden with a claim to be heard (7:5–6a). That God is the God of all consolation bespeaks his special relationship with those who are in need.

For Paul and other biblical authors, both OT and NT, joy results from the experience of God's presence among human beings, particularly but not exclusively in circumstances of affliction (7:4; 8:2; see 1 Thess. 1:6; James 1:2; 1 Pet. 1:6–8; cf. Heb. 10:34). That joy is a consequence of experiencing the divine presence means that God provides the initiative in the human experience of true joy. Thus Paul can speak of joy as a fruit of the Holy Spirit (Gal. 5:22) and as a quality of the kingdom of God (Rom. 14:17).

The consolation that God gives is granted through human experience. Paul, who was afflicted in all sorts of ways, was consoled by the arrival of Titus. A fearful Titus was consoled by the reception that he received from the Corinthians. Paul was consoled by the news about the Corinthians that Titus brought. From the standpoint of those who are consoled, experiencing divine consolation can be described as having one's spirit refreshed, as through rest when there has previously been restlessness. In simple language, receiving divine consolation is an experience of being cheered up.

Since consolation is experienced as a result of a divine intervention, consolation results in joy. Thus Paul can write that he rejoiced all the more because of the conversion that the Corinthians have experienced. Titus was consoled by the reception that he received from the Corinthians. That brought him joy, a joy in which Paul could share. Paul's joy brought him confidence. Rejoicing, he knew that he could rely on the Corinthians because God was at work among them.

The careful reader of Paul's missive should not psychoanalyze Paul's experience of consolation and joy, but it is difficult to miss the exuberance that issues from Paul's experience of consolation and joy. He describes the Corinthians' conversion experience with seven terms, barely distinguishable from one another, but they do add up to seven, the number that signified fullness in the ancient world. Using paronomasia, the word "all" echoes throughout. Paul says that Titus was well received and encouraged by all of you and that all of you were obedient. And Paul has confidence in every way (*en panti*, 6:16), whereas previously he was afflicted in every way (*en panti*, 7:5). Paul's language may be hyperbolic, but there is no lack of enthusiasm on his part.

The way Paul describes how he was consoled and encouraged by the arrival of Titus and the things that the latter had to say—all this serves as a reminder that God works through human beings. Titus's consolation of Paul was the expression and incarnation of divine consolation.

PART 4

2 Corinthians
8:1–9:15

Service to God's Holy People

The apostle changes the subject and the tone of his writing in 8:1. He introduces a new topic, ostensibly a wonderful gift of God to the Macedonians. This proves to be introduced as a motivating factor to prompt the Corinthians to resume the collection on behalf of the poor in Jerusalem. The project has apparently been interrupted as a result of the estrangement between the Corinthians and Paul.

2 Corinthians 8:1–9:15 in Context

The letter opening (1:1–2)

Ministerial crises (1:3–2:13)

Paul explains and defends his apostolic ministry (2:14–7:4)

The arrival and report of Titus (7:5–16)

▶ Service to God's holy people (8:1–9:15)

An aggressive taskmaster (10:1–13:10)

The letter closing (13:11–13)

2 Corinthians 8:1–24

The Collection

Introductory Matters

In the Letter to the Galatians, Paul describes a visit to Jerusalem during which he met with James, Cephas, and John (Gal. 2:1–10). These acknowledged pillars of the Jerusalem church recognized the authenticity of Paul's ministry to the Gentiles, the uncircumcised. Before returning to Antioch, Paul reached a gentleman's agreement, signed with a handshake, that he should remember the poor. Paul says that this is something that he was eager to do.

Paul's eagerness to remember the poor remained with him throughout his ministry. Both of the extant letters to the Corinthians and the Letter to the Romans bring up the topic of a collection on behalf of believers in Jerusalem. It is a moot question whether the collection represents Paul's response to the agreement that he had made with the three leaders of the Jerusalem church, or whether it was simply a manifestation of Paul's eagerness to help the poor. What is beyond any doubt is that Paul spoke about the collection in the Roman provinces of Asia, Macedonia, and Achaia—as well as in Rome itself, via the letter that he would write to that community.

The First Letter to the Corinthians contains Paul's first mention of a collection (1 Cor. 16:1–4), about which he had previously spoken to them. The collection is identified in matter-of-fact fashion as "the collection for the holy ones" (16:1 NAB). Perhaps in response to the Corinthians' query about the practicalities of the collection, Paul tells them that they are to follow the same procedures as he had spelled out for the Galatians. Lest a major fund-raising effort wait until Paul's visit, the Corinthians are encouraged to put aside some extra money on the first day of each week (16:2). When Paul arrives, he will organize the delivery of the collected monies to Jerusalem. The gift (*hē charis*, 16:3) is to be brought to Jerusalem by delegates of the Corinthian church who will be bearing letters of recommendation. If it appears advantageous for Paul to accompany the delegation, he is willing to do so (16:4).

Apparently the Corinthians' interest in the collection has flagged, undoubtedly as a result of the difficult circumstances surrounding Paul's visit to their city (2 Cor. 2:1). Titus's enthusiastic report about the Corinthians' renewed zeal for Paul and his work has given Paul hope that this important work can proceed. Christians in Jerusalem are in need (8:14). In his letter to Rome, Paul says that the resources are to be shared with the poor among God's holy people in Jerusalem (15:26). The poor are not people living on the brink of poverty or who are marginally poor; they are people who are truly destitute, who are suffering from a deeply entrenched poverty.

Any number of factors could have contributed to their poverty. To begin, believers in Jerusalem were not, for the most part, drawn from among the wealthy class. Living in a fairly arid area of Palestine, people in Jerusalem bore the brunt of periodic famines (see Acts 11:27–30). The Sanhedrin had the leading disciples arrested (Acts 4:1–3; 5:21b–41); Paul himself had persecuted the church (1 Cor. 15:9; Gal. 1:13; see Acts 8:1; 9:1–2). It is not unlikely that this open hostility toward believers was accompanied by a more subtle hostility that took an economic toll on believers. Intra-Christian factors may have exacerbated the situation. Some support had to be found for the Galilean leaders of the church who settled in Jerusalem. Hospitality was needed for missionaries and pilgrims. There seems to have been a number of widows who needed support (see Acts 6:1–7). Perhaps the common possession of material goods (see Acts 2:44–45) contributed to the situation insofar as the practice reduced the "capital" that some possessed. In any case, the poverty of the church in Jerusalem was real, deep-seated, and prolonged.

Tracing the Train of Thought

The Example of the Macedonians (8:1–6)

8:1–6. With **and we want you to know, brothers and sisters** (8:1), Paul begins this new section of his letter by calling upon the Corinthians as his brothers and sisters and telling them that there is something that they should know. This "disclosure formula," "we want you to know," is well known to the readers of Paul, who uses it as he transitions from one topic to another lacking close connection to the previous topic (see 1 Cor. 12:3; 15:1; Gal. 1:11; cf. 1:8). Paul typically calls upon his addressees as his brothers and sisters, but this formula of direct address is virtually absent from 2 Corinthians (see 1:8; 13:11). Its presence in 8:1 is a sign that the sibling relationship that was broken as a result of Paul's painful visit has been restored. Paul can once again call upon the Corinthians as his brothers and sisters. That he does so here has the added rhetorical advantage of enabling Paul to appeal to the family ties that bind him and them together as he seeks to remind them about the all-but-forgotten collection.

Before getting to the point, Paul tells the Corinthians about **the grace of God [*tēn charin tou theou*] given to the churches of Macedonia**. God's gift is, in fact, the topic that Paul wants to discuss. Mention of the gift introduced as the gift of God in 8:1 (see 1:12) will dominate the discourse of this chapter, in which "gift" appears seven times. Paul continues to speak about the gift in the next chapter of this letter, where *hē charis* appears three times.

> **2 Corinthians 8:1–24 in the Rhetorical Flow**
>
> **The letter opening (1:1–2)**
> **Ministerial crises (1:3–2:13)**
> **Paul explains and defends his apostolic ministry (2:14–7:4)**
> **The arrival and report of Titus (7:5–16)**
> **Service to God's holy people (8:1–9:15)**
> ▶ The collection (8:1–24)
> > The example of the Macedonians (8:1–6)
> >
> > The appeal (8:7–15)
> >
> > Titus and his delegation (8:16–24)

The churches of Macedonia were communities founded by Paul, certainly the churches in Philippi and Thessalonica and, most likely, a gathering of believers in Beroea as well (see Acts 17:10–15; 20:4). Before describing God's gift to these churches, Paul describes their situation. To motivate the Corinthians, he emphasizes their difficult circumstances. **In a great ordeal of affliction, their overflowing joy and their truly deep poverty flowed over into a richness of generosity on their part** (8:2). The Macedonian churches suffered a great amount of affliction and were almost destitute. Paul emphasizes the extent of their affliction by describing it as a great ordeal. The affliction that they endured was a true test of their mettle. As for their poverty, they were in deep need. They were poor to the depths of poverty. They were truly indigent.

Their situation was, nonetheless, paradoxical. Despite their severe affliction, they possessed overflowing joy. Joy, as has been noticed, is often contrasted with affliction in Paul's writings. In the Macedonians' situation described by Paul, the overflowing of joy contrasts sharply with the extent of their affliction. To compound the paradox, Paul says that from the depths of the Macedonians' poverty flowed a richness of generosity. Affliction is juxtaposed with joy, poverty with riches. Each of the four terms is qualified in such a way that the readers understand how Paul wants them to know that all four realities—affliction, joy, poverty, and riches—abounded, almost to the point of excess.

The surfeit of Paul's language continues as he describes what the Macedonians did: **They gave according to their means and, so I can testify, beyond their means** (8:3). Paul adds a mild oath, "so I can testify" (cf. Rom. 1:9; Phil.

1:8; 1 Thess. 2:5, 10), to confirm that the Macedonians gave beyond their expected ability to do so. And this was not because they were commanded or even urged to do so. It was they who urged Paul to let them participate in this important endeavor. He describes them as **begging us, with much urging, for the grace to participate in this service to the saints** (8:4). The Macedonians pleaded with Paul to allow them a part (*tēn koinōnian*) in this service to the saints, which they regarded as a God-given opportunity, a grace (*tēn charin*).

Earlier in the letter Paul used "ministerial language" (the verb *diakoneō*, "serve" [3:3]; the noun *diakonia*, "service" [3:7, 8, 9 (2x); 4:1; 5:18; 6:3]; and the noun *diakonos*, "server" [3:6; 6:4]) in reference to his ministry among the Corinthians. Now he writes about a service in which the Macedonians could participate and were eager to do so, the service to the saints. That Paul does not need to explain the nature of this service or the identity of the holy people means that the Corinthians know what Paul is talking about. The service to God's holy people is a way of identifying the collection of money to support the poor among believers in Jerusalem (see 8:19, 20; 9:1; Rom. 15:31).

The Macedonians' plea to Paul apparently met with a favorable response on the part of Paul since they did this, **not as we had hoped** (8:5). Paul's Greek text lacks any explicit mention of his response to their request, nor does it mention that the churches in Macedonia made a collection. Paul says only "and not as we had hoped," implying that what the Macedonians gave to help

Service to "the Saints"

In the three extant letters in which Paul writes about the collection, he identifies the project as a "service to the saints" (*tēs diakonias tēs eis tous hagious*, 8:4; 9:1; see Rom. 15:25, 31; 1 Cor. 16:1). Who are the saints, God's holy people (see "Ecclesiology," after my comments on 2 Cor. 1:1–2)? Paul uses the language of holiness to speak about believers in Corinth (1 Cor. 1:2) and elsewhere in the province of Achaia (2 Cor. 1:1), the colony at Philippi (Phil. 1:1), and the imperial capital (Rom. 1:7). The collection is, however, not intended for universal distribution. Paul intends that the proceeds of the collection be brought to Jerusalem, where the service to the saints will be rendered (Rom. 15:25, 26, 31; 1 Cor. 16:3).

In the context of the collection, the service to the saints is a service to God's holy people, believers, in Jerusalem. In the Septuagint, God's holy people are the chosen people, those who belong to God. The terminology was appropriately used of early Jewish-Christian believers in Jerusalem, who could be considered as the faithful remnant of God's holy people. The language, first used in reference to the first generation of believers in Jerusalem, was later applied to all believers. The honorific epithet "saints," or "holy people," properly belongs to believers in Jerusalem. By extension it applies to all believers, not only in the first century CE but also in the twenty-first century.

Figure 9. Coins of the Realm. Coins like these were gathered in the collection about which Paul writes in 2 Cor. 8–9.

God's holy people exceeded even his own expectations. From personal experience Paul knew about the generosity of the church in Philippi (11:8–9; see Phil. 4:10, 15), but the generosity of that community and the other Macedonian churches was more than what he had expected.

But they gave themselves generously, writes Paul, **first to the Lord and then to us by the will of God.** With these words Paul not only explains their bounteousness but also contrasts it with his previous expectations. He makes a point of saying that their response was first of all a response to God; only secondarily was it an expression of loyalty to Paul. It may well be that, as Paul is preparing to send Titus back to Corinth to reignite the spark of their generosity toward God's holy people, he wants the Corinthians to know that the appeal that Titus is about to make is not to be a test of their loyalty to Paul. They have already proved their loyalty to Paul (7:7, 11). No further proof is necessary. The generosity of the churches in Macedonia was in the first instance a demonstration of their response to the will of God.

Encouraged by this experience and buoyed up by Titus's favorable report about the current situation in Corinth, Paul has decided to send Titus back to Corinth to continue the welfare work on behalf of the church in Jerusalem: **We urged Titus, that as he had already started so he should likewise finish this grace among you** (8:6). Once again the work of the collection is identified as a grace, a gift of God (*tēn charin tautēn*). Who better to continue the work that began sometime in the past than Titus, who has so recently been favorably received by the Corinthians (7:13, 15) and who was previously involved in the task of organizing the collection in Corinth? When was Titus active in the collection at Corinth? Perhaps the previous year (8:10)!

With the announcement that Titus will be his delegate to Corinth for the purpose of the collection, Paul brings a long and somewhat labored sentence to a close. In Greek, 7:1–6 is a long, ninety-four-word sentence, whose style contrasts with the typical pithiness of Paul's composition.

Although it is somewhat useless to speculate on why Paul wrote this way, it is clear why he wrote. In Hellenistic rhetoric the giving of examples (*epideigmata, exempla*) was considered to be an important means of persuading people. Familiar as he was with rhetorical techniques, Paul does not hesitate to cite the example of the Macedonian churches as he urges the church at Corinth to take up once again the all-but-abandoned collection.

The Appeal (8:7–15)

8:7–15. A little flattery never harms. Rhetoricians considered examples, models to be followed, as logical arguments in demonstrative rhetoric. They considered an appeal to the emotions or advantage of the addressees as another kind of argument, an argument from *pathos*. Now Paul takes this tack as he writes, **But just as you exceed in every way, in faith, and speech, and knowledge, and all zeal, and our love for you** (8:7). The initial "but" can be construed as making a contrast between one type of rhetorical contrast and another. More likely, however, the adversative conjunction simply points to a shift in Paul's thought.

Paul flatters the Corinthians as he speaks about their many qualities, just as he did when he began 1 Corinthians by telling them that "in every way [*en panti*] you have been enriched in him, in speech [*en panti logō*] and knowledge of every kind [*pasē gnōsei*]" (1:5). Now he tells the Corinthians that they are blessed in every way (*en panti*) and illustrates the abundance of their assets by citing five of them. He begins with their faith, speech, and knowledge. Two of these have been cited in the flattering thanksgiving of 1 Corinthians, at 1:5; all of them are mentioned in that letter's reflections on the gifts of the Spirit: faith in 1 Cor. 12:9; 13:2, 13; speech in 12:8; 14:9; and knowledge in 12:8; 13:2, 8; 14:6. In addition to these gifts of the Spirit, Paul's addressees have been enriched by the relationship that they have with Paul. Presently, at least, they are zealous for Paul (see 2 Cor. 7:11, 12). And Paul loves them (cf. 2:4; 6:6; 7:1; 12:15, 19) with a love that he repeatedly professes in 1 Corinthians (4:14;

"Our Love for You"

Instead of "our love for you" (*tē ex hēmōn en hymin agapē*) in 2 Cor. 8:7, many ancient manuscripts, including the Codex Sinaiticus (‭א‬) and the Codex Ephraemi Syri Rescriptus (C), have the personal pronouns in reverse order and read "your love for us" (*tē ex hymōn en hēmin agapē*). This latter reading is reflected in the translations found in the King James Version, New English Bible, Revised English Bible, Revised Standard Version, and New International Version; but a majority of the committee that worked on the Greek text of the NT found in NA²⁸/UBS⁴ preferred the former reading. The reading that attests to Paul's affection for the Corinthians is found in the oldest manuscript of 2 Corinthians (𝔓⁴⁶), several ancient versions, and the writings of two important biblical scholars of the patristic era, Origen and Ephraim the Syrian.

A Proof of Love

In the first of his extant letters, Paul indicates that the work of love is a hallmark of ecclesial existence (1 Thess. 1:3). Love-in-action is an essential characteristic of the church. For the Christian "the only thing that counts is faith working through love" (Gal. 5:6). Paul writes about love as the gift of the Spirit (Rom. 5:5; 1 Cor. 13), but when he writes about love as a human virtue, he always has in mind love in the concrete, love expressing itself in action, love that comes at a price. In 2 Cor. 8:8, 24 Paul writes about the Corinthians showing their love-in-action and giving proof of their ecclesial status by participating in the collection for God's holy people in Jerusalem.

10:14; 15:58), a letter that concludes with a postscript, "My love be with all of you in Christ Jesus" (16:24), the only such postscript in the extant Pauline correspondence.

Reprising the verb with which he began his flattery of the Corinthians, Paul makes his plea: **so also exceed in this grace** [*tē chariti*]. As the Corinthians have been abundantly gifted, so they should be willing to give abundantly. Paul's Greek text does not use the imperative; rather, he uses a "so" (*hina*) clause with a verb in the subjunctive, which may express more of a wish than a command for **I do not speak to you by way of command** (8:8). Paul's expression suggests a contrast (see 1 Cor. 7:6, 25). If he is not speaking by way of command, why is he speaking as he does? Paul answers the unasked question with **I am testing the genuineness of your love by means of the zeal of others.** Paul uses the zeal of the Macedonian churches to goad the Corinthians to show their generosity, thereby making it more than clear to them why he has spoken about the Macedonians' enthusiastic participation in the collection. Will the Corinthians be as enthusiastic and as generous as the Macedonians were? The collection will prove just how genuine is the love of the Corinthians.

If the example of the Macedonian churches is not enough to move the church at Corinth to a generous response to Paul's appeal, Paul gives another model, one that they already know: **For you know the grace of our Lord Jesus Christ** (8:9). Using the full christological title (see 1:3), Paul writes about the presence of the Lord Jesus Christ as God's gift (*charis*), explaining **that he who was rich became poor for your sake so that you might be enriched by his poverty.**

In his christological reflection, Paul exploits the contrast between rich and poor. Contrasted with his preexistence, the earthly existence of Jesus can only be described as a condition of dire poverty, the purpose of which is that the Corinthians (and we!) might be enriched. Their riches are spiritual (see 8:7) rather than material. Paul's language is obviously metaphorical, but it will be easy for the Corinthians to grasp Paul's point. As Christ was willing to become poor for the sake of the Corinthians, so they should be willing to share their material possessions, thereby becoming a bit poorer, for the sake of God's holy people in Jerusalem.

Having cited two examples to provide the Corinthians with motivation, Paul then offers some advice: **And I give you my opinion about this** (8:10). In somewhat tortuous Greek, Paul then says, **What** I am about to say **is appropriate for you** since you are **the sort of people who, last year, began to do this and to do it willingly. So now finish the task so that, as [your] desire to do it will be satisfied, so the project will be completed from what you have** (8:11). Paul has advised the Corinthians to complete the work that they have begun. Then he offers a second bit of advice, that they give according to their means: **For if desire is present, a gift is acceptable in proportion to what a person has, not in proportion to what one doesn't have** (8:12).

Paul explains what he means by this as he writes, **For the idea is not that others have relief and you hardship, but that there be equity** (8:13). The collection is not a matter of impoverishing the Corinthians so that the people in Jerusalem can be rich. Rather, it is a matter of equity. The financial situation of the Corinthian faithful should be comparable to the financial situation of believers in Jerusalem. The Corinthians are being urged not to enrich those in Jerusalem but to take care of their present needs; **at present your abundance satisfies their needs** (8:14).

As Paul writes, the Corinthians are relatively well off, but the situation might change. There may come a day when they are in need. That being a possibility, it is to the Corinthians' advantage to come to the support of believers in Jerusalem. In Hellenistic rhetoric, arguments from pathos often focus on the advantage that will accrue to the addressees if they respond to the plea of the one who is speaking to them. So Paul adds that it is to the Corinthians' self-advantage to be generous **so that their abundance** (the *perisseuma* of the people in Jerusalem) **might satisfy your needs** (the *hysterēma* of the Corinthians) if the present situation should be reversed. This would not be a matter of the people in Jerusalem paying the Corinthians back when their situation

---

Romans 15:26–27

The idea of reciprocity between Corinth and Jerusalem suggested by 2 Cor. 8:13–14 may lead contemporary readers to remember the kind of reciprocity between the Gentile churches of Macedonia and Achaia and God's holy people in Jerusalem, reciprocity that Paul discusses when he writes about the collection in the Letter to the Romans. In 15:26–27, Paul mentions that the Jerusalem community has shared its spiritual riches with Gentile believers, so Gentile believers should share their material riches with the Jerusalem community. In 2 Cor. 8:13–14 Paul is concerned only with financial resources.

improves; rather, it is **so that there will be equity** (*isotēs*). A comparable standard of living is the goal, now and in the future.

Greek rhetoricians frequently quoted sages and philosophers, authority figures, as they tried to persuade their addressees. Paul uses passages from the Jewish Scriptures in much the same way. Hence, as a final argument in his plea to the Corinthians, he adds a passage of Scripture: **For so it is written, "The one who had much did not have too much; the one who had little did not have too little"** (8:15). Taken out of its biblical context, verse 18 of the Exodus story about the gift of manna (16:1–36) serves as a final argument in Paul's appeal to the Corinthians. According to the biblical narrative, the Israelites who gathered more manna did not have a surplus while those who gathered less did not experience any shortage of food to eat.

Paul has goaded the Corinthians by citing the example of the Macedonians' generosity. He has cited the example of Jesus. He has appealed to the Corinthians' self-interest and urged them, perhaps appealing to their pride, to finish what they have started. And finally, he uses a scriptural argument. Thus, with a plethora of arguments, the master rhetorician develops his appeal on behalf of God's holy people in Jerusalem.

Titus and His Delegation (8:16–24)

8:16–24. Urging the Corinthians to take part in the collection is one thing; getting it organized is another. Paul is not disinclined to interrupt his flow of thought with a brief prayer of thanksgiving (see 2:14; Rom. 7:25). So now he thanks God that Titus is ready and willing to take on the organizational task. **Thanks be to God,** he writes, **who placed this same zeal for you in the heart of Titus because he accepted this appeal and, being very eager, went to you willingly** (8:16–17). Titus wants the Corinthians to participate in the collection as much as Paul does. Paul urges Titus to go to the Corinthians (8:6), but Titus is so enthusiastic about the project that he goes virtually of his own accord.

Reverting to the use of the editorial first-person plural, Paul adds, **And we sent with him the brother who is praised by all the churches in regard to the gospel** (8:18). Since Christian missionaries rarely traveled alone in those times, Paul appointed a traveling companion for him. He does not identify the traveling companion by name but commends him in laudatory and almost hyperbolic terms. Titus's companion is obviously a believer; he is identified as a brother, a member of a church. Paul has confidence in him since he is the person whom Paul has chosen to send. And he enjoys a good reputation in all the churches because of his zeal for the gospel. Taken literally, "all the churches" is an overstatement; Paul probably means that the man is highly regarded in the churches of Macedonia that have taken part in the collection.

Paul's commendation of the anonymous believer continues with mention of a task to which he has already been appointed. **Moreover,** Paul says, **he has been appointed by the churches as our traveling companion with the gift that** we are administering for the glory of the Lord and our desire [*prothymian hēmōn*] (8:19). It is appropriate that someone from the community or communities that have contributed to the collection accompany Paul as he makes his way to Jerusalem. It is, after all, their gift (see 1 Cor. 16:3–4), even if Paul is in charge of its administration. And Paul gladly participates in this work for the glory of the Lord.

Aware that some have called his integrity into question (see 6:3; 12:16–17), Paul adds an aside: **We want to avoid something [*stellomenoi*] (hapax in Paul), namely, that anyone blame us in regard to this extravagant gift that we are administering** (8:20). Previously Paul lauded the eagerness and the generosity of the Macedonians, who gave even beyond their means (8:2–3), but this is the first time that he draws attention to the extraordinary amount that has been collected by using a term, *adrotēti* ("lavish gift"), that does not otherwise appear in the NT. That the collection thus far has proved to be so successful makes it all the more important for Paul to assure the Corinthians that he is not dipping into the till. **For,** he explains, **we are careful about what is good** and honorable **not only in the sight of the Lord but also in the eyes of men and women [*enōpion anthrōpōn*]** (8:21). Paul's phrase echoes Prov. 3:4 LXX, but for Paul "the Lord" refers to Christ rather than to God.

And we sent with them our brother whom we have tested in many ways (8:22). This third member of the traveling delegation is someone to whom Paul has apparently entrusted a variety of tasks. Paul has found him to be **zealous and now even more zealous because of his great confidence in you.** The language that Paul uses in commendation of the third member of the delegation is similar to that used for Titus in 8:16–17. In sum, the delegation consists of three persons, two who are particularly close to Paul and someone who represents the churches from which a collection has already been taken. That the anonymous delegate tested by Paul is said to have confidence in the church at Corinth implies that he, like Titus and Paul himself, has been party to at least some aspects of Paul's tense relationship with the Corinthians.

Having identified the members of the delegation that he is sending to Corinth, Paul makes a formal recommendation: **With regard to Titus,** he is **my partner and coworker on your behalf. With regard to our brothers,** they are **apostles of the churches, the glory of Christ** (8:23). Paul's commendation of Titus and the two other members of the delegation is clear even though his Greek text omits the verb "to be." Titus is described as Paul's "partner" (*koinōnos emos*), a rare use of the term by Paul (cf. Philem. 17). As far as the Corinthians are concerned, Titus is Paul's coworker for their sake, as the Corinthians have already experienced. As far as the unnamed members of the delegation are concerned, they have been sent by the churches; they are emissaries of the churches (*apostoloi ekklēsiōn*). Paul adds a particular laudatory note to their commendation. They are "the glory of Christ," most likely a reference to their service, which redounds to the honor and glory of Christ.

The Commendation

The way Paul writes about Titus and the two other delegates in 8:16–24 reflects many traits of letters of recommendation in the Hellenistic world (see 3:1).

The letter of recommendation praised those who were commended in such a way that they became familiar to those who were receiving the letter. Pseudo-Demetrius's model letter of recommendation suggests that mention might be made of the commended person's having been tested by the author of the letter. Typically the letter of recommendation concludes with a request. These characteristics of the letter of recommendation abound in 8:16–24.

Letters of recommendation often served to introduce the letter carrier and included a closing request that hospitality be extended to the carrier. The similarities between 8:16–24 and the letter of recommendation suggest that Paul may have intended that the delegation carry his letter to the Corinthians.

Paul uses a past tense (aorist), to refer to Titus's leaving for Corinth (8:17) and Paul's sending the other delegates (8:18, 22). It may well be that these are "epistolary aorists." The events in the past to which they refer are not past at the time that the letter is being written; they are past with respect to the time when the letter is being read. Instead of using an epistolary aorist, Paul could have written, "Titus is leaving" and "we are sending."

Understandably Paul has written about the composition of the delegation at some length. First of all, there is safety in numbers. It would not have been safe for a single person to carry a large sum of money, or any money, along Roman highways or byways. Banditry was always a concern. That is why travelers grouped themselves into caravans. Paul, however, seems to be as concerned with the integrity of the project as he is with the safe passage of the funds. His own integrity has recently been called into question at Corinth. By sending a delegation whose principal was well known to the Corinthians, an appointee of the Macedonian churches, and a person who had been well tested by Paul, the apostle distances himself somewhat from the actual collection of the monies. Well-regarded and responsible persons will be on hand to oversee the collection, rather than the apostle himself.

The identity of the unnamed members of the delegation has puzzled commentators during the course of the centuries. Paul has contributed to the puzzle not only by not naming these delegates but also by making reference to only one of them in 12:18. Different commentators have proposed any number of persons known to Paul, among whom the names of Barnabas and Silas are the most prominent, as being one or the other of the unnamed delegates. Hans Lietzmann (1949, 137) once suggested that Paul's letter originally mentioned

Baker Photo Archive

Figure 10. The Lechaion Road. This was one of the principal routes into the city of Corinth.

the names of the delegates but that the names were later deleted from copies of the letter because they had fallen out of favor.

All of this is only speculation. Paul's way of writing about the delegation is just to let the Corinthians know that Titus is the one in charge. The anonymity of his two companions may owe to Paul's expectation that Titus will introduce them to the Corinthians. In any case, the unnamed legates enjoy the confidence both of the churches and of Paul. This is all that needed to be said about them. Titus can introduce them to the church at Corinth when he arrives.

This section of Paul's letter concludes with a request that is virtually a command: **Therefore show the churches proof of your love and [show] them proof of our boasting about you** (8:24). In 2 Corinthians Paul often makes use of a participle rather than a principal verb to express his thought. Now, in a kind of motivational peroration, he uses a participial phrase (*endeixin . . . endeiknymenoi*) as an imperative to repeat the plea of verse 7, that the Corinthians participate generously in the collection. Paul has told the

> ### The Anonymous Brothers
>
> "There are plausible grounds for identifying the first of the two unnamed 'brothers' as Apollos, whom Paul mentions by name in 1 Corinthians but not in 2 Corinthians, and the second as Timothy, whom Paul mentions by name in Romans, 1 Corinthians, 2 Corinthians, Philippians, 1 Thessalonians, and Philemon." (W. Walker 2011, 319–20)

Corinthians that the collection is to be a test of their love (8:8); now he tells them that a generous response to his appeal will be a demonstration of their love. It will show the churches that their love is genuine.

The tenor of Paul's argument suggests that the churches to whom the Corinthians should give proof of their love are primarily the churches of Macedonia (8:1), but the thought of the Corinthians' love for the church in Jerusalem is not to be excluded. A generous response on the part of the Corinthians will also prove to Titus and the other members of the delegation the truthfulness of what Paul has been saying about the Corinthians (see 7:14).

Theological Issues

Christology

In 8:9, Paul cites the Lord Jesus Christ as an example for the Corinthians to follow. Thereafter Christ continues to remain as the frame of reference in Paul's appeal and the decisions that he makes in regard to practicalities.

The hortatory use of the example of Christ in verse 9 is a singularly important christological piece that evokes a comparison with the christological hymn in Phil. 2:6–11. Alluding to the preexistence of Christ, both texts speak about the incarnation. They are the only two texts in the Pauline corpus that do so. Both describe the human condition of Jesus in graphic terms. Second Corinthians uses the metaphor of abject poverty to do so; Philippians speaks about the obedience and the death by crucifixion of Christ. Although both texts underscore the lowliness of the human condition of Christ, both texts use the full range of christological epithets to identify the Christ. Finally, Paul uses both texts for hortatory purposes (see Phil. 2:5, "let the same mind be in you that was in Christ Jesus").

Paul does not write as he does in 8:9 in order to develop a Christology; rather, he uses a Christology to motivate the Corinthians. Nonetheless, the passage played an important role for the teaching and life of the church from the second century to the sixth, especially in the church fathers' theology of exchange. For example, Ambrosiaster, the anonymous author of a series of commentaries on Paul's Letters once attributed to Ambrose, writes, "Christ was made poor because God deigned to be born as a man, humbling the power of his might so that he might obtain for man the riches of divinity and thus share in the divine nature" (Ambrosiaster, *Commentary on Paul's Epistles* 3.259).

The mention of "the Lord" in 2 Cor. 8:21 is allusive insofar as the reference is found within a biblical passage. Paul echoes the language of Prov. 3:4. Because the Scripture speaks of the Lord (*kyrios*), the title that he normally uses for Jesus, Paul is able to use the biblical passage in reference to Christ. Paul often employs the Scriptures in this way.

Verses 19 and 23 speak about Christ's glory as "the glory of the Lord" in verse 19 and "the glory of Christ" in verse 23. Attentive to the glory of the one whom he acknowledges to be Lord, Paul willingly administers the collection, and then he uses the somewhat enigmatic "glory of Christ" in praise of the unnamed delegates whom he is sending to Corinth.

Within the extant Pauline correspondence, only 2 Corinthians speaks about the glory of Christ. Paul's use of "glory" in reference to Christ is an acknowledgment of his exalted status since "glory" properly belongs to God. Indeed, in the OT "glory" commonly evokes the idea of a theophany. The divine glory is reflected on the face of Jesus Christ (4:6). Hence, Paul can write about the glory of the Lord, in reference to Christ, thereby intimating the divine origin of the glory of Christ (3:18; see 1 Cor. 2:8). The reflection of the glory of God on Christ is so overwhelming that at the present we can experience it only as if in a mirror. We experience but a reflection of the reflection of God's glory.

Paul's gospel is a proclamation of the glory of Christ (4:4), whom Paul immediately identifies as the image of God. Since the proclamation of the glory of Christ is the proclamation of the gospel, it is likely that the unnamed brothers of 8:23 are lauded for their work of proclaiming the gospel.

A Gracious Gift (charis)

The word *charis* is a refrain echoing throughout these two chapters (2 Cor. 8–9) dealing with the collection that Paul sponsors and administers (8:19, 20; see 9:3). The word appears seven times in chapter 8 (vv. 1, 4, 6, 7, 9, 16, 19) and three times in chapter 9 (vv. 8, 14, 15). The word is a characteristic part of Paul's vocabulary (see 1:2, 12, 15; 2:14; 4:15; 6:1; 12:9; 13:13), appearing in all of his letters as well as in all the deuteropauline letters that bear his name.

Typically, the word *charis* appears in the greetings of Paul's Letters (2 Cor. 1:2; Rom. 1:7; 1 Cor. 1:3; Gal. 1:3; Phil. 1:2; 1 Thess. 1:1; Philem. 3) and their final salutations (2 Cor. 13:13; Rom. 16:20, 24; 1 Cor. 16:23; Gal. 6:18; Phil. 4:23; 1 Thess. 5:28; Philem. 25). In these passages *charis* is generally translated as "grace." The term collectively describes the gifts that a benevolent God gives to his people. Paul also uses the term in short prayers of thanksgiving to God such as those in 2 Cor. 8:16 and 9:15 (see 2:14; Rom. 6:17; 7:25; 1 Cor. 15:57), where *charis* is appropriately rendered as "thanks."

In ordinary parlance, *charis* designates either a personal quality such as beauty, favor, or gratitude, or a gift given or received. As such, the term is appropriately used in reference to the gift that the churches of Macedonia and the church in Corinth will give to God's holy people in Jerusalem (see 1 Cor. 16:3). Thus "gift" seems to be the best rendering of the term in 8:19, but in 8:1, 6, and 7 *charis* is a comprehensive term designating the entire project of the collection, a project in which the Corinthians were previously involved (8:6) and are now urged to finish.

In his motivational piece about the willingness and generosity of the churches of Macedonia, Paul speaks of the project as "the grace of God" (8:1; see 1:12; 4:15; 6:1; 12:9). The work of the collection is ultimately God's project. It is the result of God's gift. God gave the Macedonians the desire and ability to participate in his project. The theological meaning of *charis* as the gift of God is not beyond Paul's purview as he talks about the collection as a *charis*, a "grace."

As Paul continues to write about the collection in chapter 9, he uses the term *charis* not only in a prayer formulary (9:15), but also in 9:8, 14. In these latter instances, Paul makes clear that *charis* is a gift of God. In 9:8 and perhaps in 9:14 as well, God's gift includes the material gifts that God has given to the Corinthians.

The theological sense of *charis* is most evident in 8:9, where Paul refers to the incarnation of our Lord Jesus Christ as a *charis*, as God's gracious gift. Christ himself is God's gift to believers. Rhetorically, Paul references the incarnation in metaphorical terms, as the one who was rich yet became poor for our sakes, to urge the Corinthians to emulate the generosity of Christ. Underlying Paul's use of the term *charis* is, however, another motivational factor. As God has graciously given to them, the Corinthians should graciously give to others. God's gift is requited in their generosity (see 9:8).

As a personal quality, *charis* connotes favor or goodwill. This connotation comes to the fore when Paul describes the Macedonians as begging for the grace (*tēn charin*) to participate in the project (8:4). They are begging Paul to permit them to participate. He would grant them a favor if he did so. The Greek of verse 4 might be translated literally as they "asked for the favor and participation in the service" to God's holy people. They asked for the favor of being allowed to participate in the collection. Paul's favor, his goodwill, his *charis*, is part of the bigger picture that Paul identifies as "the grace of God" (8:1), about which he wants his addressees to be informed.

The way Paul uses the term *charis* to cover all aspects of a seemingly mundane collection for the poor is a reminder that Paul considers the entire life of the believer to be the result of God's grace. Some aspects of the Christian life are more religious; some seem to be more spiritual and therefore clearer manifestations of the grace of God at work. Yet, for Paul, everything that the believer does is due to the grace of God at work.

2 Corinthians 9:1–15

A Further Appeal

Introductory Matters

Hans Dieter Betz's 1985 commentary on 2 Cor. 8–9 (the German translation appeared eight years later) was significant in many respects, not the least of which was that he studied the two chapters as substantial fragments of two separate administrative letters written by Paul to the church at Corinth.

The opening verse of chapter 9 is both introductory and transitional. "For concerning the service to the saints" begins with the formulaic "concerning" (*peri*; see 1 Cor. 7:1, 25; 8:1, 4; 12:1; 16:1, 12) and suggests that the author is taking up a new topic or responding, in sequence, to topics that have been raised in a letter that he has received.

On the other hand, the initial "for" (*gar*) indicates that the author is offering (further) explanation of something about which he has just written. Moreover, the language of the first few verses of chapter 9 reprises the vocabulary that Paul used in chapter 8. In verse 1 he writes about the service to the saints (*diakonia*, 8:4; see

8:19, 20). In verse 2 he writes about the Corinthians' goodwill (*prothymia*, 8:11, 12, 19), his boasting about them (*kauchaomai*, 8:24), and the effort of last year (*apo perusi*, 8:10). And in verse 3 he writes about his sending the brothers to them (*pempō tous adelphous*, 8:18, 22).

These elements of close connection make the preterition of 9:1 difficult to understand. How can he say that there is no need to write about the collection when he has already said so much about it?

Tracing the Train of Thought

Concerning the Delegation (9:1–5)

9:1–5. Paul begins with a classic figure of speech, preterition. **For, to be sure, it is superfluous for me to write to you about the service to the saints** (9:1). By saying that there is really no need to write about the service to the saints, Paul draws attention to the project and emphasizes its importance. The order of Paul's Greek text is such that he announces the topic (cf. 1 Cor. 16:1) before he says that there is no need to write about it. The initial "for" suggests that what Paul is about to do is to explain the service to the saints a little bit more. Paul's use of the Greek particle is virtually antithetical to the preterition that follows. In any case Paul draws attention to the topic at hand, the service of the saints, both by the classic fashion in which he announces the topic and his use of the rhetorical device of preterition. In context "it is superfluous for me to write to you" really literally means that there is no need to write anything more, but Paul does so anyway.

For, says Paul, explaining why he does not need to write, **I know your goodwill, with regard to which I boast about you to the Macedonians** (9:2). Paul has told the Corinthians that he has been boasting about them to Titus and

---

Preterition

From the Latin *praeteritio*, preterition (also known as paralipsis, from the Greek *paraleipsis*) is a rhetorical device in which an author or orator states that he is going to pass over a subject but ends up discussing and thus emphasizing the very subject he said he would not mention. The language of preterition is performative: an author who claims not to need to mention something actually brings up that very topic.

Paul uses the device for the sake of emphasis in 2 Cor. 9:1; 1 Thess. 1:8; 5:1; and Philem. 19. Use of the figure of speech continues to the present day as, for instance, when a person says, "I don't have to tell you that . . ." or "There's no need to talk about this, but . . ." Saying that there is no need to mention something is a way to mention the topic and draw attention to it.

the other members of the delegation (7:4, 14). Now he tells them that he is also boasting about them to believers in Macedonia, where he is presently located (9:2–5). Specifically, he is boasting about the Corinthians' goodwill, a noble trait that Paul mentions only with regard to the Corinthians (see *prothymia* also in 8:11, 12, 19). The term, notes Spicq (*TLNT* 2:181), suggests fervor, enthusiasm, and generosity. Paul capitalizes on the nuances of the term to tell the Corinthians that he is telling the Macedonians **that Achaia was ready last year** (see 8:10). They have been ready to participate in the collection for a year. Paul flatters the Corinthians (see 1:1) by subtly naming the province of which Corinth was the political and commercial center.

Your zeal, evidenced by the Corinthians' readiness about which Paul has bragged, **motivated most of them**. Paul was enough of a realist to recognize that not everyone who belonged to one of the churches of Macedonia was moved to participate in the collection, but most of them did. Paul knew how to motivate people. He bragged about the Corinthians to incite the generosity of the Macedonians. Now he boasts about the Macedonians' willingness and almost extravagant generosity to encourage the Corinthians' generous participation in the collection. He plays the pride of one community over and against the other.

Ever confident of the Corinthians' generosity, Paul writes, **I sent the brothers lest our boasting about you in regard to this prove to be empty** (9:3a). Paul's sending the three-member delegation is all that remained to be done in order to give the Corinthians opportunity to prove their generosity and the accuracy of Paul's boast about them, his actual pride in them. **So that—since I had said that you were prepared—in case [some] Macedonians come with me and find you unprepared, we be put to shame in regard to this undertaking** (9:3b–4). Paul is especially concerned that he might lose face in the sight of the Macedonians if any of them come with him on his next visit to Corinth and find that the Corinthians have not responded generously to his appeal for their participation in the collection. So Paul sends the delegation as an advance team to make sure that the project is well under way by the time he arrives. Paul is well aware that a successful collection is one that takes place over time (see 1 Cor. 16:1–4), so he is very much concerned that the Corinthians prepare for the collection before his visit.

For Paul, this is a matter of his apostolic honor. In the Greco-Roman world, honor (*timē*) and shame (*aischynē*) were among the most important social realities and significant motivational values. Paul would be shamed in the eyes of the Macedonians if the Corinthians do not respond generously to the appeal of the one who is their apostle (1 Cor. 9:2). His shame would be compounded because he bragged so much about the Corinthians, as he recalls in an aside that complicates the grammar of this complex sentence. That Paul puts his apostolic honor on the line adds yet another element to the multilayered rhetoric of his appeal.

To uphold his honor, **it was therefore necessary for me to urge the brothers to go on ahead of me and prepare the promised gift in advance** (9:5). "Therefore" shows that Paul has arrived at his conclusion. The task entrusted to the delegation is that they get the promised gift ready before Paul's arrival. Paul expects the Corinthians' contribution to the collection to be generous. He uses a new term to speak about the collection. He calls the Corinthians' expected gift a *eulogia*, a term that usually means "blessing" but was sometimes used in Hellenistic Greek in reference to a bounteous gift (cf. 8:7). Paul reminds the Corinthians that they have already promised the gift. Since he has not previously drawn attention to their promise of a gift, it is most likely that he takes their previous participation in the collection as a sign that the work will be finished.

Lest they miss the nuance of Paul's saying that he expects the proceeds of the collection to be a generous gift, Paul repeats himself and draws attention to the nuance of the term. A pointed contrast underscores how generous he expects the Corinthians to be. He has sent the team **so that** [*houtōs*] **it** (the gift) **would be ready as** [*hōs*] **a generous gift** [*eulogian*] **and not as a miserly one** [*pleonexian*]. *Pleonexia* is an abstract term meaning "greed" or "avarice." Here an abstract is used for the concrete. A gift that comes from a giver who is ever attentive to the satisfaction of his/her own greed is miserly. Paul's thought echoes what he writes in 8:15, citing Exod. 16:18's warning against taking too much, hoarding for oneself.

Final Motivation (9:6–15)

9:6–15. The final argument in Paul's appeal focuses on the qualities of the Corinthians' gift as a generous donation (*eulogia*) and as given willingly. **Be aware of this,** he writes, **the one who sows sparingly also reaps sparingly; and the one who sows plentifully also reaps plentifully** (9:6). Paul exploits a proverb that expresses the perennial wisdom of the farmer. The harvest corresponds to what is sown. If good seed is sown, there will be harvest of good grain. If only a little seed is sown, the harvest will not be very abundant.

The proverb was widely used for rhetorical purposes. It appears in Gorgias, Aristotle, and Cicero, as well as in the book of Proverbs and *3 Baruch*. Because the proverb was so commonly used, it is hardly likely that the Corinthians would miss Paul's point in using it. The antithetical proverbs are so arranged that the emphasis lies on reaping, either disastrously or in abundance. The apostle cites the double proverb to encourage the Corinthians to be generous, but he does not immediately indicate what the Corinthians might expect in return for their generosity (see 8:14; cf. Deut. 15:10).

And, says Paul, **let each one [give] as had previously been decided in the heart, not reluctantly or under duress** (9:7). His Greek lacks the verb "give," but an exhortation to give needs to be supplied. In 1 Corinthians, Paul wrote about how much they should give (see 1 Cor. 16:2). "Previously decided" might

---

Sowing and Reaping

"You have sown shame and reaped misfortune." (Gorgias, as cited by Aristotle, *Rhet.* 3.3.4 [1406b])

"Those who have sown well, harvest well." (*3 Bar.* 15.2)

"Those that sow righteousness get a true reward." (Prov. 11:18b)

"Whoever sows injustice will reap calamity." (Prov. 22:8a)

---

refer to the decisions made on the occasion of Titus's previous visit; alternatively the verb could refer to decisions made on the arrival and initial plea of the delegation that he had sent. His point is that the Corinthians should willingly give as much as they have decided.

They should not give with a heavy heart or under pressure, perhaps not even the pressure of "keeping up with the Joneses." The language of Paul's exhortation echoes that of his contemporary, the Stoic philosopher Epictetus, who writes about the importance of free human decision and observes that not even the fear of death should compel a person (*Diatr.* 1.17.20–29).

Paul adds a maxim in support of his exhortation: **for God loves the cheerful giver.** The maxim is a proverb that echoes Prov. 22:8a LXX (not in MT), but Paul cites the maxim as a simple proverb rather than as a passage of Scripture. If he wished to acknowledge that the proverb was a passage of Scripture, he would use the customary "as it is written" (8:15; 9:9) to introduce the citation.

The proverb's mention of God (in 9:7c) brings God—strikingly absent from Paul's exhortation since the initial identification of the collection in Macedonia as a "grace of God" (8:1)—back into focus. **God has the power to make every grace abound in you** (9:8), Paul reminds the Corinthians. The affirmation has general significance, but in context the use of "grace" evokes either the gift (see 8:19) that the Corinthians are expected to give or the entire project (see 8:1, 6, 7). The theological affirmation subtly suggests that God will richly reward the Corinthians if they participate in the project.

So that, having enough of everything at all times and in every way, you abound in every good work, adds Paul as he elucidates the innuendo. Through the sequence of repeated *p* sounds in the Greek words *en panti pantote pasan autarkeian*, Paul uses alliteration to emphasize the greatness of God's gift, and the thrice-repeated "all" draws attention to the idea that God will equip the Corinthians for "every [*pan*] good work" (see 2 Tim. 3:17).

The implications of having enough (*pasan autarkeian*) should not be overlooked. Self-sufficiency (*autarkeia*; used by Paul only in 9:8; see Phil. 4:11) was a quality of life highly esteemed by the popular moralists of the day, Aristotle, Socrates, Plato, Marcus Aurelius, and Epictetus, among others. Self-sufficiency was a common topic in ethical discussion. For Paul, the only sufficiency that matters is the "self-sufficiency" that comes from God.

As it is written, "He scattered, he gave to the poor; his justice remains forever" (9:9, quoting Ps. 111:9 LXX [112:9 Eng., MT]). Paired with Ps. 110 LXX (111 Eng.), which speaks of God's righteousness, Ps. 111 (112 Eng.) is an extended beatitude that extols the blessings of the righteous person. Paul uses the passage in the way that the author of the psalm intended—not, as some authors contend, to speak about God, but to praise those who give generously. Their generosity is a good work that is made possible by the sufficiency that God has given them.

> ### Epictetus on Self-Sufficiency
>
> *"But one ought nonetheless to prepare for this also, that is, to be able to be self-sufficient, to be able to commune with oneself, even as Zeus communes with himself, . . . not to be in need of others."* (Diatr. 3.13.6–7)

Returning to the agricultural imagery of verse 6, Paul describes God as **the one who provides seed for the sower and bread for food** (9:10). As God provides seed for the sower, so he provides the Corinthians with the wherewithal to be able to come to the assistance of the Jerusalem poor. Paul's agricultural imagery echoes the language of Isa. 55:10–11, where God's word is compared to precipitation that comes down from heaven and does not return until it has accomplished its purpose, "giving seed to the sower and bread to the eater." The imagery of seed and the harvest (9:6, 10) allows Paul to describe God's benefaction to the Corinthians in crescendo fashion. God **will provide and will multiply your seed and will increase the fruits of your righteousness.** Paul does not use the proper name "God," but God, the giver of every grace, has been the unexpressed agent in Paul's reflection since verse 8.

The harvest that the Corinthians will reap is "the fruits of your righteousness." The expression comes from the book of Hosea, in a passage in which the prophet uses agricultural imagery to urge Israel to pursue righteousness. Having used the language of sowing and reaping in the first part

---

"He Scattered"

The literary genre of Ps. 111 (112 Eng.) is such that it refers to righteous persons by using a generic third-person masculine singular. I have retained the singular in my translation in order to preserve its gnomic character, not to restrict its applicability to one gender. The NRSV uses the plural "they" to capture the general applicability of the psalmist's words of praise. If I were to use "one who," as in my translation of the agricultural proverb, or "he or she" or "they," to render adequately the sense of the psalm, I would unduly complicate the translation of the psalm as an element in the development of Paul's rhetorical argument.

of the verse (Hosea 10:12a), the prophet concludes his exhortation with "seek the Lord till the fruits of justice come to you" (10:12b LXX, Brenton 1986).

Paul's use of the phrase "of your righteousness" can be differently interpreted. Is the genitive to be taken as a subjective genitive, so that Paul is talking about the results of "righteousness"? Or is he using a genitive of definition, so that Paul is saying that the harvest is righteousness? In the former case, "fruits" metaphorically describes the blessings that will accrue to the Corinthians as a result of their righteousness. In the end, the resolution of the grammatical issue does not bring about different understandings of what Paul is really saying.

The Corinthians' right relationship with God and God's people is manifest in their generous participation in the collection. The fruits of this righteousness are the material well-being (8:14) and the spiritual gifts that God will give them. Paul has already referred to many gifts that God gave to the Corinthians (8:7; 1 Cor. 1:5, 7) and to every grace that God gave (9:8). Now he says, **You are being enriched in every way for [your] every generosity** (9:11). The qualifying adjectives echo the "all/every" of verse 8. God's gifts to the Corinthians have enabled them to be generous. God is ultimately the enabler of the Corinthians' service to God's holy people in Jerusalem.

Describing the Corinthians' generosity as that **which produces thanksgiving to God through us,** Paul introduces the theme of thanksgiving, which will dominate the rest of the chapter. Thanksgiving will be offered by believers in Jerusalem, but Paul is the instrument of their thanksgiving since he is a key player in the organization of the collection and its delivery to Jerusalem.

The service of this public work not only satisfies the needs of the saints but also overflows into abundant thanksgiving to God (9:12) continues Paul's explanation. With a genitive of definition, Paul speaks of the collection as a "public work" (*leitourgia*). Religious connotations are not absent from Paul's use of this terminology to describe the collection since he describes the public work as resulting in thanksgiving to God and the glorification of God. Not only does the collection meet the needs of God's holy people in Jerusalem

---

A Public Work (*leitourgia*)

Leitourgia suggests an activity undertaken for the common good, the benefit of the greater society. The person in charge of distributing bread or grain to those in need was sometimes identified as a *leitourgos* in Hellenistic literature (see P.Oxy. 2925, 2941). The word group was occasionally used in a broader sense in reference to those who assisted the needy. Paul uses the vocabulary in this way to describe the work of Epaphroditus, who acts on behalf of Philippian believers to help Paul in various ways (see Phil. 2:25, 30).

As far back as Aristotle, the terminology sometimes enjoyed religious connotations. It is sometimes used in the Greek Bible in reference to the work of Levites (e.g., Num. 4:41).

Glorifying God

The participle *doxazontes* ("glorifying") belongs to the same word group as *doxa* ("glory"), whose use is a feature of NT doxologies, for example, the Pauline doxologies in Rom. 16:25; Gal. 1:5; and Phil. 4:20. In effect, Paul's use of the participle in 9:13 describes an activity that is a prayer of praise. But whose action is it?

In 2 Corinthians participles are frequently used in passages where the reader would normally expect a principal verb. Taking the place of the principal verb in the single forty-four word sentence of verses 13–14 is the participle *doxazontes*. The participle, used instead of a principal verb, makes it difficult for the commentator to ascertain who it is that Paul is talking about. Is he saying that the Corinthians are glorifying God, as I have suggested, or that Jerusalem believers are glorifying God?

It may be that the apostle's language is deliberately ambiguous, as it often seems to be in this letter. Many commentators and translators—Alfred Plummer (1915, 266) and Charles Kingsley Barrett (1973, 240), for example—think that Paul is continuing to reflect on the prayer of the holy people in Jerusalem; others (Lambrecht 2006, 145, 148; Matera 2003, 207, 210; Minor 2009, 178; NAB, NRSV) think that Paul is describing the church at Corinth. The 1984 edition of the NIV avoids the issue by translating the participial clause as "Men will praise God," which the 2011 NIV changes to the gender-neutral "others."

Located among references to the Corinthians' service, their evangelical obedience, and their generosity, the participle most likely refers to the Corinthians. The collection that they will undertake, if successful, is a way for them to glorify God.

(see 8:14); it also leads to much thanksgiving being offered to God. Paul emphasizes the immense outpouring of thanksgiving on the part of believers in Jerusalem in three ways: his use of the verb "overflow" (*perisseuousa*), the adjective "abundant" (*pollōn*), and the noun "thanksgiving" in the plural (*eucharistiōn*, lit., "thanksgivings").

There is also a theological dimension to the activity of participating in the collection itself: **Through the evidence of this service, you glorify God** (9:13). The Corinthians' generous participation in the collection, which redounds to the glory of God, is done **in obedience to your confession of the gospel of Christ and the sincerity of your fellowship with them** [*haplotēti tēs koinōnias eis autous*] **and with all.** Participation in the collection is an expression of faith. It results from the Corinthians' obedience to the gospel and their authentic fellowship community with other believers.

In each of his extant letters, Paul writes about the gospel, which he often identifies as "the gospel of Christ" (see 2:12; 10:14; Rom. 15:19; 1 Cor. 9:12; Gal. 1:7; Phil. 1:27; 1 Thess. 3:2), but the extant correspondence does not yield any other evidence of Paul's having used the word "confession." In the phrase "in obedience to your confession," "confession" is obedience and vice

---

Fellowship (*koinōnia*)

Koinōnia is an important term in Paul's theological lexicon (2 Cor. 6:14; 8:4; 9:13; 13:13; Rom. 15:26; 1 Cor. 1:9; 10:16 [2x]; Gal. 2:9; Phil. 1:5; 2:1; 3:10; Philem. 6), as are its cognates, the verb *koinōneō* (e.g., Rom. 15:27) and the adjective *koinōnos* (2 Cor. 1:7; 1 Cor. 10:18, 20), used substantively in 2 Cor. 8:23 and Philem. 17. Derived from the root *koino-*, meaning "common," the noun *koinōnia* is an abstract term. The term may connote a shared relationship among persons, thus yielding the translation "fellowship" or "community." Alternatively, the term might connote something that is shared in common. Hence come the translations "participation" or "sharing."

Most commentators and translators take the use of the term in 9:13 to have the latter sense. Accordingly, they render *koinōnia* as "sharing" (Harris 2005; NIV, NRSV) or "contribution" (Lambrecht 2006; REB). Consequently *haplotēti* is construed as "generosity," the connotation of the term in 8:2 and 9:11 (see Rom. 12:8). Interpreting Paul's phraseology in this fashion raises the question of the meaning of "and with all" (*kai eis pantas*). Jan Lambrecht considers it as a bolt out of the blue and writes, "Paul's horizon is suddenly broadening" (2006, 148).

Used of persons and personal relationships, the word *haplotēs* connotes sincerity and has this meaning in 1:12 and 11:3 (see Eph. 6:5; Col. 3:22). If *haplotēs* should be taken as "sincerity" and *koinōnia* as "fellowship," the addition of "and with all" makes full sense. Paul's ecclesiology often looks beyond the immediate horizon (1:1; 13:12; 1 Cor. 1:2; 16:19–20; Phil. 4:22; 1 Thess. 4:9–10). In this regard, Margaret E. Thrall (2000, 591) observes, "Perhaps Paul would intend the additional phrase to be seen as expressing praise of the Corinthians for their 'ecumenical' outlook."

---

versa. Paul is saying that the Corinthians' confession of faith is not merely a confession on the lips but a confession that also takes the form of action (cf. Gal. 5:6). This is the form that their obedience takes. Their confession of faith is embodied in their service to God's holy people. This service is a real expression of their fellowship with believers in Jerusalem and elsewhere.

Paul's reference to God's holy people in Jerusalem, to which he has appended the ecclesial note "and with all," leads the apostle to reflect on what he presumes will be the Jerusalemites' response to the Corinthians' generosity. **And in their prayer for you, they long for you because of the immeasurable gift of God to you** (9:14). As a result of God's gracious activity among the Corinthians, the Jerusalem believers' prayer will be one of thanksgiving (9:12), yet it will also be a prayer of petition for their Corinthian benefactors. Their longing for the Corinthians is expressed in their prayer. Since Paul has introduced the topic of the Corinthians' fellowship with God's holy people in Jerusalem, of which the collection is an expression, the prayerful longing of believers in Jerusalem can be seen as an expression of their fellowship with the Corinthians and, by implication, with the churches in Macedonia as well.

With his mention of the gift of God to the Corinthians, whose extravagance he has underscored by describing it as immeasurable, Paul has come full circle. He began the first part of his appeal by speaking about the gift of God to the churches of Macedonia (8:1). Now he speaks about the gift of God to the Corinthians (9:14). This gift is not only the economic wealth that God has afforded to the Corinthians, thus making their generosity to God's holy people in Jerusalem a possibility; it is also God's manifold gracious activity among the Corinthians, which is about to make their generosity a reality.

For all of this, Paul adds his own prayer of thanksgiving (see 8:16) to that of the believers in Jerusalem: **Thanks be to God for his indescribable bounty!** (9:15). With "indescribable bounty" Paul introduces new terminology into his appeal to the Corinthians. He does not otherwise use the word "indescribable" and does not use "bounty" in this letter apart from this one instance. "Bounty" does not so much connote the generous gift that will be brought to Jerusalem as it does the whole reality of salvation (see Rom. 5:15, 17; Eph. 3:7; 4:7), of which the Corinthians' service to God's holy people in Jerusalem is but one element. Words cannot be found that adequately describe God's wonderful gift of salvation.

Theological Issues

The Significance of the Collection

Paul's final words of thanksgiving place the collection for God's holy people in Jerusalem in the broadest possible context. It must be seen within the context of God's gift of salvation.

To ensure its success, Paul employs a number of rhetorical arguments. They run the gamut from the argument from *ēthos* to the argument from *logos* and include the argument from *pathos*. Paul's own honor is involved. He does not want to be ashamed. He does not want his boasting about the Corinthians shown to be without foundation. His logical arguments begin with his mention of the example of the Macedonians' and Christ's own self-inflicted poverty. He cites a well-known proverb and quotes Scripture. He uses Prov. 22:8a LXX simply as a proverb rather than as an argument with the authority of a scriptural text.

The argument from *pathos*, subtle at times, pervades his entire plea. Paul flatters the Corinthians by telling them repeatedly that he has boasted about them. He flatters them by saying how gifted they are and reminding them that they abound in good works. Paul talks about their generosity and the extravagance of their gift. Perhaps he appeals to a sense of competition as he speaks about the Macedonians. Cannot Achaia keep up with or perhaps outpace

Macedonia (see 8:8)? Paul appeals to the Corinthians' sense of honor as he reminds them that they have already begun the work. Finishing it will serve the Corinthians' own advantage. If the Corinthians fall into need, Jerusalem believers will help them out. And even now God's holy people in Jerusalem will pray for the Corinthians. And let the Corinthians not forget that God looks kindly on those who give generously!

Hyperbolic language pervades Paul's entire appeal. From the initial description of the situation of the Macedonians in 8:2—"In a great ordeal of affliction, their overflowing joy and their truly deep poverty flowed over into a richness of generosity on their part"—until he speaks about the incredible bounty of God in his final thanksgiving (9:15), Paul's language is enthusiastic.

Paul uses different terms to designate the collection. Each of them has its own nuance and contributes to our understanding of how Paul views the collection, yet it seems that "the service to the saints" (8:4; 9:1; cf. Rom. 15:25; 1 Cor. 16:1) is the name of the project. Repeatedly Paul uses the language of "service" to talk about the collection, either as a noun (*diakonia*, 2 Cor. 8:4; 9:1, 12, 13) or as a verb (*diakoneō*, 8:19, 20; Rom. 15:25). Paul is the administrator of this service (2 Cor. 8:19, 20), but he avoids any mention of the possibility of his taking the collection to Jerusalem (see Rom. 15:25; 1 Cor. 16:3–4), perhaps out of regard for the recently tense situation between himself and the church at Corinth. Nonetheless, he takes pains to organize the collection very carefully.

The people who will do the on-site collection are, to a person, well-respected individuals. Employing them to make the collection ensures the integrity of the project. The collection will begin before Paul's visit so that there is an adequate period of time in which to collect the monies (see 1 Cor. 16:2). Paul is also attentive to the amount to be given. Whatever is given must be given freely, without any coercion. The Corinthians must make a decision, but they should not put themselves into a situation of penury. Generosity is appropriate insofar as it is proportionate to what a person has (8:12). In 1 Corinthians Paul has told them to put aside whatever extra they have each week (1 Cor. 16:2). Paul does not repeat that language in the present missive. On the horizon is the example of the Macedonians, who gave beyond their means (8:3).

In Paul's view, the collection has ethical, ecclesial, christological, and theological dimensions. Ethically, at least some of the believers in Jerusalem are poor. In Rom. 15:26 Paul says that the collection taken up among the Macedonians and Achaians is for the benefit of the "poor among the saints at Jerusalem" (Rom. 15:26). The language that he uses there speaks of their dire poverty rather than mere need (2 Cor. 8:14; 9:12), as Paul describes their situation in this missive. Thus the collection is an act of Christian charity, an expression of the love that proceeds from the believer's faith. Indeed, Paul calls their participation a "proof of love" (8:24; see 8:8). Their participation in the collection is a sign of their righteousness (9:9–10).

Ecclesially, Paul exploits the idea that there is a wider community of believers who enjoy *koinōnia* with one another. Paul points to the unity among churches in citing the example of the Macedonians to the Corinthians. Their generosity will be an expression of their *koinōnia* with believers in Jerusalem and beyond. The Corinthians give evidence of this *koinōnia* by their generosity; God's holy people in Jerusalem give witness to it by their prayer. Paul's awareness of the wider community of believers is also evident in the way he speaks about the churches of Macedonia and the fashion in which he describes the members of the delegation as legates of the churches.

Identifying the recipients of the Corinthians' generosity as God's holy people, "saints," Paul uses language that he otherwise uses in reference to the Corinthians themselves (1:1; 13:12 [2x]; see 1 Cor. 1:1–2). Does this extended theological use of "saints" suggest that the Corinthians are aware that the language properly belongs to the mother church at Jerusalem, implicitly suggesting that the Corinthians' generosity is a recognition of their debt to Jerusalem? The question cannot be answered. In Rom. 15:27, Paul writes that it is appropriate that material gifts be given in response to spiritual benefits received. In that same passage of Romans, Paul implies that the collection plays a role in the relationship between Gentiles and Jews within the community of believers. These issues are not explicitly brought to the fore in 2 Corinthians.

The christological dimension of the collection is principally heard in the echo of the christological hymn of Phil. 2:5–11 in 2 Cor. 8:9. Paul offers the example of Christ—who was rich and became poor so that the Corinthians (and others) might become rich—to urge the relatively well-off Corinthians to come to the assistance of their fellow believers in Jerusalem, especially those in poverty. In 9:13, Paul notes that their generosity is an expression of their obedience to the gospel of Christ; in 8:5 he says that the Macedonians' response was a matter of their giving themselves to the Lord. Paul's observation about the gospel of Christ suggests in general fashion that the Corinthians' response to his plea is a manifestation of their Christian faith. Might Paul have something specific in mind, perhaps Christ's emptying himself for our sake (8:9; see Phil. 2:7) or even the love command (see Rom. 13:8)?

Ever solicitous for what is good in the Lord's eyes (2 Cor. 8:21), Paul says that he has gladly taken on the task of administering the collection for the glory of the Lord in 8:19. And, using an extraordinary turn of phrase, he praises those whom he has sent to Corinth as "the glory of Christ" (8:23), indicating thereby that what they are doing redounds to the glory of the Lord.

Paul's final prayer (9:15) puts the entire project into a theological perspective. He sees the collection as an element in God's incredible gift of salvation. The "grace of God" (8:2; 9:13) is a bookend-like phrase that draws attention to what the collection really is, God's gracious gift at work (see 9:8). The Macedonian churches responded to the will of God (8:5). Paul can give thanks to God because Titus is so willing to participate in the endeavor (8:16). God has been abundantly generous to the Corinthians (8:7; 9:8, 14), enabling them, spiritually and materially, to be able to take part in the collection. By their participation, the Corinthians glorify God (9:13), and God looks favorably on those who are generous (9:7). What can Paul say except "Thanks be to God for his indescribable bounty"?

PART 5

2 Corinthians
10:1–13:10

An Aggressive Taskmaster

Paul's appeal to the Corinthians that they participate generously in the collection on behalf of the saints in Jerusalem ends with a brief prayer of thanksgiving. Then Paul's tone changes once again. He echoes an apparent accusation against him to the effect that his letters are strong but that he himself is a sad figure.

Throughout this part of the letter, Paul defends himself vigorously, writing with a seemingly uncharacteristic harshness. Why does he do so? "You made me do it," says he in 12:11. The severity of this part of the letter seems out of place after Titus's report that things are going well in Corinth (7:5–16). Moreover, its tone contrasts sharply with the conciliatory tone of the defense that Paul has mounted in the first part of the letter (1:3–2:13) and the relatively mild defense of his ministry in 2:14–7:4.

Since the passage is but loosely connected to what precedes it and differs in tone from the rest of 2 Corinthians, many commentators hold that this and the following chapters (2 Cor. 10–13) were not originally part of the same Pauline epistolary effort as the rest of the letter. Even some who reject the various versions of a radical composite hypothesis (e.g., Barrett 1973; Furnish

193

2 Corinthians 10:1–13:10 in Context

The letter opening (1:1–2)

Ministerial crises (1:3–2:13)

Paul explains and defends his apostolic ministry (2:14–7:4)

The arrival and report of Titus (7:5–16)

Service to God's holy people (8:1–9:15)

▶ An aggressive taskmaster (10:1–13:10)

The letter closing (13:11–13)

1984) think that 2 Cor. 10–13 was originally part of a letter distinct from 2 Cor. 1–9. If 10:1–13:10 was written independently of the rest of the text, it could have been the apparently lost "letter of tears" (2:3–4, 9), as was suggested in the late nineteenth century by authors such as Adolf Hausrath (1870) and James H. Kennedy (1897; 1900).

2 Corinthians 10:1–18

Paul's Missionary Task

Introductory Matters

After Paul's reasoned appeal for the Corinthians to participate in the effort to aid believers in the mother church in Jerusalem, his letter takes on a new tone. As the new chapter begins, Paul draws attention to himself in a manner unparalleled in any other of his extant letters; this move is a first indication that what he is about to write represents a change in the way in which he has been writing to the Corinthians.

Barely has Paul begun what appears to be a hortatory exhortation when he breaks off the development of his thought to again talk about himself (10:1b). He is on the defensive and appears to be rather agitated. His thought switches from one subject to another. Several times he introduces an aside into the free-flowing exposition of his thought. Sometimes it is difficult to determine precisely what constitutes the aside and what is the principal thought that he is expressing. The syntax of some of his wording is difficult to decipher. And some of his vocabulary is unusual. Not only does the appearance of several hapax legomena punctuate the expression of his thought, but also the protracted images of warfare (10:3–6) and measurement (10:13–16) do not appear elsewhere in his correspondence. Paul makes a point of telling the Corinthians about what he has not done and about what he has no intention of doing (vv. 12a, 13a, 14a, 15a).

The agitation that shows through Paul's language appears to be due to the fact that he is responding to accusations that his rivals have leveled against him. Since we do not possess documentation to verify those accusations, we know about them only from what Paul has written and cannot identify the particulars of the accusations. Among them appear to be accusations that Paul has been acting in a merely human fashion (10:1–6), that in missionizing the Corinthians he has not really acted as an agent of Christ (10:7–8), that there is marked discrepancy between the tone of Paul's correspondence with the Corinthians and the way that he deals with them when he is present among them (10:9–11), and that he refuses to compare himself with his rivals (10:12–18). The implied accusation is that he knows he does not measure up to them.

In passing, Paul criticizes his opponents. He resorts to ad hominem arguments that are sometimes explicit but sometimes only implicit. Paul makes reference to their sophistry and alludes to their pride (vv. 4–5). He refers to their claim to be apostles of Christ (v. 7). They presume that they have courage and strength (implicit, argues Bultmann [1985, 183–92], in Paul's use of "dare" in v. 12a). They compare themselves to one another (v. 12a) rather than by the standards that God has established. Lacking in understanding, they are mindless (v. 12b). They intrude on another's territory (vv. 12–13). At bottom they are boastful and are engaged in self-commendation (vv. 13, 15, 18).

The heart of the passage is the central section, verses 7–11, where Paul reflects on the apostolic power and authority given to him by God. The surrounding passages, verses 1–6 and 12–18, use metaphorical language to talk about Paul's ministry, but they are just as much a critique of Paul's rivals as they are an exposition of Paul's ministry. Consequently, the chapter has a loosely constructed A-B-A′ structure. Its final two verses constitute a kind of rhetorical peroration in which Paul cites a scriptural maxim about boasting (vv. 17–18) that gives meaning to the entire passage.

Tracing the Train of Thought

Strategic Warfare (10:1–6)

10:1–6. This new section, loosely connected to the preceding material by the particle *de*, begins with Paul emphatically drawing attention to himself: **And I, Paul** [*autos de egō Paulos*], **appeal to you** (10:1). Paul uses a deictic first-person pronoun for emphasis. The use of the relative pronoun (*autos*) adds even further emphasis. And then Paul adds his own name, something that he rarely does in the body of his letters (see Gal. 5:2; 1 Thess. 2:18). It is clear that Paul wants to make an appeal to the Corinthians in his own name, perhaps distinguishing himself from the emissaries about whom he has been writing. Perhaps he even wants to leave his fellow evangelists out of what appears to be a cat-and-dog fight with the interlopers.

"Appeal to you" (*parakalō*) is a phrase that Paul typically uses to introduce moral exhortation (Rom. 12:1; 1 Thess. 4:1). He uses the formula to suggest that he is making a tactful appeal rather than commanding his correspondents or asking them to do something. The formula, especially as it appears in Hellenistic diplomatic letters, often suggests that the appeal is being made on the basis of an alien authority, the one making the appeal doing so on behalf of some other, unnamed but well-known, authority. This being so, Paul's emphasis on himself is truly unusual. Perhaps Paul is intimating that he really is qualified to speak on behalf of another, the other being God.

> ### Meekness and Gentleness
>
> "Boldness and arrogance and audacity are for those cursed by God; but graciousness and humility and gentleness are with those who are blessed by God." (1 Clem. 30.8)
>
> "Perhaps he sent him, as one might suppose, to rule by tyranny, fear, and terror? Certainly not! On the contrary, he sent him in gentleness and meekness, as a king might send a son who is a king." (Diogn. 7.3–4)

The apostle continues his thought by telling the Corinthians that he is appealing to them **because of the meekness and graciousness of Christ**. Paul's mention of such qualities of Christ is a rare occurrence in his letters. The pair of terms recurs in later but still early Christian texts. The terms describe a person who is kindly condescending but not overbearing. Paul rarely mentions the earthly Jesus in his letters, and here he identifies Jesus as "Christ," an epithet that normally points to Christ's death and resurrection. He appears to be telling the Corinthians that he is modeling his authoritative behavior toward them on that of the earthly and risen Lord Jesus.

Making this claim on his own behalf, Paul begins to think about how others perceive him, anticipating the self-defense that will follow in the next few chapters. Some in the community—undoubtedly the superapostles with whom Paul will contend and probably some members of the community as well—hold that there are two different modalities in Paul's relationship with the community. He is gentle enough while he is among them but harsh and demanding in his letters. I, he writes, **who am humble [*tapeinos*] when I am with you face-to-face [*kata prosōpon*] and bold [*tharrō*] toward you when not present [*apōn*]**. Paul considers humility to be a virtue, the opposite of haughtiness (Rom. 12:16). He has self-consciously acted in humble fashion when among

197

the Corinthians (2 Cor. 11:7). In his lowliness, Paul has been the beneficiary of God's goodness, expressed in the arrival of Titus (2 Cor. 7:6). Paul's humility is his way of putting on the meekness and graciousness of Christ.

On the other hand, when Paul is away from the Corinthians, he is bold toward them. This is, of course, a reference to the attitude that Paul evinces in his letters, specifically, in the letter that he wrote with tears (2:3–4, 9). Not only are presence (*parousia*) and absence (*apousia*) typical epistolary motifs (10:11), but the idea of presence and absence was also much in evidence the previous time that Paul referred to the sorrowful letter in this missive (7:8).

Paul always has a specific purpose in mind when he writes a letter. Recalling the boldness that some people in Corinth find in his letter(s), Paul says that he hopes it will not be necessary for him to be similarly frank and confrontational on the occasion of his next visit. **I beg you that when present** among you, **I need not be bold with the confidence that I count on to be courageous toward some who think that we are acting according to the flesh** (10:2). Buoyed up by Titus's report of the renewed esteem with which the Corinthians regard him (7:7–16), Paul does not want to be confrontational with the Corinthians. He wants to reserve that boldness to take on those who have been spreading false rumors about him.

Some accuse him of acting according to worldly standards, "walking according to the flesh," rather than according to the Spirit. For those who make that false accusation against Paul and his fellow missionaries—note the plural in Paul's account of the accusation—Paul is ready to act boldly and with confidence. Paul's confidence in God (3:4) is characteristic of his apostolic endeavors. From that confidence comes the courage that Paul will need and will show in dealing with his accusers.

Like some of the philosophical moralists who compared their doing verbal battle with their opponents to warfare, Paul says that he is about to do battle with his accusers. It may be that Paul was inspired by what the sage had noted in Prov. 21:22, "One wise person went up against a city of warriors and brought down the stronghold in which they trusted," but even John Chrysostom (*Hom. 2 Cor.* 21) noted that Paul prolonged the metaphor. He was ready to do battle, ready to wage war.

Acting in the flesh, Paul informs the Corinthians and cautions his accusers, **we do not wage war according to the flesh** (10:3). Paul and his companions are only human; their abilities are constrained by their human condition (*en sarki*). Nonetheless, they do not fight as ordinary humans do. **For our weapons for warfare are not fleshy [*sarkika*] by nature** (10:4). Theirs are not merely human weapons. This negative statement provides the background for, and allows Paul to make, an emphatic statement. **Rather** our weapons **are powerful because of God**. It is possible to take Paul's Greek as if he is saying that his weapons are powerful because they are used in God's service, but it is better to take his words as meaning that God enables Paul to use his armaments

The Military Metaphor

Paul's use of the military metaphor has a place within the rich and ancient tradition of philosophical discourse. Using agonistic language to describe his defense of the gospel (cf. 6:7), Paul employs the military motif in a way that is similar to how it is used in the writings of Cynics and Stoics. Cynics claimed that they had armaments received from the gods (e.g., Pseudo-Crates, *Epistles* 19, 23). They used the image of a city's fortifications against siege to describe the sage's rationale (see Malherbe 1989, 91–103). Paul's Jewish contemporary, Philo of Alexandria, similarly wrote about Justice as razing cities that those filled with self-love had fortified so as to menace the unhappy soul (*Confusion* 128–32). He mentions a stronghold and its destruction, using the very words employed by Paul in 10:4.

powerfully. The power of God contrasts with the weakness inherent in human existence. Empowered by God, Paul is ready for battle.

Roman armies followed a time-honored battle plan. Success in battle depended on success in all three stages of the battle plan: (1) demolishing fortifications; (2) taking prisoners; (3) punishing resistance. Paul's language is replete with military imagery, language that he does not otherwise use or rarely uses. He has talked about warfare. He may even have anticipated his use of the agonistic metaphor when he wrote about boldness (*tharrēsai*) and being courageous (*tolmēsai*) in verse 2. The former was sometimes used of a soldier's bravery in battle (Plutarch, *Them.* 8.2; *Tim.* 9.1), and the latter of military leaders who showed courage in battle (Plutarch, *Apoph. Lac.* 213C).

Paul follows the battle plan to a T. The powerful arms with which he fights are **for the destruction of strongholds**. The language that describes a fortified enclave occurs only here in Paul's extant correspondence. Paul immediately explains that he is using the term in a metaphorical sense. Reprising the language of destruction, he says, **We demolish sophistries and every barrier that rises up against the knowledge of God** (10:4c–5a). "We demolish" is in the form of a participle that has the force of an indicative, one of many such usages in 2 Corinthians. This participle is the first of three correlated participles employed by Paul in his exposition of the metaphor. Each of them pertains to a stage in Paul's and the Romans' battle plan.

The strongholds that Paul is about to demolish are sophistries (*logismous*, v. 4c). The term normally connotes a reasoned argument, but Paul uses the term with a negative connotation, as his explanation suggests. The intruders' specious arguments are a barrier erected against true knowledge of God. A "barrier" is an elevation (see Rom. 8:39). Evoking the militarily advantageous high ground, barriers metaphorically suggest the haughty attitude of the apostle's opponents. Paul's accusers do not know God as he has been revealed

---

Homoeoteleuton

The term "stronghold" (*ochyrōma*, v. 4b) properly belongs to the domain of military construction. It is one of three terms in this passage that have *ma* as their ending. "Barrier" (*hypsōma*, v. 5a) and "thought" (*noēma*, v. 5b) are the other two. Of the three, only "thought" is part of Paul's usual vocabulary. The apostle uses the term *noēma* almost exclusively in 2 Corinthians (2:11; 3:14; 4:4; 10:5; 11:3; cf. Phil. 4:7). Paul's use of terms with the same ending in relatively close proximity to one another is an example of the figure of speech known as homoeoteleuton, "similar ending."

---

in Christ. Paul aims to destroy the barriers that they have raised against the true knowledge of Christ.

Moving on to **We make captives of every thought** to bring it **to obedience to Christ,** Paul articulates the second part of the battle plan. The agonistic language of taking captives (cf. Rom. 7:23)—the second participle as Paul maps out his battle plan—gives way to plain language as Paul says that his goal is not to take prisoners; it is rather to subject every thought to obedience to Christ.

The third stage in the plan of battle is to wipe out residual resistance. A third participle appears when Paul writes, **We are ready to punish** [*ekdikēsai*] (elsewhere for Paul only in Rom. 12:19, quoting Deut. 32:35) **every** kind of **disobedience** (10:6). In a military campaign, mopping up pockets of resistance occurs after the basic conquest. In Paul's case, he will punish residual disobedience **once your obedience is complete,** that is, after the body of Corinthian believers is firmly entrenched in Christ's camp. "Every" is an all-inclusive adjective similar to the "every" that Paul uses to qualify "barrier" and "thought." He is looking for a complete victory in his war against his opponents. This is the kind of boldness that Paul is ready to demonstrate to the Corinthians, even if he hopes that it will not be necessary for him to do so.

A Warning (10:7–11)

10:7–11. Paul began to make an appeal to the Corinthians in 10:1. Then he abruptly interrupted his appeal to prepare his self-defense. Now, in verse 7 Paul initiates an exhortation that has a minatory tone: **Look at what you can see** [*ta kata prosōpon blepete*] (10:7). Ancient writers used the expression in the same way that Paul does (see Thucydides, *Peloponnesian War* 1.106; Xenophon, *Cyr.* 1.6.43). Look at what's in front of you, says Paul; face the facts.

If anyone is really confident that he belongs to Christ. The conditional clause appears to be a generalization, but it is probable that Paul has his adversaries, or perhaps a specific adversary, in mind. "Belong to Christ" means something more than just being a Christian. The letter gives no indication whatsoever that Paul's adversaries ever denied that he is a believer. The expression probably means something like "Christ's man," that is, a person who exercises authority in Christ's name.

Let that person seriously think again. Paul's words are equivalent to our mildly confrontational "think again." What that person should seriously ponder is **that just as that person belongs to Christ, so do we.** If someone or some group among Paul's opponents seriously thinks that they can claim apostolic authority for themselves, they should be aware that Paul and his fellow evangelists have no less a claim to wear the mantle of Christ's authority.

Paul has no doubt that he has a legitimate claim to apostolic authority and has made the decision to start boasting about that authority: **For if I boast excessively about the authority [*tēs exousias*] that the Lord has given to us** (10:8). The conditional clause is loaded. Authority is a major theme in chapter 10; Paul's boasting is a major theme in this fifth part of the letter. "Boast," used as a verb, appears seventeen times in chapters 10–12. The interaction of the players is also significant. Paul is the one who will boast, and he will do so even to excess. "The Lord" grants him the authority about which he will boast. The christological epithet "Lord" is to be taken seriously (cf. 13:10). It is not merely a way of referring to Christ. The term designates someone who has ultimate authority over another. That authority is "given to us." Paul will boast that the Lord has granted authority not only to him personally but also to those who are his coworkers in evangelization.

Every exercise of authority has its purpose. Paul is aware that the Lord has conferred authority upon the missionaries for a specific purpose, **for building you up, not for tearing you down.** Paul's military metaphor used language of destruction to describe the campaign he is about to wage. He was provided with arms for the destruction of strongholds. He was ready to demolish specious arguments. Now he says that this is not the real purpose of the power (*tēs exousias*) that the Lord has given him. The Greek noun *exousia* is generally translated as "authority" or "power." The connotation of the term is not raw power, which the Greek *dynamis* would indicate, but authority that has the power or capability to achieve its purpose. The weapons with which Paul was provided are capable of destroying sophistries constructed as strongholds against the truth.

But destruction is not the real purpose of the authority and power that God has given Paul. That authority was ultimately given for the purpose of building up the Corinthians, not for tearing them down. The antithesis, whose stress is on the negation, is used for emphasis (cf. Jer. 24:6). Paul wants the Corinthians to know that what he is doing is not for the sake of destruction; it is

Boasting

The verb *kauchaomai* occurs in 10:8, 13, 15, 16, 17 (2x); 11:12, 16, 18 (2x), 30 (2x); 12:1, 5 (2x), 6, 9. The noun *kauchēsis* appears in 11:10, 17.

Inclusio/Ring Construction

Ring construction, the literary device known to the ancients as *inclusio*, is a technique in which key words or expressions appear at the beginning and the end of a literary passage. Mathew's version of the Beatitudes is a well-known NT example (Matt. 5:3–10). The clause "for theirs is the kingdom of heaven" appears in the first and the eighth beatitude.

Ring construction is used for a double purpose. First, it delineates a discrete passage, generally part of a longer literary unit. Second, it draws attention to and emphasizes a key idea, often the theme, of the passage.

Paul uses the technique not only in this passage but also elsewhere in his letters. In the first paraenetic unit of 1 Thessalonians, the words "God," "holy," and "us" set off 1 Thess. 4:3–8 as a discrete literary unit. His letter to the Galatians is encompassed by the *adelphoi* ("brothers and sisters") that appears in Gal. 1:2 and 6:18.

rather that the Corinthians might be built up. The thought weighs so heavily on Paul that at the end of his letter he reprises language almost identical to that of verse 8: "This is why I am writing these things to you while I am away from you, that when I arrive, I will not have to deal severely with you according to the authority that the Lord gave me for building up, not for tearing down" (13:10). The related ideas that Paul's power and authority are for building up, not for tearing down, and that he doesn't want to act with severity when he arrives—these thoughts stand as a pair of bookends marking the beginning and the end of the fifth part of the letter.

If Paul boasts not about his own achievement but about the gift that the Lord has given to him, namely, the authority and power to build up the community, then, he says, **I shall not be put to shame** [*aischynthēsomai*]. Paul returns to talking about himself, as he did in verse 2. Boasting is something that he will do. It is usually shameful to boast, but if Paul boasts about God's gift to him (cf. v. 17), he will not be put to shame. The voice of the verb is a theological passive. If Paul boasts about God's gift, God will not put him to shame.

Verse 2 alluded to Paul's correspondence with the Corinthians; now he returns to the subject since he wants to set the Corinthians straight about his letters: **Lest I appear as frightening you with letters** (10:9). Paul declares that his purpose in writing to the Corinthians is not to frighten them.

Paul sets the stage for what he is about to say with an oblique reference to his accusers: for his **letters are weighty and strong indeed, they say, but his bodily presence is weak, his speech contemptible** (10:10). "They say" is virtually equivalent to "if someone says," as is made clear by the singular in verse 11, when Paul resumes his train of thought. The aside consists of a somewhat imbalanced sentence that contrasts letters as strong with physical presence and speech as weak.

Both physical presence and speech are contrasted with letters. The latter are weighty and strong; the former are respectively weak and contemptible. The double contrast is noteworthy. By definition, letters are a mode of communication of someone who is absent. In effect, presence is contrasted with absence, oral communication with written communication. Paul's unnamed interlocutor is described as saying that Paul's physical presence is feeble and weak while what he has to say is worthless. Only from afar, says the anonymous accuser, does Paul appear to be serious and strong. Perhaps Paul's stated meekness (v. 1) was an allusion to the kind of accusation leveled against him that is spelled out in fuller detail in the aside (v. 10). The accusation was serious. Physical appearance and rhetorical skill were highly valued in Hellenistic and Corinthian society. Paul was accused of being highly deficient on both counts.

The broad strokes of Paul's aside provide the setting for what Paul says next. He is willing to confront the accusers head-on. Paul denies that there is any difference between his written word and his spoken word in the quality of his communication. There is, he continues, no difference between how he

10:9 as an Interpreter's Challenge

Verse 9 is a negative purpose clause beginning with *hina mē*, "in order that not, lest." The challenge is to determine how it relates to its immediate context.

1. Has Paul omitted something like "I say this," so that the statement is elliptical (Barrett 1973; Thrall 2000)?
2. Should *hina* be taken as an imperative particle, so that Paul is saying, "I do not want to seem as if I were frightening you" (Lambrecht 2006; NRSV, NAB)?
3. Does the purpose clause qualify verse 8 as if Paul were suggesting that he is not exercising his God-given authority in such a way as to frighten people with his letters?
4. Does the clause relate to verse 11, with the result that verse 10 is a parenthetical remark (Matera 2003)?

The first and second interpretations imply that the purpose clause has the force of an independent statement. The third and fourth interpretations take the purpose clause as a true purpose clause. Admittedly, the verse is a true crux. Any interpretation is not without its difficulties. On balance, however, it seems that the verse should be taken as a purpose clause that is linked with verse 11, with the result that verse 10 ("for they say that [our] letters are weighty and strong, but his bodily presence is weak and his speech contemptible") is to be read as a parenthetical observation.

acts from afar and how he acts when present. **Let that person consider this** [*touto logizesthō*] (the expression used in v. 7), he writes, **that just as we are in word by letters when absent; so we are in deed when present** (10:11). The chiastic structure of Paul's Greek highlights the contrast between absence and presence, word and deed. But, says Paul, it doesn't matter. There is no inconsistency in the way that he relates to the Corinthians. Present or absent, he relates to them in exactly the same way.

Self-Commendation (10:12–18)

10:12–18. Paul has just mentioned (v. 8) his boasting about the power and authority that God has given him. Now he returns to the subject of boasting in the first of three passages in which he takes up the subject in some detail (see 11:18; 12:5–10). Given the similarity of vocabulary and theme between this passage and what he has written in verse 8, we should read verses 12–18 as Paul's commentary on verse 8. Kasper Ho-yee Wong (1998, 70, 72) sees the passage as containing the clue to Paul's foolish boasting (cf. Forbes 1986, 1). The passage is delineated as a discrete literary unit by means of the verb "commend," which appears in verse 12 and twice in verse 18—another instance of Paul's use of a literary inclusion.

Paul begins on the defensive: **Indeed we do not presume to class or compare ourselves with some of those who commend themselves** (10:12). Comparison was a rhetorical device, called *synkrisis*, often used by rhetoricians of old, but Paul says that he is not going to get into that game. He may have been accused of refusing to compare himself with the interlopers, but he adamantly refuses to do so. The interlopers, he suggests—at least some of them—are people who commend themselves, and Paul will have none of that. His refusal to get into the comparative argument is ultimately a denial of the fact that he is not on the same level as his antagonists. With this denial Paul begins an overview of things that he will not do. He will not boast beyond limits (vv. 13, 15). He will not overextend himself (v. 14). He will not boast about what others have done (v. 16).

In what appears to be yet another Pauline aside, the apostle turns to those who build themselves up with self-commendation. What they are doing is comparing themselves with one another, thus proving that

---

Paronomasia Once Again

Paul's "class or compare" (*enkrinai ē synkrinai*) ourselves is a classic example of paronomasia. Only the prefixed preposition distinguishes the two verbs, which are separated by a simple conjunction. Some commentators try to reflect Paul's use of the literary device in their translations. Thus Alfred Plummer (1915, 286) renders the Greek as "pair or compare" while Philip Edgcumbe Hughes (1962, 364) suggests "compete or compare." This figure of speech is sometimes used for the sake of irony, but Paul uses the device for the sake of emphasis in 10:12. It strengthens his use of rhetorical contrast.

A Textual Issue

The critical apparatus of Greek editions of the NT shows considerable variation in how the Greek of verses 12–13 is to be read. My translation follows the Greek that appears in NA²⁸/UBS⁴ and is generally reflected in most translations of the verse. A good number of Western witnesses omit the final two words of verse 12 and the first two words of verse 13: "They are not wise; we, however."

This shorter reading requires that the two participles of verse 12 describe Paul and his coevangelists, saying that they measure themselves and compare themselves with one another. Rudolf Bultmann (1985, 193), holding that this reading is consistent with Paul's presentation of himself as a fool, is one of the few modern scholars who opt for the shorter reading.

---

they are not very intelligent. **But, measuring themselves by one another and comparing themselves with one another, they are not wise.** Abruptly dismissing his adversaries in this manner, Paul in effect compares himself with them, as suggested by the adversative "but." They have their own standards: they measure themselves against one another.

"Measuring themselves" introduces the measurement motif that redounds throughout the passage. The interlopers have a self-contained system of measurement, but this is a foolish way to act. Paul's opponents are not wise. The language has a biblical ring. The psalmist and the prophets frequently describe those who do not "know" the Lord as being foolish (see, e.g., Pss. 14:1; 53:1).

Paul considers his opponents' practice of using one another as a standard by which to be measured as a form of self-commendation. Their boasting contrasts with Paul's practice. He begins his reflection on boasting—the verb *kauchaomai* ("boast") appears five times in this passage—with an emphatic denial: **We, however,** (an emphatic "we") **do not boast beyond measure** (10:13). He is not going to boast beyond the appointed limits.

Paronomasia comes into play once again as Paul takes up the topic of "measuring," which he has used regarding his adversaries in his descriptive aside. He says that he is not going to boast beyond measure (*ouk eis ta ametra*), using a noun that is not used elsewhere in the NT apart from 10:15. The verb "measure" (*metreō*) is a hapax in Paul's writing at 10:12. The related noun "measure" (*metron*) appears twice in 10:13, but Paul uses the term elsewhere only in Rom. 12:3. Thus the idea of standards of measurement is largely confined to 2 Cor. 10:12–18 in Paul's writings, but it is a key idea in this passage.

What are Paul's standards? Paul answers the question when he writes, **but we boast according to the measure, the standard of measurement [*tou kanonos . . . metrou*] that God has given to us.** Commentators universally note that Paul's wording is extremely difficult. Wanting to emphasize "measure," he places *metrou* at the end of the phrase. But what does he mean by "standard" (*tou kanonos*)? Paul uses the term three times in this passage (vv. 13, 15, 16) but only once elsewhere (Gal. 6:16). Paul's "standard" appears to be the area or territory that God has assigned to him. The interlopers have their standard: one another. Paul has his standard: the standard established by God.

The verb "give" (*emerisen*) basically means "divide, partition, or apportion." God has assigned Paul a particular area in which to exercise his apostolate. From the time of his Damascus experience, Paul knew that he was a missionary to the Gentiles (Gal. 1:16; cf. Acts 9:15; 26:17). The Greco-Roman city of Corinth fell within Paul's sphere of competence, so he adds **to reach as far as to you.** Corinth was included in Paul's territory. Paul confirms the idea by saying that he was not reaching beyond the divinely established boundaries when he went to Corinth: **For we are not overextending ourselves, as not being able to reach you** (10:14). Paul is an apostle to the Gentiles; hence, it is appropriate for him to be the apostle to the Corinthians (1 Cor. 9:2). On the other hand, the interlopers overextended themselves by acting as they did in Corinth. Since Paul does not use the verb "overextend" elsewhere in his correspondence, it is likely that he chose the word in order to direct a mild criticism toward his opponents, perhaps using the very terminology that they had used against him.

Paul's being the apostle to the Corinthians means that he was sent to evangelize the Corinthians. With **for even to you we came first with the gospel of Christ,** he states that he has accomplished his mission. Paul rarely uses the verb "come first" (see Rom. 9:31; Phil. 3:16; 1 Thess. 2:16; 4:15), a verb that sometimes means do something before others do it. Paul was well aware of his foundational role in having first preached the gospel to the Corinthians. In an earlier letter, he has used the image of someone who plants seed (1 Cor. 3:6) and the image of someone who lays a cornerstone (1 Cor. 3:10) to underscore his start-up role at Corinth.

Paul's initial visit to Corinth is in the past. What about the future? Although verse 15 is part of a relatively long—at least for Paul—sentence in Greek, it is best to consider it as expressing a new idea since it begins with a phrase that is parallel with a similar phrase in verse 13: **We are not boasting beyond measure about others' efforts** (10:15). Paul's participle ("boasting") is almost equivalent to an indicative, as is frequently the case in 2 Corinthians. What Paul considers to be out of bounds is boasting about others' efforts. In ordinary usage the noun (*kopos*) and its related verb (*kopiaō*) refer to hard and difficult work, or even trouble, and Paul uses the terms in this way. More often than not, however, Paul uses the terms in reference to the work of evangelization, either his own (1 Cor. 15:10; Gal. 4:11; Phil. 2:16; 1 Thess. 3:5) or that of others (1 Cor. 3:8; 15:58; 16:16; 1 Thess. 1:3). Use of the term suggests that the work of evangelization demands personal effort. In Rom. 15:20–21 Paul uses a passage from Isa. 52:15 to bolster his assertion that he does not build on someone else's work. He would like the interlopers to follow the same principle.

Corinth is part of Paul's assigned territory. He has hopes for the Corinthians and for himself: **but we hope that, as your faith increases, we will be greatly praised [*megalynthēnai*]** (cf. Phil. 1:20 and also Luke 1:46) **by you in accordance with our standards [*kata ton kanona hēmōn eis perisseian*]**. As the Corinthians' faith is deepened, probably to the point where it is no longer troubled by the intrusive efforts of Paul's rivals, he and his work will be more fully appreciated by the Corinthians. The praise by the Corinthians, their positive response to Paul's evangelization, is within the limits that God has established.

Adding **that we will proclaim the gospel beyond your borders** (10:16), Paul suggests that the deepening of the Corinthians' faith will allow him to think of further expansion of his apostolic efforts. **And not boast about what has been prepared in another's territory**, says Paul, implicitly comparing himself with those who have blatantly commended themselves as they have intruded into Paul's territory. He himself is not going to boast about or take advantage of others' efforts; rather, he is going to move on to virgin territory. He will be preaching the gospel where others have not preached.

Paul is not going to boast beyond acceptable limits. He is not going to boast about other missionaries' efforts. He is not going to boast about doing something in a territory that someone else has evangelized. What Paul will do is boast in the Lord in accordance with the scriptural maxim **"Let the one who boasts, boast in the Lord"** (10:17; Jer. 9:22–23 LXX [9:23–24 Eng.]). Paul previously used these words to criticize those who boast about their intellectual, social, and economic prowess (see 1 Cor. 1:31). Now he applies the words to himself, creating a kind of apostolic motto. Paul is willing to boast about the authority and power that the Lord has given to him (v. 8), but that is boasting about something that the Lord has done.

Paul then offers an explanatory observation. **For it is not the one who commends himself that is approved, but the one whom the Lord commends** (10:18). Paul's rivals have been engaged in self-commendation; that does not mean that they have measured up. The Lord's commendation is what matters. Those whom the Lord commends are those who are approved and tested. "The Lord" refers to God, as it does in verse 8 and in Paul's modified scriptural

---

Boast in the Lord

In 1 Cor. 1:31, the hortatory formula "Let the one who boasts, boast in the Lord" is introduced with a formal *lemma*, "as it is written," which identifies the exhortation as a passage of Scripture. However, the precise sequence of words does not actually appear in Scripture. It is likely that this is a pithy summary of Jer. 9:22–23 LXX, drawing from one of Paul's favorite books of the Bible. The prophetic text contains a criticism of those who boast in their wisdom, their might, and/or their wealth. Criticizing that sort of boasting, the prophet says, "Let those who boast boast in this, that they understand [*syniein*] and know me, that I am the Lord" (Jer. 9:23 LXX [9:24 Eng.]).

The verb *syniēmi* ("understand") was used by Paul in his dismissal of his adversaries as being foolish (2 Cor. 10:12), a likely indication that the scriptural maxim dominated Paul's thought as he was composing 10:12–18.

---

citation. Early on in his apostolate, Paul affirmed that he had indeed been approved and tested by God (see 1 Thess. 2:4).

Theological Issues

Paul's Authority

At the heart of Paul's self-defense is the assertion in verse 8 that the Lord God has given him authority for building up, not for tearing down. In the epistolary context of chapter 10, the phrase provides a neat contrast with Paul's use of military imagery that was to be used for tearing down (v. 4). While suitable in its context, Paul's description of the purpose of his authority is more than an obiter dictum. It is what defines his authority and provides *the* criterion for his use of apostolic authority.

Every exercise of apostolic authority is to be judged according to how it builds up. That this is so is evident when we consider that "authority which the Lord has given to me for building up and not for tearing down" is reiterated as the final word of this missive (13:10). The assertion is followed only by customary closing conventions (13:11–13). In 12:19, Paul tells the Corinthians, addressed as his beloved, that everything that he does is for the sake of building them up. He is telling them that he uses his apostolic authority to pursue the purpose for which it was given to him.

The noun "building up" (*oikodomē*) and the related verb "build up" (*oikodomeō*) are construction terms. The noun was used in ancient times in reference to a structure, something that has been built, or to the act of building the structure. The verb means build something or have it built. Hardly ever were the terms used in a metaphorical sense in ancient literature. Paul, however, always uses the words, especially in the Corinthian correspondence, metaphorically. For Paul both the noun and the verb refer to the church. In Paul's vocabulary the words are not construction terms; they are ecclesial terms.

The church at Corinth is "God's building" (*theou oikodomē*, 1 Cor. 3:9), a building that belongs to God, a building that is constructed by means of the gifts that God has given, a building in which Paul's foundational role is to lay the cornerstone (3:10). The image is closely related to Paul's use of "house" or "house of God" in reference to the church. Paul's building up the Corinthians is a matter of preparing them as a community in which God can dwell. He is not alone in that endeavor. Although he uses the first-person singular when he writes about the authority that the Lord has given to him in 2 Cor. 13:10, in 10:8 he qualifies that authority as given to "us," using a plural pronoun.

Building up the church is an idea in Paul's correspondence with the Corinthians. Prophets are to use the gift of prophecy so that the church might be built up (lit., so that it might receive a "building up," *oikodomēn*, 1 Cor. 14:3, 5). Indeed, he exhorts the Corinthians to seek after charisms (*charismata*) in order to build up the church (14:12) and urges that everything "be done for building up" (14:26).

When Paul says in 2 Cor. 10:8 and again in 13:10 that the authority the Lord has given him is an authority to build up and not to tear down, he may well be hurling a subtle accusation at the interlopers. What they are doing is tearing down the church of God at Corinth, not building it up.

Paul's self-defense contains an important observation about the use of power and authority in the church of God. Authority within the church is not given so that pastors and other leaders can lord it over the faith of the flock (1:24), telling them exactly what they should do and should not do and demanding loyalty and obedience from them. Rather, a church leader's sole authority is to be used in building up the community as the church of God, a community of faith, loyal to Christ, and following the example of Jesus.

2 Corinthians 11:1–15

On the Attack

Introductory Matters

The impassioned language of 10:1–18 continues and intensifies in 11:1–15, but the focus is different. In the previous chapter, Paul has been on the defensive, responding to various objections that the interlopers have raised against Paul's conduct of his ministry. That gave Paul the opportunity to write about his ministry, defining the parameters within which he would preach the gospel.

In 11:1–15 Paul continues to defend himself against the accusations brought against him, particularly his lack of rhetorical skill (11:5–6) and his financial independence from the Corinthians, which was construed as a lack of trust in or lack of love for the Corinthian community. The tone of this unit is different from the tone of 10:1–18. Now Paul is on the attack. He engages in ad hominem argumentation. He accuses the interlopers into the church of God at Corinth of introducing a different Jesus, a different spirit, and a different gospel into the community. Paul does not hesitate to resort to name-calling. The tactic includes coining new terms like "superapostles" (v. 5) and "pseudo-apostles" (v. 13) to describe the status of the interlopers. He compares them with the serpent of Gen. 3 (v. 3) and calls them servants of Satan (v. 15). He says that they are preachers full of guile, who have only disguised themselves as apostles of Christ. They have tried to pass themselves off on the Corinthians as being something they are not.

The passion of Paul's attack is evident in the number of hapax legomena. Words and phrases that are not otherwise used by Paul, some of which do not appear elsewhere in the NT or even in the entire Bible, mark this passage.

Paul's impassioned tone is also evident in the mild oaths that appear in verses 10–11: "The truth of Christ is in me"; "God knows." There is little doubt that it is an angry apostle who has written these verses.

The passage has an A-B-B′-A′ structure. The central sections, B (vv. 5–6) and B′ (vv. 7–12), contain Paul's rebuttal of two accusations made against the way he has conducted his ministry, namely, that his rhetorical skills are inferior (vv. 5–6) and that his failure to receive support from the Corinthians is offensive (vv. 7–12). Reading between the lines, Paul is taking on the interlopers, who claim superior oratorical skill and are quite content to be supported by the Corinthian community.

The encompassing sections, A (vv. 1–4) and A′ (vv. 13–15), correspond to one another. Both refer to the serpent/ Satan (vv. 3, 14), deception/falsehood (vv. 3, 13–15), and the interlopers. Particularly noteworthy in Paul's references to Satan is the similarity between what he says and descriptions of Satan's tempting Eve in Jewish apocalyptic literature contemporary with Paul, *The Life of Adam and Eve* and the *Apocalypse of Moses*. Similarities between Paul's Letters and these two works are not elsewhere evident in the extant Pauline correspondence.

> **2 Corinthians 11:1–15 in the Rhetorical Flow**
>
> **The letter opening (1:1–2)**
>
> **Ministerial crises (1:3–2:13)**
>
> **Paul explains and defends his apostolic ministry (2:14–7:4)**
>
> **The arrival and report of Titus (7:5–16)**
>
> **Service to God's holy people (8:1–9:15)**
>
> **An aggressive taskmaster (10:1–13:10)**
>
>   Paul's missionary task (10:1–18)
>
> ▶On the attack (11:1–15)
>
>   The Corinthians' betrothal (11:1–4)
>
>   Paul is not inferior to the super-apostles (11:5–6)
>
>   The gospel for free (11:7–12)
>
>   The pseudo-apostles (11:13–15)

A The Serpent and the Superapostles (vv. 1–4)
   B Response to an Accusation (vv. 5–6)
   B′ Response to an Accusation (vv. 7–12)
A′ Satan and the False Apostles (vv. 13–15)

Tracing the Train of Thought

The Corinthians' Betrothal (11:1–4)

11:1–4. Lest he give offense to anyone by what he is about to say, Paul expresses a wish: **Would that you put up with me, in a little bit of foolishness!** (11:1). What could be offensive is the foolishness that is about to flow from Paul's lips as he dictates to a scribe. Foolishness is a dominating motif in what

---

Paul's "Foolish" Language

Foolishness (*aphrosynē*):
11:1, 17, 21 (and in no
other place)
Foolish, fool (*aphrōn*):
11:16 (2x), 19; 12:6, 11;
Rom. 2:20; 1 Cor. 15:36
Be out of one's mind
(*paraphroneō*): 11:23
(hapax in the NT)

Paul dictates from 11:1 until 12:10. And then he says that the Corinthians themselves made him speak foolishly (12:11).

Paul's Greek construction suggests that his wish is unusual, perhaps unobtainable. However, the Corinthians have put up with interlopers who preach another Christ (v. 4). They put up with fools (v. 19). They have put up with all sorts of abuse (v. 20). So why shouldn't they put up with a little bit of foolishness on Paul's part? They should, and he tells them so: **Yes, put up with me.** Tolerating Paul in his foolishness appears to be a major theme in chapter 11. Paul employs the verb "tolerate," "put up with," in verses 1 (2x), 4, 19, 20 (cf. 1 Cor. 4:12).

Paul explains why he wants the Corinthians to put up with his foolishness: **For I am zealous for you with the zeal of God** (11:2). Paul's protective jealousy is personal—note the use of the first-person singular—and it is a divine jealousy. He explains why he is so jealous, writing, **for I have betrothed you to** only **one man, to present you as an unsullied virgin to Christ.** The metaphorical explanation reflects Jewish marriage customs. Betrothal of a woman to a man was arranged by their parents or the clan's elders. Once betrothed, the young woman belonged to her husband, but she was not yet introduced into her husband's home, nor did she have sexual relations with him. Any voluntary sexual intercourse of the betrothed woman with a man other than her husband was considered to be adultery (see Deut. 22:13–15). Her father assumed responsibility for protecting her virginity (see Sir. 42:9–10) until such

---

Grammatical Matters in 2 Cor. 11:1

Apart from the difficult construction (*ophelon aneichesthe mou*, "Would that you put up with me"), with a verb (*aneichesthe*) in the imperfect tense in Paul's expression of his wish, two other matters need resolution.

Does *mou* ("me") in the genitive serve as the object of the verb? Or does it qualify "a little bit of foolishness"? Since the pronoun recurs at the end of verse 1 as the object of the verb, it is best to take its appearance in the first part of the verse as having the same grammatical function that it has in the latter part of the verse. Thus, "Would that you put up with me!" rather than "Would that you put up with a little bit of my foolishness!"

Should the final "put up with" (*anechesthe*) be read as an indicative or as an imperative? It seems best to take the verb as a command. Paul wants the Corinthians to do something that they are not yet doing.

---

time as she moved into her husband's house, generally at least a year after the betrothal.

Paul's marital imagery recalls the biblical metaphor that describes Israel as Yahweh's spouse (Isa. 50; 54; Jer. 3; Ezek. 16; Hosea 1–3). His language reflects the two stages in the marital relationship. Paul considers himself to be the matchmaker in the spousal relationship between the Corinthian church and Christ. He initiated the marital relationship with Christ through his preaching of the gospel. He betrothed the Corinthian church to Christ for a purpose, that the church might one day be presented to Christ.

Church as Bride

Second Corinthians 11:2 is the first literary evidence of the use of the image of the church as the spouse of Christ in Christian tradition. The imagery reappears some time later and is developed in Eph. 5:25–27; Rev. 19:7–8; 21:2, 9; 22:17.

The Seduction of Eve

"Now the serpent [ho ophis] was more crafty than any other wild animal that the Lord God had made. . . . Then the Lord God said to the woman, 'What is this that you have done?' The woman said, 'The serpent tricked me [ho ophis ēpatēsen me], and I ate.'" (Gen. 3:1, 13 NRSV, LXX)

"Just as the serpent deluded [ho ophis exēpatēsen] Eve with his cunning, . . . Satan disguised himself [metaschēmatizetai] as an angel of light." (2 Cor. 11:3, 14)

"Who is the one who seduced Eve? . . . The impiety of their behavior unto perdition, Azazel himself." (Apoc. Ab. 23.1, 11; Origen identifies Azazel with Satan [cf. Cels. 6.3])

"Then Satan was angry and transformed himself into the brightness of angels and went away to the Tigris River to Eve and found her weeping. . . . 'Come out of the water, and I will lead you to the place where your food has been prepared.' Now when Eve heard this, she believed this and came out of the river." (L.A.E. 9.1; 9.5–10.1)

"The devil said to him [the serpent] . . . 'I will speak a word through your mouth by which you will be able to deceive him.' . . . Then Satan came in the form of an angel and sang hymns to God as the angels. And I saw him bending over the wall, like an angel. And he said to me, 'Are you Eve?' . . . He said these things, wishing in the end to entice and ruin me. . . . And I bent the branch toward the earth, took of the fruit, and ate." (Apoc. Mos. [L.A.E.] 16.5; 17.1–2; 19.1, 3 [100 BCE–200 CE])

"But the devil, not having found an opportunity with Adam, came to the Tigris River to Eve. Taking the form of an angel, he stood before her weeping. . . . Thus he deceived me, and I stepped out of the water." (Apoc. Mos. [L.A.E.] 29.15, 17)

213

Seduction

The verb *phtheirō*, which Paul uses to describe Satan's possible seduction of the Corinthians, was commonly used to mean lure or entice in the active voice, drift or go astray in the passive voice. In the ancient papyri, it appears in marriage contracts and was sometimes used in reference to the seduction of unmarried women.

Paul has a paternal responsibility to maintain the integrity of that relationship.

The betrothal period is an image of the eschatological situation of the Corinthian church. The church belongs to Christ, but its relationship with Christ has not yet been consummated; it is not yet fulfilled. The fulfillment of the relationship will come with the parousia. In the meantime, Paul feels obliged to protect the purity of the church. He is jealous lest anyone interfere with the integrity of the Corinthian church's relationship with Christ.

Paul's jealousy is not unfounded. Biblical lore tells the story of a woman who belonged to God but was seduced by someone else. **For I am fearful lest, just as the serpent deluded [*ho ophis exēpatēsen*] Eve with his cunning, your minds be seduced away from pure devotion to Christ** (11:3). This is the only time in the extant correspondence that Paul mentions Eve. His allusion to the Genesis story of her seduction by the serpent (Gen. 3:1–13, 20) is of a piece with the use of the tale in Jewish haggadah (*Apoc. Ab.* 23; *L.A.E.* 9–11; cf. 1 Tim. 2:14).

Paul's words allude to Eve's answer to the Lord God, "The serpent tricked me [*ho ophis ēpatēsen me*], and I ate" (Gen. 3:13 LXX). Unlike his anonymous

---

Pure Devotion (*tēs haplotētos kai tēs hagnotētos*, "Devotion and Purity")

The manuscript tradition at 11:3 shows significant variety among the words *apo tēs haplotētos kai tēs hagnotētos*, "from devotion and purity." Some manuscripts, including the corrected Codex Sinaiticus (ℵ) and corrected Codex Claromontanus (D), have only the first noun, "devotion." Some, especially Latin patristic witnesses such as Ambrose and Augustine, read only the second noun. Some Western witnesses, such as the original reading of Codex Claromontanus, have the nouns in reverse order. The editorial committee for NA[28]/UBS[4] opted for the variant *apo tēs haplotētos [kai tēs hagnotētos]* (with the latter phrase in brackets to show its textual uncertainty) because of the importance of the ancient manuscript evidence ($\mathfrak{P}^{46}$, Vaticanus [B], and the original reading of Sinaiticus) and because it easily explains the origins of the other variants. "Purity" (*tēs hagnotētos*) recalls the spousal imagery of verse 2, where the community at Corinth is described as an "unsullied [*hagnēn*] virgin."

I take the pair of nouns as an example of Paul's use of hendiadys, a figure of speech in which two nouns are connected by the conjunction "and" (*kai*) to express a single idea. Hence my translation "pure devotion."

---

disciple who wrote 1 Tim. 2:14, Paul does not denigrate Eve. He simply affirms that she was deceived by the cunning serpent. Paul's words remind us that he himself has been accused of acting cunningly (2 Cor. 4:2).

With Wis. 2:24, Paul identifies Genesis's serpent with Satan (see Rev. 12:9), the very same Satan with whom Paul and his fellow missionaries are in a struggle (2:11), the same Satan who is the power behind the interlopers (11:14–15; cf. 1 Thess. 3:5). Paul's "deluded" prepares for what he is about to say. Satan—the implied agent in the seduction—is at work among the interlopers, who are tricking the Corinthians away from Christ. Paul is worried lest "your minds be seduced away from pure devotion to Christ." "Minds" (*noēmata*) refers to the whole human person, not simply a person's mental capacity.

Paul's anxiety lest the Corinthians be led astray from their single-hearted devotion to Christ is the reason why he told them to put up with him. A little bit of boldness on his part is the tactic that he is going to employ in order to ensure his objective: the Corinthians' fidelity to Christ. Paul argues that the Corinthians should have no difficulty in putting up with him, **for you put up with it easily enough when someone arrives and proclaims a different Jesus, whom we did not proclaim** (11:4). "Put up with it easily enough" is the point of Paul's emphasis. The phrase comes at the end of Paul's sentence after the three hypothetical situations that Paul urges the Corinthians to ponder.

Typically Paul uses "Jesus" in reference to the human Jesus. In no other place in his writings does he speak of Jesus without the honorific title "Christ" as the object of proclamation (the verb *kēryssō*; see 1:19; cf. 1 Cor. 1:23; 15:12). Paul's use of the name Jesus without further qualification may imply that the interlopers are proclaiming an exalted Christ, with little or no reference to his suffering and death. Paul proclaims Jesus as Lord (4:5), suggesting that total obedience to Jesus is necessary for those who accept Paul's gospel.

Switching from the third-person singular to the first-person plural and using a different adjective, Paul describes the situation of the Corinthians in a different way: **or if you receive another spirit that you did not receive, or if you accept another gospel that you did not accept.** Paul is fond of triads, but the three elements in the triad of verse 4—Jesus, spirit, and gospel—do not appear as a triad in any other of Paul's writings. They are obviously intertwined. One whose Jesus is different from the Jesus preached by Paul has accepted a gospel other than that preached by Paul (cf. Gal. 1:6–8). The spirit received is therefore different from the gift of the Spirit that accompanies the reception of Paul's gospel. That different spirit is not the Spirit of Jesus. The Corinthians put up with that. Why then shouldn't they put up with Paul?

Paul Is Not Inferior to the Superapostles (11:5–6)

11:5–6. The interlopers, who seem to pride themselves on their rhetorical skills, apparently chided Paul for having inferior rhetorical powers (cf. 11:6). Paul is not willing to admit that he is inferior to the interlopers, whom he styles as "superapostles." **For I think that I am in no way inferior to the superapostles** (11:5; cf. 12:11). The "superapostles" are not the leaders of the church in Jerusalem—James, Cephas, and John (Gal. 1:17–19; 2:9)—nor are they any others of the traditional Twelve. Neither are they any of the other preachers of the gospel whom Paul calls apostles. Rather, "superapostles" (*tōn hyperlian apostolōn*; only here and 12:11) appears to be a derogatory epithet that Paul has coined to describe the interlopers. They accuse Paul of inferiority; with his accusatory epithet, Paul accuses them of pride (cf. 10:5).

And even if I am unskilled in speech (11:6), he writes, conceding that he lacks formal rhetorical training (cf. 1 Cor. 2:1, 4) and most likely also acknowledging the better rhetorical skills of the interlopers. Josephus (*Ant.* 2.271) used the same expression in reference to Moses, whose verbal skills were such that he had to make use of Aaron, his brother, to speak on his behalf. Notwithstanding his lack of rhetorical expertise, Paul's verbal adequacy is more than enough for the effective proclamation of the gospel. This is because **I am not lacking in knowledge.** Cynic philosophers used the contrast between speech and knowledge in their polemic against Sophists, but Paul raises the distinction to another level. He contrasts human rhetorical skills with the gift of knowledge that God has given to him (see 1 Cor. 12:8; 13:2; 14:6). With regard to this gift of the Spirit, Paul is not inferior to the superapostles. His assertion is an understatement; with regard to spiritual gifts, Paul is not merely on a par with the superapostles—he far exceeds them (see 12:1–5, 7).

The Corinthians should be aware of this for **we have made** this **clear to you in every way in all things.** Paul uses a participle, as he does so often in this letter, as a principal verb. It is flanked by the generalizing qualifiers "in every way . . . in all things," which suggest that the Corinthians should already be fully aware that Paul is not lacking in knowledge. Using a verb in the singular, "I think," Paul is speaking about himself in the first part of the verse. The participle's plural form suggests that Paul's fellow missionaries are associated with him in clarifying things for the Corinthians.

The Gospel for Free (11:7–12)

11:7–12. What! **Did I commit a sin because I humbled myself** (cf. 10:1) **so that you might be exalted because we preached the gospel of God to you without a fee?** (11:7). The context of Paul's speaking like this is that philosophers and other trained orators were sometimes supported by their patrons. They were, in effect, clients of their patrons. Paul prefers to support himself by working at his trade. The interlopers apparently consider this to be self-demeaning. For them, this is yet another example of Paul's weakness. Some may even have taken umbrage if Paul rejected the Corinthians' offer of financial support.

Paul's rhetorical question is sarcastic in tone. It begins with "What!" (*ē*) to show that Paul is about to make a forceful objection. Apart from the quotation of Ps. 31:2 LXX (32:2 Eng.) in Rom. 4:8, this is the only time Paul uses

---

The Gospel of God

More often than not, Paul uses the term "gospel" (*euangelion*) absolutely, without further qualification. Sometimes pronouns in the form of a subjective genitive indicate who the preachers are, thus "our" in 2 Cor. 4:3 and 1 Thess. 1:5; and "my" in Rom. 2:16 and 16:25 (cf. Gal. 1:11). Earlier in 2 Corinthians, Paul uses "Christ" as an objective genitive to say that the Christ event, his death and resurrection, is the content of the gospel (2:12; 9:13; 10:14; cf. 4:4; Rom. 1:9; 15:19; 1 Cor. 9:12; Gal. 1:7; Phil. 1:27; 1 Thess. 3:2). When he writes about "the gospel of God," as he does in 11:7, Paul is saying that the content of the good news is what God has accomplished in the Christ event. The genitive *tou theou* is an objective rather than a subjective genitive (see Rom. 1:1; 15:16; 1 Thess. 2:2, 8, 9).

"sin" (*hamartia*) to connote an individual sin (cf. Rom. 14:23; see the sidebar "Sin" at 5:19). While one may speculate that Paul's "sin" is his lack of love (11:11) or that his manual labor violates the Lord's command (1 Cor. 9:14; Luke 10:7), it is more likely that Paul is speaking ironically. He concedes that he is lacking in rhetorical skill, but he does not concede that he has sinned in offering the gospel free of charge (*dōrean*; cf. Rom. 3:24).

He is, nonetheless, willing to assert that his manual labor is a kind of self-abasement. In addition to recognizing that some Corinthians might consider the exercise of his trade to be demeaning, servile labor, Paul may be thinking of Christ, who humbled himself (*etapeinōsen heauton*), only to be exalted by God (*hyperypsōsen*; see Phil. 2:8–9).

Using the rhetorical device of comparison, Paul observes that the reason for his own self-abasement was the exaltation (*hypsōtēte*) of Corinthian believers. Their exaltation was the result of their having received the gospel of God as a free gift. Paul's Greek is such that "freely" (*dōrean*) and "God" (*theou*) are side by side. "The gospel of God" is different from the "other gospel" preached by the interlopers (v. 4).

The apostle, who is not disinclined to use military language to speak about his preaching of the gospel (see 10:3–6), uses another military image to describe how he obtained the funds to support himself: **For I robbed other churches, taking booty in order to serve you** (11:8). Paul's ironical remark uses forceful language. His Greek uses a verb that from the time of Homer was used to describe the actions of soldiers profiting from their military exploits. Taking the weapons of captured or fallen enemies, despoiling the bodies of the fallen, and pillaging captured cities and towns—these were some of the denotations of the verb "rob" (*sylaō*; found only in 11:8 in the entire NT). Paul's "booty" (*opsōnion*) is a term that originally connoted a soldier's rations but had the extended meaning of military pay or reward (see 1 Cor. 9:7).

217

Figure 11. Spoils from the Jerusalem Temple. This relief from the Arch of Titus shows articles from the temple being carried in triumphal procession after the destruction of Jerusalem in 70 CE. In 11:8 Paul compares himself to a soldier taking booty, when he writes about his receiving support from other churches yet rejecting financial support from the Corinthians.

Paul's strong language, not devoid of hyperbole, is intended to show the Corinthians the lengths to which the apostle would go in order to be of service to them. His taking support from other churches while serving the Corinthians might be construed as a kind of injustice. After all, he was serving the Corinthians, not those from whom he was receiving support. Oddly enough, Paul says that he robbed other churches, in the plural. In Phil. 4:15–16, he protests that he received support only from the Philippians, who wanted to share in his distress.

The result of Paul's taking support from elsewhere was that **while I was present among you and in need, I burdened you in no way whatsoever** (11:9).

"Not a Burden"

In 2 Cor. 11:9 Paul uses a medical term, *katanarkaō* (an intransitive verb meaning "become numb"), to say that he was not and will not be a burden to the Corinthians. Among NT authors, Paul alone uses the term, which does not appear in any of the extant papyri. Unusual among Greek authors is Paul's use of it as a transitive verb and his giving it a metaphorical meaning. Paul reprises the expression, with the same meaning in 12:13, 14.

Jerome (*Epist.* 121.10) suggests that the usage was regional, particular to Paul's native Cilicia. Chrysostom (*Hom. 2 Cor.* 23.5) and Theodoret (*2 Cor.* 343) assume that the verb is a synonym of *barynō* (see 1 Thess. 2:7, 9). A popular contemporary Greek translation of the NT, published in Athens in 2004, renders Paul's Greek with *epibaryna*, a verb derived from *barynō*. Toward the end of verse 9, Paul uses the related term *abarē* (*a-barē*; unused elsewhere in the Greek Scriptures) to describe his not being a burden.

While present among the Corinthians, Paul was in a situation of poverty (6:10; cf. 6:5; 11:27), a condition to which he was no stranger (see Phil. 4:12). Nonetheless, he chose not to burden those whom he evangelized.

Paul received support from Philippi and probably others in the Macedonian region; **for brothers coming from Macedonia fulfilled my needs.** Generous Macedonians (see 8:1–2; 9) helped Paul out. Paul's choice of verb (*prosaneplērōsan*, "fill up"; cf. 9:12) suggests that what the Macedonians contributed supplemented the meager income that he obtained as a result of his leatherwork. So, **I kept myself from being burdensome to you in every way, and I will continue to do so.** The generalizing "in every way" corresponds to the "in no way whatsoever" earlier in the verse. There was absolutely no way that Paul was going to impose on the Corinthians.

> **Theodoret of Cyr**
>
> *"This is the greatest condemnation of the Corinthians imaginable. For, while he was benefiting them, Paul was being funded by others elsewhere."* (2 Cor. 343)

Paul confirms his financial independence from the Corinthians, with a mild oath: **The truth of Christ is in me** (11:10). Oaths such as this occasionally punctuate Paul's Letters. Paul tells the truth as he sees it. In similar fashion, he says in Rom. 9:1 that "I am speaking the truth in Christ—I am not lying." Similarly he proclaims that God is faithful (2 Cor. 1:18; 1 Cor. 1:9; 10:13; cf. 1 Thess. 5:24) or that God is his witness (2 Cor. 1:23; Rom. 1:9; Phil. 1:8; 1 Thess. 2:5). "God knows that I do" (2 Cor. 11:11) functions in much the same way (cf. 11:31; 12:2, 3). The oath affirms, with some solemnity, the truth of what Paul is saying.

Paul's mild oath underscores the idea that he has no intention of forgoing his practice of not accepting financial support from the Corinthians, something about which he is willing to boast. **This boasting,** he says, **will not be silenced in me in the regions of Achaia.** I am going to continue with my boasting. I am not going to shut up about the fact that I do not take money for preaching the

---

Brothers from Macedonia

The brothers (*adelphoi*) coming from Macedonia are those who brought financial support to Paul, much in the same way that Epaphroditus was the emissary of the Philippian community in rendering assistance to Paul (Phil. 2:25; 4:18). My use of the masculine plural "brothers" to render the Greek *adelphoi* suggests that the Macedonian emissaries were probably a small group of men. The translation does not imply that men only were the source of Paul's support. In Rom. 16:2, Paul acknowledges that the deacon Phoebe was his patron.

gospel. Paul's mention of the Roman province of Achaia, of which Corinth is the capital, recalls his earlier reflection on boasting within appropriate limits (10:12–18). That he brings up his boasting once again prepares for what Margaret E. Thrall (2000, 707) calls Paul's "boasting project." From 11:16 onward, boasting becomes a dominant theme in what Paul is writing.

Some may take umbrage at the fact that Paul does not accept financial support from the Corinthians, counting it as an indication that he does not love them. Perhaps some feel that the apostle does not trust them because he refuses to accept their financial support. Yet if he had done so, he would have had a client relationship with them and would have been, according to dominant social practice, beholden to them, his patrons. The apostle meets the objection head-on: **Why? Because I don't love you? God knows** that I do (11:11). If there is any community for which Paul expresses his love, it is the church at Corinth (2:4; 6:6; 7:1; 8:7; 12:15, 19; cf. 1 Cor. 16:24). Paul's emotional language is a sign that he is offended by the suggestion that he does not love his beloved Corinthians.

Having dispatched the suggestion that he refused financial support because he does not love the Corinthians, Paul answers his rhetorical "why" by giving the real reason why in the present situation he wants to be financially independent. **I will continue to do what I am doing so that I might cut off an opportunity for those who are seeking an opportunity so that in their boasting they may be found just as we are** (11:12). Their boasting reveals their true selves. The interlopers would like to boast that Paul operates the same way that they do. Paul will have none of that. He is different from them. His financial independence from the Corinthians is one indication of the difference between him and them. Paul intends to make his behavior a criterion for theirs.

The Pseudo-Apostles (11:13–15)

11:13–15. Then, in what seems to be almost an angry outburst, Paul describes the interlopers. His earlier critique (11:3–4, 5) appears mild in comparison with what he now writes. Resorting to a type of name-calling that is characteristic

---

"Disguised Themselves"

The verb that Paul uses (*metaschēmatizō*) is one that is used by him alone among NT writers. Three of the five occurrences of the verb appear in 11:13–15, twice in reference to the false apostles and once in relation to Satan (cf. 1 Cor. 4:6; Phil. 3:21). Literally, the verb means "change the form of," but in this passage it has the meaning of "disguise." Josephus (*Ant.* 8.267) used the verb with the same connotation when he wrote about King Jeroboam's encouraging his wife to disguise herself by wearing a peasant's dress in order to trick the prophet Achias (Ahijah). God enabled the almost-blind prophet to see through the ruse.

of people in heated arguments, he writes, **For such people are pseudo-apostles, deceitful workers, who have disguised themselves as apostles of Christ** (11:13). "Pseudo-apostles" (*pseudapostoloi*; hapax in the NT) is probably of Pauline coinage and may be compared to his earlier description of them as "super-apostles" (11:5; cf. 12:11). They are deceitful workers. "Workers" is part of the Pauline vocabulary used to describe evangelists, but the interlopers are deceitful workers. The adjective suggests slyness and treachery. Paul's strongest accusation is that they have transformed themselves into something that they are not. They have disguised themselves as apostles of Christ.

It's no wonder! (11:14) underscores the idea that their trickery is to be expected. After all, **Satan disguises himself as an angel of light**. The idea that Satan appears in the form of an angel is found in a number of Jewish texts. For the most part, the precise date of the composition of these works is difficult to determine, but they come from the same era in which the apostle wrote. These texts not only speak about Satan's angelic disguise but also mention the serpent and the deception of Eve, as cited by Paul in 11:3.

If Satan is able to disguise himself as an angel of light, it is little wonder that his minions can also disguise themselves. Like master, like servants. **It's not a great thing, then, if his servants disguise themselves as servants of righteousness** (11:15). The last of the demeaning epithets that Paul hurls at the interlopers is that they are servants of Satan. These servants of Satan pawn themselves off as servants of righteousness. Paul and his fellow missionaries are servants of God (*theou diakonoi*, 6:4). The intruders are servants of Satan, and Satan is Paul's ultimate opponent (cf. 2:11; 12:7).

Paul concludes his description of the deceptive interlopers with an affirmation of eschatological judgment: **Their end [*to telos*] will be according to their works** (see Rom. 2:6; Phil. 3:19; cf. Rom. 12:19, with its reference to Deut. 32:35; 1 Cor. 3:12–15; 4:4). In 5:10 Paul declares that everyone must appear before the judgment seat of Christ, to be judged on the basis of their good or evil behavior. Now he affirms that judgment will be brought to bear on those who have intruded into his territory and preached a gospel other than the one that he preached.

Theological Issues

Paul's Financial Independence

From the outset of his ministry Paul preferred to be self-employed, toiling at his leatherworker's trade, so that he can preach the gospel free of charge and not be a financial burden to those to whom he preaches (cf. 1 Thess. 2:9). Luke's story of the Pauline mission recounts that during the second missionary voyage, Paul came to Corinth, where he met Aquila, a fellow Jew, and his wife, Priscilla. Paul stayed with them, and "they worked together—by trade they

Figure 12. The Corinthian Agora. In Paul's day, this street was lined with shops selling goods and services, including items made of leather such as Paul made.

were tentmakers" (Acts 18:3). "Tentmakers" may be a restrictive translation. The trio were most likely leatherworkers.

Paul worked for a living instead of receiving compensation from those to whom he preached (1 Cor. 9:6–7). The work was hard and not well paid. Paul tells the Corinthians that he grew weary as a result of his manual labor (1 Cor. 4:12). Two of the lists of hardships in 2 Corinthians mention Paul's hard work and toil (6:5; 11:27). Indeed he introduces his long catalog of hardships with a mention of his far greater labor (11:23). The vocabulary that he uses to speak of his work shows that it was really hard work. And it was not well paid. Lucian speaks about the difficulties that artisans had in making ends meet. They often did not make enough to eat properly (cf. Lucian, *Gall.* 1; *Cat.* 20; *Sat.* 20). Paul recognizes that he has nothing (6:10; cf. Phil. 4:11) and sometimes nothing to eat (6:5; 11:27).

Despite the hardship entailed in exercising his leatherworker's trade, Paul wanted to work. Undoubtedly part of his determination to work was due to his Jewish heritage. In the light of Gen. 1:28, a man's exercise of a trade was very important in Jewish tradition. Later tradition underscored a father's responsibility not only to find a wife for his son but also to teach his son a trade (*m. 'Abot* 4.5; *t. Qidd.* 1.11). Rabbis exercised a trade, concerning which the great rabbi Gamaliel said, "Excellent is the study of the Law together with worldly occupation" (*m. 'Abot* 2.2). Jesus, like Joseph his father, was a carpenter (Matt. 13:55; Mark 6:3).

Another factor in Paul's decision to work was undoubtedly the opportunities for evangelization that it provided. In 1 Thess. 2:9 Paul intimates that he preached while he worked. A leatherworker's shop located on the agora, the marketplace, afforded a place to meet people. Paul could have spoken about Jesus while he worked. Those who visited the shop would include not only the locals but also visitors who came in to have their sandals and, less frequently, their tents repaired.

Paul's working at his trade distinguished him from many of the teachers of his day. Although some philosophers, particularly among the Stoics and the Cynics, supported themselves by working or by begging, most did not. Philosophers and other trained orators were sometimes supported by their patrons. At other times they were paid on an ad hoc basis. This financial arrangement was society's way of recognizing their value.

As in Thessalonica, so in Corinth, Paul was determined that he was not going to be a burden on those to whom he preached. Rarely did he accept any gifts; indeed, apparently only from the Philippians would he accept any financial help (2 Cor. 11:9; Phil. 4:15–16), but it is unlikely that he did so while he was in Philippi.

The interlopers of 2 Corinthians apparently consider Paul's manual labor to be self-demeaning, affirming that any worthwhile orator would receive compensation for what he has to say. To the affluent and free citizens of Corinth, Paul's work as an artisan has the appearance of his working as a slave (R. Hock 1980, 60). Paul is willing to concede that he is humbling himself in the eyes of the Corinthians (11:7; cf. 10:1), but this does not deter him from working so as not to impose a burden on them.

Some of them might even have been offended by Paul's refusal to accept a potential offer of financial support. This rejection might have been construed as a lack of appreciation, a lack of love for the Corinthians—something that Paul adamantly denies (11:11). Rejecting patronage and supporting himself, Paul was able to preach the gospel free of charge (11:7). As a good Jew, that was something he could be proud of. At bottom, there was a conflict of cultures. Beyond that, Paul was a servant of Christ. He chose not to be a client of the Corinthians.

2 Corinthians 11:16–12:13

Boasting like a Fool

Introductory Matters

In 1 Cor. 4:10, Paul says, "We are fools for the sake of Christ" (*mōroi dia Christon*). He compares himself to the Corinthians, of whom he says, "You are wise in Christ" (*phronimoi en Christō*). Continuing the comparison, Paul speaks of his being weak (*astheneis*) and in disrepute (*atimoi*). Thereupon follows a nine-item hardship catalog (1 Cor. 4:11–13).

Similar experiences are cited in the "fool's speech" of 2 Corinthians (11:21b–12:13). The speech takes a different tack from the way Paul describes himself as a fool in 1 Corinthians. In 2 Corinthians Paul does not explicitly compare himself with his addressees, as he did in the earlier letter; rather, he compares himself with the interlopers. At the beginning of the speech, the comparison is implicit. At first Paul claims parity with the interlopers. They are Hebrews, Israelites, and descendants of Abraham, but so is Paul.

It is as a minister of Christ that Paul exceeds them. Remarkably, however, Paul with some irony does not appeal to his apostolic successes to make his point; rather, he makes the point by saying that he has labored much more, been more often in prison, been beaten more severely, and been in danger of death more often than they.

The fool's speech consists of an introduction, three principal parts, and an epilogue. In Hellenistic rhetoric the introduction to a speech, its *prooi-mion*, or *exordium*, typically establishes the speaker's *ethos*, the person's authority for speaking in such a way. The introduction prepares the audience to lend a sympathetic ear to the speech. Paul's introduction departs from

224

the classic rhetorical pattern. He distances himself somewhat from what he is about to say and acknowledges that he is not speaking according to the Lord, whose authority he normally invokes. As far as his audience is concerned, instead of flattering them with a *captatio benevolentiae* (lit., "the seizing of goodwill"), a rhetorical device used to elicit someone's sympathy or support, he reminds them that they already tolerate fools—hardly a flattering observation!—so they might as well put up with one more fool. After all, Paul has been weak.

> **The Fool's Speech**
>
> Introduction (11:16–21a)
> Part 1: The List of Hardships (11:21b–29)
> Part 2: The Escape from Damascus (11:30–33)
> Part 3: The Rapture to the Third Heaven (12:1–10)
> Epilogue (12:11–13)

The first part of the speech (11:21b–29) consists for the most part of a long list of hardships. Such lists were a classic part of many rhetorical speeches. Speakers used them to enhance their personal *ethos*. Use of a catalog of hardships implicitly spoke of the speaker's endurance, perhaps his bravery under fire. Paul uses a list of hardships to illustrate his poverty and his weakness. His mention of innumerable hardships is virtually a concession to the interlopers, who accused him of being weak in mien and poor in speech (10:10). He almost seems to embrace some of the charges that they have directed against him.

Today's readers of Paul's discourse about his hardships might hope that Paul had included some more detail, since these lists offer an intriguing picture of the circumstances in which Paul carried out his apostolic ministry. Modern readers might experience frustration insofar as the various hardships receive little confirmation in Luke's narrative account of Paul's apostolic activity in Acts.

The second part of the speech (11:30–33) describes Paul's escape from Damascus. Paul considers his down-the-wall departure from Damascus to be an example of his weakness. This second part of the speech begins with "If I must boast, I will boast about things that pertain to my weakness." The use of examples was an important feature of ancient rhetoric. Examples generally functioned as proofs. Concrete examples were typically introduced after the main argument. This seems to be the case with Paul's mention of his escape from Damascus. Aristotle observes that examples are of two sorts, historical and invented (cf. *Rhet.* 2.20.2), and that lessons derived from facts are particularly useful for deliberative rhetoric (2.20.8).

Paul's escape from Damascus is clearly an example of his weakness. He did not escape on his own. He needed the help of others in order to escape from the clutches of the ethnarch. Because it is an example of his weakness, Paul can boast about it, as he does. He has, however, said that he boasts in the Lord (10:17). Paul may be boasting about his escape not only because it is an example of his weakness but also because he believes that it was the Lord who enabled him to escape as he did.

The third part of the speech (12:1–10) offers another example, Paul's rapture to the third heaven. The narrative occupies the climactic position in Paul's account of his weakness. On first reading, Paul's narrative seems out of place in an account of his weakness. Paul seems to acknowledge that it is out of place. Of itself, it is the kind of experience that Paul might use to exalt himself, but he distances himself from the experience by means of a narrative in the third person and states his reluctance to talk about it.

In any case, his telling of the story serves to substantiate his thesis (*prothesis*; cf. Aristotle, *Rhet.* 3.13.1–2) that he is even more a servant of Christ than are the interlopers (11:23). The account has an apologetic purpose insofar as the interlopers apparently spoke about their spiritual experience. Paul's ecstatic experience tops anything that they could offer. He has bested them at their game of one-upmanship. The narrative serves as a refutation (*elenchus*) of their claims.

As Paul's narrative continues, it appears that the real reason for Paul's telling about the rapture is that it was the occasion for his experience of a particularly difficult hardship, the thorn in his side, the only hardship from which he prayed to be delivered, at least insofar as he tells us. His prayer was answered, but not in the way he expected. The answer came in the form of a revelation from the Lord about the meaning of weakness. When Paul is weak, it is then that he is powerful, since the power of Christ dwells in him and is at work in him.

This brings Paul to the peroration (*epilogos*) of his speech. Aristotle says that among the purposes of the peroration are that it seeks to dispose the hearer favorably to the speaker and unfavorably toward the adversary and that it excites the emotions of the hearer (*Rhet.* 3.19.1). This Paul does as he compares himself to the interlopers for one last time. His final words remind the Corinthians of how well off they are in comparison with others. With some irony, Paul appeals to them for a sympathetic understanding of his situation.

Tracing the Train of Thought

Putting Up with Paul (11:16–21a)

11:16–21a. After the digression in which he describes and attacks the interlopers (11:1–15), Paul returns to the line of thinking that he initiated in 11:1, but he begins with a demur. He wants the Corinthians to know that, even though he might appear to be a fool because what he is about to say is so much foolishness, he is not really a fool. **And I repeat, let no one think me to be a fool; otherwise, accept me as a fool so that I can boast a little** (11:16). Paul seems to have adopted the language of Hellenistic philosophical debates. Sophists accused philosophers of being fools and saying foolish things. Could some of the interlopers, in their attempts to denigrate Paul's apostolic authority, have suggested that Paul is a fool? Paul is hoping that none of the Corinthians consider him to be a fool, but if they do, so what? Paul's boasting is really so much foolishness, so even if some of the Corinthians consider him to be a fool, that is okay so long as they listen to what he has to say.

In formally introducing his topic, **With regard to boasting** (11:17), Paul is ready to begin his speech. He thinks that it is so much foolishness since it is not according to the Lord: **what I am saying is not according to the Lord; it is like foolishness.** Paul's Greek clearly describes his boasting as foolishness. The use of "like" suggests that Paul is distancing himself somewhat from the sort of foolishness that he is about to begin (cf. 11:16a). Foolishness is not according to the Lord: it is according to the flesh. Boasting is a way in which weak human beings speak about themselves.

Acting according to the flesh is not Paul's usual modus operandi, but he adopts the tactic because many others—the interlopers are surely included—do so. **Many boast according to the flesh, so I too will boast** (11:18). Paul will engage in the same kind of boasting that the interlopers perpetrate. By his estimation, that is boasting "according to the flesh." "According to the flesh" has negative overtones. The interlopers boast in a merely human way; theirs is not boasting in the Lord (see 10:17). Paul will boast in similar fashion.

Paul addresses the Corinthians directly with a bit of sarcastic irony. **Since you are wise, you gladly put up with fools** (11:19). This is hardly the *captatio benevolentiae* that one expects to find at the beginning of a speech. Thinking themselves to be wise (cf. 1 Cor. 4:10; 10:15), the Corinthians readily tolerate fools. If they put up with fools, they should certainly tolerate Paul's speaking foolishly. But that is not really Paul's point. His sarcasm intensifies in tone as he uses a series of hyperbolic metaphors to describe what is happening to the Corinthians as they put up with the foolish interlopers. Metaphor upon

---

Anaphora

Anaphora (or *epanaphora*) is a figure of speech characterized by the repetition of the same expression at the beginning of a series of successive statements. Often the statements are synonymous. Paul's use of this figure of speech is characterized by his use of *ei tis* ("when someone") to introduce each of his five images in 2 Cor. 11:20. The series uses the personal pronoun "you" in the opening and closing image.

The rhetorical device generally adds gravity to an argument, but some ancient rhetoricians believed that it was used merely to embellish the argument. Indeed, some consider anaphora to be contrived, an example of so-called Gorgian assonance.

The kind of bombastic language used by Paul enjoyed popular appeal. Demosthenes, the great Athenian political orator, used anaphora to mount a successive attack (see also Longinus, *On the Sublime* 20.13). This is what Paul does in 11:20.

---

metaphor describes what happens to the Corinthians when they fall victim to the seduction of false teachers. Hans Windisch (1970, 347) writes that "each clause of this splendid series of anaphorae operates as a whiplash."

Paul's opening salvo is **You put up with it, when someone enslaves you** (11:20). Paul begins by saying that the Corinthians have become enslaved (see Gal. 2:4) as a result of the interlopers' intrusion. The idiom of slavery describes the human situation of the Corinthians. The interlopers have lorded it over the faith of the Corinthians (cf. 1:24). The Corinthians have become their slaves. Yet there may be more to Paul's use of the idiom. He may be implying that the Corinthians have fallen victim to the ominous power of sin, that they have become enslaved to sin.

The series continues with **when someone eats you up**. The Corinthians have been eaten up alive (*katesthiei*), as it were. "Preys upon" (NRSV) does not convey the full sense of a verb that was normally used to describe animals devouring their prey (Gal. 5:15; Homer, *Il.* 17.542; etc.). The world of wild animals also provides Paul with his next metaphor, **when someone takes hold of you**. Paul portrays the Corinthians as being grabbed (*lambanei*), in much the same way that lions and predatory birds take hold of their prey and carry it away. With **when someone puts on airs** (*epairetai*), Paul may be evoking the thought of the interlopers' rising up (*epairomenon*) against the knowledge of God (10:5; the only other use of the verb *epairō* in Paul's correspondence). Paul's series comes to a close with **when someone slaps you on the face**. Added to everything else is the personal insult of being slapped in the face (*eis prosōpon hymas derei*).

Continuing to speak with irony, Paul confesses his own weakness in not acting as the interlopers do. **I am saying this to my shame: we have been weak** [*ēsthenēkamen*] (11:21a). The interlopers accuse Paul of being weak (10:10) because he has not acted as they do. The interlopers have lorded it over the Corinthians: they have taken advantage of them and insulted them. In contrast, Paul did not lord it over their faith (1:24); nor did he take advantage of them. Indeed, he robbed other churches so as not to burden them (11:8). He acted as a father to them. By their standards, he was weak. This is the first time that Paul talks about being "weak" in this part of his missive. The language of weakness will resonate throughout the fool's speech that is about to begin. As Paul develops his argument, he will show that he is weak but in a way that is quite different from the "fault" of which he was accused.

A Telling Comparison (11:21b–23)

11:21b–23. For some time Paul had been intimating that he would be speaking like a fool. He was going to boast, and that would be speaking like a fool, speaking in a merely human way. On more than one occasion, he has expressed some hesitancy about what he is going to say. About to begin the speech, Paul once again expresses his embarrassment. He is willing to speak foolishly only because others have dared to do so (cf. 11:18): **So if anyone dares** to speak **in this way—I am speaking in foolishness—I too will dare** (11:21b). The parenthetical remark betrays Paul's embarrassment as he is about to begin (see 11:1, 17). He is going to be bold (see 10:2, 12) and will dare to do what others have done. "If anyone" refers generically to the interlopers, just as it did in Paul's imaginative description of them in verse 20.

With a series of rhetorical questions, arranged in a rising crescendo, Paul lists the titles that the interlopers have appropriated to themselves. The titles point to their qualifications, but Paul argues that he is every bit as qualified as they are. Indeed, as far as the last title is concerned, the high point of the crescendo, Paul says that he is even more qualified than they are.

Paul begins by speaking about their ethnic heritage. **Are they Hebrews? So am I** [*kagō*] (11:22). The interlopers can claim to be full-blooded Hebrews, but Paul is no less a pure-blooded Hebrew than they are. He is a Hebrew, born of Hebrews (Phil. 3:5). **Are they Israelites? So am I.** They claim to be Israelites, with all that that implies in salvation history (see Rom. 9:4–5). Paul, a member of the tribe of Benjamin and circumcised on the eighth day, is no less a member of the nation of Israel. Then, raising his questions to a theological level, Paul asks, **Are they the seed of Abraham?** With the emphatic **so am I**, Paul responds once again to his rhetorical question. It was to Abraham and his seed that the promises were made (Gal. 3:16). Paul lays claim to those promises, but he may also have had in mind that Abraham was a blessing for the nations. Mention of Abraham suggests that the blessings of the covenant are to be extended to the Gentiles. The interlopers may have described themselves as the seed of Abraham to say that even though they were Jews, they had a legitimate right to go to the Gentiles in Corinth.

With the next rhetorical question, **Are they servants of Christ?** (11:23), Paul moves his discourse into the realm of Christian commitment. The question, like the preceding three questions, calls for a positive response. Yes, the interlopers are servants of Christ, but Paul will not intimate that they might be apostles of Christ. He has previously stated that they are false apostles who disguise themselves as apostles of Christ (11:13). As such, they are servants of Satan (11:15). Despite the interlopers' divided loyalty, Paul is willing to concede that they are servants of Christ because he has reached the climax of his comparative crescendo and now proclaims that he is even more a servant of Christ than they are. **Speaking as a madman**, he writes, **I am even more so.** The thrice-repeated "so am I" now gives way to "I am even more so" (*hyper egō*). This is Paul's point. He has a greater claim to be called a servant of Christ than the interlopers do, and he will prove it. Yet when he speaks in this way, he acknowledges that he is virtually out of his mind, almost delirious.

Nonetheless, he is going to justify his claim to be more of a servant of Christ than the interlopers. To justify his claim, he gives a résumé of his apostolic sufferings, beginning with a comparison between himself and the interlopers. Compared with them, he is a servant of Christ **with far more labor, more often in prison, beaten more severely, and in danger of death more often** than they.

The comparison serves as an introduction to the list of hardships that Paul is about to enumerate, but some ambiguity arises with regard to the specifics that Paul has in mind. Does far more labor refer to Paul's apostolic efforts or to the manual labor in which he was engaged as he preached the gospel? Paul uses "labor" (*kopos*) with both meanings (see 10:15; 11:27). On balance, it appears that here Paul is writing about the manual labor by means of which he earns his living. Not only does the appearance of labor in the expression "hard work and toil" (11:27) suggest that "labor" refers to Paul's manual labor, but also the fact that Paul works to support himself is a bone of contention between himself and the interlopers. Moreover, it is hardly likely that Paul would begin his hardship catalog by boasting about his having preached far more often than the interlopers had. That would be the meaning of his words if "labor" were taken to mean apostolic labor.

Paul says that he has been imprisoned more than once (cf. 6:5), but Luke's narrative account of Paul's apostolic activity mentions only the imprisonment at Philippi (Acts 16:22–24) as having occurred before this juncture in Paul's "career." Could it be that whatever happened in Ephesus (see 1:8; 1 Cor. 15:32) was an imprisonment? Prisoners were often flogged. So Paul mentions that he was severely beaten, but does the adverb (*hyperballontōs*) refer to the quantity or the quality, as I have suggested with the translation "more severely," of Paul's beatings? Finally Paul mentions his many brushes with death (cf. 1:8–9), the high point of his introduction, but the modern reader of Paul's letter remains in the dark about when and where these brushes with death occurred (cf. Acts 15:26).

Paul's Hardships (11:24–29)

11:24–29. Paul follows up his introduction with a detailed list of his apostolic sufferings. This is the third such listing of Paul's hardships in this letter (see 4:8–12; 6:4–10). A fourth will follow in the next chapter (12:10). This list is the longest of the four and contains some vocabulary that does not appear elsewhere in Paul's correspondence as well as other words that he rarely uses. Like the other catalogs, this list demonstrates Paul's endurance and his steadfastness in preaching the gospel, despite the difficulties that he encountered at virtually every turn.

The list begins with a series of hardships in which Paul's very life was at risk, illustrating thereby the many dangers of death that he mentions in his summary introduction: **From the Jews five times I received forty lashes minus one, three times I was beaten with rods, once I had rocks thrown at me, three times I was shipwrecked, for a day and a night I was adrift in the sea** (11:24–25). His own people were the first source of danger. Acts frequently mentions Paul's attempts to preach the gospel in the synagogue, the result being that Jews turned against him (Acts 9:20–23; 13:44–45, 50; 14:1–2; 17:1–5, 10–13; 18:4–6; cf. 22:19; 26:11). Luke does not mention that the apostle received the forty-lashes-but-one five times, but it was a classic Jewish punishment. The maximum legal punishment meted out to the loser in a civil case was forty lashes, but the law contained a stern warning against anything beyond that number (Deut. 25:1–3). Hence, it was customary to flog the offender only thirty-nine times. That Paul received the maximum penalty five times shows the widespread offense that his own people took at his preaching and his own determination to preach the gospel first to his fellow Jews.

Paul was also punished by Roman authorities. Three times he was beaten with rods. According to both the Lex Portia and the Lex Julia, this kind of punishment was not to be inflicted on Roman citizens (cf. Acts 16:37–39), but there were exceptions (see Thrall 2000, 740). Luke recounts that magistrates at Philippi ordered that Paul and Silas be flogged in this fashion, "with rods" (Acts 16:22–23).

Paul also had rocks thrown at him, perhaps by an angry mob that tried to stone him (Acts 14:19). That Paul was shipwrecked three times is not surprising considering the number of sea voyages that he undertook. One of the shipwrecks left Paul adrift in the sea for almost a full twenty-four hours. Luke mentions Paul suffering shipwreck off the island of Malta (Acts 27:39–44), but that shipwreck occurred long after the writing of this letter.

With his **many different trips** (11:26), Paul was constantly in danger. Eight times he mentions the dangers that he faced; the phrase *en kindynois* ("in dangers") is repeated eight times. Traveling with only a few companions, as he forded streams and traveled roads in isolated areas, the apostle faced **dangers from rivers** and **dangers from bandits.** Just as he suffered punishment from Jewish and Gentile authorities, he encountered **dangers from my countrymen**

and **dangers from Gentiles**. Neither his ethnicity nor his Roman citizenship protected him as he traveled about to preach the gospel. No matter where he was, there was the possibility of danger. Neither urban areas, deserted areas, nor the sea afforded him safe passage. There were **dangers in the city, dangers in the wilderness**, and **dangers at sea**. The climax of this list of dangers is danger of another sort. There were **dangers from false brethren** (*en pseudadelphois*, cf. Gal. 2:4). For the apostle, the most serious danger of all came from fellow believers who tried to undermine his apostolic work. The intrusive false apostles at Corinth are certainly among them.

Other hardships that Paul endured were self-imposed, at least to some degree. He did not hesitate to push himself to the limit in order to proclaim the gospel of Jesus Christ. **With hard work and toil** (11:27) he preached the gospel. The combination also appears in 1 Thess. 2:9 (cf. 2 Thess. 3:8) in reference to Paul's working night and day to support himself as he preached the gospel. Its appearance here is particularly relevant insofar as the interlopers apparently criticized Paul for his refusal to receive financial support from the Corinthians. The combination suggests that the "far more labor" in his summary introduction relates to the exercise of his trade (cf. 1 Cor. 4:12).

That Paul **often** lived **with sleepless nights** (see 6:5) and **in hunger and thirst** (cf. 1 Cor. 4:11, linking hunger and thirst) were probably consequences of his decision to be self-supporting. Manual laborers and artisans often did not make enough to feed themselves properly. Paul was **often without food, in the cold, and poorly clothed**. Paul's being without food could be a reference to a religious fast, but in the context of a catalog of hardships, the expression more likely refers to the fact that Paul was hungry because he was poor (6:5). In 1 Cor. 4:11 Paul complains about being clad in rags (*gymniteuomen*, hapax in the NT). Now he says that he was poorly clothed (*en gymnotēti*; cf. Rom. 8:35), a sure sign of his poverty (cf. Epictetus, *Diatr.* 3.22.45). The verb and the noun denote nakedness, but those who were poorly clothed and in rags were said to be naked (cf. Seneca, *Ben.* 5.13.3).

Before beginning the fool's speech, Paul tells the Corinthians that despite being in poverty (11:9), he has refused to take any money from them. In the last several phrases of this long catalog of hardships, Paul spells out some of the consequences of his poverty.

Apart from all the rest, there is my daily pressure, my anxiety for all the churches (11:28). There is no need for Paul to go on. He has written enough: the point has been made. As a minister of Christ, he has suffered hardship for the sake of the gospel. But there is one more thing that he wants to mention, his worrisome concern for the communities that he has evangelized. Every day he experiences pressure (*epistasis*, hapax in Paul). He is torn apart (*merimna*, a noun likewise hapax in Paul) by his concern for the churches. "All the churches," the several communities that Paul has evangelized, are a constant source of worry for him (see Gal. 4:19–20; 1 Thess. 3:1–5). The interlopers apparently boasted about many things, but it is hardly likely that they were able to boast about a concern for the churches. Paul's reference to the churches provides a context for all his hardships. What he has endured is for the sake of the communities that he evangelized.

Paul brings the first part of his foolish boast to a close with a pair of rhetorical questions: **Who is weak, and I am not weak? Who is made to fall** [*skandalizetai*]**, and I am not set on fire** [*pyroumai*]**?** (11:29). Continuing with the ecclesial note of verse 28, Paul uses these questions to identify with the members of the Corinthian church. In 1 Corinthians he writes at length about the weak members of the community, those whose consciences are not fully formed with regard to the matter of eating food that has once been offered to idols (e.g., 1 Cor. 8:7, 9, 11). In this letter, Paul may have a wider variety of weaknesses in mind, including those of a physical nature. Whatever the weakness, Paul identifies with the weak (cf. 1 Cor. 9:22a). In 1 Corinthians, Paul urges the strong not to scandalize the weak (8:9) and expresses his own willingness to forgo meat lest he scandalize the weak (8:13).

When people are scandalized, when they are led astray, when they stumble over the obstacles that are put before them, Paul becomes indignant; he is set on fire. An emphatic "I" underscores Paul's personal indignation. The two metaphors, stumbling and setting on fire, are found only here in 2 Corinthians. It may be, as Michael Barré (1975) suggests, that Paul's use of "be weak" is based on the connotation of the verb in the Greek Bible and intertestamental literature, where the expression is found in contexts that speak of persecution and oppression. Paul sees his own apostolic sufferings in the context of the great eschatological struggle in which the forces of evil are attacking him.

The Escape from Damascus (11:30–33)

11:30–33. Paul begins the second part of his speech by saying that he can only boast about his weakness: **If I must boast, I will boast about things that pertain to my weakness** (11:30). Within the next few verses he will reiterate that it is necessary for him to boast (*ei kauchasthai dei*; lit., "if it is necessary to boast"; cf. 12:1, 3). Barré (1975, 513) suggests that the noun "weakness" (*astheneia*), related to the verb "be weak" in the rhetorical question of 11:29a, connotes concrete events that show how a person is subject to overt hostility, not merely various ways in which a person might lack strength.

Although Paul expressed serious reservations about boasting as he was about to do so, he wants the Corinthians to know that he is telling them the truth, and so he interrupts his speech with another oath. **The God and Father of the Lord Jesus—he who is blessed forever—knows that I do not lie** (11:31; see 11:10). The expanded epithet used of God (see 1:3) underscores the serious tone and solemnity of the oath. The short blessing (cf. 1:3) incorporated into the oath reflects Paul's piety. Use of such short blessings seems to have been common practice in Paul's day and is continued among pious Jews to this day.

233

King Aretas

Aretas IV Philopatris ruled Nabataea in Roman Arabia for almost fifty years (ca. 9 BCE–39 CE), a time of great prosperity for the territory. Around 65 BCE, Rome had taken control of the city of Damascus, where the Nabataeans had established their capital for about twenty years. As a result, the king's unnamed ethnarch (*ethnarchēs*, hapax in the NT) most probably enjoyed only limited responsibility, that is, he was probably responsible for only the city's Nabataean quarter.

Josephus says that Alexandrian Jews, in somewhat similar circumstances, had a series of ethnarchs who were responsible for various legal matters. The practice was condoned by Augustus in keeping with the emperor's respect for local customs (see Josephus, *Ant.* 14.117; 19.283).

A good example of Paul's weakness is what happened to him **in Damascus** (11:32). The **ethnarch of King Aretas guarded the city of Damascus in order to arrest me**. The Nabataean governor took steps to have Paul arrested, but providence intervened, and **I was let down in a basket through a window in the wall of the city and escaped from his hands** (11:33). The casement walls of ancient cities often had openings from which approaching forces could be seen and defensive arms employed. Paul was lowered in a large basket (*en sarganē*) from an opening in the Damascus wall and made his escape. Luke describes the whole affair as part of a Jewish plot, adding that Paul escaped by night with the help of some believers (see Acts 9:23–25). With their help, Paul escaped from the ethnarch's clutches.

Corinth was an important Roman colony. Consequently some commentators, including Edwin Arthur Judge (1966) and Thomas D. Stegman (2009, 261–72), read Paul's description of his escape from the city against the background of Roman commanders awarding the *corona muralis* to the first soldier to scale the wall of a besieged city (see Aulus Gellius 5.6.4; Livy, *History* 26.4). This high military decoration was a golden crown decorated with turrets. During the time of the empire, it was bestowed only on centurions and those of superior rank. Paul's lowly descent from the wall in

Luke on Paul's Hardships

This is one of the rare occasions when Luke's account substantiates with particulars the hardships cited by Paul.

"After some time had passed, the Jews plotted to kill him, but their plot became known to Saul. They were watching the gates day and night so that they might kill him; but his disciples took him by night and let him down through an opening in the wall, lowering him in a basket." (Acts 9:23–25)

a basket is in sharp contrast to the conduct of brave soldiers mounting a wall in combat. The reverse image contrasts with the apostle's proud use of military imagery in such passages as 10:3b–6 and 11:8 and contributes to his self-deprecation as someone who is weak. Paul uses the example of his escape to illustrate his helplessness. Boasting in the Lord, he can boast of his almost miraculous escape from Damascus.

Rapture to the Third Heaven (12:1–5)

12:1–5. Paul came down the wall at Damascus, but he went up to the third heaven to paradise. The interlopers have forced Paul to boast, so he continues to boast in this third part of his speech. In many ways this phase of his boasting is the climax of his verbal battle with the interlopers. Apparently they have spoken about their spiritual experiences. Paul is reluctant to boast of his own spiritual experience, but he will do so, even if his account may not prove to be convincing. **Although it's of no use, I'll come to the visions and revelations of the Lord** (12:1).

Figure 13. Paul Being Let Down in a Basket. This engraving done by artist Bernhard Rode in 1783 depicts Paul's escape from Damascus at night to avoid capture by an ethnarch of the Nabataean king Aretas IV.

Paul and the anonymous author of Ephesians describe Paul's experience on the road to Damascus as a revelation (*apokalypsis*, Gal. 1:12; Eph. 3:3). In Acts 26:19 the Damascus experience is identified as a vision (*optasia*), to which Paul was responsive (cf. Acts 16:9). In addition to the thrice-described Damascus experience, Luke offers a few additional accounts of visions experienced by Paul (Acts 16:9; 22:17–21; 27:23–25).

Paul himself does not use the word "vision" elsewhere in his letters, and neither does he use the word "revelation" in the plural, so it is likely that his talking about visions and revelations is his way of addressing a matter about which the intruders are boasting. The expression "visions and revelations" is a hendiadys; Paul does not intend to separate the visual from the auditory part of his experiences. These visual and auditory experiences came from the Lord, but in the light of Paul's stating that he saw the Lord at the time of his

235

Figure 14. A *Corona Muralis*. This mural (Latin *murus*, "wall") crown is similar to the Roman military decoration awarded to the first soldier to successfully scale the wall of a besieged enemy city. In 10:30–33 Paul may be implicitly contrasting his descent from the wall of Damascus with a soldier's attempt to scale a wall and thus merit the *corona muralis*. The soldier's would be a glorious action; Paul's a lowly one.

Jocélio/Wikimedia Commons

Damascus experience (see 1 Cor. 9:1, which uses *kyrios*; 15:8; Gal. 1:12, 16), Paul wants his readers to know that it was the Lord Jesus himself who was the object of his visions.

Using the third-person singular, he describes his vision almost as if it had happened to someone else. **I know someone [*anthrōpon*] in Christ who fourteen years ago—whether in body I do not know or outside the body I do not know, God knows—was snatched up to the third heaven** (12:2). The third-person narrative allows Paul to distance himself somewhat from the vision and present it as an apocalyptic experience.

That the experience happened fourteen years earlier (*pro etōn dekatessarōn*; cf. Gal. 2:1) means that the vision was not that of the Damascus experience; nor was it the temple vision described in Acts 22:17–21. The temporal reference gives the narrative a tone of similitude: it really happened. Apocalyptic writers, as the prophets before them, used geographical (cf. Rev. 9:1) and temporal references (cf. Isa. 6:1; Jer. 1:2–3; Ezek. 1:1–3; Amos 1:1; Mic. 1:1; Zeph. 1:1; Hag. 1:1) to establish the reality of their narrative. Paul's "fourteen years ago" serves a similar function. Unfortunately, since the ecstatic experience that Paul describes is neither the Damascus experience nor the temple vision, "fourteen years ago" does not offer enough precision for modern commentators to date the experience, which most likely occurred in the early forties.

Jewish apocalyptic literature includes narrative accounts of ascents into heaven by various figures—including Enoch, Levi, Moses, Ezra, and Baruch—but we do not know whether the apostle was familiar with any of them. In the

A Translation Issue

Paul does not use the relative pronoun "who" in 12:2. Rather, he has a strange construction: the phrase "such a person was snatched up" (*harpagenta ton toiouton*) is in apposition to "someone" (*anthrōpon*), the direct object of "I know" (*oida*), with which the sentence begins. I have rendered *ton toiouton* as "who" to make it easier to understand Paul's words. When Paul repeats himself in verse 3, *ton toiouton* qualifies *anthrōpon* immediately, resulting in my translation "such a person." In Paul's Greek, the reference to his being snatched up is found in the subordinate clause.

long run it does not really matter because Paul is describing his own personal experience, an experience that was so overwhelming that he does not know what really happened to him. His aside acknowledges that the experience was beyond his ability to comprehend it. Only God knows what really happened.

The antithetical "in body or out of body" (*en sōmati . . . ektos sōmatos*) does not so much suggest an alternative as it indicates that the ecstatic experience was a total experience. The reader of Paul's letter, however, might have been aware that the Jewish tradition was familiar with in-body experiences, whereas the Hellenistic tradition was more familiar with out-of-body experiences. No matter the kind of experience it was, Paul wants his readers to know that he was unable to fully understand it.

Paul describes the experience as rapture. He was caught up to the third heaven. Apart from 1 Thess. 4:17, Paul uses the verb "snatched up" only in verses 2 and 4. The passive voice indicates that Paul's being caught up into heaven was a divine action. The apostle shares with many of his contemporaries the idea that there were several levels of heaven. He says that he was caught up to the third heaven. Most likely that third heaven is in paradise. In *2 Enoch*, the longer version of which begins, "The story of Enoch, how the Lord took him to heaven," Enoch says, "And the men took me from there, and they brought me up to the third heaven, and they placed me in the midst of Paradise" (*2 En.* [A] 8.1). The *Apocalypse of Moses* says that God instructed the archangel Michael to take Adam "up into Paradise, to the third heaven" (*L.A.E.* 37.5).

Seemingly overwhelmed by his experience, Paul immediately repeats himself. **And I know such a person—whether in body or outside the body I do not know, God knows—that he was snatched up to paradise** (12:3–4a). Some older commentators, among whom Alfred Plummer (1915, 344) should be named, take the apparent repetition as describing a sequential action on the part of God. Paul would have experienced rapture to the third heaven and then rapture from the third heaven to paradise. In light of the cited parallels in Jewish apocalyptic literature and the Semitic literary device of synonymous

---

Paradise in *2 Enoch*

"And that place has an appearance of pleasantness that has never been seen. Every tree was in full flower. Every fruit was ripe, every food was in yield profusely; every fragrance was pleasant. And the four rivers were flowing past with gentle movement, with every kind of garden producing every kind of good food. And the tree of life is in that place, under which the Lord *takes a rest when the* Lord *takes a walk in Paradise. And that tree is indescribable for pleasantness of fragrance."* (*2 En.* [A] 8.1c–3 [of the two extant versions of the Slavonic *2 Enoch*, A is shorter than J]; cf. Gen. 1:11–12; 2:9–14)

parallelism in which a separate phrase repeats and slightly moves the thought of the first sentence forward, it is best to take verses 2 and 3a as synonymous. "Paradise" is a synonym for the third heaven, which is in paradise.

This is the only time in his extant correspondence where Paul mentions paradise. He does not offer a description of paradise as *2 Enoch* does; rather, he describes what he experienced in paradise. **And he** [Paul really means I] **heard unspeakable sounds that a human is not allowed to utter** (12:4b). It is impossible to know exactly what it was that Paul heard. "Unspeakable sounds" (*arrēta rhēmata*, another play on words by Paul) could mean sounds that a human is unable to pronounce, but in view of the qualifying clause, "that a human is not allowed to utter," the words most likely refer to a message that a human being receives but is not allowed to communicate to others. In similar fashion, Enoch says, "I saw the face of the LORD. But the face of the LORD is not to be talked about, it is so very marvelous and supremely awesome and supremely frightening" (*2 En.* [J] 22.1). It may be that Paul appropriated language that was associated with the oracles of mystery religions, but it is not to be excluded that he has angelic voices in mind (cf. 1 Cor. 13:1). *Second Enoch* speaks of "the angelic songs which it is not possible to describe" (*2 En.* [J] 17.1). Since Paul was not permitted to express what he heard, it is impossible to do anything but speculate about the nature of his auditory experience.

With regard to the beneficiary of the visions and revelations, Paul writes, **I will boast about such a person** (12:5). He can do so because they are the work of the Lord. With regard to himself, **however**, Paul writes, **I will not boast about myself except about my weaknesses.** The distinction between such a person and himself is another indication of Paul's hesitancy to boast, especially to boast about his ecstatic experience. That it happened fourteen years earlier and is not mentioned in any of Paul's other letters suggests that this may well be the first time that Paul has spoken about it. He was reluctant to do so, but the interlopers' boasting about their experiences "forced" Paul to do so. On the other hand, he is willing to boast about his weaknesses (cf. 11:30; 12:9). As for "yours truly," he says, I can only boast about the things that show that I am weak.

A Thorn in the Flesh (12:6–9a)

12:6–9a. Even while boasting, Paul maintains his truthfulness (cf. 6:7; 7:14; 11:10; 13:8). **If I want to boast, I will not be a fool since I will be speaking the truth** (12:6). The Corinthians should not take Paul's boasting like a fool to mean that he is not telling the truth. Insofar as he is telling the truth, he is not a fool. The reason why Paul refrains from boasting is not because boasting might lead him to be untruthful. **Rather, I forgo doing so lest anyone consider me more than what he sees in me or hears from me.** Paul wants the Corinthians to evaluate him on the basis of his conduct and the truth of the message that he proclaims, not on the basis of what he might have to say about himself.

In fact, despite having given Paul an overwhelming ecstatic experience, God took the initiative in keeping Paul humble. **Therefore, because of the abundance of revelations, lest I exalt myself, a thorn in the flesh was given to me, a messenger of Satan, to torment me so that I might not exalt myself** (12:7). Lest Paul be carried away because of the overwhelming revelatory experience (*tē hyperbolē tōn apokalypseōn*), God gave him "a thorn in the flesh." This was to keep Paul from having any undue pride (*hyperairōmai*, used by Paul only in 12:7) because of what he had experienced. "Was given," a divine passive, corresponds to the divine passive "was snatched up" (*ēpargē*) of verse 4 (cf. v. 2). Both experiences are the result of God's action. It is likely that both occurred in the same time frame.

"Thorn in the flesh" is the traditional translation of the Greek phrase *skolops tē sarki*, but "thorn for the flesh" might better express the metaphor. *Skolops* is not used elsewhere in the NT. The word properly describes any pointed object, but commentators generally take the term to mean a thorn or splinter since that is the meaning of the term in the Greek Bible (Num. 33:55; Ezek. 28:24; Hosea 2:6 [2:8 Eng.]; Sir. 43:19).

Some see in Paul's use of the term an allusion to the text in Num. 33:55, "barbs [*skolopes*] in your eyes and thorns [*bolides*] in your sides," in which barbs and thorns metaphorically describe the enemies of Israel. Some patristic authors therefore take Paul's metaphor to be a reference to his enemies or the persecutions that he suffered, all the more so since Satan is God's cosmic adversary.

The Vulgate's translation of the Greek as "thorn of the flesh" (*stimulus carnis*) gave rise to an interpretation, dominant in Western Christianity until the Reformation, which took the metaphor as a reference to erotic thoughts and sexual desires. This interpretation requires that "flesh" have a sexual nuance that Paul's "flesh" (*sarx*) does not have.

Thorn in the Flesh

"There are some who have said that Paul is referring to a pain in the head caused by the devil, but God forbid! . . . Paul was attacked by adversaries. . . . These were the messengers of Satan." (Chrysostom, *Hom. 2 Cor.* 26.2)

"Many people think this was some kind of headache, but in reality Paul was referring to the persecutions that he suffered, because they came from diabolical powers." (Severian of Gabala, *Pauline Commentary from the Greek Church*; Bray 1999, 301)

"By 'messenger of Satan' Paul means the insults, attacks, and riots that he had to face." (Theodoret of Cyr, *2 Cor.* 349)

Various physical ailments and disabilities as well as all sorts of psychological difficulties—enough to fill a dictionary of pathology!—have also been proposed as the referent of Paul's metaphor. Difficulties with speech or sight are most commonly proposed (cf. Gal. 4:13–15; 6:11). If Paul suffered from some sort of obvious physical disability, he may have been mocked by the interlopers, who accused him of being weak in physical appearance (see 10:10). In the end, it is impossible to know what Paul meant by this intriguing image. The Corinthians themselves may not have known the real meaning of the metaphor.

Paul personifies the image by describing it as a messenger of Satan (*angelos satana*; see 11:14). The thorn was given to torment Paul (*hina mē kolaphizē*). That "torment" really means "beat" adds to the personification. Satan's messenger was sent to Paul to flog him. Whatever Paul suffered was comparable to a beating that he might receive (cf. 11:24–25a). If Paul suffered from a physical ailment, the metaphor could imply that the suffering is demonic, since many of Paul's Jewish contemporaries considered physical illness to be the result of sin or demonic possession. On the other hand, the reference to Satan may suggest that God was allowing Satan to impede Paul's apostolic activity (see 1 Thess. 2:18). Paul hopes that sometime in the near future God will crush Satan, bringing his malevolent interventions to an end (Rom. 16:20).

Whatever he may mean by the image, the thorn is problematic for him. He does not understand his suffering. So, **with regard to this**, Paul writes, **three times I called on the Lord that it** [the thorn in my flesh] **might leave me** (12:8). It was the Lord Jesus Christ to whom Paul prayed (see vv. 9b–10), the only place in his extant correspondence where he acknowledges making a prayer of petition to Jesus (cf. 1 Cor. 16:22). Moreover, this is the only time that Paul uses the verb "call on" (*parakaleō*) in reference to petitionary prayer. Typically he uses this verb with the meaning of "appeal," as he does in the interrupted appeal in 10:1.

Paul's calling on the Lord several times is in keeping with early Christian tradition that a once-only appeal is not enough. Petitionary prayer must be repeated (see Matt. 7:7–8; Luke 11:5–10). A contemporary reader of Paul's letter might compare Paul's thrice-repeated prayer to be freed from his ordeal to the thrice-repeated prayer of Jesus in Gethsemane (Matt. 26:39–44; cf. Mark 14:35–41a).

Paul received a response to his prayer, but it was not what he expected. **And he**, the Lord Jesus, **said to me, "My grace is sufficient for you, for power is perfected in weakness"** (12:9a). The perfect tense of "said" indicates that Jesus's words fit Paul's ministry during the fourteen years that have passed since the ecstasy-thorn experience. The words about the sufficient grace and the fulfillment of power in weakness are the only words of the risen Lord cited in the extant Pauline correspondence.

The initial part of the Lord's response is a denial of Paul's appeal. The thorn would not be removed. Paul must bear with it, but he will be able to do so since the Lord's grace (*hē charis*), that is, his power (*hē dynamis*), is all that Paul needs. The gift of Christ's power has been granted to Paul since his calling to apostolic ministry. Paul may not have been fully aware of this, especially when he was so conscious of his own weakness and the adversity that he suffered during the course of his apostolic ministry.

Explaining the sufficiency of his grace, the Lord to whom Paul prayed said, "Power is perfected in weakness." Power becomes effective in weakness. When Paul cites these words, his readers realize that it is the Lord's power and his own weakness that he is writing about.

There is, nonetheless, a paradigm that best illustrates the truth of the maxim that power is perfected in weakness. For the Christian, the paradigm is that the Christ, who was crucified in human weakness (cf. 1 Cor. 1:23; 2:2), was raised in power (2 Cor. 13:4; cf. Rom. 1:4). The paradox of the cross makes sense of Paul's weakness. The Lord is able to use Paul's weakness in order to manifest the power experienced in the faith of the communities that Paul has evangelized.

> **"My Power Is Perfected in Weakness"**
>
> In 12:9a "my" (*mou*) qualifies "power" in most of the medieval Greek manuscripts and was added by a later corrector to some of the older manuscripts—the Sinaiticus (א), Alexandrinus (A), and Claromontanus (D) Codices—to make clear that it is the Lord's power (see v. 9b), not Paul's, that is perfected in weakness.

Power in Weakness (12:9b–10)

12:9b–10. Ultimately Paul is able to boast about his weakness since it is through his weakness that the power of the Lord is manifest: **Therefore I will quite gladly rather boast about my weaknesses so that the power of Christ might dwell in me.** "Rather" is a comparative that qualifies Paul's boasting. Paul seems to be comparing something else with his boasting about his personal experiences of weakness, his hardships, the humbling escape from Damascus, and suffering a thorn in the flesh, but he leaves the comparison unfinished. The reader is left to wonder whether the implicit point of comparison is Paul's possibly boasting about his apostolic success, or whether he is saying that after Christ's revelation to him, he is content to suffer weakness rather than pray that the thorn might be removed. Ultimately clarification matters little since what is important is expressed in Paul's purpose clause. He speaks of his weaknesses so that the power of Christ might abide in him. In Gal. 2:20 Paul makes a deeply personal christological affirmation: "It is no longer I who live, but it is Christ who lives in me." Here he concentrates on the powerful grace that has been given to him, shining forth in and through his weaknesses.

Not only does Paul boast about his weaknesses (cf. 11:30; 12:5); knowing that through them the power of Christ is manifest, Paul is also able to take satisfaction in his weaknesses. **So I delight in my weaknesses, in mistreatments** (cf. 1 Thess. 2:2), **in hardships, in persecutions, in my dire straits** (12:10). This relatively short list of Paul's apostolic difficulties is the last of the four hardship catalogs in 2 Corinthians (see 4:8–12; 6:4–10; 11:24–29). Now the reader

241

understands why Paul has dwelled so much on his hardships. Not only do they establish his apostolic credentials; they also allow the power of Christ to be manifest. Appropriately, the five-item list begins with Paul's weaknesses, but this is the only time that "weaknesses" appears on one of the hardship lists in 2 Corinthians. In fact, among the five hardships of 12:10, only "hardship" and "dire straits" appear on one of the other lists (cf. 6:4).

All of this Paul was willing to suffer **for the sake of Christ**. The use of the Christ title shows that the paradigm of the cross is very much on Paul's mind. In his writings, "Christ" is a title normally associated with the death and resurrection of Christ. The risen Lord made Paul understand why he suffered so much hardship. Paul understands that his hardships are not wonderful in themselves; Paul is not a masochist. He can delight in his hardships: **for when I am weak, then I am powerful**. What a contrast! What Paul has come to understand belies the conventional wisdom that "what is weak proves itself to be useless" (Wis. 2:11b). With this paradox of power in weakness applied to himself, Paul brings the body of the fool's speech to its end. He has rehearsed his weakness, but he knows that he is powerful—not with his own power but with the power of Christ that abides in him.

The Peroration of a Fool's Speech (12:11–13)

12:11–13. In the epilogue to his speech, Paul speaks about his foolishness for the last time in the letter. He acknowledges that he was foolish in speaking as he did: **I became foolish**, but adds, **you forced me** (12:11). You made me do it. Only on this occasion does Paul ever say that the Corinthians made him do something. They made him become foolish. The coercion was moral, not physical. Paul's concern for the church (see 11:28) led him to the tactic that he adopted.

The emphatic "you" reminds the Corinthians that they are ultimately responsible for Paul's boasting as he did. Instead of commending him as they should have (cf. 5:12), they forced him to act like a fool. **For I should be commended by you**, he writes. Since the Corinthians did not boast about Paul, Paul had to boast about himself (see 6:4), but it was foolish to do so. He does not want to be like the interlopers (see 10:12).

In no way am I inferior to the superapostles, even if I am nothing. The comparison with the superapostles (see 11:5) serves a dual purpose. First of all, it recapitulates the fool's speech, whose theme is that Paul is even more a servant of Christ than they are (11:23). Second, it reminds the Corinthians that they should have been boasting about Paul rather than about the super-apostles, as apparently they were wont to do.

What does he mean by adding "even if I am nothing"? Some suggest that Paul may be using the formula in response to an accusation that the interlopers leveled against him (thus Martin 1986, 427). Others opine that the words are a philosophical formula, used in ancient philosophical debates (see Plato, *Phaedr.* 234C–F; Epictetus, *Diatr.* 3.9.14; 4.8.25), to say that humans are like nothing when compared with the gods (thus Betz 1972, 122–28; Furnish 1984, 552–53, 555). Paul has used the words before (1 Cor. 13:2; cf. v. 3), and there is no reason why he would not use them again here to recapitulate the main thrust of the fool's speech: that without Christ's power Paul is weak, almost nothing. In the context of Paul's epilogue, his words have a meaning akin to the meaning that the words enjoyed in the philosophical debates.

The reason Paul is not inferior to the superapostles is that **apostolic signs were done among you in all perseverance, signs, and wonders, and manifestations of power** (12:12). The Corinthians should know that Paul is not inferior to the superapostles because they have witnessed the "signs" that Paul performed among them. "Signs" are a proof of one's credibility or authority, much in the way that a passport establishes credibility or a medical degree posted in a doctor's office points to certified authority and expertise. Paul qualifies the signs that he demonstrated to the Corinthians as "apostolic" not only because they establish his qualifications as an apostle, but also because he wants to counter the effect of whatever wondrous deeds the superapostles might have done among the Corinthians.

That he performed such signs "in all perseverance" suggests that Paul's miraculous activity was not a single occurrence. Rather, he performed miracles more than once. Since "perseverance" usually implies patience in the face of difficulty, Paul might be alluding to his reluctance to perform miraculous deeds,

---

"Signs and Wonders"

"Signs and wonders" (*sēmeiois te kai terasin*) is a classic biblical formula used particularly in reference to the wondrous deeds that accompanied the exodus (Exod. 7:3; Deut. 4:34; 6:22; 7:19; cf. Acts 7:36).

The formula is used several times in the NT in reference to miracles performed by Jesus's disciples (Acts 2:19, quoting Joel 2:30 [3:3 LXX]; Acts 2:43; 4:30; 5:12; 6:8; 14:3; 15:12). The Johannine Jesus acknowledges that he works signs and wonders (John 4:48). Acts 2:22 and Heb. 2:4 recall that Jesus performed signs and wonders. Luke tells his readers that Paul and Barnabas performed signs and wonders in Iconium (present-day Konya; Acts 14:3) and describes Paul and Barnabas as telling the Jerusalem assembly about their signs and wonders (15:12). Luke also attributes signs and wonders to the apostles (Acts 2:43; 5:12).

The performance of signs and wonders of itself does not, however, establish one's apostolic credentials. Since Matt. 24:24; Mark 13:22; and 2 Thess. 2:9 show that signs and wonders were performed beyond the parameters of Jesus's disciples, discernment is necessary in order to interpret signs and wonders properly. Indeed, although some signs and wonders are done through God's power, others, like those done by the Egyptian magicians of Pharaoh's court, have some other power as their source.

even if he did them often. That was not his forte, not the specific vocation to which he was called (see 1 Cor. 1:17). He seems not to be have been thrilled by the thought of Jews looking for signs (1 Cor. 1:22).

In addition to the signs and wonders that he accomplished in Corinth, Paul acknowledges that he performed such feats from Jerusalem to Illyricum (Rom. 15:19). With characteristic predilection for groups of three, Paul adds manifestations of power (*dynamesin*; cf. Acts 2:22; Heb. 2:4) to the mention of his signs and wonders. "Manifestations of power" (*dynameis*) is the term used throughout the NT to speak of what we today call miracles. In 1 Cor. 12:28–29 Paul includes manifestations of power among the Spirit's charismatic gifts.

All three terms—signs, wonders, and manifestations of power—are generic rather than specific. Although each of the terms has its specific nuance, all three refer, in general, to the marvelous deeds that Paul did by the power of God while he was with the Corinthians.

In Acts, Luke attributes several individual miracles to Paul, but the apostle himself does not do so. Luke tells stories about Paul performing miracles on Cyprus (Acts 13:8–11), in Lystra (14:8–10), in Philippi (16:18), in Ephesus (19:11–12), in Troas (20:8–10), and on Malta (28:8–9), but Paul cites none of these occurrences. Paul's reluctance to speak about the wondrous deeds that God has done is evident in the fool's speech, where he defers any mention of visions and revelations and of signs and wonders until the very end. But it is also evident in 1 Cor. 12–14. In 1 Cor. 13:1–2 Paul conditionally admits that he is a charismatic, but only toward the end of a long discussion of spiritual gifts does Paul admit that he speaks in tongues (1 Cor. 14:6, 14, 18, 19), the gift that led some Corinthians to become puffed up.

Arriving at the end of his speech and having compared himself with the superapostles, Paul directly addresses the Corinthian church, asking them to compare themselves with other churches. **How were you less well off than other churches, except that I didn't burden you?** (12:13). The rhetorical question demands an immediate negative response. The Corinthian church was in no way less devotedly served than were other churches. The Corinthians have nothing to complain about, except the fact that Paul didn't look to them for financial support (see 11:7–12), and that is really nothing to complain about even if the interlopers did so. Nonetheless, ironically and almost sarcastically, Paul begs their forgiveness: **Forgive me this injustice!** His decision to support himself was hardly an injustice to the Corinthians. Neither was it sinful (11:7)!

Theological Issues

Paul's Apostolic Weakness

In 1 Corinthians and again in Romans, Paul writes about weakness (*astheneia*) in the context of his paraenesis to those respective communities. In his long discussion of meat offered to idols (1 Cor. 8–10), Paul urges the members of the church to be sensitive to the delicate consciences of converts who previously have eaten food offered to idols. Now as believers, their consciences would be defiled if they were to eat food that they considered to have been offered to idols (see 1 Cor. 8:7, 11). In Romans, Paul urges those whose faith is strong not to disdain or scandalize those who are weak in faith and continue to observe Jewish dietary laws (see Rom. 14:1–2). In these two letters the overarching issues are believers' love for one another and the unity of the community.

In 2 Corinthians, Paul uses the language of weakness in reference to himself. His weakness is clearly different from the weakness of the believers to whom Paul makes reference in 1 Corinthians and the believers in Rome. In this final part of 2 Corinthians, Paul develops a theology and Christology of what can be called "apostolic weakness." The notion appears in none of his other letters. As is the case with most of Paul's theological concepts, his idea of apostolic weakness was developed during his interaction with those whom he evangelized—in this case, the Corinthians—and in particular with the interlopers, who were disturbing the solidarity between the apostle and the church at Corinth. Accordingly, three levels can be discerned in the exposition of Paul's thoughts on weakness.

To begin, the interlopers made the accusation that Paul's "bodily presence is weak"—the only use of the adjective *asthenēs* in this letter—"and his speech contemptible" (10:10). Paul is willing to concede that he is weak, at least according to the understanding of weakness entertained by the interlopers. To his shame, he says, we have been weak (11:21a), at least according to their understanding of weakness. They disdained his manual labor, about which Paul does not hesitate to speak in the course of his fool's speech. His decision to support himself left him relatively impoverished; he acknowledges that poverty and the consequences thereof. His accusers claimed that his physical appearance was weak and that his speech was despicable. The rags that he wore did not contribute to the image of a strong man. Although it is all but impossible to determine the exact nature of the thorn in his flesh, the most likely interpretations elicit the taunting observation that his appearance is weak or his speech impaired.

On another level, Paul expresses solidarity with those in the community who are weak. "Who is weak, and I am not weak?" he writes in 11:29. As phrased, the matter of principle is of general application. In an epistolary context, the formula expresses Paul's solidarity with the weak members of the Corinthian community. The verb has the same connotation in both parts of the sentence. The weakness rhetorically attributed to some members of the Corinthian community is not the kind of weakness evoked in Paul's earlier discussion of food offered to idols (1 Cor. 8–10). Coming as the conclusion to the long list of hardships in 11:24–28, "weak" certainly connotes one or more of the difficulties listed by Paul. Some within the community suffered from one of the forms of oppression, physical pain, physical exertion, or personal distress from which Paul has suffered. These constitute the circumstances with which Paul can identify.

This apostolic nuance of Paul's identification must not be overlooked, even if it is not yet the fullest expression of the apostolic character of Paul's weakness. Using the Semitic device of synthetic parallelism, Paul pairs the question "Who is weak, and I am not weak?" (11:29a) with another rhetorical question, "Who is made to fall, and I am not set on fire?" (11:29b). That some members of the community should be scandalized and led astray sets Paul's apostolic zeal on fire. Reaching out to them, he reacts to their situation. In similar fashion, Paul's acknowledgment of his own weakness is a way of reaching out to the weak members of the community. It is an empathetic reaction to their weakness. In 1 Cor. 9:22 Paul articulates the apostolic intention of such empathy: "To the weak I became weak, so that I might win the weak."

A third level of Paul's understanding of weakness is theological, christological, and apostolic. To put this aspect of Paul's understanding of weakness in proper perspective, one should note that the noun "weakness" appears six times in the fifth part of the letter, four times in the plural (11:30; 12:5, 9, 10) and twice in the singular (12:9; 13:4). The plural denotes particular experiences of weakness, the experiences that illustrate Paul's weakness. These are the experiences about which Paul can boast (11:30; 12:5, 9, 10) even if it is foolish to boast about such things. Typically, wise persons would not boast about their experiences of weakness, but Paul boasts about these experiences and takes delight in them (12:10).

Weakness in the singular is qualitatively different from weakness in the plural and has a christological referent. The singular first appears in 12:9, among the words of the Lord. The Lord Jesus reveals to Paul that power is "perfected in weakness." This seems almost to be an "autobiographical" reflection from the risen Lord. Paul again uses the singular of weakness in 13:4, where he says that the Christ "was crucified from weakness." He goes on to say that the (risen) Christ "lives by the power of God." In 12:9 and 13:4 "power" (*dynamis*) is antithetically opposed to weakness (*astheneia*). God's power stands over and against the weakness of the crucified Christ (13:4). The Lord Jesus's power stands over and against Paul's weakness (12:9).

About Christ's weakness, Paul writes, "Christ is not weak toward you" and continues by saying that Christ "is powerful among you" (13:3). Once again there is a contrast between weakness and power, but Paul can say that Christ is not weak since the weakness of Christ manifest in the crucifixion has been trumped by the power of God manifest in the resurrection (13:4). Christ's power is particularly at work in the weakness of Paul. In effect the risen Lord tells Paul, "My power is effective in your weakness." Just as the power of God was operative in the weakness of Jesus's humanity at the moment of the crucifixion, so Christ's power—with which he was endowed at the resurrection—was operative in the weakness of Paul. That weakness is manifest in the various weaknesses that Paul has rehearsed.

Paul embraces the notion that Christ's power is operative in his weakness. In the concluding words of the fool's speech, Paul affirms with regard to himself, "When I am weak, then I am powerful" (12:10). These words constitute a gripping and paradoxical peroration. Almost by way of explanation and just before his concluding words, Paul says, "Therefore I will quite gladly rather boast about the manifestations of my weaknesses so that the power of Christ might dwell in me" (12:9).

Since it is the power of God that inheres in the risen Christ, it is ultimately the power of God that abides in Paul. In 13:4 Paul associates his own weakness with the weakness of the crucified Christ. Paul says, "He was crucified from weakness but lives by the power of God; we too are weak in him [Christ], but we live with him by the power of God for you." The final "for you" expresses the apostolic quality of the power of God active in Paul. Alternatively phrased, Christ is powerful among you (13:3). Christ is powerful among the Corinthians through the instrumentality of Paul, minister of Christ (11:23) and apostle to the Corinthians (1 Cor. 9:2). In Paul's weakness, Christ is powerful among the Corinthians, making them powerful in their weakness in a manner similar to the manner in which Christ's power was powerful in Paul. This gives Paul reason to rejoice. "We rejoice," he writes, "when we are weak and you are powerful" (13:9).

On the literary level there is remarkable irony in Paul's expression of his theology of power in weakness. In the way Paul uses terms, they have an oxymoronic quality. The paradox is resolved theologically in the light of Paul's understanding of the cross. The mystery of the cross can be articulated as the weakness of the crucified Christ being met by the power of God operative in the resurrection.

This reality is key to the understanding of an apostolic chain. As the power of God was operative in the weakness of the cross, so the power of Christ is operative in the weakness of Paul. As the power of Christ, God's power, is operative in Paul, so the power of Paul is operative among the Corinthians. As the power of Paul, Christ's power, God's power, is operative among the Corinthians, so their power is operative. . . .

The apostolic chain continues to be realized in the church at Corinth. It continues to be realized in the church of today. When the church, its ministers, and its faithful are conscious of their own weakness, the power of God is effective in them.

2 Corinthians 12:14–13:10

Paul's Third Visit to Corinth

Introductory Matters

As Paul was wrapping up his First Letter to the Corinthians, he expressed the hope that he would make a return visit to the Corinthians and stay with them for a while, perhaps for the entire winter (1 Cor. 16:5–9). That trip was to take place after Paul passed through Macedonia, where he had established churches in Philippi and Thessalonica.

Paul changed his travel plans, deciding to go to Corinth on his way to Macedonia and then to make another visit on his way back (2 Cor. 1:16). This second visit did not go well for Paul. His change of plans made him appear fickle in the eyes of some. A troublemaker caused him some personal grief. So Paul went back to Ephesus rather than continuing on to Macedonia. Then, in order to avoid another painful experience in Corinth, Paul sent the letter of tears rather than visit the Corinthians in person (2:1–4).

The tearful letter produced some good results, as Titus's report indicated. Paul becomes confident. He hopes that the current letter will also have good results. So now he is ready to make his third visit to the Corinthians.

Tracing the Train of Thought

The Announcement (12:14–15)

12:14–15. **Now I am ready to come to you for a third time** (12:14). After having his say, Paul shares with the Corinthians his decision to come visit them.

248

The introductory "now" (*idou*, "behold") indicates that Paul is moving on to a new topic. Paul visited the Corinthians for the first time when he evangelized the community (1 Cor. 2:1–5; Acts 18:1–17). His second visit (cf. 2 Cor. 13:2) was a painful experience, to which he briefly alludes in 2:1. The pain of that visit was such that Paul put off a third visit (1:23–2:1). Paul is already in Macedonia, where he has learned about the Corinthians' longing for him (7:5–7). Earlier he had told the Corinthians that he would pass through Macedonia on his way to visit them (1 Cor. 16:5–6). The conditions were ripe for another visit, perhaps one that would enable him to spend some time with the Corinthians, as he had hoped to do at one time (1 Cor. 16:7). But there remains the issue of Paul's self-support.

Paul confronts the issue head-on. **And I will not burden you.** Paul has no intention of receiving financial support from the Corinthians. For one final time in this letter, he discusses the matter of his monetary self-support and cites his paternal relationship with the Corinthians as the

> **2 Corinthians 12:14–13:10 in the Rhetorical Flow**
>
> The letter opening (1:1–2)
>
> Ministerial crises (1:3–2:13)
>
> Paul explains and defends his apostolic ministry (2:14–7:4)
>
> The arrival and report of Titus (7:5–16)
>
> Service to God's holy people (8:1–9:15)
>
> An aggressive taskmaster (10:1–13:10)
>
> > Paul's missionary task (10:1–18)
> >
> > On the attack (11:1–15)
> >
> > Boasting like a fool (11:16–12:13)
> >
> > ▶ Paul's third visit to Corinth (12:14–13:10)
> >
> > > The announcement (12:14–15)
> > >
> > > A final defense (12:16–18)
> > >
> > > Paul's fears (12:19–21)
> > >
> > > Paul is ready nonetheless (13:1–4)
> > >
> > > Exhortation and a prayer (13:5–10)

reason why he will not accept monetary help from them. **For I am not seeking what is yours, but you; for children ought not save up for their parents, rather parents** should save up **for their children.**

Earlier in the letter, Paul has spoken to the Corinthians as his children, chiding them for the immaturity of their emotions (6:13). In 1 Corinthians he uses both paternal (4:14–21) and maternal imagery (3:1–2) to talk about his relationship with them. The imagery is apropos since Paul was the founder of the community. As a father he taught them, and as a mother he nurtured them, yet kinship language is notably absent from 2 Corinthians. In this missive Paul does not speak of himself as father or mother to the Corinthians. Even here he speaks about "parents." The language is generic. Paul writes about parents almost as if he were citing an abstract principle. Nonetheless, the implication is that Paul considers himself to have a parental relationship, albeit somewhat strained, with the Corinthians. As a parent, he seeks the well-being of the Corinthian community. He is looking out for them. The contrast between "what is yours" and "you" underscores his point.

Since the matter of Paul's financial support has been such a bone of contention—and the reader of Paul's letter, then and now, is surely aware that the continuation of the collection for Jerusalem remains on the horizon—Paul offers a simple example from day-to-day economics. Parents save up their resources to take care of their children, not vice versa. So added to all the other reasons why Paul did not accept financial support from the Corinthians is the fact that he is a parent to the community.

Continuing the economic metaphor and pursuing his assumed parental role, Paul writes, **Quite gladly I will spend and be spent for your sakes** (12:15; cf. 1 Thess. 2:8). Both verbs, "spend" (*dapanēsō*) and "be spent" (*ekdapanēthēsomai*), are hapax in Paul's writings.

A rhetorical question then interrupts the flow of Paul's thought: **If I love you more**, Paul says in his appeal to the Corinthians, **am I loved less?** Paul loves the Corinthians (2:4; 6:6; 7:1; 8:7; 11:11; 12:15; see v. 19). His willingness to pour himself out for them and his desire not to take any of their possessions for his own use are signs of Paul's love for them. He expects his love to be requited (7:2). Hence arises his question, "Am I to be loved less?" The question awaits a positive response. "Of course not," the Corinthians are expected to say; "we love you all the more."

A Final Defense (12:16–18)

12:16–18. So be it. I have not burdened you (12:16). Paul hopes that the matter has been put to rest. But some might object that all that is just a facade. **But being clever**, they might say, **I took you by deceit.** Paul does not identify who is trying to raise this suspicion among the Corinthians, but it is most likely the interlopers or some among them. They may have suggested that Paul had designs on the collection. In 4:2, Paul said that he does not act cunningly. Now he is going to counter head-on the objection that lies in the background. He asks a series of rhetorical questions designed to make the Corinthians reflect on their experience of Paul.

The first two questions await a quick "no" as their response. **I didn't take advantage of you by means of anyone I sent to you, did I?** (12:17). "Sent" is in the perfect tense, suggesting that more than one delegation was sent to the Corinthians by Paul. They should know that no one in those delegations defrauded them. "Took advantage" (*epleonektēsa*, related to *pleonexia*, "greed") is an expression that has financial overtones.

This language recurs in the next rhetorical question, which pertains to a delegation whose purpose was designedly financial: **I asked Titus, and I sent a brother with him. Titus hasn't taken advantage of you, has he?** (12:18). If 2 Corinthians is a single composition, "asked" and "sent" might be taken as epistolary aorists rather than as true aorists. In this case, the delegation to which Paul is referring could well be the delegation that he mentions in 8:16–24; 9:3. That delegation includes two brothers (8:18, 22) with Titus. It could be that in his zeal Paul forgets to mention Titus's second companion in 12:18. On the other hand, the mission that Paul is referencing here could be Titus's earlier mission (8:6, 10). In any case, "hasn't taken advantage" uses a true aorist. Paul is appealing to the Corinthians' past experience.

The next two questions expect "yes" for an answer. **Haven't we acted with the same spirit? Haven't we followed the same path?** Asking the Corinthians to consider that he acted in a way similar to the way that his emissaries acted, Paul uses a pair of metaphors. In Greek, Paul's "acted" is *periepatēsamen*, literally, "walked." He uses a common Semitic idiom. His "spirit" does not refer to the Holy Spirit; rather, it is his way of referring to the human sense of responsibility and integrity. The parallel question continues the metaphor for following an example (cf. Rom. 4:12; 1 Pet. 2:21). Paul asks, "Haven't we walked in the same footsteps?" I have rendered the elliptical question—the verb "walk" must be supplied—"Haven't we followed the same path?"

Paul's Fears (12:19–21)

12:19–21. Although Paul has made the decision to travel to Corinth, he remains somewhat apprehensive and continues to defend himself. **You have been thinking all along that we have been defending ourselves [*apologoumetha*] to you** (12:19). "All along" introduces Paul's commentary on what he thinks his addressees will be thinking as they listen to what he has written since 10:1. Paul anticipates that there will probably be some reaction. He assumes that they probably think that he has been engaged in a lengthy *apologia pro vita mea*.

But that is not the reason he writes as he does. With an oath-like affirmation—a verbatim repetition of a formula that he uses in 2:17—Paul emphasizes the truth of what he is going to say about his purpose in writing: **In the presence of God we are speaking in Christ.** The words do not have the literary form of an oath, but their function is similar to that of formulas found in 1:23; 11:11, 31; 12:2, 3. In 11:11 he writes, "The truth of Christ is in me." When Paul says that he is speaking in Christ, he states the obvious. He is speaking to the Corinthians by means of his letter.

Paul was speaking to the Corinthians in order to build them up as a community of believers. **All these things, beloved, are to build you up,** he writes. That Paul addresses the community as "beloved" (cf. 7:1; 1 Cor. 4:14; 10:14; 15:58) is appropriate after his repeated expressions of love for them. The authority that the Lord has

> ### "All along" (*palai*)
>
> The word *palai* occurs only here in Paul's extant writings. It is found in the oldest manuscript of 2 Corinthians, $\mathfrak{P}^{46}$, but in place of *palai* some ancient manuscripts and the majority of medieval Greek manuscripts read *palin* ("again"), an adverb that Paul often uses. Because of the rarity of its occurrence, preference must be given to the reading *palai* in 2 Cor. 12:19.

given to Paul is for building up the community (10:18; cf. 13:10). Even as he was taking issue with the accusations of the interlopers, seemingly boasting about himself, what he really intended to do was build up the community.

Building up the community is also the purpose of Paul's forthcoming visit to them. He is ready for the visit (12:14), but neither Paul's decision nor his reason for the visit have totally banished his apprehension. The last visit did not go well (2:1). Despite Titus's assurance that the community is longing for him (7:7), Paul continues to experience some uneasiness. He suspects that the Corinthians might not be living in accordance with their holiness, their call to be God's own people. Paul also suspects that they may be expecting him to arrive among them and act with clemency, but he is ready to act boldly if need be (13:2, 10). **For I am afraid that when I come to you**, he writes, **I may not find you** to be **the sort of people that I am wishing for, and that I will not be for you the sort of person that you are wishing for** (12:20).

That Paul might not be the sort of person that the community wants to see may be an expression of his pastoral outreach to them. But the relationship between Paul and the community is two-way. So Paul cites his concern about the Corinthians, who may not be in the situation that Paul would like them to be in. I am afraid, he explains, **that there may be division, envy, anger, strife, slander, gossip, conceit, unruliness.** The list of eight vices is a classic example of a catalog of vices. Nonetheless there is a common theme. Each of the vices mentioned by Paul undermines the unity of a community. Paul's primary concern is that the community experience unity (cf. 1 Cor. 1:10). He has spoken about most of these vices in 1 Corinthians. All of them appear elsewhere in his correspondence, most often in catalogs of vices. The first two vices in this catalog are in the singular; the other six are in the plural. Paul has in mind outbursts of anger, strife, slander, gossip, conceit, and unruliness.

As for himself, Paul says, **I fear that when I come again, my God will humble me before you** (12:21). What kind of humbling experience is Paul thinking about? The experience that he fears is something of which the Corinthians themselves would be aware. Paul fears that his visit is going to be another humiliating experience. Does

---

Vices That Undermine the Unity of a Community

division (*eris*): 1 Cor. 1:11; 3:3; Rom. 1:29; 13:13; Gal. 5:20; Phil. 1:15

envy (*zēlos*): 1 Cor. 3:3; Rom. 13:13; Gal. 5:20

anger (*thymoi*): Gal. 5:20

strife (*eritheiai*): Rom. 2:8; Gal. 5:20; Phil. 1:17; 2:3

slander (*katalaliai*): Rom. 1:30 (a related form)

gossip (*psithyrismoi*): Rom. 1:29 (a related form)

conceit (*physiōseis*): The noun is found only here in the NT, but the related verb appears in 1 Cor. 4:6, 18, 19; 5:2; 8:1; 13:4; cf. Col. 2:18

unruliness (*akatastasiai*): 1 Cor. 14:33

---

he fear a recurrence of something similar to what happened during his previous visit (2:1)? Is he afraid that the Corinthians will again find his supporting himself humiliating for him (11:7)? Is God going to send him another thorn in the flesh (12:7), and would the Corinthians find that repugnant? Whatever it might be, Paul attributes it to God, who is responsible for Paul's missionary activity, with all its attendant circumstances.

Paul expresses concern that on arriving in Corinth he may find evidence of disruption within the community, but there is something else that concerns him. **And** I fear **that I will grieve [*penthēsō*]** (hapax in 2 Corinthians) **over many who sinned before and have not turned from the impurity, and sexual immorality, and licentiousness that they practice.** The way Paul talks about these sinners indicates that he thinks their sinful behavior is

Sexual Misconduct

impurity (*akatharsia*): Rom. 1:24; 6:19; Gal. 5:19; 1 Thess. 2:3; 4:7

sexual immorality (*porneia*): 1 Cor. 5:1; 6:13, 18; 7:2; Gal. 5:19; 1 Thess. 4:3

sexually immoral person (*pornos*): 1 Cor. 5:9, 10, 11; 6:9.

act in a sexually immoral manner (*porneuō*): 1 Cor. 6:18; 10:8

licentiousness (*aselgeia*): Rom. 13:13; Gal. 5:19

continuing. They have not taken the opportunity to change their ways, perhaps on the occasion of one of Paul's previous visits.

As there was a common thread in the list of vices found in the previous verse, so is there a common thread in the way Paul describes the sinful behavior of some of the Corinthians. All three vices—impurity, sexual immorality, and licentiousness—are forms of sexual misconduct.

These three sins are cited in the catalog of vices found in Gal. 5:19–21. As is often the case with such terms mentioned in a list of vices, it is difficult to distinguish one vice from another. Nor is there any need to do so. Paul has already written to the Corinthians about sexual immorality (1 Cor. 5:1, 9–11; 6:9–10, 13, 18; 7:2). The apostle to the church at Corinth fears that this kind of behavior is still going on, despite his two visits to the community and repeated warnings in his correspondence (cf. 1 Cor. 5:9).

Paul Is Ready Nonetheless (13:1–4)

13:1–4. In 12:14 Paul announces his readiness to return to Corinth for a third visit, yet he has some apprehension at the prospect. Despite his lingering concerns, Paul's decision to go to Corinth remains firm. **I am coming to you a third time** (13:1), he writes. Then he quotes Deut. 19:15 without any introduction. **Let every case be established on the testimony of two or three witnesses.** The legal prescription is quoted in Matt. 18:16 and alluded to in Matt. 26:60 and John 8:17. Apparently this legal norm was well known among the members of early Christian communities.

It is hardly likely that Paul intends to convene a courtroom session to deal with either antisocial or sexually immoral persons among the Corinthians. In fact, in 1 Cor. 5:1–6 he takes the Corinthians to task for not adequately dealing with a sexually immoral individual. They, not Paul, are the ones who really should be addressing the issue of sexual immorality in the community. Since Paul is unlikely to preside over a court session—neither his letters nor Acts indicates that Paul ever did anything of this sort—"two or three witnesses" probably does not refer to individuals who might be called to testify in a trial. It is more likely that the expression is to be taken metaphorically.

The legal adage speaks of two or three. Paul mentions a second and third visit in 13:1–2. Given the likelihood of some correlation between the numerical expressions, the "witnesses" are most probably Paul's second and third visits to the Corinthians. With Paul's second visit the Corinthians should have set their affairs in order with regard to their lack of unity and the issue of sexual misconduct. They didn't do so. Now Paul is giving them fair warning. His forthcoming visit should convince them of what they should do.

"I told you so" is the thought that runs through what Paul says next: **When present for the second time, I said, and now absent, I say again** (13:2). The verbs "said" (*proeirēka*) and "say" (*prolegō*), respectively in the perfect and the present, are compound verbs whose prefix (*pro-*) connotes "say beforehand." Paul's perfect tense indicates that what Paul said during the second visit is still valid. What he said seems to have fallen on deaf ears, so he is going to say it again. The expression that Paul uses to speak about his presence and his absence is epistolary language. Paul is well aware of the difference between physical presence and the extended presence conveyed by means of a letter. In 10:11 Paul reminds the Corinthians that there is no difference between what he says in person and what he writes. Thus 13:2 is just one example.

Paul has spoken before and now is speaking again **to those who sinned before and to everyone else**. Those who sinned before—in Paul the verb "sin before," *proamartanō*, appears only here and in 12:21—are undoubtedly those who are continuing in their lives of impurity, sexual immorality, and licentiousness. "Everyone else" is the rest of the community, those who have not come to grips with their disunity, those who haven't been dismayed by the sexual immorality in their midst.

The message for everyone is **that when I come again, I will not refrain**. On his next visit he is not going to hold back; he is not going to restrain himself; he will not be discouraged by the reception that he received on the occasion of his second visit. The interlopers exploited his "weakness" in an attempt to undermine his authority. Their accusations will not deter Paul. He will not hold back. He will not be lenient if the situation calls for him to be bold (cf. 10:2).

With **since you seek proof of Christ's speaking in me** (13:3), Paul alludes to the situation. Paul has already mentioned the apostolic signs that he has produced (12:12), but he is well aware that the interlopers have so poisoned

the atmosphere at Corinth that some
Corinthians are still looking for "proof."

The Corinthians want proof that Paul
is the spokesperson for Christ (see 12:9,
19), **who is not weak toward you but is
powerful among you.** This characterization of Christ is most likely Paul's own
formulation. It allows him to reprise the
theme he began to develop in 12:9. A
chiastic construction—with the prepositional phrases on the outside and verbs
connected by the conjunction "but" at
the center—highlights the contrast between "not weak" and "powerful."

The traditional core of Christian
belief is that "Christ died . . . and was
raised" (1 Cor. 15:3–4), but for pastoral
reasons pertaining to the situation at
Corinth, Paul emphasizes the modality
of Christ's death in preaching the gospel
to the Corinthians. In 1 Corinthians he writes, "We proclaim Christ crucified [*Christon estaurōmenon*], a stumbling block to Jews and foolishness to
Gentiles" (1:23; cf. 1:27). Furthermore, "I decided to know nothing among
you except Jesus Christ, and him crucified" (2:2).

Now Paul picks up on the way he preached about Christ during his first
visit and declares, **For indeed he was crucified from weakness** (13:4), the only
mention of the cross in 2 Corinthians. Death is a consequence of the manifest
condition of human weakness. Death at the hands of others is a sign of their
power and one's own weakness. Thus, Christ was crucified from weakness.
Early Christian creedal formulas proclaim that Christ's death is not to be
separated from his resurrection. Together they form one salvific event (see
5:15; Rom. 1:3–4; 1 Cor. 15:3–5; 1 Thess. 4:14).

Since death contrasts with life, Paul speaks about the resurrection in terms of
life. Weakness contrasts with power. So Paul writes, **but he lives by the power of
God.** "Of God" creates an imbalance in the tight formulaic contrast between
"crucified from weakness" and "lives by power," but Paul wants his readers to
know that the life of the resurrected Christ is from the power of God. In a sense,
the apostle is affirming that the weakness of the crucified Christ is due to his
humanity, but the power by which the risen Christ lives is alien to him. It is with
that power, the power of God, that Christ is powerful among the Corinthians
(13:3b). Christ is, as Paul has written earlier, the power of God (1 Cor. 1:24).

The contrast between weakness and power continues as Paul applies the
just-stated truth about Christ to his own situation. The emphatic "we" with

---

Proof

Discourse about proof and passing the
test is much in evidence in 13:1–10 as
the presence of the *dokim-* word group
indicates:

The verb *dokimazō* ("scrutinize")
appears in 13:5 (cf. 8:8, 22).
The noun *dokimē* ("proof") appears in 13:3 (cf. 2:9; 8:2; 9:13).
The adjective *dokimos* ("passed
the test, qualified") appears in
13:7 (cf. 10:18).
The adjective *adokimos* ("failed
the test, unqualified") appears
in 13:5, 6, 7.

which the sentence begins draws attention to Paul's personal appropriation of the christological truth: **For indeed we too are weak in him, but we will live with him by the power of God.** The expression "for indeed," which introduces this second part of verse 4, also similarly introduces the first part of the verse, showing that Paul develops a single interlocking argument by way of commentary on the powerful Christ whom the Corinthians seek to find speaking in Paul.

Admittedly Paul is weak, but in his weakness he identifies with the weakness of the crucified Christ. Paul will also live with Christ, by the very same power with which Christ lives. He will live by the power of God. As Christ lives by the power of God, so Paul lives by the power of Christ. The "with him" phrase denotes "association in activity" (Stegman 2005, 210). As Christ is powerful among the Corinthians (v. 3), so Paul will live by God's power for them, **for your sake** (*eis hymas* is absent from a few ancient manuscripts, including Codex Vaticanus [B]). The future life to which Paul makes reference—the verb "will live" is in the future tense—is not Paul's eschatological life after death. Rather, it is the life that he will be living when he is among the Corinthians on the occasion of his third visit. Then, he says, he will be living—and acting—by the power of God.

Exhortation and a Prayer (13:5–10)

13:5–10. Rather than testing Paul, trying to find proof that Christ is speaking through him, the Corinthians should be testing themselves. **Test yourselves to see if you are in the faith** (13:5; cf. 1:24); **scrutinize yourselves.** "Test yourselves" is almost formulaic. The verb is a hapax in 2 Corinthians; the initial "yourselves" draws attention to the Corinthians just as the initial "we" in the previous sentence focused attention on Paul. **Don't you realize that Jesus Christ is among you?** The rhetorical question calls for a positive answer. If the Corinthians look deep within themselves, they should surely realize that Christ is among them. If they don't, then they don't measure up to the standard of someone who is in the faith. **If not, you have failed the test.** If they do not realize that Christ is among them, they have failed the test.

Paul adds, **I hope you know that we have not failed the test** (13:6). Surely the Corinthians realize that Christ is among them; if they do, then just as surely they should realize that Paul has not failed the test (cf. 2 Cor. 3:3). He is living his apostolic calling. The fact that they have faith attests to Paul's being in the faith, for he is the one who evangelized them.

Paul continues with an expression of his pastoral solicitude: **We pray to God that you do no wrong** (13:7). The prayer is offered to God, the usual addressee (albeit sometimes implicit) of Paul's prayers. The verb "pray" (*euchometha*) is in the present tense and is performative: as Paul writes about his prayer, he is in fact engaged in prayer. He is praying for his beloved Corinthians.

The Christian life is evident in the way Christians act. Paul has expressed concern lest there be evidence of disharmony and sexual immorality in the community. Since the test of a genuine life in faith is doing what is right, Paul prays that the Corinthians are doing nothing evil, that they are not engaged in behavior that disrupts the community, whether sexual immorality or anything else that is evil.

Paul's concern is for the Corinthians. Paul does not want the Corinthians to live morally just so that people will recognize that his apostolic ministry has been successful. Lest anyone think along those lines, Paul issues a disclaimer. The intention of his prayer is **not that we might appear to have passed the test.** The emphatic "we" makes clear that Paul doesn't want attention drawn to himself. Despite his vigorous defense of his ministry, he wants the Corinthians to live a life of faith, no matter what people think of him. Corinthian believers should know that Paul has passed the test of apostolic fidelity. If others, perhaps the interlopers, think that he has not, so what?

Paul's desire that his beloved Corinthians avoid evil and do what is good is so strong that he resorts to a literary contrast to reiterate his point. **But** we pray **that you do what is good.** Once again Paul adds a disclaimer containing another emphatic "we": **even if we seem to have failed the test.** Paul does not care if people think he has failed the test as long as the Corinthians do what is good. The fourth-century Ambrosiaster (*Commentary on Paul's Epistles* 81.3.312) suggests that if the Corinthians do what is good and avoid evil, Paul will appear to have failed the test insofar as there would be no need for him to chastise sinners when he arrives in Corinth. This could be construed as a lessening of Paul's apostolic authority. Yet the apostle is not concerned about himself; his only concern is for the Corinthians. He does what he does because he cannot act contrary to the truth. **For,** he writes, **we are unable to do anything against the truth** (13:8). We act **rather for the sake of the truth.**

Paul has much to say about power. Paradoxically he has said that it was when he was weak that he was powerful (12:10). The paradox is resolved with the realization that Paul's power is an alien power. He has written about the power of Christ as dwelling in him (12:9b). Paul lives by the power of God (13:4b; cf. 6:7). In verse 8 he returns to the topic of his power. He has no power against the truth. The only power that he has is for the sake of truth. Paul has been empowered for the sake of truth.

"We cannot act contrary to the truth" appears to be a commonplace of moral wisdom, but the words have a deeper meaning in Paul. The contrast between not acting against the truth and acting on behalf of the truth expresses a norm for Paul's apostolic behavior. What he does is for the sake of the truth, the truth of Christ that is in Paul (11:10). In 4:2 and again in 6:7 he uses the word "truth" in reference to the word of God, the gospel. The word of God, the gospel, is the norm of Paul's apostolic ministry.

Confident that in his weakness he has been acting with the power of God for the sake of the gospel, Paul has reason to be glad. **For,** he writes, **we rejoice when we are weak and you are powerful** (13:9). The contrast brings to mind what Paul said in 4:12, "Death is at work in us, while life is at work in you," as well as the "We are weak, but you are strong" of 1 Cor. 4:10b. If the gospel message preached by Paul in his weakness takes hold among the Corinthians, they are powerful with the power of God and his Christ. Energized by that power, the Corinthians do what is good and avoid evil. This brings joy to Paul's heart. Throughout the letter, he repeatedly tells the Corinthians that it is their situation of living in faith, in fidelity to the gospel, that makes him joyful (see 2:3; 6:10; 7:7, 9, 16).

Paul recapitulates the thought of this short subunit on the content of his prayer for the Corinthians (13:7–10) with **and we pray for this, that you get things together**. In 12:20 he identifies a number of vices that can disrupt the unity of a community and expresses his fear that the well-being of the community might continue to be threatened in this way. In this summary of his prayer (13:9b), he expresses a hope, a wish that the Corinthians get their act together.

With thoughts of the upcoming visit on the horizon, Paul brings the letter to a close. **This is why I am writing these things to you while I am away from you** (13:10). Paul is self-consciously aware that he is writing a letter and that a letter is a means of communication when one is absent. An explicit contrast between absence (*apousia, apeimi*) and presence (*parousia, pareimi*) belongs to the domain of epistolary literature; it is the language one uses when writing letters. For the fourth time in this letter (see 10:1–2, 11; 13:2), Paul exploits the contrast as he says, so **that when I arrive [*parōn*], I will not have to deal severely with you**. Paul's purpose in writing the letter is so that he will not

---

"That You Get Things Together"

In Greek this phrase appears as a noun (*katartisin*), with a qualifying pronoun in the second-person plural (*hymōn*). The noun has been variously translated as "completion, perfection, restoration, or improvement." The appearance of the noun as the very last word in the prayer stresses its importance, but it appears nowhere else in the NT. Since it comes after Paul has said that he is praying that the Corinthians act in a morally appropriate fashion, the word seems to have a moral connotation.

The related verb, *katartizō*, is a technical term used in moral exhortation. Paul uses the verb with paraenetic import and will do so again in 13:11 (cf. 1 Cor. 1:10; Gal. 6:1). The verb has, however, a wide range of applicability. It was used in reference to a broad range of spheres, as diverse as meal preparation and architecture (*EDNT* 2:271–74). Its basic meaning seems to be to adjust something so that it fits its purpose.

In 1 Cor. 1:10, Paul uses the verb with a connotation similar to its use in political discourse, to refer to the appeasement of factions and the restoration of unity. This idea may well capture the main thrust in Paul's use of the noun in 13:9.

need to act harshly when he goes to them. He is ready to do so (10:2; 13:2; cf. 10:10), but he hopes that his letter motivates the Corinthians to get their lives together and their church unified (13:9).

If it should be necessary for Paul to deal severely with the Corinthians, his action would be **in keeping with the authority that the Lord gave me for building up, not for tearing down.** Paul has no authority except the authority that the Lord has given him. Using the same phrase that appeared in 10:8, Paul reminds the Corinthians that the purpose of his authority is to build them up, not tear them down. If he has had harsh things to say in this letter, it was to build them up (12:19). These are the last words in the body of Paul's letter. He hopes that when he arrives in Corinth, he will not need to use his authority severely. That is why he has written this letter in advance of his arrival. He hopes that the Corinthians take his message to heart and prepare for his visit.

Theological Issues

Paul's Credentials

As Paul announces his intention to make a third visit to the Corinthians, he is aware that some among them are still seeking proof that Christ is speaking in him. What are the credentials that Paul can show to prove that he is an apostle, authorized to speak in the name of Christ? Paul's citation of a legal norm, Deut. 9:15, shows that he is, as it were, on trial. The interlopers have sought to undermine his apostolic authority. Paul strives to provide convincing evidence that he is an apostle.

One line of argument is defensive. Paul does not concede that the interlopers are apostles of Christ Jesus (cf. 1:1). With no small irony, Paul labels them "superapostles" (11:5; 12:11), apparently because they claim that they are apostles based on their producing signs of an apostle, using their ability to work wonders. In Paul's judgment, however, they are false apostles who have disguised themselves as apostles of Christ (11:13).

Paul does, however, concede that they are servants of Christ. Nonetheless, he claims that he is more a servant of Christ than they are (11:23). In fact, he is in no way inferior to them (11:5; 12:11). Ironically, to demonstrate that he is more a servant of Christ than they are, he cites a long list of hardships. The list begins with a comparison: Paul says that he worked harder and was more frequently in prison than they were. He implies that he was beaten more than they were and experienced brushes with death that they didn't experience. The long list of hardships culminates with Paul's mention of two experiences that illustrate his weakness: his flight-by-night escape from Damascus and his suffering a protracted thorn in his flesh. Ironically these hardships qualify Paul as an apostle of Christ because they allow him to identify with Christ in his weakness (cf. 4:8–12; 12:9b–10). In somewhat similar fashion, the list of hardships in 6:4–10 allows Paul to commend himself as a servant of God.

Comparing himself with the superapostles in 11:5, Paul concedes that his oratorical skill might be inferior to theirs (cf. 10:10), but with regard to the charismatic gift of knowledge, he is not inferior. That is an understatement. If Paul's spiritual experiences are to be compared with those of the super-apostles, his ecstatic experience and the abundance of revelation that he has received from the Lord—about which he is hesitant to boast but cites because these experiences come from the Lord (cf. 10:17)—are beyond any spiritual experience about which the interlopers can boast.

Then there is the matter of charismatic activity. Paul speaks about signs and wonders in the context of comparing himself with the superapostles (12:11–12). That he does so suggests that the superapostles boasted about the wondrous deeds that they had performed. They may have appealed to these miracles to establish their credentials, calling them "apostolic signs." Paul is reluctant to talk about the miracles that he has performed. His hesitancy to do so is evident in that he does not speak about them in any of his letters except at 12:12 and Rom. 15:19. Among the Corinthians he has given evidence of signs and wonders and manifestations of power. That he does so in all persever-ance must be understood in the context of the polemical argument with the interlopers. Does it mean that Paul is hesitant to perform miracles, or does it imply that Paul comes out ahead in the battle of miracles?

The interlopers have apparently cited their suffering, their spiritual experi-ences, and their ability to perform miracles in order to establish their credibility. Using these criteria, Paul shows that in the battle of credentials he is in no way inferior to the superapostles. For Paul, however, providing the Corinthians with a demonstration of these sorts of credentials is not what matters. The only credential that matters is the faith of the community. Paul first addressed this issue in 3:1–3. He has the letters of credence that are important, the Christian community itself, a letter of Christ.

Using other language and different imagery, Paul returns to this idea in 13:5–7. The Corinthians are looking for proof that Paul is Christ's spokes-person. The Corinthians should know that Paul has not failed the test. Let them scrutinize themselves. That Christ is among them and that they have a dynamic faith are proof that they have not failed the test, nor has Paul.

Paul's Prayer

In 13:7–9, Paul offers a short prayer to God, asking that the Corinthians do what is good and avoid evil. He brings his prayer to a close by saying that he is praying that the Corinthians get their house in order and improve their lives: "We pray to God that you do no wrong, . . . rather, that you might do what is good. . . . We pray for this, that you may get things together."

The appearance of "we pray" in verses 7 and 9 constitutes a literary inclusion and makes of the three verses a distinct subunit in Paul's letter. The
intervening clauses remind the Corinthians that Paul's prayer is not motivated
by self-interest. In his prayer, Paul is concerned for the best interests of the Corinthians. The emphatic position that he accords to "this" in speaking about
his prayer for the second time confirms that this is indeed the case.

Paul is praying to God—the verb is in the present tense—asking God to
bring something to pass among the Corinthians. His use of the verb *euchomai*
(13:7, 9) to speak about his prayer is his only use of the verb with this meaning
(cf. Rom. 9:3). Similar prayers of petition are not found anywhere else in the
extant correspondence.

Use of the verb to connote petitionary prayer has a long history in Greek
literature and is echoed in the Greek Bible (cf. *EDNT* 2:147–54). For example, it
was said of a priest of Dionysus that "he shall pray prayers for the city of the Prie-
niens" (I.Priene 174.19). Plato defined this sense of the verb: "To pray is to address
requests to the gods" (*Euthyphr.* 14c). Paul's Hellenistic Jewish contemporary
Philo defined the related noun "prayer" in similar fashion. "Prayer [*euchē*]," he
writes, "is a request of good things from God" (*Sacrifices* 53; *Unchangeable* 87).

In the ancient papyri roughly contemporary with Paul, the verb is an epistolary expression. It sometimes appears at the end of a letter (P.Tebt. 41.53),
particularly in letters that begin "to A from B" rather than "A to B," the
standard form used by Paul and most Hellenistic letter writers (cf. 1:1–2). Far
more often, however, the formula is found at the beginning of a Hellenistic
letter (P.NYU 25.2; P.Oxy. 3314.3; P.Brux. 17.94), especially when the letter
writer prays for the well-being of the addressee.

In praying for the well-being of the community at Corinth, however, Paul
prays not for their physical welfare but for
their spiritual well-being. He asks God to enable their being in faith to manifest itself in
their conduct: in their doing what is good,
avoiding evil, and repairing potential ruptures
in the community. The presence of the qualifying pronoun "your" in the second-person
plural in verse 9's summary of Paul's prayer
clearly shows that the Corinthians are the intended beneficiaries of Paul's prayer of petition. The prayer stands out as the only extant
example of Paul's prayer of petition, a pastor's
prayer for a troubled community.

The embedded instruction to the Corinthians
suggests that Paul's prayer is as much a prayer
report as it is an actual prayer. In this respect it is
akin to the epistolary thanksgivings of Romans,

> ### The Prayer for Good Health
>
> A letter writer's prayer for the
> good health of the recipient is
> found in several ancient papyri,
> including P.Aberd. 71.3; P.Mert.
> 28.3; 81.2; 82.2, 3, 5; 85.2; P.Yale
> 78.3; P.Wisc. 71.3; 72.4; P.Oslo 52.3;
> P.Alex. 24.3; 30.4; BGU 1673.3;
> P.Laur. 20.3. In the NT, 3 John 2 is
> the only place with the customary
> epistolary prayer for good health.
> The prayer for good health typi-
> cally uses the verb *euchomai*.

Paul's Wish-Prayers

Wish-prayers, such as those found in Rom. 15:5–6, 13; 1 Thess. 3:11, 12–13; 5:23–24 (cf. Rom. 15:33; 16:20a), are also prayers for the community, but this sort of prayer belongs to another literary genre, and none of them appears in 2 Corinthians except, perhaps, for the formularies at the end of the letter (13:11b, 13). Like the other final greetings in Paul's letters (Rom. 16:20; 1 Cor. 16:23; Gal. 6:18; Phil. 4:23; 1 Thess. 5:28; Philem. 25), 2 Cor. 13:13 is virtually an epistolary benediction.

1 Corinthians, Philippians, 1 Thessalonians, and Philemon. Nonetheless, the present tense of the verb, "we are praying," suggests that Paul's language is in some ways performative. Just as the present tense of the verb "we give thanks" in the epistolary thanksgivings not only reports on Paul's thanksgiving but is also an expression of Paul's present thanks to God, so "we are praying" suggests that Paul is praying even as he writes. In this regard, a multitasker he certainly was.

Paul concludes the body of this letter with a prayer for the Corinthians. For the most part the letter has been an extended reflection on Paul's ministry, specifically on his ministry among the Corinthians. As he brings his letter to a close, his prayer for the Corinthians is a reminder that Paul is praying for those whom he has evangelized.

Those who preach the gospel today have much to learn from the way Paul conducted his ministry among the Corinthians. They should remember that the successful preacher of the gospel preaches the gospel in word and in deed. Ministers of the gospel should also remember to pray for those to whom they preach.

2 Corinthians 13:11–13

The Letter Closing

Introductory Matters

In addition to being a preacher and pastor, Paul is a writer of letters. Letters are one way in which he exercises his evangelistic and pastoral roles. Like all letter writers, Paul uses a number of epistolary conventions to bring his letters to a close.

We customarily bring our letters to a close with a final salutation and the signing of our name. A signature block generally follows the signature in business letters and more formal correspondence. Hellenistic letter writers also employed standard conventions in bringing their letters to a close. Most commonly this was a simple farewell (*errōso, errōsthai*), to which was added a signature—often in the author's own hand when the letter had been dictated—and/or a descriptive epithet expressing the relationship between the author and the addressee. Some longer letter closings included health wishes, greetings, and/or the date of the letter. Occasionally there was a postscript— Paul uses one in 1 Cor. 16:24—and/or a note from the scribe who penned the text on behalf of an illiterate letter writer.

Paul developed his own style of signing off his letters. In the earliest of his letters, a final greeting in the form of a wish-prayer harks back to the opening salutation (1 Thess. 5:28; 1:1). In that letter he asks that his greetings be extended to everyone (5:27). From that "experiment in Christian letter writing," as Helmut Koester (1979, 34) once called it, Paul developed his personal epistolary style. Eventually his letters would be brought to a close with a variety of conventions, including not only greetings and a final greeting, but also doxologies,

263

prayers for peace, an exhortation, and the postscript that appears in 1 Cor. 16:24. Occasionally he begins his closing remarks with an adverbial "finally." Typically he initiates the epistolary closing by directly addressing as "brothers and sisters" those to whom he is writing. Some papyrus letters also use kinship language to express a writer's relationship with the one addressed (see P.Oxy. 1296, 2980; P.Princ. 69).

Second Corinthians' epistolary closing uses four of the standard conventions: a hortatory remark (13:11a), a peace prayer (13:11b), greetings (13:12), and a final greeting in the form of an epistolary blessing or wish-prayer (13:13). These remarks have been carefully crafted. In various ways they underscore the community's need for harmony and recapitulate some of the themes of the letter to which they have been appended.

Tracing the Train of Thought

Exhortation (13:11a)

13:11a. With the words, **finally, brothers and sisters** (13:11a), Paul announces his intention to bring the letter to a close. In several of his letters he uses "finally" to say that he is coming to the end of the letter (see Phil. 4:8; cf. Phil. 3:1; 1 Thess. 4:1). Addressing the recipients of his letters as "brothers and sisters" is also typical of his letter-writing style. It is found at the end of all of his letters, with the exception of his note to Philemon (see Rom. 16:17; 1 Cor. 16:15; Gal. 6:18; Phil. 4:8 mg; 1 Thess. 5:14 mg, 25 mg; cf. Philem. 20). Its presence at the end of this letter, in which the familiar formula of direct address has been notably scarce (cf. 1:8; 8:1), suggests that Paul is continuing to seek reconciliation with the Corinthian community.

The epistolary closing formula introduces Paul's final exhortation to his addressees. Sometimes Paul's closing hortatory remarks are expressed in a staccato-like series of short individual exhortations. That is the case here (cf. 1 Cor. 16:13–14; 1 Thess. 5:14–22). **Rejoice, mend your ways, be encouraged, be of the same mind, live in peace.** "Rejoice" occasionally appears in letters as an epistolary farewell, but here the verb is to be taken as a true exhortation. The early part of Paul's letter spoke of the sadness and grief that overtook him and the community. He hopes that all that is behind them. In fact, Paul himself expresses his joy that the Corinthians will be strong in their faith in answer to his prayer (13:9), and he has often mentioned that the Corinthians have brought him joy (1:24; 2:3; 6:10; 7:4, 7, 9, 13, 16).

The five verbs are in the present imperative, showing that Paul wants the Corinthians to respond to his urging with an ongoing effort. "Mend your ways" echoes the object of Paul's prayer of petition for the Corinthians (13:9). The exhortation "be encouraged" is expressed by the polyvalent Greek verb *parakaleisthe*. Paul urged the Corinthians to encourage a malefactor (2:7–8) and used the same verb to write about how he had been consoled and encouraged by God (1:3–7). In 1 Thess. 4:18 and 5:11 he urges the Thessalonians to console and encourage one another. The verb is particularly apropos in a situation in which there has been some grief. The idiomatic "be of one mind," that is, agree with one another, also appears in Rom. 12:16; 15:5; and Phil. 2:2; 4:2. Finally, Paul urges the Corinthians to "live in peace" with one another. A similar exhortation appears in Rom. 12:18 and 1 Thess. 5:13.

The dominant theme of all five tersely phrased exhortations is reconciliation and unity. The thematic and verbal links between these exhortations and various passages in the letter make them an appropriate peroration at the end of the letter, a letter that some, such as Victor Paul Furnish (1984) and Nigel Watson (1993), identify as a letter fragment largely preserved in our present chapters 10–13. The exhortations recapitulate some of the most important motifs of these chapters but also some of the important themes of the first part of the missive.

Peace Prayer (13:11b)

13:11b. Paul adds a wish-prayer to his exhortation: **And the God of love and peace will be with you** (13:11b). Jeffrey A. D. Weima (1994, 209; 2010, 310–13) calls the prayer a "peace benediction," but it has been called by many other names. The initial "and" closely links the prayer with the preceding exhortations.

"God of peace" is a Pauline epistolary epithet, appearing at the end of letters (Rom. 15:33; 16:20; Phil. 4:9; 1 Thess. 5:23). It reminds the reader of the letter's opening greeting (1:2; Rom. 1:7; Phil. 1:2; 1 Thess. 1:1). Apart from Paul, the epithet occurs only in *T. Dan* 5.2 and Heb. 13:20. The formula recalls that God is the source of peace, which the Semites understood to be *shalom*, the fullness of God's covenantal blessings upon his people. Paul's words are a prayerful wish that God would grant peace to the Corinthians.

Paul inserts a mention of "love" into his customary wish-prayer. That God is the source of love is made clear in 1 Cor. 13, where love is described as God's greatest gift (12:31; 13:13). In no other passage of the NT is God identified as "the God of love." That Paul has added "of love" to the familiar prayer suggests that Paul thinks the Corinthians need God's love if they are to mend their ways and live in faith and peace.

Greetings (13:12)

13:12. Much as we might add a few words to the end of a letter, perhaps in the form of a postscript, asking someone to give the kids a hug or tell the addressee that someone wants to be remembered, so Paul adds greetings. The greetings that he extends in his own name are what Jeffrey Weima (1994, 105–8) calls first-person greetings. Greetings such as "Say hello to your mom" are second-person greetings, and those in the form "Tom says hi" are third-person greetings. All three types of greetings are found in Paul's Letters:

Figure 15. Final Lines of 2 Corinthians from Codex Sinaiticus. This page from a fourth-century uncial manuscript shows the ending of 2 Corinthians (column 2) and the beginning of Paul's Letter to the Galatians.

first-person greetings (Rom. 16:22; 1 Cor. 16:21)

second-person greetings (Rom. 16:3–16; 1 Cor. 16:20; Phil. 4:21; 1 Thess. 5:26)

third-person greetings (Rom. 16:21, 23; 1 Cor. 16:19–20; Phil. 4:21–22; Philem. 23)

Second Corinthians contains one second-person greeting and one third-person greeting, both of which are general in scope.

Paul begins with a second-person greeting, **Greet one another with a holy kiss** (13:12). The intention of this type of greeting is that the recipients of the letter serve as intermediaries between the letter writer and those others to whom greetings are extended. Early church fathers—such as Justin (*1 Apology* 65.2), Hippolytus (*Apostolic Tradition* 4.1; 22.6), and Cyprian (*Unity of the Catholic Church* 9) in the West and Cyril (*Commentary on Romans* 10.33) in the East—speak about the kiss of peace that takes place in a liturgical setting. The liturgical kiss of peace is a later liturgical development that may be based on Paul's Letters (Rom. 16:16; 1 Cor. 16:20; 1 Thess. 5:26; cf. 1 Pet. 5:14).

Early papyri suggest that the reference to "give a hug" employs an epistolary formula. The embrace is holy not because it is a liturgical gesture but insofar as the gesture of goodwill is to be exchanged among God's holy ones (see 1:1). This kind of greeting is particularly apropos in a letter written to a conflicted community. The request might also suggest that Paul wants greetings to be extended to those who are not physically present for the reading of the letter, that is, all the holy people throughout Achaia (cf. 1:1).

The same understanding of holiness resonates in Paul's third-person greeting, **All the holy ones greet you.** Presumably these holy ones are the Macedonian Christians who are with Paul as he is writing the letter (cf. Phil. 4:21, "The brothers and sisters who are with me send greetings" [NIV]). Does Paul's "all" (cf. 1 Cor. 16:20) have any particular significance? Pelagius suggests that the qualifier means "all the saints, . . . not just the leaders" (*Commentary on the Second Epistle to the Corinthians* 13). It could mean that all those who knew that Paul intended to write the letter wanted to greet the Corinthians. Yet again, Paul might consider himself to be a spokesperson for all the communities that he has evangelized and to be speaking on their behalf when he says "All the holy ones greet you." In any event, Paul's extension of greetings to the Corinthians on behalf of all the saints is a reminder to the Corinthians that they belong to a group of believers that extends beyond the boundaries of their city.

Epistolary Benediction (13:13)

13:13. Paul's final words to the Corinthians, **The grace of the Lord Jesus Christ and the love of God and the fellowship of the Holy Spirit be with you**

all (13:13), are his way of saying good-bye to them. Each of his letters contains a similar but much shorter formula, "The grace of our Lord Jesus Christ be with you" (Rom. 16:20; 1 Cor. 16:23; 1 Thess. 5:28; with some modification in Gal. 6:18; Phil. 4:23; Philem. 25). In neither the long farewell greeting of 13:13 nor in any of the short greetings is any verb expressed; the verb "to be" must be supplied.

"The grace of the Lord Jesus Christ be with you" reprises the farewell greeting of 1 Thess. 5:28, without the "our" that qualifies "the Lord Jesus Christ" in that first letter. The formula replaces the typical "farewell" of the ordinary Hellenistic letter in Paul's day. Paul's greeting provides an artistic closing to his letter; it creates a literary inclusion with his opening greeting (see 1:2).

In comparison with Paul's customary farewell greetings, the farewell greeting of 2 Corinthians contains three significant additions: (1) "and the love of God," (2) "and the fellowship of the Holy Spirit," and (3) "all." Most probably the apostle is making these additions ad hoc (see Fee 1994, 362; Weima 2010, 344).

The first addition to Paul's customary farewell, "the love of God," expresses the wish that the Corinthians would experience God's love for them. "Of God" is a subjective genitive in Greek, indicating that God is the source of love rather than its object. It is God's love that makes the life of the church possible. God's love is the fundamental charisma (Rom. 5:5) of which the individual spiritual gifts present in the church are different articulations. The lessons of 1 Cor. 12–13 should not have been forgotten by the church at Corinth, which continues to experience the spiritual gifts that God has given them (8:7).

The Lord Jesus Christ and God are respectively identified as the source of the grace and the love that Paul wants the Corinthians to experience in the first two parts of his prayer. A question must be raised about the function of "Holy Spirit" in the third element of the benediction. Is the reference to the Holy Spirit in "fellowship of the Holy Spirit" (*hē koinōnia tou hagiou pneumatos*) formula a subjective genitive, meaning that the fellowship of the membership of the church community is from the Spirit? Or is the expression an objective genitive, as is normally the case with genitives following *koinōnia* (cf. 8:4; 1 Cor. 10:16; Phil. 3:10), meaning that the members of the church participate in the life of the Spirit, that is, have communion with the Spirit?

The term "fellowship" (*hē koinōnia*, 9:13) gives rise to the difficulty since in some uses of the term the emphasis lies on the relationship among those in fellowship, yet sometimes the emphasis is on the partners' sharing in something else. "It may be," says Frank Matera (2003, 314), "that there is a surplus of meaning here, so that Paul has in view the fellowship whereby believers are united both with each other and with the Holy Spirit." He may well be right.

"All" in the final phrase of 2 Corinthians, "be with you all," represents the third addition to Paul's customary farewell greeting. The addition may well result from Paul's awareness, even as he brings his letter to a close, that he is writing to a divided community (cf. 1 Cor. 16:24; and the textually dubious

Rom. 16:24). Paul does not want any of its members to think that they are being omitted from his prayerful wish.

Some of the ancient manuscripts add additional data at the end of a manuscript. This is the case with 2 Corinthians. The oldest manuscript of 2 Corinthians ($\mathfrak{P}^{46}$) and one of the most reliable manuscripts (Codex Sinaiticus [ℵ]) append "Second to the Corinthians" (*Pros Korinthious B'*). Codex Vaticanus (B) adds "written from Philippi" (*egraphē apo Philippōn*). These additions are later scribal notations, not the words of Paul.

Theological Issues

The Economy of Salvation

The emphasis in 13:13 is on the gifts of grace, love, and fellowship. Paul prays that God would grant these gifts to the Corinthians. These gifts are respectively attributed to the Lord Jesus Christ, God, and the Holy Spirit. The triad of "personal names" appears in one other place in Paul's writings, in 1 Cor. 12:4–6, where Paul writes about the Spirit, the Lord, and God.

The fathers of the church use the image of household management (*oikonomia*) to describe God's activity in the world, particularly with regard to creation and God's plan of salvation. They speak of an "economy of salvation." Paul's closing benediction prepares the way for this feature of patristic theology and should not be read as an expression of trinitarian theology, which had not yet developed in the Christian church. At most, Paul's language might be called proto-trinitarian, insofar as his mention of the Lord Jesus Christ, God, and the Holy Spirit employs a triad that will, centuries later, be appropriated into the church's doctrine of the Trinity.

Paul begins with the Lord Jesus Christ, not only because this is a common feature of his epistolary closings but also because he has been writing about the Lord Jesus Christ throughout the letter. It is through the reconciliation effected by means of the Lord Jesus Christ and the ministry of Paul that the Corinthians have experienced the grace of God. Grace is an expression of the love of God. The Spirit is God's abiding gift to the community, dwelling within them (1 Cor. 3:16). The Spirit is the source of their unity, creating bonds among them such that they form a fellowship, a single community (*koinōnia*). Paul's final words are a prayer for the unity of a fractured and conflicted church.

Ecclesiology, Once More

The language of Paul's opening salutation (1:1–2) is the bearer of a rich theology. The same can be said about the remarks with which Paul brings his missive to an end. The way he addresses the Corinthians, as brothers and sisters, is a reminder that the ties binding the members of the church together are similar to family ties, with all that this implies. The Corinthians are brothers and sisters to Paul, and they are brothers and sisters to one another. Nothing should be allowed to break the unity of the family. Joy, agreement, and peace should qualify their existence as a family.

The community owes its ongoing existence to the love of God, through which it came into existence and by which it is sustained. God's love for the community is manifest in God's many and varied gifts, not least of which are those spiritual gifts, the charismata, which for the most part are sources of ministry within the community.

Established by God, the church of God at Corinth is a community that belongs to God. Its members are God's holy people. Their holiness is a given, but it needs to be reflected in the way Corinthian believers lead their lives.

As contemporary believers read Paul's letter, they cannot help but think that the church described by Paul at the end of his letter is similar to the church of today. What the apostle said about the church of God at Corinth almost twenty centuries ago should be able to be said about the church of today each time that Paul's letter to the church of God is read.

Bibliography

Abernathy, David. 2001. "Paul's Thorn in the Flesh: A Messenger of Satan?" *Neotestamentica* 35:69–79.

Adewuya, J. Ayodeji. 2001. *Holiness and Community in 2 Cor. 6:14–7:1: Paul's View of Communal Holiness in the Corinthian Correspondence*. Studies in Biblical Literature 40. New York: Lang.

Aejmelaeus, Lars. 2000. *Schwachheit als Waffe: De Argumentation des Paulus in Tränenbrief (2 Kor. 1–13)*. Schriften der Finnischen Exegetischen Gesellschaft 78. Göttingen: Vandenhoeck & Ruprecht.

Allo, E.-B. 1956. *Saint Paul: Seconde Épître aux Corinthiens*. Études bibliques. Paris: Gabalda.

Amador, J. David Hester. 2000. "Revisiting 2 Corinthians: Rhetoric and the Case for Unity." *New Testament Studies* 46:92–111.

Anderson, R. Dean, Jr. 1996. *Ancient Rhetorical Theory and Paul*. Contributions to Biblical Exegesis and Theology 18. Kok: Pharos.

———. 2000. *Glossary of Greek Rhetorical Terms Connected to Methods of Argumentation, Figures and Tropes from Anaximenes to Quintilian*. Contributions to Biblical Exegesis and Theology 24. Louvain: Peeters.

Angers, Dominique. 2007. "The Pauline Expressions 'Until This Very Day' and 'Until Today' (Rom. 11,8 and 2 Cor. 3,14–15) in the Light of the Septuagint." In *Voces biblicae*, edited by Jan Joosten and Peter J. Tomson, 115–54. Contributions to Biblical Exegesis and Theology 49. Louvain: Peeters.

Arzt-Grabner, Peter. 2011. "Gott als verlässlicher Käufer: Einige papyrologische Anmerkungen und bibeltheologische Schlussfolgerungen zum Gottesbild der Paulusbriefe." *New Testament Studies* 57:392–414.

Aune, David E. 2003. *The Westminster Dictionary of New Testament and Early Christian Literature and Rhetoric*. Louisville: John Knox.

Aus, Roger David. 2005. *Imagery of Triumph and Rebellion in 2 Corinthians 2:14–17 and Elsewhere in the Epistle: An Example of the Combination of Greco-Roman and Judaic Traditions in the Apostle Paul*. Studies in Judaism. Lanham, MD: University Press of America.

Back, Frances. 2002. *Verwandlung durch Offenbarung bei Paulus: Eine religions-geschichtlich-exegetische Untersuchung zu 2 Kor 2,14–4,6*. Wissenschaftliche Untersuchungen zum Neuen Testament 2/153. Tübingen: Mohr Siebeck.

Baldanza, Giuseppe. 2007. "*Osmē e euōdia* in 2 Cor. 2,14–17: Quale interpretazione?" *Laurentianum* 48:477–501.

Banks, Robert. 1987. "Walking as a Metaphor of the Christian Life." In *Perspectives on Language and Text*, edited by Edgar W. Conrad and Edward G. Newing, 303–13. Winona Lake, IN: Eisenbrauns.

Barnett, Paul. 1997. *The Second Epistle to the Corinthians*. New International Commentary on the New Testament. Grand Rapids: Eerdmans.

Barré, Michael L. 1975. "Paul as 'Eschatologic' Person: A New Look at 2 Cor. 11:29." *Catholic Biblical Quarterly* 37:500–526.

Barrett, Charles Kingsley. 1973. *A Commentary on the Second Epistle to the Corinthians*. Black's New Testament Commentaries. London: Black.

Bassler, Jouette M. 1992. "2 Corinthians." In *The Women's Bible Commentary*, edited by Carol A. Newsome and Sharon H. Ringe, 330–32. London: SPCK; Louisville: Westminster John Knox.

Becker, Eve-Marie. 2004. *Letter Hermeneutics in 2 Corinthians: Studies in Literarkritik and Communication Theory*. Journal for the Study of the New Testament: Supplement Series 279. London: T&T Clark.

Beckheuer, Burkhard. 1997. *Paulus und Jerusalem: Kollekte und Mission im theologische Denken des Heidenapostels*. Europäische Hochschulschriften 23. Theologie 611. Frankfurt: Lang.

Beker, J. Christiaan. 1980. *Paul the Apostle: The Triumph of God in Life and Thought*. Edinburgh: T&T Clark.

———. 1982. *Paul's Apocalyptic Gospel: The Coming Triumph of God*. Philadelphia: Fortress.

Belleville, Linda L. 1991. *Reflections of Glory: Paul's Polemical Use of the Moses Doxa Tradition in 2 Corinthians 3.1–18*. Journal for the Study of the New Testament: Supplement Series 52. Sheffield: Sheffield Academic Press.

———. 1993. "Tradition or Creation? Paul's Use of the Exodus 34 Tradition in 2 Corinthians 3.7–18." In *Paul and the Scriptures of Israel*, edited by Craig A. Evans, 165–85. Biblical Seminar 34. Sheffield: Sheffield Academic Press.

———. 1994. "Gospel and Kerygma in Paul in 2 Corinthians." In *Studies on Corinthians, Galatians and Romans for Richard N. Longenecker*, edited by L. Ann Jervis and Peter Richardson, 110–33. Journal for the Study of the New Testament: Supplement Series 108. Sheffield: Sheffield Academic Press.

———. 1996a. "Paul's Polemic and the Theology of the Spirit in Second Corinthians." *Catholic Biblical Quarterly* 58:281–304.

———. 1996b. *2 Corinthians*. IVP New Testament Commentary Series. Downers Grove, IL: InterVarsity.

Best, Ernest. 1987. *Second Corinthians*. Interpretation. Louisville: John Knox.

————. 1995. "Paul's Apostolic Authority." In *The Pauline Writings*, edited by Stanley E. Porter and Craig A. Evans, 13–34. Biblical Seminar 34. Sheffield: Sheffield Academic Press.

Betz, Hans Dieter. 1972. *Der Apostel Paulus und die sokratische Tradition: Eine exegetische Untersuchung zu einer "Apologie"; 2 Korinther 10–13*. Beiträge zur historische Theologie 45. Tübingen: Mohr Siebeck.

————. 1985. *2 Corinthians 8 and 9: A Commentary on Two Administrative Letters of the Apostle Paul*. Hermeneia. Philadelphia: Fortress.

Bieringer, Reimund, ed. 1996. *The Corinthian Correspondence*. Bibliotheca ephemeridum theologicarum lovaniensium 125. Louvain: Leuven University Press / Peeters.

Bieringer, Reimund, and Jan Lambrecht. 1994. *Studies on 2 Corinthians*. Bibliotheca ephemeridum theologicarum lovaniensium 112. Louvain: Leuven University Press / Peeters.

Bieringer, Reimund, Emmanuel Nathan, and Dominika Kurek-Chomycz, eds. 2008. *2 Corinthians: A Bibliography*. Biblical Tools and Studies 5. Louvain: Peeters.

Blanton, Thomas R., IV. 2007. *Constructing a New Covenant: Discursive Strategies in the Damascus Document and Second Corinthians*. Wissenschaftliche Untersuchungen zum Neuen Testament 2/233. Tübingen: Mohr Siebeck.

————. 2010. "Spirit and Covenant Renewal: A Theologoumenon of Paul's Opponents in 2 Corinthians." *Journal of Biblical Literature* 129:129–51.

Boring, M. Eugene, Klaus Berger, and Carsten Colpe, eds. 1995. *Hellenistic Commentary to the New Testament*. Nashville: Abingdon.

Bornkamm, Günther. 1962. "The Authority and Integrity of the New Testament." *New Testament Studies* 8:258–64.

————. 1971. "Die Vorgeschichte des sogenannten Zweiten Korintherbriefes." In *Geschichte und Glaube II: Gesammelte Aufsätze 4*, 162–92. Beiträge zur evangelische Theologie 53. Munich: Kaiser.

Bouttier, Michel. 1989. "La souffrance de l'apôtre: 2 Co 4,7–18." In *The Diakonía of the Spirit (2 Co 4:7–7:4)*, edited by Lorenzo de Lorenzi, 29–49. Monographic Series of "Benedictina." Biblical-Ecumenical Section 10. Rome: Benedictina.

Bray, Gerald, ed. 1999. *1–2 Corinthians*. Ancient Christian Commentary on Scripture: New Testament 7. Downers Grove, IL: InterVarsity.

Brenton, Lancelot C. L., trans. 1986 (1851). *The Septuagint with Apocrypha: Greek and English*. London: Samuel Bagster and Sons. Repr., Peabody, MA: Hendrickson.

Breytenbach, Cilliers. 1990. "Paul's Proclamation and God's θρίαμβος: Notes on 2 Corinthians 2:14–16b." *Neotestamentica* 24:257–71.

Brondos, David A. 2006. *Paul on the Cross: Reconstructing the Apostle's Story of Redemption*. Minneapolis: Fortress.

Bruce, F. F. 1971. *1 and 2 Corinthians*. New Century Bible. London: Oliphants.

Bultmann, Rudolf. 1910. *Der Stil der paulinischen Predigt und die kynisch-stoische Diatribe*. Forschungen zur Religion und Literatur des Alten und Neuen Testaments 13. Göttingen: Vandenhoeck & Ruprecht.

————. 1985. *The Second Letter to the Corinthians*. Edited by Erich Dinkler. Minneapolis: Augsburg.

——. 1987. *Der zweite Brief an die Korinther*. Edited by Erich Dinkler. 2nd ed. Meyers Kritisch-exegetischer Kommentar über das Neue Testament. Göttingen: Vandenhoeck & Ruprecht.

Burke, Trevor J., and J. K. Elliott, eds. 2003. *Paul and the Corinthians: Studies on a Community in Conflict; Essays in Honour of Margaret Thrall*. Supplements to Novum Testamentum 109. Leiden: Brill.

Byrnes, Michael. 2003. *Conformation to the Death of Christ and the Hope of Resurrection: An Exegetico-Theological Study of 2 Corinthians 4,7–14 and Philippians 3,7–11*. Tesi Gregorian: Serie Teologia 99. Rome: Pontifical Gregorian University.

Campbell, Douglas A. 2009. "2 Corinthians 4:13: Evidence in Paul That Christ Believes." *Journal of Biblical Literature* 128:337–56.

Carrez, Maurice. 1980. "Le '*nous*' en 2 Corinthiens." *New Testament Studies* 26:474–86.

Collange, Jean-François. 1972. *Enigmes de la deuxième épître de Paul aux Corinthiens*. Cambridge: Cambridge University Press.

Collins, Raymond F. 1998. *Letters That Paul Did Not Write: The Epistle to the Hebrews and the Pauline Pseudepigrapha*. Good News Studies 28. Wilmington, DE: Glazier.

——. 1999. *First Corinthians*. Sacra pagina 7. Collegeville, MN: Liturgical Press.

——. 2000. "'I Command That This Letter Be Read': Writing as a Manner of Speaking." In *The Thessalonians Debate: Methodological Discord or Methodological Synthesis?*, edited by Karl P. Donfried and Johannes Beutler, 319–39. Grand Rapids: Eerdmans.

——. 2004. "'The Field That God Has Assigned to Us' (2 Cor. 10:13)." In *Orientale Lumen VII Conference Proceedings*, edited by Jack Figel, 123–42. Fairfax, VA: Eastern Christian Publications.

——. 2008. *The Power of Images in Paul*. Collegeville, MN: Liturgical Press.

Conrad, Edgar W., and Edward G. Newing, eds. 1987. *Perspectives on Language and Text*. Winona Lake, IN: Eisenbrauns.

Crafton, Jeffrey A. 1991. *The Agency of the Apostle: A Dramatistic Analysis of Paul's Responses to Conflict in 2 Corinthians*. Journal for the Study of the New Testament: Supplement Series 51. Sheffield: Sheffield Academic Press.

Dautzenberg, Gerhard. 1989. "'Glaube' oder 'Hoffnung' in 2 Kor 4,13–5,10." In *The Diakonía of the Spirit (2 Co 4:7–7:4)*, edited by Lorenzo de Lorenzi, 75–104. Monographic Series of "Benedictina." Biblical-Ecumenical Section 10. Rome: Benedictina.

Debanné, Marc J. 2006. *Enthymemes in the Letters of Paul*. Library of New Testament Studies 303. London: T&T Clark.

De Lorenzi, Lorenzo. 1987. *Paolo: Ministro del Nuovo Testamento (2 Co 2,14–4,6)*. Monographic Series of "Benedictina." Biblical-Ecumenical Section 9. Rome: Benedictina.

——. 1989. *The Diakonía of the Spirit (2 Co 4:7–7:4)*. Monographic Series of "Benedictina." Biblical-Ecumenical Section 10. Rome: Benedictina.

deSilva, David A. 1998. *The Credentials of an Apostle: Paul's Gospel in 2 Corinthians 1–7*. Bibal Monograph Series 4. North Richland Hills, TX: Bibal.

DiCicco, Mario M. 1995. *Paul's Use of Ethos, Pathos, and Logos in 2 Corinthians 10–13*. Mellen Biblical Press Series 31. Lewiston, NY: Mellen.

Dooling, D. 2008. "2 Corinthians 11:22: Historical Context, Rhetoric, and Ethnicity." *Hervormde Teologiese Studies* 64:819–34.

Duff, Paul D. 2008. "Transformed 'from Glory to Glory': Paul's Appeal to the Experience of His Readers in 2 Corinthians 3:18." *Journal of Biblical Literature* 127:759–80.

Ecumenical Task Force. 2012. *The Biblical Foundations of the Doctrine of Justification: An Ecumenical Follow-Up to the* Joint Declaration on the Doctrine of Justification. New York and Mahweh, NJ: Paulist.

Emmerling, Christian August Gottfried. 1823. *Epistola Pauli ad Corinthios*. Leipzig: J. A. Barth.

Evans, Craig A., and James A. Sanders. 1993. *Paul and the Scriptures of Israel*. Journal for the Study of the New Testament: Supplement Series 83. Sheffield: Sheffield Academic Press.

Fee, Gordon. 1994. *God's Empowering Presence: The Holy Spirit in the Letters of Paul*. Peabody, MA: Hendrickson.

Finney, Mark T. 2010. "Honor, Rhetoric, and Factionalism in the Ancient World: 1 Corinthians 1–4 in Its Social Context." *Biblical Theology Bulletin* 40:27–36.

Fitzgerald, John T. 1998. *Cracks in an Earthen Vessel: An Examination of the Catalogues of Hardships in the Corinthian Correspondence*. Society of Biblical Literature Dissertation Series 99. Atlanta: Scholars Press.

Fitzmyer, Joseph A. 1993. "Glory Reflected on the Face of Christ (2 Cor. 3:7–4:6)." In *According to Paul: Studies in the Theology of the Apostle*, compiled by Joseph A. Fitzmyer, 64–79. New York: Paulist Press.

Forbes, Christopher. 1986. "Comparison, Self-Praise and Irony: Paul's Boasting and the Conventions of Hellenistic Rhetoric." *New Testament Studies* 32:1–30.

Furnish, Victor Paul. 1984. *II Corinthians*. Anchor Bible 32A. Garden City, NY: Doubleday.

———. 1993. "Theology in 1 Corinthians." In *Pauline Theology*, vol. 2, *1 and 2 Corinthians*, edited by David M. Hay, 59–89. Minneapolis: Fortress.

Gargano, Guido Innocenzo. 2007. *Lectio divina sulla Seconda Lettera ai Corinti*. Coversazioni bibliche. Bologna: Dehoniane.

Garland, David E. 1999. *2 Corinthians*. New American Commentary. Nashville: Broadman & Holman.

Gaventa, Beverly Roberts. 1993. "Apostle and Church in 2 Corinthians: A Response to David M. Hay and Steven J. Kraftchick." In *Pauline Theology*, vol. 2, *1 and 2 Corinthians*, edited by David M. Hay, 182–99. Minneapolis: Fortress.

Gerber, Christine. 2005. "Krieg und Hochzeit in Korinth: Das metaphorische Werben des Paulus um die Gemeinde in 2 Kor 10,1–6 und 11,1–4." *Zeitschrift für die neutestamentliche Wissenschaft und die Kunde der älteren Kirche* 96:99–125.

Gignilliat, Mark. 2007. *Paul and Isaiah's Servants: Paul's Theological Reading of Isaiah 40–66 in 2 Corinthians 5.14–6.10*. Library of New Testament Studies 330. London: T&T Clark.

Gloer, William Hulitt. 1996. *An Exegetical and Theological Study of Paul's Understanding of New Creation in 2 Cor. 5:14–21*. Mellen Biblical Press Series 42. Lewiston, NY: Mellen.

Gnilka, Joachim. 1968. "2 Cor. 6:14–7:1 in the Light of the Qumran Texts and the Testaments of the Twelve Patriarchs." In *Paul and Qumran: Studies in New Testament Exegesis*, edited by Jerome Murphy-O'Connor, 48–68. London: Geoffrey Chapman.

Gooder, Paula R. 2006. *Only the Third Heaven? 2 Corinthians 12:1–10 and Heavenly Ascent*. Library of New Testament Studies 313. London: T&T Clark.

Goulder, Michael D. 2001. *Paul and the Competing Mission in Corinth*. Library of Pauline Studies. Peabody, MA: Hendrickson.

Gräbe, Petrus J. 2000. *The Power of God in Paul's Letters*. Wissenschaftliche Untersuchungen zum Neuen Testament 2/123. Tübingen: Mohr Siebeck.

Grässer, Erich. 2002. *Der zweite Brief an die Korinther: Kapitel 1,1–7,16*. Ökumenischer Taschenbuchkommentar 8/1. Gütersloh: Gütersloher-Verlagshaus.

———. 2005. *Der zweite Brief an die Korinther: Kapitel 8,1–13,13*. Ökumenischer Taschenbuchkommentar 8/2. Gütersloh: Gütersloher-Verlagshaus.

Grindheim, Sigvid. 2005. *The Crux of Election: Paul's Critique of the Jewish Confidence in the Election of Israel*. Wissenschaftliche Untersuchungen zum Neuen Testament 2/202. Tübingen: Mohr Siebeck.

Hafemann, Scott J. 1990. *Suffering and Ministry in the Spirit: Paul's Defense of His Ministry in II Corinthians 2:14–3:3*. Grand Rapids: Eerdmans.

———. 2000. *2 Corinthians*. NIV Application Commentary. Grand Rapids: Zondervan.

———. 2005. *Paul, Moses, and the History of Israel: The Letter/Spirit Contrast and the Argument from Scripture in 2 Corinthians 3*. Paternoster Biblical Monographs. Milton Keynes, UK: Paternoster.

Hall, David R. 2003. *The Unity of the Corinthian Correspondence*. Journal for the Study of the New Testament: Supplement Series 251. London: T&T Clark.

Hanson, Anthony Tyrrell. 1995. "The Midrash in 2 Corinthians 3: A Reconsideration. In *The Pauline Writings*, edited by Stanley E. Porter and Craig A. Evans, 98–123. Biblical Seminar 34. Sheffield: Sheffield Academic Press.

Harris, Murray J. 2005. *The Second Epistle to the Corinthians: A Commentary on the Greek Text*. New International Greek Testament Commentary. Grand Rapids: Eerdmans; Milton Keynes, UK: Paternoster.

Harvey, Anthony Ernest. 1996. *Renewal through Suffering: A Study of 2 Corinthians*. Edinburgh: T&T Clark.

Hausrath, Adolf. 1870. *Der Vier-Capitel-Brief des Paulus an die Korinther*. Heidelberg: Bassermann.

Hay, David M. 1993. "The Shaping of Theology in 2 Corinthians." In *Pauline Theology*, vol. 2, *1 and 2 Corinthians*, edited by David M. Hay, 135–55. Minneapolis: Fortress.

Hentschel, Anni. 2007. *Diakonia im Neuen Testament: Studien zur Semantik unter besonderer Berücksichtigung der Rolle von Frauen*. Wissenschaftliche Untersuchungen zum Neuen Testament 2/226. Tübingen: Mohr Siebeck.

Héring, Jean. 1958. *La Seconde Épître aux Corinthiens*. Commentaire du Nouveau Testament 8. Neuchâtel: Delachaux et Niestlé.

Hock, Andreas. 2007. "Christ Is the Parade: A Comparative Study of the Triumphal Procession in 2 Cor 2,14 and Col 2,15." *Biblica* 88:110–19.

Hock, Ronald F. 1980. *The Social Context of Paul's Ministry: Tentmaking and Apostleship*. Philadelphia: Fortress.

Hodgson, Robert. 1983. "Paul the Apostle and First Century Tribulation Lists." *Zeitschrift für die neutestamentliche Wissenschaft und die Kunde der älteren Kirche* 74:59–80.

Hogeterp, Albert L. A. 2006. *Paul and God's Temple: A Historical Interpretation of Cultic Imagery in the Corinthian Correspondence*. Biblical Tools and Studies 2. Louvain: Peeters.

Hooker, Morna D. 2008. "On Becoming the Righteousness of God: Another Look at 2 Cor. 5:21." *Novum Testamentum* 50:358–75.

Horrell, David G. 1996. *The Social Ethos of the Corinthian Correspondence: Interests and Ideology from 1 Corinthians to 1 Clement*. Studies of the New Testament and Its World. Edinburgh: T&T Clark.

Hubbard, Moyer V. 2002. *New Creation in Paul's Letters and Thought*. Society for New Testament Studies Monograph Series 119. Cambridge: Cambridge University Press.

Hughes, Philip Edgcumbe. 1962. *Paul's Second Epistle to the Corinthians*. New International Commentary on the New Testament. Grand Rapids: Eerdmans.

Hurtado, Larry W. 1998. *One God, One Lord: Early Christian Devotion and Jewish Monotheism*. 2nd ed. Edinburgh: T&T Clark.

———. 2003. *Lord Jesus Christ: Devotion to Jesus in Earliest Christianity*. Grand Rapids: Eerdmans.

Infante, Renzo. 1985. "Imagine nuziale e tensione escatologica nel Nuovo Testamento: Note a 2 Cor. 11,3 e Eph. 5,25–27." *Rivista biblica* 33:45–61.

Jackson, T. Ryan. 2010. *New Creation in Paul's Letters: A Study of the Historical and Social Setting of a Pauline Concept*. Wissenschaftliche Untersuchungen zum Neuen Testament 2/272. Tübingen: Mohr Siebeck.

Jervis, L. Ann, and Peter Richardson, eds. 1994. *Studies on Corinthians, Galatians and Romans for Richard N. Longenecker*. Journal for the Study of the New Testament: Supplement Series 108. Sheffield: Sheffield Academic Press.

Jones, Ivor H. 2008. "Rhetorical Criticism and the Unity of 2 Corinthians: One 'Epilogue,' or More?" *New Testament Studies* 54:496–524.

Joosten, Jan, and Peter J. Tomson, eds. 2007. *Voces biblicae: Septuagint Greek and Its Significance for the New Testament*. Contributions to Biblical Exegesis and Theology 49. Louvain: Peeters.

Judge, Edwin Arthur. 1966. "The Conflict of Educational Aims in NT Thought." *Journal of Christian Education* 9:32–45.

———. 1968. "Paul's Boasting in Relation to Contemporary Professional Practice." *Australian Biblical Review* 16:37–50.

Käsemann, Ernst. 1971. "Some Thoughts on the Theme 'The Doctrine of Reconciliation in the New Testament.'" In *The Future of Our Religious Past: Essays in Honor of Rudolf Bultmann*, edited by James M. Robinson, 49–64. London: SCM; New York: Harper.

Keener, Craig S. 2005. *1–2 Corinthians*. New Cambridge Bible Commentary. Cambridge: Cambridge University Press.

Kennedy, James H. 1897. "Are There Two Epistles in 2 Corinthians?" *The Expositor*, 5th series, 6:231–38, 285–304.

———. 1900. *The Second and Third Epistles of St. Paul to the Corinthians*. Studies in the Gospels and Epistles. London: Methuen.

Koester, Helmut. 1979. "1 Thessalonians—Experiment in Christian Writing." In *Continuity and Discontinuity in Church History: Essays Presented to George Huntston Williams on the Occasion of His 65th Birthday*, edited by F. Forrester Church and Timothy George, 34–44. Studies in the History of Christian Thought 19. Leiden: Brill.

Koskenniemi, Heikki. 1956. *Studien zur Idee und Phraseologie des griechischen Briefes bis 400 nach Christus*. Annales Academiae scientiarum Fennicae, Series B, 102/2. Helsinki: Akateeminen Kirjakaupaa.

Kraftchick, Steven J. 1993. "Death in Us, Life in You: The Apostolic Medium." In *Pauline Theology*, vol. 2, *1 and 2 Corinthians*, edited by David M. Hay, 156–81. Minneapolis: Fortress.

Kuschnerus, Bernd. 2002. *Die Gemeinde als Brief Christi: Die kommunikative Funktion der Metaphor bei Paulus am Beispiel von 2 Kor 2,5*. Forschungen zur Religion und Literatur des Alten und Neuen Testaments 197. Göttingen: Vandenhoeck & Ruprecht.

Kwon, Yon-Gyong. 2008. "*Arrabōn* as Pledge in Second Corinthians." *New Testament Studies* 54:525–41.

Lambrecht, Jan. 1978. "The Fragment of 2 Cor. vi 14–vii 1: A Plea for Its Authenticity." In *Miscellanea Neotestamentica II*, edited by Tjitze Baarda, A. F. J. Klijn, and W. C. van Unnik, 143–61. Supplements to Novum Testamentum 48. Leiden: Brill. Reprinted in *Studies on 2 Corinthians*, by Reimund Bieringer and Jan Lambrecht, 531–49. Bibliotheca ephemeridum theologicarum lovaniensium 112. Louvain: Leuven University Press / Peeters, 1994.

———. 1986. "The *Nekrōsis* of Jesus: Ministry and Suffering in 2 Cor. 4,7–15." In *L'apôtre Paul: Personnalité, style et conception du ministère*, edited by Albert Vanhoye, 120–43. Bibliotheca ephemeridum theologicarum lovaniensium 73. Louvain: Leuven University Press / Peeters. Reprinted in *Studies on 2 Corinthians*, by Reimund Bieringer and Jan Lambrecht, 309–33. Bibliotheca ephemeridum theologicarum lovaniensium 112. Louvain: Leuven University Press / Peeters, 1994.

———. 1994a. "The Eschatological Outlook in 2 Corinthians 4,7–15." In *To Tell the Mystery: Essays on New Testament Eschatology*, edited by Thomas E. Schmidt and Moisés Silva, 122–39. Sheffield: Sheffield Academic Press. Reprinted in *Studies on 2 Corinthians*, by Reimund Bieringer and Jan Lambrecht, 335–49. Bibliotheca ephemeridum theologicarum lovaniensium 112. Louvain: Leuven University Press / Peeters, 1994.

———. 1994b. *Pauline Studies: Collected Essays*. Bibliotheca ephemeridum theologicarum lovaniensium 115. Louvain: Leuven University Press / Peeters.

———. 2003. *Understanding What One Reads: New Testament Essays*. Louvain: Peeters.

————. 2006. *Second Corinthians*. 2nd ed. Sacra pagina 8. Collegeville, MN: Liturgical Press.

Lietzmann, Hans. 1949. *An die Korinther I/II*. Edited by Werner Georg Kümmel. 4th, expanded ed. Handbuch zum Neuen Testament 9. Tübingen: Mohr Siebeck.

Lim, Kar Young. 2009. *"The Sufferings of Christ Are Abundant in Us" (2 Corinthians 1.5): A Narrative Dynamics Investigation of Paul's Sufferings in 2 Corinthians*. Library of New Testament Studies 399. London: T&T Clark.

Lindgård, Fredrik. 2005. *Paul's Line of Thought in 2 Corinthians 4:6–5:10*. Wissenschaftliche Untersuchungen zum Neuen Testament 2/189. Tübingen: Mohr Siebeck.

Litwa, M. David. 2008. "2 Corinthians 3:18 and Its Implications for Theosis." *Journal of Theological Interpretation* 2:117–33.

Long, Frederick J. 2004. *Ancient Rhetoric and Paul's Apology: The Compositional Unity of 2 Corinthians*. Society for New Testament Studies Monograph Series 131. Cambridge: Cambridge University Press.

Lorusso, Giacomo. 2001. *Il ministero pasquale di Paolo in 2 Cor. 1–7: Le implicazione del soffrire e gioire per il Vangelo*. Rome: Edizione Vivere.

————. 2007. *La Seconda lettera ai Corinzi: Introduzione, versione, commento*. Scritti delle origini cristiane 8. Bologna: Dehoniane.

MacRae, George W. 1968. "Anti-Jewish Polemic in 2 Cor. 4,6?" In *Studia evangelica*, vol. 4, *Papers Presented to the Third International Congress on New Testament Studies Held at Christ Church, Oxford, 1965*, edited by Frank L. Cross, 420–31. Texte und Studien 102. Berlin: Akadamie Verlag.

Malherbe, Abraham J. 1988. *Ancient Epistolary Theorists*. Society of Biblical Literature Sources for Biblical Study. Atlanta: Scholars Press.

————. 1989. *Paul and the Popular Philosophers*. Minneapolis: Fortress.

Malin, François S. 2010. "Moral Language in the New Testament: Language and Ethics in 2 Corinthians 3." In *Moral Language in the New Testament*, vol. 2, edited by Ruben Zimmermann and Jan G. van der Watt, 245–54. Wissenschaftliche Untersuchungen zum Neuen Testament 2/296. Tübingen: Mohr Siebeck.

Malina, Bruce, and John Pilch. 2006. *Social Science Commentary on the Letters of Paul*. Minneapolis: Fortress.

Manzi, Franco. 2002. *Seconda lettera ai Corinzi*. I libri biblici: Nuovo Testamento. Milan: Pauline.

Marshall, Peter. 1987. *Enmity in Corinth: Social Conventions in Paul's Relations with the Corinthians*. Wissenschaftliche Untersuchungen zum Neuen Testament 2/23. Tübingen: Mohr Siebeck.

Martin, Ralph P. 1986. *2 Corinthians*. Word Biblical Commentary 40. Waco: Word.

Martyn, J. Louis. 1967. "Epistemology at the Turn of the Ages: 2 Cor. 5:16." In *Christian History and Interpretation: Studies Presented to John Knox*, edited by William R. Farmer et al., 269–87. Cambridge: Cambridge University Press.

Matera, Frank J. 2002. "Apostolic Suffering and Resurrection Faith: Distinguishing between Appearance and Reality (2 Cor. 4,7–5,10)." In *Resurrection in the New Testament: Festschrift J. Lambrecht*, edited by Reimund Bieringer et al., 387–405.

Bibliotheca ephemeridum theologicarum lovaniensium 165. Louvain: Leuven University Press / Peeters.

———. 2003. *II Corinthians*. New Testament Library. Louisville: Westminster John Knox.

McCant, Jerry W. 1999. *2 Corinthians*. Readings: A New Biblical Commentary. Sheffield: Sheffield Academic Press.

Metzger, Bruce M. 1994. *A Textual Commentary on the Greek New Testament*. 2nd ed. Stuttgart: Deutsche Bibelgesellschaft / United Bible Societies.

Mills, Watson Early. 1997. *2 Corinthians*. Bibliographies for Biblical Research: New Testament Series. Lewiston, NY: Mellen.

Minor, Mitzi L. 2009. *2 Corinthians*. Smyth & Helwys Bible Commentaries. Macon, GA: Smyth & Helwys.

Murphy-O'Connor, Jerome. 1987. "Relating 2 Corinthians 6.14–7.1 to Its Context." *New Testament Studies* 33:272–75.

———. 1988. "Faith and Resurrection in 2 Cor. 4:13–14." *Revue biblique* 95:543–50.

———. 1989. "A Ministry beyond the Letter (2 Cor 3:1–6)." In *The Diakonía of the Spirit (2 Co 4:7–7:4)*, edited by Lorenzo de Lorenzi, 105–29. Monographic Series of "Benedictina." Biblical-Ecumenical Section 10. Rome: Benedictina.

———. 1991. *The Theology of the Second Letter to the Corinthians*. New Testament Theology. Cambridge: Cambridge University Press.

———. 1993. "Co-authorship in the Corinthian Correspondence." *Revue biblique* 100:562–70.

———. 2010. *Keys to Second Corinthians: Revisiting the Major Issues*. Oxford: Oxford University Press.

Nguyen, V. Henry T. 2008. *Christian Identity in Corinth: A Comparative Study of 2 Corinthians, Epictetus and Valerius Maximus*. Wissenschaftliche Untersuchungen zum Neuen Testament 2/243. Tübingen: Mohr Siebeck.

Olbricht, Thomas H., and Jerry L. Sumney, eds. 2001. *Paul and Pathos*. Society of Biblical Literature Symposium Series 16. Atlanta: Society of Biblical Literature.

O'Mahoney, Kieran J. 2000. *Pauline Persuasion: A Sounding in 2 Corinthians 8–9*. Journal for the Study of the New Testament: Supplement Series 199. Sheffield: Sheffield Academic Press.

Peterson, Brian K. 1998. *Eloquence and the Proclamation of the Gospel in Corinth*. Society of Biblical Literature Dissertation Series 163. Atlanta: Scholars Press.

Pickett, Raymond. 1997. *The Cross in Corinth: The Social Significance of the Death of Jesus*. Journal for the Study of the New Testament: Supplement Series 143. Sheffield: Sheffield Academic Press.

Pitta, Antonio. 2006. *La seconda lettera ai Corinzi*. Commenti biblici. Rome: Borla.

Plevnik, Joseph. 2000. "The Destination of the Apostle and of the Faithful: Second Corinthians 4:13b–14 and First Thessalonians 4:14." *Catholic Biblical Quarterly* 62:83–95.

Plummer, Alfred. 1915. *A Critical and Exegetical Commentary on the Second Epistle of St. Paul to the Corinthians*. International Critical Commentary. Edinburgh: T&T Clark.

Polaski, Sandra Hack. 2005. *A Feminist Introduction to Paul*. St. Louis: Chalice.

Porter, Stanley E., and Sean A. Adams, eds. 2010. *Paul and the Ancient Letter Form*. Pauline Studies 6. Leiden: Brill.

Porter, Stanley E., and Craig A. Evans, eds. 1995. *The Pauline Writings*. Biblical Seminar 34. Sheffield: Sheffield Academic Press.

Rensberger, David K. 1978. "2 Corinthians 6:14–7:1—A Fresh Examination." *Studia biblica et theologica* 8:5–49.

Roetzel, Calvin J. 2007. *2 Corinthians*. Abingdon New Testament Commentaries. Nashville: Abingdon.

———. 2009. "The Language of War (2 Cor. 10:1–6) and the Language of Weakness (2 Cor. 11:21b–13:10)." *Biblical Interpretation* 17:77–99.

Romaniuk, Kasimir. 1990. "Résurrection existentielle ou eschatologique en 2 Co 4,13–14." *Biblische Zeitschrift* 34:248–52.

Sabourin, Léopold, and Stanislaus Lyonnet. 1970. *Sin, Redemption, and Sacrifice: A Biblical and Patristic Study*. Rome: Pontifical Biblical Institute.

Sampley, J. Paul. 2000. "The Second Letter to the Corinthians." In *The New Interpreter's Bible*, edited by Leander E. Keck, 11:3–180. Nashville: Abingdon.

Savage, Timothy B. 1996. *Power through Weakness: Paul's Understanding of the Christian Ministry in 2 Corinthians*. Society for New Testament Studies Monograph Series 86. Cambridge: Cambridge University Press.

Schmeller, Thomas. 2010. *Der zweite Brief an die Korinther*. Vol. 1, *2 Kor 1,1–7,4*. Evangelisch-katholischer Kommentar zum Neuen Testament 8/1. Neukirchen: Neukirchener Verlag.

Schrader, Karl. 1835. *Uebersetzung und Erklärung der Briefe des Apostels Paulus an die Corinther und an die Römer*. Vol. 4 of *Der Apostel Paulus*. Leipzig: Kollmann.

Scott, J. M. 1998. *2 Corinthians*. New International Biblical Commentary: New Testament 8. Peabody, MA: Hendrickson.

Stanley, David M. 1973. *Boasting in the Lord: The Phenomenon of Prayer in Saint Paul*. New York: Paulist Press.

Stegman, Thomas D. 2005. *The Character of Jesus: The Linchpin to Paul's Argument in 2 Corinthians*. Analecta biblica 158. Rome: Pontificio Istituto Biblico.

———. 2007. "*Episteusa, dio elalēsa* (2 Corinthians 4:13): Paul's Christological Reading of Psalm 115:1a LXX." *Catholic Biblical Quarterly* 69:725–45.

———. 2009. *Second Corinthians*. Catholic Commentary on Sacred Scripture. Grand Rapids: Baker Academic.

Stockhausen, Carol K. 1989. *Moses' Veil and the Story of the New Covenant: The Exegetical Substructure of II Cor. 3.1–4.6*. Analecta biblica 116. Rome: Pontifical Biblical Institute.

———. 1993. "2 Corinthians 3 and the Principles of Pauline Exegesis." In *Paul and the Scriptures of Israel*, edited by Craig A. Evans and James A. Sanders, 143–64. Journal for the Study of the New Testament: Supplement Series 83. Sheffield: Sheffield Academic Press.

Sumney, Jerry L. 1999. *"Servants of Satan," "False Brothers" and Other Opponents of Paul*. Journal for the Study of the New Testament: Supplement Series 188. Sheffield: Sheffield Academic Press.

Swanson, Reuben J., ed. 2005. *New Testament Greek Manuscripts: Variant Readings Arranged in Horizontal Lines against Codex Vaticanus; Corinthians*. Vol. 2, *2 Corinthians*. Wheaton: Tyndale House; Pasadena, CA: William Carey International University Press.

Szypuła, Wojciech. 2007. *The Holy Spirit in the Eschatological Tension of Christian Life: An Exegetico-Theological Study of 2 Corinthians 5,1–5 and Romans 8,18–27*. Tesi Gregoriana: Serie Teologia 147. Rome: Pontifical Gregorian University.

Thrall, Margaret E. 1977. "The Problem of II Cor. vi. 14–vii. 1 in Some Recent Discussion." *New Testament Studies* 24:132–48.

———. 1994. *A Critical and Exegetical Commentary on 2 Corinthians*. Vol. 1, *1–7*. International Critical Commentary. London: T&T Clark.

———. 2000. *A Critical and Exegetical Commentary on 2 Corinthians*. Vol. 2, *8–13*. International Critical Commentary. London: T&T Clark.

Tomson, Peter J. 2007. "Blessing in Disguise: *Eulogeō* and *Eucharisteō* between Hebrew and Greek Usage." In *Voces biblicae*, edited by Jan Joosten and Peter J. Tomson, 35–61. Contributions to Biblical Exegesis and Theology 49. Louvain: Peeters.

Vegge, Ivar. 2008. *2 Corinthians—A Letter about Reconciliation: A Psychological, Epistolographical and Rhetorical Analysis*. Wissenschaftliche Untersuchungen zum Neuen Testament 2/239. Tübingen: Mohr Siebeck.

Vogel, Manuel. 2006. *Commentatio mortis: 2 Kor 5,1–10 auf dem Hintergrund antiker ars moriendi*. Forschungen zur Religion und Literatur des Alten und Neuen Testaments 214. Göttingen: Vandenhoeck & Ruprecht.

Walker, Donald Dale. 2002. *Paul's Offer of Leniency (2 Cor. 10:1): Populist Ideology and Rhetoric in a Pauline Letter Fragment*. Wissenschaftliche Untersuchungen zum Neuen Testament 2/152. Tübingen: Mohr Siebeck.

Walker, William O. 2001. *Interpolations in the Pauline Letters*. Journal for the Study of the New Testament: Supplement Series 213. London: Sheffield Academic Press.

———. 2011. "Apollos and Timothy as the Unnamed 'Brothers' in 2 Corinthians 8:18–24." *Catholic Biblical Quarterly* 73:318–38.

Wan, Sze-kar. 2000. *Power in Weakness: Conflict and Rhetoric in Paul's Second Letter to the Corinthians*. New Testament in Context. Harrisburg, PA: Trinity Press International.

Watson, Nigel M. 1983. "'To Make Us Rely Not on Ourselves but on God Who Raises the Dead': 2 Cor. 1,9b as the Heart of Paul's Theology." In *Die Mitte des Neuen Testament: Einheit und Vielfalt neutestamentlicher Theologie; Festschrift für Eduard Schweizer zum siebzigsten Geburtstag*, edited by Ulrich Luz and Hans Weder, 384–98. Göttingen: Vandenhoeck & Ruprecht.

———. 1993. *The Second Epistle to the Corinthians*. Epworth Commentaries. London: Epworth.

Webb, William J. 1993. *Returning Home: New Covenant and Second Exodus as the Context for 2 Corinthians 6.14–7.1*. Journal for the Study of the New Testament: Supplement Series 85. Sheffield: Sheffield Academic Press.

Weima, Jeffrey A. D. 1994. *Neglected Endings: The Significance of the Pauline Letter Closings*. Journal for the Study of the New Testament: Supplement Series 101. Sheffield: Sheffield Academic Press.

———. 2010. "Sincerely, Paul: The Significance of the Pauline Letter Closings." In *Paul and the Ancient Letter Form*, edited by Stanley E. Porter and Sean A. Adams, 307–45. Pauline Studies 6. Leiden: Brill.

Welborn, Laurence L. 1997. *Politics and Rhetoric in the Corinthian Epistles*. Macon, GA: Mercer University Press.

———. 2005. *Paul, the Fool of Christ: A Study of 1 Corinthians in the Comic-Philosophic Tradition*. Early Christianity in Context. London: T&T Clark.

———. 2009. "Paul's Caricature of His Chief Rival as a Pompous Parasite in 2 Corinthians 11.20." *Journal for the Study of the New Testament* 32:39–56.

White, John L. 1986. *Light from Ancient Letters*. Foundations & Facets: New Testament. Philadelphia: Fortress.

Williamson, Lamar. 1968. "Led in Procession: Paul's Use of *Thriambeuō*." *Interpretation* 22:317–32.

Windisch, Hans. 1970. *Der zweite Korintherbrief*. Kritisch-exegetischer Kommentar über das Neue Testament 6. Göttingen: Vandenhoeck & Ruprecht.

Witherington, Ben, III. 1995. *Conflict and Community in Corinth: A Socio-Rhetorical Commentary on 1 and 2 Corinthians*. Grand Rapids: Eerdmans; Carlisle: Paternoster.

Wong, Emily. 1985. "The Lord Is the Spirit (2 Cor. 3:17a)." *Ephemerides theologicae lovanienses* 61:48–72.

Wong, Kasper Ho-Yee. 1992. "'Lord' in 2 Corinthians 10:17." *Louvain Studies* 17:243–53.

———. 1998. *Boasting and Foolishness: A Study of 2 Cor. 10,12–18 and 11,1a*. Jian Dao Dissertation Series 5. Bible and Literature 3. Hong Kong: Alliance Bible Seminary.

Wray, T. J., and Gregory Mobley. 2005. *The Birth of Satan: Tracing the Devil's Biblical Roots*. New York: Palgrave Macmillan.

Wright, N. T. 1993. "On Becoming the Righteousness of God." In *Pauline Theology*, vol. 2, *1 and 2 Corinthians*, edited by David M. Hay, 200–208. Minneapolis: Fortress.

Young, Frances, and D. F. Ford. 1987. *Meaning and Truth in Second Corinthians*. Biblical Foundations in Theology. Grand Rapids: Eerdmans.

Zeilinger, Franz. 1992. *Krieg und Friede in Korinth: Kommentar zum 2. Korintherbrief des Apostels Paulus*. Vol. 1, *Der Kampfbrief, der Versöhnungsbrief, der Bettelbrief*. Vienna: Böhlau.

———. 1997. *Krieg und Friede in Korinth: Kommentar zum 2. Korintherbrief des Apostels Paulus*. Vol. 2, *Die Apologie*. Vienna: Böhlau.

Index of Subjects

Page numbers followed by f *refer to figures.*

Index of Modern Authors

Index of Scripture and Ancient Sources

4Q225

frg. 2, col. 2, line 14
  146

4Q253

frg. 3, 2 146

4Q286

frg. 7, 2.1–6 146

4Q390

frg. 2, col. 1, line
  4 146

5Q13

frg. 5.2 146

11Q13

2.13 146
2.25 146
3.7 146

RABBINIC WORKS

Babylonian Talmud

Berakot

32a 31

Ketubbot

7b 32

Soṭah

7b 32

Genesis Rabbah

92.7 84

Mishnah

'Abot

2.2 222
4.5 222

Pesiqta Rabbati

10.6 83

Tosefta

Qiddušin

1.11 222

APOSTOLIC FATHERS

1 Clement

5.6–7 131
30.8 197

Diognetus

7.3–4 197

ANCIENT AUTHORS

Alexander

De figuris

1.4 87

Ambrosiaster

Commentary on Paul's Epistles

3.259 177
81.3.312 257

Aristotle

Rhetoric

2.20.2 225
2.20.8 225
3.3.4 184
3.13.1–2 226
3.19.1 226

Cyprian

Unity of the Catholic Church

9 267

Cyril

Commentary on Romans

10.33 267

Demetrius

De elocutione

223 6
226 6
227 5
229 10

Demosthenes

1 Philippic

4.51 86

2 Philippic

6.31 86

4 Philippic

10.53–54 86

Dio Chrysostom

Ad Alexandrinos

11 86

Epictetus

Diatribai

1.17.20–29 184
2.15.4–8 42
2.19.24 100
3.9.14 242
3.13.6–7 185
3.22.45 232
4.8.25 242

Euripides

Orestes

307–8 152

Hermogenes

De inventione

4.12 87

Hippolytus

Apostolic Tradition

4.1 267
22.6 267

Homer

Iliad

2.319 90
17.542 228

Horace

Odes

3.9.24 152

Jerome

Epistulae

121.10 218

John Chrysostom

Homiliae in epistolam II ad Corinthios

7.5 88
8.2 93
10.1 106
13.17 149
14.1 152
21 198
23.5 218
26.2 239

Josephus

Antiquities of the Jews

2.271 216
4.123 150
6.144 58
8.267 220
9.273 150
14.117 234
19.283 234

Jewish War

7.119–57 70

Justin

1 Apology

65.2 267